Yugoslavia
a country study

Foreign Area Studies
The American University
Edited by
Richard F. Nyrop
Research Completed
September 1981

On the cover: Bridge at Mostar, Bosnia and Hercegovina; built by Romans in first century A.D.

Second Edition, First Printing, 1982.

Library of Congress Cataloging in Publication Data
Main entry under title:

Yugoslavia, a country study.

   (Area handbook series) (DA pam ; 550–99)
   Rev. ed. of: Area handbook for Yugoslavia.   1973.
   Bibliography: p.
   Includes index.
   1. Yugoslavia.   I. Nyrop, Richard F.   II. American
University (Washington, D.C.).   Foreign Area Studies.
III. Area handbook for Yugoslavia.   IV. Series.
V. Series: DA pam ; 550–99.
DR1214.Y83   1982   949.7   82–11632

Headquarters, Department of the Army
DA Pam 550–99
Supersedes 1970 edition

For sale by the Superintendent of Documents, U.S. Government Printing Office
Washington, D.C. 20402

Foreword

This volume is one of a continuing series of books prepared by Foreign Area Studies, The American University, under the Country Studies/Area Handbook Program. The last page of this book provides a listing of other published studies. Each book in the series deals with a particular foreign country, describing and analyzing its economic, national security, political, and social systems and institutions and examining the interrelationships of those systems and institutions and the ways that they are shaped by cultural factors. Each study is written by a multidisciplinary team of social scientists. The authors seek to provide a basic insight and understanding of the society under observation, striving for a dynamic rather than a static portrayal of it. The study focuses on historical antecedents and on the cultural, political, and socioeconomic characteristics that contribute to cohesion and cleavage within the society. Particular attention is given to the origins and traditions of the people who make up the society, their dominant beliefs and values, their community of interests and the issues on which they are divided, the nature and extent of their involvement with the national institutions, and their attitudes toward each other and toward the social system and political order within which they live.

The contents of the book represent the views, opinions, and findings of Foreign Area Studies and should not be construed as an official Department of the Army position, policy, or decision, unless so designated by other official documentation. The authors have sought to adhere to accepted standards of scholarly objectivity. Such corrections, additions, and suggestions for factual or other changes that readers may have will be welcomed for use in future new editions.

William Evans-Smith
Director, Foreign Area Studies
The American University
Washington, D.C. 20016

Acknowledgments

The authors are indebted to numerous individuals in various agencies of the United States government and in international and private organizations in Washington, D.C. who gave of their time, research materials, and special knowledge on Yugoslav affairs to provide data and perspective. The authors also wish to express their appreciation to members of the Foreign Area Studies staff who contributed directly to the preparation of the manuscript. These include Karen R. Sagstetter, Kathryn R. Stafford, and Dorothy M. Lohmann, who edited the manuscript with the assistance of Janet B. Connors; Harriett R. Blood, who prepared the graphics; and Gilda V. Nimer, who provided valuable bibliographic assistance. The authors appreciate as well the contributions of Ernest A. Will, publications manager.

Special thanks are owed to Carlyn Dawn Anderson who designed the book cover and the illustrations on the title page of each chapter. The inclusion of photographs in this study was made possible by the generosity of various individuals and public and private organizations. We acknowledge our indebtedness especially to those who provided work not yet published.

Contents

Chapter 1. Historical Setting 1
Vlad Georgescu

PRE-SLAV HISTORY—EARLY SLAV HISTORY—The
Slovenes—The Croats—The Serbs—Bosnia and Herce-
govina—The Montenegrins—The Macedonians—THE
YUGOSLAV MOVEMENT AND WORLD WAR I—
THE YUGOSLAV KINGDOM, 1918–41—Economic
Developments—From Democracy to Dictatorship (1918–
34)—The Regency (1934–41)—The War: Occupation and
Resistance—COMMUNIST YUGOSLAVIA—The Ortho-
dox Years—The Break with Stalin—The Yugoslav Way—
The Policy of Nonalignment—Tito's Last Years

Chapter 2. The Society and Its Environment 51
Patricia A. Kluck

GEOGRAPHY AND POPULATION—Topography—
Drainage Systems—Climate—Population—PEOPLES
OF YUGOSLAVIA—Overview—Serbs—Croats—Slo-
venes—Montenegrins—Ethnic Muslims—Macedonians
—Albanians—SOCIAL GROUPS—Peasants—Workers
—Intelligentsia—Family Organization—MIGRATION
AND URBANIZATION—Migration—Urbanization—
RELIGION—Roman Catholicism—Serbian Orthodox
Church—Islam—EDUCATION—HEALTH AND SO-
CIAL WELFARE

Chapter 3. The Economy 113
Darrel R. Eglin

ROLE OF GOVERNMENT—The Beginning of Workers'
Self-Management—Self-Management in the 1970s—Fiscal
Policy—Problems of Workers' Self-Management—
GROWTH AND STRUCTURE OF THE ECONOMY—
LABOR—INDUSTRY—Energy—Mining—Manufactur-
ing—AGRICULTURE—Land Use—Land Tenure and
Agrarian Reform—Cropping Patterns and Production—
Livestock—Fishing—Forestry—BANKING AND IN-
FLATION—FOREIGN TRADE AND BALANCE OF
PAYMENTS—THE 1981–85 PLAN

Chapter 4. Government and Politics 169
Steven L. Burg

THE DEVELOPMENT OF THE CONTEMPORARY
POLITICAL ORDER—THE CONSTITUTIONAL
ORDER—THE PROCESS OF GOVERNMENT—THE
LEAGUE OF COMMUNISTS—OTHER SOCIOPO-
LITICAL ORGANIZATIONS—THE DOMESTIC
POLITICAL AGENDA—FOREIGN POLICY

Chapter 5. National Security 229
Robert E. Bartos

DEVELOPMENT OF MODERN FORCES—ATTI-
TUDES TOWARD THE MILITARY—NATIONAL
SECURITY CONCERNS—MISSIONS AND ORGANI-
ZATION—High Command—Army Organization—Navy
Organization—Air Force Organization—Frontier Guard
Organization—The Territorial Defense Force—Civil
Defense—MILITARY TACTICS—LOGISTICS—
MANPOWER—Source and Quality—Procurement—
Service Obligations—TRAINING—Training in Military
Schools—Enlisted Training—Officer Training—PER-
SONNEL SERVICES AND SUPPORT—Grades and
Rank—Commendations, Decorations, and Ratings—
PAY, WORKING HOURS, AND LEAVE—MILITARY
JUSTICE—SPECIAL SERVICE-RELATED RIGHTS
AND DUTIES—SERVICE IN THE YUGOSLAV
PEOPLE'S ARMY AND IN THE RESERVE BY CIVIL-
IANS—PUBLIC ORDER AND INTERNAL SECURITY
—Public Order and Rights—The Police System—Crim-
inal Procedures—Criminal Courts—The Penal System

List of Figures

Preface

The death in May 1980 of Josip Broz Tito, who since World War II had been the dominant figure in all aspects of the Yugoslav society, made essential a new study on this important Balkan state. *Yugoslavia: A Country Study* replaces the *Area Handbook for Yugoslavia*, which was published in 1971. This study contains some material from the 1971 edition but is almost entirely a new book. Like its predecessor, the present country study is an attempt to treat in a compact and objective manner the dominant social, political, economic, and national security aspects of contemporary Yugoslav society. Sources of information included scholarly journals and monographs, official reports of governments and international organizations, foreign and domestic newspapers, numerous periodicals, and interviews with individuals who have special competence in Yugoslav and East European affairs. Chapter bibliographies appear at the end of the book; brief comments on some of the more valuable sources as possible further reading appear at the end of each chapter. Measurements are given in the metric system; a conversion table is provided to assist those readers who are unfamiliar with metric measurements (see table 1, Appendix). A Glossary is also included.

The contemporary place names used in this study are generally those approved by the United States Board on Geographic Names with the exception that the authors employed the conventional spelling for many place names, i.e., Belgrade, Croatia, and Montenegro rather than Beograd, Hrvatska, and Crna Gora, respectively. In addition the authors followed the practice of most publishers and did not use the diacritical marks of Serbo-Croatian in the Latin alphabet. The reader will therefore find, for example, *ustasa* rather than *ustaša* and Pristina rather than *Priština*.

A word of caution is in order with respect to the terms *nationalism* and *nationalistic*. Although the 1974 Constitution, in common with its several predecessors, recognizes the six nations (see Glossary) and various nationalities of which the nation is composed and, within a federal system of government grants extensive powers to the republic and provincial governments, excessive loyalty to a republic, province, or nationality at the expense of the federal government and the nation-state is categorized as nationalism (see Glossary) or as nationalistic activity and is a crime against the state.

Country Profile

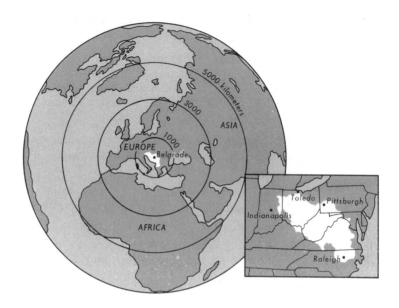

Country

Formal Name: Socialist Federal Republic of Yugoslavia.

Short Form: Yugoslavia.

Term for Citizens: Yugoslav(s).

Capital: Belgrade.

Geography

Size: Approximately 255,892 square kilometers.

Topography: Two principal regions are coastal and interior high-lands and the Pannonian Plains. Highlands a mountainous area that extends northwest-southeast from the border with Austria to Greek border. Plains a continuation of the Great Hungarian Plains, which extend northwest-southeast from the border with Austria to Romanian border.

Climate: Generally temperate but varies from moderate Mediterranean along the Adriatic Coast to colder continental conditions in the mountains and plains of the east central and northern sections of the country.

Society

Population: Census spring 1981 reported population of 22,352,162 that was growing at annual rate of slightly more than .08 percent.

Education and Literacy: Education compulsory between ages of seven and fifteen. Literacy 85 percent in 1971. Extensive growth in the educational system throughout post-World War II era.

Health: Republic/provincial constitutions stipulate rights of citizens to health care. General health insurance program covers most of population. Substantial expansion of health care resources in the 1960s and 1970s, but disparities between rural and urban areas, richer and poorer regions remained significant.

Languages: Serbo-Croatian, Slovenian, and Macedonian. Albanian, Hungarian, and Italian main national minority languages.

Ethnic Groups: Serbs, Croats, ethnic Muslims, Slovenes, Macedonians, and Montenegrins (all South Slavs and constituting together over four-fifths total population) the main ethnic groups. Albanians and Hungarians the principal minority groups.

Religion: Roman Catholic (approximately 30 percent), Serbian and Macedonian Orthodox (35 percent), Sunni Muslim (12 percent).

Economy

Gross National Product (GNP): Estimated US$61.5 billion in 1979, US$2,430 GNP per capita. Economic growth slow in 1980 (2.5 to 3 percent) and 1981 because of balance of payments constraints.

Energy and Mining: Country energy short although large deposits of low calorie coal and some crude oil and gas. Substantial ferrous and nonferrous mining industry.

Industry: Largest sector accounting for 37 percent of GDP in 1980. Relatively broad base with considerable metal fabricating.

Agriculture: Consists of small, highly developed socialized sector and large private sector (95 percent of farm employment). Private farms averaged 3.5 hectares and fragmented. Main crops corn and wheat but variety of additional produce. Livestock more important than cropping but short of fodder.

Exports: US$9 billion in 1980, of which 45 percent were manufactured products, 41 percent raw and semifinished materials, and 11 percent agricultural commodities. Communist countries largest export market followed by West European countries.

Imports: US$15.1 billion in 1980, 62 percent of which were raw or semifinished materials, 31 percent machinery and equipment, and 7 percent agricultural commodities. Western Europe largest source of imports, followed by communist countries. Crude oil about one-fifth of total imports in 1980.

Balance of Payments: Deteriorated during the 1970s. Became a serious constraint on growth in 1980 that was likely to continue during early 1980s.

Exchange Rate: Dinar devalued twice in 1980 totaling 28 percent against United States dollar. Average conversion value for 1980 was 24.9 dinars to US$1 and exchange rate was 33.4 dinars to US$1 in May 1981.

Fiscal Year: Calendar year.

Fiscal Policy: Governmental system highly decentralized. Federal budget expenditures, mainly defense and administration, only about one-fifth of that of total public sector and not used to influence economic activity.

Inflation: Retail prices increased an average of 30 percent in 1980 and inflation remained a serious problem in early 1980s.

Transportation

Railroads: 9,909 kilometers, of which 9,762 kilometers standard gauge (1.435 meters); 794 kilometers double tracked; and 2,911 kilometers electrified (1978). Total freight 69 million tons in 1978.

Highways: 112,200 kilometers, of which 50,200 kilometers modern surfacing; 40,100 kilometers macadam; and 21,900 kilometers earth (1978). Total freight 179 million tons in 1978.

Inland Waterways: 2,600 kilometers. Total freight 52 million tons in 1978.

Ports: Nine major, of which Rijeka, Split, Koper, Bar, and Ploce were most important, and twenty-four minor ports. Total ocean freight 27.7 million tons in 1978. Belgrade most important river port.

Pipelines: 1,373 kilometers for crude oil; 2,760 kilometers for natural gas; and 150 kilometers for refined products.

Government and Politics

Government: Federal system in which power and authority shared by federal government and governments of six republics and two autonomous provinces. After death of Josip Broz Tito in May 1980 the eight-member presidency of the republic under an annually rotating president became head of state; president of Federal Executive Council is premier and de facto head of government. Decision-making slow, often cumbersome, and subject to veto by a republic government that decides that its vital interests damaged.

Politics: Sole political party League of Communists of Yugoslavia (LCY), which embraces a league of communists in each republic and province and in the Yugoslav People's Army (YPA). Front organization for LCY is Socialist Alliance of the Working People of Yugoslavia (SAWPY).

Foreign Relations: After break with Soviet Union and its East European satellites in 1948, Yugoslavia adopted nonaligned policy. Tito, India's Prime Minister Jawaharlal Nehru, and Egypt's President Gamal Abdul Nasser were prime movers in establishment of the Movement of Nonaligned Nations, in which Tito remained pivotal figure until his death.

International Agreements and Memberships: In addition to nonaligned movement, member of United Nations and most of its specialized agencies; observer status in Council for Mutual Economic Assistance (Comecon); World Bank; International Monetary Fund; and participates in some activities of the Organisation for Economic Co-operation and Development.

National Security

Armed Forces: Yugoslav People's Army (YPA) includes army, navy, air force, and Frontier Guard. In mid-1981 ground forces numbered 190,000 (140,000 conscripts); navy, 17,500 (6,000 conscripts); air force, 45,000 (8,000 conscripts); and Frontier Guard, 20,000. Navy force included about 2,500 marines. Estimated 500,000 reservists at any given time. Paramilitary Territorial Defense Force (TDF) composed of over 1 million in 1981, perhaps as many as 3 million. TDF units largely funded by and in peacetime under control of republic and provincial governments but designed to fight independently or under command of YPA command during an invasion.

Major Military Units: Ground forces in mid-1981 organized into eight infantry divisions, eight independent tank brigades, sixteen independent infantry brigades, and other specialized brigades and regiments. Navy's submarines, corvettes, and frigate are center of Adriatic fleet; smaller craft in both river and Adriatic command. Air force's 341 combat aircraft grouped in twelve fighter, ground-attack squadrons, nine interceptor squadrons, and various support and training squadrons. Most aircraft and naval vessels domestically manufactured, as are growing range of infantry weapons.

Military Budget: In 1981 defense expenditures were listed as equivalent of US$3.47 billion, nearly 8 percent of gross national product (GNP). TDF costs estimated between .05 and 1 percent of GNP in early 1980s.

Internal Security Forces: Consist of Public Security Service (regular police force) and State Security Service (an intelligence and secret police service).

Figure 1. Administrative Divisions, 1982

Introduction

THE LITERATURE ON contemporary Yugoslavia—whether by scholars or journalists, Yugoslavs or foreigners—tends to focus on one or more aspects of a few interrelated issues. Central to all issues is the pronounced heterogeneity of the society. Distinctions based on ethnicity, language, region, and religion crosscut the society, producing several separate communities, each marked by strong internal loyalty and solidarity. The cleavages thus produced constitute a strong centrifugal force that complicates economic and political questions and poses a continuing threat to the stability of the state.

Largely as a result of the social heterogeneity, the country's leaders have since the 1950s instituted various measures that decentralized decisionmaking, not only within the federal system of government but also within the sole political party, the League of Communists of Yugoslavia (LCY). In addition the economic system that evolved in the 1960s and 1970s is neither capitalist nor communist, and in early 1982 the concept of self-management (see Glossary) remained central to the functioning of the country's economic enterprises and social institutions (see Role of Government, ch. 3). Because of the social heterogeneity and the economic and political heterodoxy, British scholar David A. Dyker asserted in 1979 that "the sheer complexity of the Yugoslav system is such that the most experienced students of South Slav affairs are reluctant to claim comprehension, even at a given point in time."

The overwhelming majority of the population consists of South Slavs, hence the name Yugoslavia—the land of the South Slavs. Croats, ethnic (or Bosnian) Muslims, Macedonians, Montenegrins, Serbs, and Slovenes are the South Slavs. They are constitutionally identified as nations (see Glossary) inasmuch as most of their traditional homelands lie within the country's borders. There are in addition several national minorities, such as Albanians, Bulgarians, Hungarians, Italians, and Turks, whose homelands are largely outside the country (see Peoples of Yugoslavia, ch. 2).

The cleavages and in some instances bitter animosities between and among the South Slavs reflect both the country's history and its terrain. In the fourth century A.D. the authorities in Rome and Byzantium agreed on a dividng line between the eastern and western branches of the empire; this line—the Theodosian—ran through what is now Yugoslavia. In the fifth, sixth, and seventh centuries various South Slav tribes entered the area and settled in often widely separated and sometimes isolated valleys and plains (see fig. 2). In due course the Slovenes, Croats, and Bosnians became Roman Catholics and, among other things, adopted the Latin alphabet. The Serbs, Macedonians, and Montenegrins embraced the Eastern Orthodox faith and with it the Cyrillic alphabet (see Religion, ch. 2).

Moreover, from the late 1300s to the 1800s the Ottoman Empire ruled large sections of the country (see fig. 4). As a result of that long and frequently repressive period of domination by an Islamic polity, in early 1982 an estimated 12 to 15 percent—and perhaps even more—of the Yugoslavs adhered to the tenets of Islam, but at the same time some members of the society, particularly the Serbs and Montenegrins, retained memories of Muslim oppression. The parts of the country not conquered by the Ottomans were, with the exception of Montenegro, subjugated by the Habsburg Empire, the predecessor of the Austro-Hungarian Empire (see Early Slav History, ch. 1).

The assassination of Austrian Archduke Franz-Ferdinand in Sarajevo in June 1914 triggered the events that culminated in World War I. At the outbreak of the war, the Austro-Hungarian army contained numerous subject peoples, among them Croats and Slovenes. One such soldier was a former metalworker who had been born in 1892 in a Croatian village to a Croatian father and a Slovenian mother. Early in the war this young man, Josip Broz, was seriously wounded and captured by Russian troops. He recovered from his wound in a hospital in Russia and at the time of the Russian Revolution was working as a prison laborer. He escaped and made his way to Saint Petersburg (now Leningrad) and was there at the time of the Bolshevik Revolution in November 1918.

In September 1920 the young man returned to his homeland as an enthusiastic, if unsophisticated, Communist. By the mid-1930s he had become a skilled party organizer and during extended periods of imprisonment in Yugoslav jails had acquired a solid grounding in Marxist-Leninist history and doctrine. In 1937 the Comintern (see Glossary) appointed him general secretary of the Communist Party of Yugoslavia (CPY).

Shortly after the Germans invaded Yugoslavia in April 1941, the CPY alerted its small, tightly knit, but countrywide organization to begin the establishment of a guerrilla force, which came to be known as the Partisans (see Glossary). In 1943 the CPY convened a congress at Jajce that established the Council of National Liberation to act as a parliament for the resistance forces. The congress designated Josip Broz—henceforth publicly known by his party name, Tito—as premier of the resistance government and as Marshal of Yugoslavia. From that time until his death on May 4, 1980, Tito dominated virtually every facet of public life.

During the war Tito and his associates rarely spoke publicly about the future of the party, focusing instead on the war against the Nazis and their allies. Non-Communists held important positions within the guerrilla forces and the resistance government. When the German army retreated from Belgrade in October 1944, Tito seized control of the capital as the commander in chief of an army of several hundred thousand and the head of an efficient, well-organized government that included representatives of most important antifascist organizations. Within a few months, however, Tito and his colleagues had forced the non-Communists out of the government and had embarked on a program designed to create a system based on the Soviet Stalinist model.

Although Tito and his associates—particularly Edvard Kardelj, Milovan Djilas, and Aleksandar Rankovic—viewed themselves as dedicated Communists, even during the war they had been disgruntled by the paucity of weapons and matériel the Soviets had provided, which was far less than that provided by the British or that captured in battle. The Yugoslavs felt strongly that they had waged a successful guerrilla war not only against the Nazis but also against such traitors within the society as the *ustase* (see Glossary) and that they had done so with scant support from the Kremlin. Furthermore Tito and his friends were persuaded that only they understood the extant society and that only they were qualified to create a new society. Therefore when Stalin complained in 1947 and 1948 that the Yugoslavs had prevented the Soviets from recruiting agents within Yugoslavia and had refused to allow the Soviets to take over the training of the Yugoslav People's Army (YPA), he was in essence voicing Yugoslav complaints about Soviet efforts to interfere in domestic affairs. The disputes between Belgrade and Moscow became increasingly acrimonious, and eventually the Cominform (see Glossary) terminated Yugoslavia's membership and urged the Yugoslavs to depose Tito and to select a new leader for the party. Ironically the Cominform acted on June 28, a date of particular importance known as Vidovdan (Saint Vitus Day); among other events, the date commemorated a battle in 1389 in which the Ottomans first defeated the Serbs and the 1914 assassination of the archduke that started World War I (see The Break with Stalin, ch. 1).

Despite their expulsion from the communist club, Tito and his associates did not at once abandon their allegiance to Stalinism, and they continued their efforts to impose the Soviet model of a command economy. In the early 1950s, however, they introduced measures that within a score of years resulted in political and economic institutions quite unlike those in any other self-described socialist or communist country. Not all of Tito's colleagues survived the evolutionary process; Djilas was expelled from the party in 1954 because of his public calls for more democratic measures and Rankovic, who at the time was viewed as Tito's probable successor, lost his party and government positions in 1966 because of his use of the secret police to increase his personal power and to thwart liberalizing reform measures.

Throughout the 1970s Tito took the initiative in preparing for the transfer of power when he died (see Tito's Last Years, ch. 1). Although he neither claimed nor exercised absolute dictatorial power, he remained until his final illness the ultimate decision-maker. The party and governmental systems that evolved after the break with the Kremlin provided special status and reserved unique powers to him—such as head of state, chief of the party, and supreme commander of the armed forces. Nevertheless his will was often thwarted and his opinions frequently challenged. Despite his positions of power and his enormous personal prestige, he frequently was forced to negotiate with other powerful individuals to secure decisions that approximated what he deemed essential. His imprint on the LCY, the federal system of government, the armed forces, and indeed the basic concepts of the Yugoslav experiment was nonetheless so decisive that Yugoslavs and foreigners alike regularly referred to "Tito's Yugoslavia," and during the 1970s a recurring question within the country and abroad was: "After Tito, what?" Two years after his death the question had not yet been completely answered.

As had been arranged under Tito's guidance, he was succeeded by a collective Presidency. The president of the Presidency serves as head of state and supreme commander of the armed forces. The office of the president rotates annually by formula among the nine members of the Presidency, and during his tenure the incumbent is the first among equals of the members of the Presidency and the spokesman for its consensually formed decisions.

The succession went smoothly, and the work of government continued without immediate problems. It soon became obvious, however, that the Presidency was too unwieldly to cope with rapid decisionmaking, particularly for a national security emergency. On April 13, 1982, the government proclaimed a new Law on Nationwide Defense, the fourth national defense law. The legislation provides that "in times of war or the immediate danger of war or any other peril to the country" and if the members of the Presidency are not immediately available to render a collective decision, the president of the Presidency is to act on behalf of the Presidency.

Of perhaps greater significance, however, the law increases the power and responsibility of the National Defense Council (sometimes cited as the Military Council), a body within the Federal Secretariat for National Defense. The law specifies that in time of war or "of any other peril" the federal government—which will determine that such a situation exists—assumes sweeping police powers. The National Defense Council as a sort of "collective military command" will become the dominant government body. The law stipulates that the federal secretary for national defense will serve as chairman. The members include the chief of staff of the YPA; the undersecretary and the deputy secretaries in the defense secretariat; the chief inspector (commander in chief) of the Territorial Defense Force (TDF—an all-peoples defense militia force); commanders of the ground, naval, and air forces; other senior military officers that the chairman may appoint; and the president of the LCY in the YPA (see The Territorial Defense Force, ch. 5). The entire membership is therefore composed of active duty officers of the YPA under the chairmanship of the commander in chief of the YPA.

Observers were generally agreed that the legislation provides a small number of military officers an astonishing and unprecedented degree of autonomy. Some observers suggested that the legislation

Josip Broz Tito: 1892–1980
Courtesy Embassy of Yugoslavia, Washington

constituted an abnegation of responsibility by civilian political leaders. Others opined that the new law simply took note of reality and the longstanding special role of the armed forces within the society. By this they meant that in an emergency the senior officers of the YPA would act with or without orders or permission from the Presidency. Analyst Robin Remington has noted that Tito described the role of the military in open-ended terms: "Our army's task is to defend the country from foreign enemies. However, it should defend the achievements of our revolution, if needed, from internal enemies too."

Moreover the YPA—the direct successor to the Partisans—continued in early 1982 to enjoy a special sociopolitical role. In a speech on December 22, 1981—the fortieth anniversary of the formation of the armed forces—Serej Kraigher, then president of the Presidency, rehearsed the wartime achievements of the Partisans. He asserted that they had killed 450,000 of the enemy, "including the quisling forces," i.e., the *ustase* and the Cetniks (see Glossary). He stated that the Partisans had suffered 305,000 deaths and another 425,000 casualties and that the overall Yugoslav deaths during World War II had exceeded 10 percent of the population. The president described the modernization and expansion of the YPA and the development of the TDF as the implementation of Tito's call for "the socialization of defense affairs." Kraigher placed particular emphasis on the politicizing role of the armed forces, noting that "as a mass school of socialist education of young generations, the army has consistently implemented LCY policy. . . ."

The role of the armed forces within the LCY remained important. In early 1982 nearly 115,000 officers and soldiers—out of a total strength of about 270,000—belonged to the LCY in the YPA; an estimated 90 percent of the officer corps were members. The YPA membership exceeded Kosovo's 96,000 and Montenegro's 79,000 (see fig. 1). For the Twelfth Party Congress in June 1982, however, the YPA was allocated fifty-eight elected delegates but only thirty additional delegates, whereas Kosovo had forty-eight elected and forty additional delegates and Montenegro had thirty-nine elected and sixty additional delegates. (Out of a total of 1,570 delegates to the congress, Serbia proper—i.e., the Republic of Serbia minus the autonomous provinces of Kosovo and Vojvodina—had by far the largest representation: 309 elected delegates and sixty additional delegates, about 24 percent.)

In early 1982 there were various indications that the process of government in the post-Tito era was functioning smoothly. The Presidium of the LCY and the Presidency announced the nominations of several key senior officials as part of the rotation of government and party posts. (Although the LCY formulates broad policy, unlike other communist states the LCY does not possess a "shadow" government that actually makes and executes decisions.) Among those named to assume office in May 1982 for four-year terms were Milka Palanic to be president of the Federal Executive Council, the de facto prime minister; Stane Dolanc, interior secretary; Lazar Mojsov, foreign secretary, and Admiral Branko Mamula, defense secretary. Palanic, a Croatian, will be the first woman to be head of government. Mamula succeeded General Nikola Ljubicic, who had served as defense secretary since 1967. The Eleventh Party Congress in 1978 elected Mamula to the LCY Central Committee as the representative of the LCY in the YPA. In 1979 Tito appointed him chief of the general staff of the YPA.

Although Mamula had earlier been identified as a Serb from Croatia, the official announcement of the composition of the Federal Executive Council that took over in May 1982 listed Mamula in the Croatian contingent. (The new council was composed of nine Serbs, five Croats, five Slovenes, four Macedonians, three Montenegrins, and one each Albanian, ethnic Muslim, and Romanian.)

In May 1982 the government released the names of several new military appointments. Colonel General Dane Petkovski, born in Macedonia in 1922, succeeded Mamula as chief of staff; he had been serving as the assistant federal defense secretary for political administration and held several positions in the LCY leadership. Colonel General Petar Gracanin, born in Serbia in 1923, was appointed deputy defense secretary; his previous posting had been that of commander, Belgrade military district. Colonel General Asim Hodzic, an ethnic Muslim born in Bosnia in 1922, became the undersecretary of the defense secretariat; in 1981 he was the chief of military counterintelligence. Retired General Ljubicic became president of the Republic of Serbia.

The economic situation in early 1982 was worrisome, however. From the early 1950s to the late 1970s the country's economic growth was remarkable. By 1979 the per capita gross national product was US$2,430, and several aspects of the economy were approaching the level of some West European countries. During the late 1970s, however, a number of problems in the economy became increasingly intractable. The rate of industrial growth declined, as did the rate of growth of exports. The public had become accustomed to a high rate of consumption, and imports remained high. Because of economic recessions in West European countries, especially the Federal Republic of Germany (West Germany), numerous Yugoslavs working in those countries were forced to return home, and the remittances by the workers still abroad steadily declined, thus worsening an already severe balance of payments deficit. In common with most energy importing countries, Yugoslavia was also severely damaged by the series of price increases for crude oil and petroleum products (see Growth and Structure of the Economy, ch. 3).

In 1981 inflation and unemployment were high and going higher, and real wages were declining. The government's austerity measures created hardships for many, particularly those in the poorest regions. This became apparent in the spring of 1981 by an outburst of the latest in a series of violent, nationalist demonstrations in

Kosovo. The riots began in Pristina University but quickly spread throughout the province (see The Domestic Political Agenda, ch. 4). The army moved in swiftly to assist the local police in firmly repressing the demonstrations, but the political impact of obvious Albanian disaffection continued to be felt in early 1982. During the summer and fall of 1981, the LCY conducted a sweeping purge of the LCY of Kosovo and of the faculties and student body of the university. Serbs and Montenegrins continued to flee the province, and animosity between the Albanians and Serbs became more pronounced.

The Albanians, almost all of whom are Muslims, constituted an overwhelming majority of the population of Kosovo (see The Development of the Contemporary Political Order, ch. 4). According to the census of March and April 1981, Albanians totaled 1,227,000 out of Kosovo's population of 1,585,000. The partial census report revealed that Kosovo's population had increased by 27 percent in the intercensal decade and that this included an increase of 311,000 Albanians (an increase of about 34 percent) but a decrease of about 18,500 Serbs (decrease of about 6 percent), the second largest community in the province. The preliminary census data showed a countrywide population of approximately 22,352,000, an increase of about 8.9 percent since 1971.

After an unprecedented delay of almost a year, the government in February 1982 finally released a detailed census report (see table 8, Appendix). The Serbs remained by far the largest nation, accounting for about 36 percent of the population. The Croats constituted a distant second with slightly less than 20 percent. The data revealed that the Albanian community in Macedonia had increased by about 35 percent in the intercensal period, far ahead of the rate of increase of the Macedonians. Perhaps the most surprising figure concerned the more than quadrupling of the number of those who identified themselves to the census takers as Yugoslavs, a total of about 5.4 percent of the population, thereby forming a group over twice the size of the Montenegrin nation of 577,298, for example. Some Yugoslav observers attributed this sharp increase to the rising number of interethnic marriages—estimated to be as high as 30 percent of all marriages in the 1970s—whose offspring frequently refuse to claim the nationality of either parent and insist on identification as Yugoslavs.

Although in the early 1980s most Yugoslavs voiced optimism about their future, there were nonetheless recurrent warnings that all was not well. In November 1981 Branko Vuksic, a close associate of the revered Kardelj who for the thirty-five years before his death in 1979 was the leading theoretician of the LCY, issued one such warning. In an article in a prominent Belgrade periodical, Vuksic reminded his readers that shortly before Kardelj died he had warned that if the country and the people "did not radically put our situation in order, we might experience 'the fate of Chile'." By this Kardelj was referring to the "economic chaos and internal destabilization" that had prevailed in Chile before the military seized power in a coup d'etat and to the radical transformation of the Chilean society by the armed forces. During Tito's lifetime the notion of the armed forces moving against him was dismissed as widely impossible. In the early 1980s the thought was no longer impossible, and some observers suggested that the TDF had been established and has continued to expand not only as an important defense in depth against an invasion but also as a counterweight to the regular military.

Richard F. Nyrop

June 1982

Chapter 1. Historical Setting

Patriarchal Monastery near Pec, Kosovo; from thirteenth to eighteenth century served as seat of administration for Serbian Orthodox Church

THE SOUTH SLAV groups in present-day Yugoslavia became linguistically and culturally differentiated after they had migrated to the Balkan Peninsula in the sixth and seventh centuries A.D. Their subjection to various non-Slav powers occupying the area during the next twelve centuries fostered even greater variations among them in religion, language, culture, and political development. For some 600 years before 1914, Croats and Slovenes were subordinated to the Germanic and Roman Catholic Habsburg Empire. The Eastern Orthodox Serbs, Macedonians, and Islamized Slavs were under the rule of the Ottoman Empire for much of the period between the fourteenth and nineteenth centuries.

Centuries of foreign rule, however, did not prevent the development of a strong sense of ethnic identity within each of the South Slav groups. Slovenes, Serbs, Croats, Montenegrins, and Macedonians sought to maintain separate characters and identities. Serbia's successful struggle to regain independence in the early nineteenth century stimulated the other groups to strive for independence.

During the nineteenth century some Slovene, Croat, and Serb intellectuals began to advocate the creation of a united and independent South Slav, i.e., Yugoslav, state. By 1914 the sentiment for a union of the South Slavs was widespread, and at the end of World War I the Western Allied Powers agreed to the concept of a Yugoslav kingdom to be formed by uniting the South Slav territories of the defeated Austro-Hungarian Dual Monarchy (the successor to the Habsburg Empire) with Serbia, Montenegro, and northern Macedonia. Until 1929 the new state was known as the Kingdom of the Serbs, Croats, and Slovenes.

After formation of the kingdom, the sense of separateness that was the legacy of the past continued to exert a significant influence on each group. Forces of unity and cohesion were counterbalanced by the influences of ethnic extremism. Threats to the internal order of the state by ethnically based political extremist groups led to the establishment of a royal dictatorship in 1929, a situation that continued until the outbreak of World War II and the occupation of Yugoslavia by the Axis Powers.

It is difficult to overemphasize the extent to which the Yugoslavia of 1981 was the creation of the late Josip Broz, known as Tito. Chief of the Communist Party of Yugoslavia from 1937 onward, Tito achieved fame and prominence during World War II as leader of a small group of dedicated Communists and commander of a large guerrilla army, popularly known as the Partisans. Under Tito the Partisans waged war not only against the Axis invaders but also against groups within Yugoslavia that collaborated with Hitler and his Nazi regime. In addition to conducting almost constant guerrilla warfare,

3

Tito and his closest associates created government institutions—executive, legislative, and judicial—that enabled them to govern large sections of the country during the war and to establish a functioning government as soon as the Germans retreated from the country.

The post-World War II history of the nation is in large part the record of the regime's evolution of its own variant of communism and the internal and external forces that molded it. During the first three years in power, the Tito government modeled itself after the governmental philosophy of the Soviet Union. But Tito's unwillingness to follow the Soviet lead on several major issues led to a break with the Soviets in 1948 and resulted in an independent course that eventually brought about important ideological and organizational deviations from the Soviet version of communism. The formerly sweeping powers of the federal government were narrowed by a system of local autonomy, and constitutional reforms were accompanied by measures that theoretically limited the dominance of the League of Communists of Yugoslavia (known as the Communist Party of Yugoslavia until 1952). In practice, however, the authority of the League of Communists continued as the basic political force, holding effective but generally indirect influence over almost all activities. The sociopolitical system that then evolved was based upon a Marxist view of society but included a high degree of decentralization, offering citizens a limited opportunity to participate at the community or enterprise level in some degree of economic and political self-management.

During the 1970s Tito and his associates refined and clarified preparations for an orderly transfer of power, and at his death on May 4, 1980, a few days short of his eighty-eighth birthday, the succession of power proceeded as planned. But Tito's country and countrymen—beset as they were by economic problems and by ethnic, linguistic, and religious disputes—will sorely miss Tito's charisma and political acumen as they confront the problems of the 1980s.

Pre-Slav History

Recent archaeological discoveries reveal that the territory of today's Yugoslavia has been inhabited since the Paleolithic era. Paleolithic sites have been researched in more than 100 places, and Neolithic and Bronze Age settlements are even more numerous, covering practically the entire Yugoslav territory.

When the Greeks began establishing colonies along the Dalmatian Coast (sixth century B.C.), the populations living north of the Epirus and west of the Vardar rivers came to be known as Illyrians, while those living east of the Vardar were referred to as Thracians (see fig. 8).

The penetration of the Romans into the Balkan Peninsula started in the third century B.C., but it was only by 168 B.C. that

Dalmatia, Macedonia, and most of Illyria became Roman provinces. In A.D. 9 Rome created the huge province of Illyricum, thus bringing under one administration the territory of contemporary Yugoslavia with the exception of northern Serbia (today's Vojvodina). The empire ruled the large area for five centuries, exposing the native population to its developed civilization. Military camps became the main centers of Roman influence, the economy made rapid progress, and the province became relatively urbanized. The western and central lands were known especially for mineral wealth and the Pannonian Plains for agricultural products. Trade with Italy was active, largely because of the remarkable network of roads built by the Romans.

The process of Romanization took place mostly in the towns and on the coast; inland, especially in the mountain areas, various indigenous groups preserved their traditions. Beginning in the fourth century A.D. Gothic, Hunic, and Avaric invaders swept through the entire region but did not control it directly. A fundamental ethnic change did not occur until the sixth century with the arrival of the Slavs and the creation of permanent Slav settlements.

From their original habitat the Slavs moved toward the Ukraine and southern Russia and from there to the lower Danube area in what is today Romania and Hungary (see fig. 2). In A.D. 602, taking advantage of a rebellion in the Byzantine army, they forced the imperial frontier on the Danube and invaded the Balkans, reaching the Peloponnesus in the south and the Adriatic Coast in the west. The early distinctions between Slav tribes are still difficult to make, but soon those covering the territory of present-day Yugoslavia split into three main branches: the Slovenes in the northwest, the Croats to their south, the Serbs in the southeast.

Some native inhabitants of the area withdrew to those cities that had remained for some time in the hands of the Byzantine Empire and were better protected; others, such as the Vlachs, isolated themselves by fleeing to the more inaccessible forests and mountains and were reduced mainly to animal husbandry—but were able nevertheless to survive for centuries as a population of Roman origin and language. The majority accepted the new arrivals and were Slavicised by them. By the end of the sixth century the stage was set for the appearance of the first Slav states.

Early Slav History

The Slovenes

By the eighth century the Slovenes had submitted to the domination of the Franks. Under Charlemagne, German Catholic missionaries converted them to Christianity and introduced German culture. German influence increased, and the Slovene peasants became serfs under the German feudal nobility. During the tenth and eleventh centuries the Slovene lands were divided into the marches (borderlands) of Carniola, Carantania (the name given in the eighth

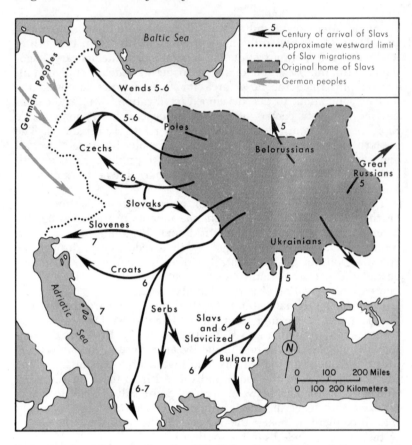

Source: Based on information from Roy E.H. Mellor, *Eastern Europe: A Geography of
the Comecon Countries*, New York, 1975, p. 41.

Figure 2. *Migrations of the Slavs, Fifth–Seventh Centuries, A.D.*

century to the region known more recently as Carinthia), and Styria
(see fig. 3).

Throughout the next two centuries the Slovenes were ruled by a
variety of petty princes until the region came under the control of
the Habsburgs in the late thirteenth century. From then until 1918
the Slovene lands were an integral part of the Habsburg domains,
although during the fifteenth to the seventeenth centuries the
Slovenes, like the Slav groups to the south, were repeatedly subjected to Turkish raids.

In the sixteenth century the Protestant Reformation had considerable influence among the Slovenes, but the severity of the Counter-
Reformation, combined with the efforts of the Austrian nobility to
retain power, reinforced both the feudal system and the discipline of
the church over the peasant population. The centralization policy of
the Habsburg rulers during the seventeenth century resulted in an

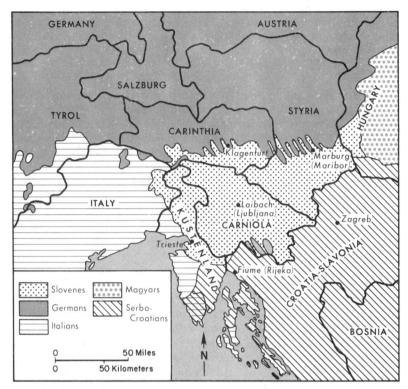

Source: Based on information from Great Britain, Admiralty, Naval Intelligence Division, *Yugoslavia, II: History, Peoples, and Administration*, London, 1944, p. 14a.

Figure 3. Slovene Lands Before 1918

even greater degree of Germanization. German was made the official language for all government affairs as well as for education, but Slovene national consciousness remained strong, and the masses continued to speak the Slovenian language.

French troops came into the Slovene regions during Napoleon's campaign against Austria, and in 1809 the Treaty of Vienna brought most of the Slovene lands and Croatia under the control of France. These areas, plus Dalmatia—the coastal region along the Adriatic Sea—were formed into the Illyrian provinces under a French proconsul. During the brief period of French control, there was substantial improvement in the material conditions of the Slovenes. Additional schools were established, and the Slovene language was given renewed status.

After the defeat of Napoleon's forces in the Russian campaign, the 1815 agreements of the Congress of Vienna restored the Slovene lands, as well as Dalmatia and part of Croatia, to the Austrian Empire. Although Slovenes were again subjected to German control,

7

Slovene national consciousness continued to grow, and sentiments developed favoring not only Slovene unity and independence but the union of all the South Slavs as well.

The Croats

During the sixth and early seventh centuries Croatian tribes migrated from the Dnieper River region (Ukraine) into the land between the Sava and Drava rivers (Slavonia), the land directly south of the Slovene area (Croatia), and into the northern Adriatic coastal region (Dalmatia). In the seventh century these tribes converted to Christianity.

Largely in response to military pressure from both the eastern and western branches of the Roman empires, organization on a family and tribal basis evolved into broader units during the eighth century. Two principal settlements developed, Dalmatian Croatia along the Adriatic, and Pannonian Croatia to the north, centering in the valley of the Sava River. During the first quarter of the ninth century, the northern Croats were brought under the hegemony of the Franks, and Dalmatian Croatia came under the nominal control of the Eastern Empire. Because of their relative isolation from the two power centers, the Croatian groups were eventually able to shake off foreign domination and by the early tenth century had begun to develop a sense of common identity.

About 924 Tomislav, a powerful *zupan* (tribal leader) from Nin, a city on the Adriatic, united the Pannonian and Dalmatian Croats and was recognized by the pope as king. He extended the borders of his territory inland to include part of Bosnia and established a kingdom that continued for nearly 200 years.

During this time the original tribal structure of Croatian society was gradually replaced by feudalism. A class system developed, based on landholdings. The leaders of the more powerful clans assumed the status of a hereditary nobility; the royal family and the church accumulated extensive properties formerly held as a common tribal land, and the peasants were reduced to serfdom.

In the late eleventh century the increasing strength of the nobility limited the authority of the king, and his power began to wane. When the throne became vacant in 1089, a long struggle ensued between rival Croatian claimants. In 1102, not having a leader strong enough to unite the Croatian lands, the Croatian nobles offered the crown—with the blessing of Pope Paschal II—to the king of Hungary. Although at times the Croats enjoyed a special status, during most of the ensuing 800 years (until 1918) Croatia remained tied to Hungary.

In the late fourteenth century the Ottoman Empire began its incursions into the more northern regions of the Balkan Peninsula, and after Bosnia fell to Turkish forces in 1463, the sultan's armies pushed into Croatian lands. For sixty years the Croats and Hungarians sought to resist the periodic raiding of the Turks, but in 1526 the Hungarian army was defeated in a disastrous encounter;

the king was killed, and Hungarian resistance ended. The next year Croatian nobles opted to submit to the Habsburg Emperor Ferdinand, who that same year had become ruler of most of Hungary. The Turks continued to press northward and by the end of the sixteenth century had absorbed much of Croatia and almost all of Slavonia.

In 1578 the Habsburg emperor established a Military Frontier Province in the depopulated southern borderland of what remained of Croatia and Slavonia. Expropriated from Croatian nobles, these lands were subject directly to the emperor, who granted them to soldier-peasants, free from feudal obligations in return for military service.

In 1699, when the Habsburgs recovered all of Croatia and Slavonia from the Turks, the Military Frontier Province was extended to include the southern half of Croatia, Slavonia, and the Vojvodina—the southern part of the Hungarian Danubian Plain directly east of Slovania (see fig. 4). The land was settled not only by Croat peasants but by Germans and a large number of Serbs who migrated into the area to escape Ottoman oppression. The descendants of these Serb immigrants later became a controversial factor in the nineteenth-century issue of Croatian nationalism.

The Croat feudal nobility opposed the emperor's efforts to retain the frontier lands under his direct control, but the system was continued until the late nineteenth century. The frontier soldier-peasants became the most loyal of the emperor's subjects; as late as World War I these frontier elements resisted Croatian nationalist sentiment in favor of the emperor.

The Dalmatian coastal area of the medieval Croatian state was the object of 300 years of conflict between Hungary and the growing power of Venice. Some Dalmatian cities changed hands repeatedly. From the fifteenth century to the end of the eighteenth, most of the coastal area was subordinate to Venice and shared in its art, commerce, and wealth. The Republic of Ragusa (see Glossary), present-day Dubrovnik, remained independent of foreign control throughout most of the period, however, and developed its own high level of economic prosperity and culture. By the eighteenth century the commercial power of Venice and Ragusa had passed to other European states, and the Dalmatian cities were in a state of decay.

Like the Slovene lands, part of Croatia was incorporated into the Illyrian provinces by Napoleon in the early years of the nineteenth century. During the four years of French control, schools were established, the first Croatian-language newspaper appeared, commerce was stimulated, and Croatian nationalist sentiment was fomented.

After Napoleon's defeat, Slovenia, Dalmatia, and the Military Frontier Province were restored to Austria; the rest of Croatia went to Hungary within the Habsburg Empire. Feudalism was formally ended by the Habsburg emperor, and Slovene and Croat peasants were permitted to buy their land from their former feudal lords.

9

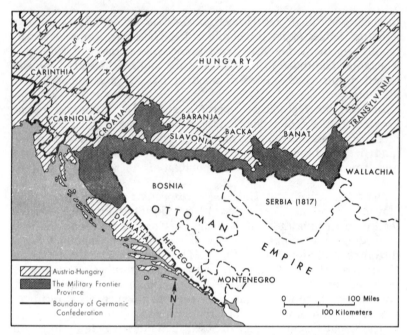

Source: Based on information from Great Britain, Admiralty, Naval Intelligence Division, *Yugoslavia, II: History, Peoples, and Administration*, London, 1944, p. 20.

Figure 4. Military Frontier Province Between the Habsburg and Ottoman Empires, ca. 1600–1800

The second half of the nineteenth century was dominated politically by two parties. In 1841 Bishop Josif Juraj Strossmayer founded the National Party. Strossmayer was a strong advocate of Slav unity within the Habsburg Empire and a supporter of the independence struggle in Serbia, which he thought could become the core of a future Yugoslav entity. Strossmayer also founded the Yugoslav Academy of Zagreb in 1867, and he was the main organizer of the first Yugoslav Congress, held in Ljubljana, Slovenia, in 1870. After the bishop's death the party split into different national groups representing Croats and other nationalities living in Croatia; of these, the Serbs were the most important (26 percent of the entire population). The Serbs created their own National Independent Party of Croatia in 1887; a similar Serbian party appeared in Dalmatia.

The other important political force was the Party of Rights, founded by Ante Starcevic in the 1860s. It promoted views totally different from Strossmayer's. Starcevic started as a pan-Slavist but eventually became an ardent Croatian nationalist. He opposed both Austrian and Hungarian dominance and was in favor of an independent Croatia, reborn in its medieval frontiers. His map of Croatia included not only Dalmatia and the Military Frontier Province but also Slovenia and Istria, which had never been part of medieval Croatia. When Bosnia and Hercegovina were put under Austrian control in 1878, the Party of Rights extended its activity into these two provinces, considering them as part of the Croatian kingdom. When some members of the party gave up their militant anti-imperial attitudes and joined the government, Starcevic in 1895 founded a new Pure Party of Rights. Supported by the middle class and the peasants, this party was more influential than any other political force in Croatia. Nationalistic and anti-Serbian, its ideas outlived the party itself and presented serious problems for the new Yugoslav state after 1918. Ante Pavelic's "independent" Croatia of 1941 represented the natural continuation of Starcevic's program.

The Serbs

Serb tribes settled in the interior of the Balkan Peninsula south and east of the Croatian lands during the seventh century. Throughout these early years clans engaged each other in a continual struggle for dominance. During most of the period from the eighth through the eleventh centuries the Serbs were under the control of either Bulgar or Byzantine rulers. In the latter half of the ninth century, Byzantine monks—the most important of whom were Methodius and Cyril—converted the Serbs to Christianity and introduced Byzantine culture into the area.

Byzantine control was weak, however, and by the twelfth century strong tribal leaders were able to unite the Serbs into two independent Serbian states: Zeta, in the mountainous region of present-day Montenegro and Hercegovina; and Raska, in Serbia proper. Shortly before 1170 Stephan Nemanja became the grand *zupan* of Raska. He shook off Byzantine hegemony, united the two states into a Serbian kingdom, and founded a dynasty that in the next 200 years made Serbia the strongest state in the Balkans.

The Serbian rulers enlisted the Eastern Orthodox Church in their efforts to unite the dissident tribes. In 1196 Nemanja abdicated the throne and with his son helped found the great Serbian Orthodox monastery of Hilander on Mount Athos in present-day Greece. The younger Nemanja later gained recognition from the Byzantine patriarch for an independent Serbian archbishopric, and in 1219 (under the name of Sava) he became the first Serbian archbishop. The Serbian rulers developed a fierce loyalty to the church among their people.

The Serbian Empire reached its zenith under its last emperor, Tsar Stephen Dusan (1331–35). Guided by Dusan's genius, Serbian economy and arts developed greatly. In 1349 he promulgated an important legal code, known as the Dusanov Zakonik, which fused Byzantine law and Serbian custom into a formal legal and political system. Dusan expanded the empire to include all of modern Albania, Macedonia, Epirus, and Thessaly. With Dusan's death, however, rebellion by subordinate nobles brought about the disintegration of the empire.

11

Encouraged by the disunity of the Serbian state, the Ottoman Turks, who had expanded into the southern Balkans in the middle of the fourteenth century, advanced against the Serbs. In 1389 the Turks met and defeated the Serbian armies in Kosovo in what was to become the most famous battle in Serbian history.

Turkish power in the Balkans steadily increased, and after the second great defeat of the Serbs at Smederevo in 1459, the Serbian lands were placed under Turkish military occupation and so remained for more than 350 years. Bosnia fell to the Turks in 1463; Hercegovina, in 1483. Only the most inaccessible mountainous Serbian area north of Lake Scutari—present-day Montenegro—was able to resist Turkish domination.

When the Ottoman Turks overran Serbia, Macedonia, and Bosnia, the Slav nobles of Serbia and Macedonia were killed or forced to flee to the mountains or into Hungary. The Turkish sultan granted large landholdings to spahis (cavalry officers), who subjected the Christian serfs to a new, oppressive feudal system. The Serbs continued to be tied to their land and were forced to pay heavy taxes in kind to the spahis and other Turkish administrators. In addition every four years they had to submit to the seizure of a portion of the healthiest and most gifted boys in each village, whom the spahis sent to Constantinople to be educated as Muslims and trained as part of the sultan's elite military corps, the Janissary. Many came to occupy high positions in the Ottoman government.

During the first 200 years of Turkish occupation, when the Ottoman Empire was expanding and the newly conquered lands were able to support the increasing numbers of Muslim aristocrats, Turkish rule was not intolerably oppressive. As long as the Christian serfs paid taxes, they were permitted to live according to Serbian customs and to govern their own local affairs without direct interference from the Turkish administration. They could not be removed from their land, which continued to be treated as private family property. The Turks were tolerant of the Christian religion, although they impoverished the Serbian Orthodox Church by seizing most of its lands and its richest buildings.

The Serbs reverted to the egalitarian rural society that had characterized their social structure before the rise of feudalism. They avoided town living, and towns were inhabited almost solely by the Turkish nobility and administrators, along with the non-Slav craftsmen and traders who supplied them. The Serb villagers retained a high degree of autonomy under the administration of village councils elected by the head of each Serbian family. In the absence of a native nobility, the members of the church hierarchy were recognized by the Serbs as their leaders, and the Serbian Orthodox Church became the major perpetuator of Serbian tradition and national consciousness.

During the late seventeenth century and the first half of the eighteenth, the Serb peasants supported several vain attempts by the Habsburg armies to force the Turks out of Serbia. Brutal reprisals by the Ottoman administrators triggered a mass migration of 30,000 to 40,000 Serb families, who moved northward in 1691 and settled in Habsburg-controlled Vojvodina. During the second half of the eighteenth century, Constantinople lost most of its control over its officials in Serbia, who then entered a period of unrestrained oppression and plundering of the defenseless Serb peasants. As the power of the Ottoman Empire declined, Habsburg Austria and tsarist Russia attempted to extend their hegemony over the Balkans. During the late eighteenth century the two powers joined together to oust the Turks, but their efforts were indecisive until the expansion of Napoleon's empire began to threaten Turkish territories.

With the sultan's forces under pressure from Napoleon in the Mediterranean area, Russia moved to occupy Turkish provinces in the eastern region of the Balkans. In 1804, sensing that the time was ripe for revolt, a Serbian peasant, Djordje Petrovic—known to his followers as Karadjordje (Black George)—led the Serbs in an uprising against their Turkish rulers. The revolution was successful for a time, and Karadjordje established a short-lived government in Belgrade. When Napoleon's forces attacked Russia in 1812, Russian troops were withdrawn from the Balkan area, and Turkey took advantage of the situation to move against the Serbs. By October 1813 the Serbs were defeated, and Karadjordje fled to Austria.

In 1817 a second revolt, led by a peasant, Milos Obrenovic, forced the Turks to grant the Serbs a considerable degree of autonomy. The mysterious murder of Karadjordje that same year began a feud between his descendants and those of Obrenovic that affected Serbian politics until the early twentieth century.

Although Serbia remained nominally a province of Turkey after 1817, the Serbs were virtually independent. By 1830, with the support of Russia, they were able to force Constantinople to establish Serbia as an autonomous principality. Russia took the new state under its protection, but it was not until 1878 that complete freedom from Turkish domination was achieved via the Treaty of Berlin. In 1882 the Serbian ruler took the title of king.

Unlike the development in Croatia where nationalist sentiment was fostered by an intellectual minority, Serbian independence was created by the peasant masses. Milos Obrenovic gained additional support among the peasants by dividing the confiscated Turkish properties among them. Under the Turkish landlords the peasant class had been given no opportunities for education, and almost none, including the leaders, were literate. Much of the leadership in the government established in 1817 was provided by educated Serb immigrants from Vojvodina, who introduced a romantic nationalist passion for the native language and folkways that strengthened the people's self-consciousness as a nation.

In 1839, after much dissension over the autocratic nature of Milos Obrenovic's rule, he was forced to abdicate in favor of his son. The sultan named a group of advisers, and in 1842 the advisers, some of whom belonged to a group called the Defenders of the Constitution, forced out the Obrenovic prince and installed Alexander Karadjordjevic, son of the first Karadjordje, on the throne. Internal conflicts were exacerbated by Russian and Austrian influences who used the Serbian rivalries as a means of keeping Serbia weak. Serbia remained neutral in the Crimean War and accepted the terms of the Treaty of Paris in 1856, which ended Russia's position as exclusive protector of the Serbs and placed Serbia under the protection of Austria, Britain, France, and Turkey. Amidst complex internal dissensions, the Serbian parliament (Skupstina) deposed Alexander in 1858 in favor of the return of the Obrenovic dynasty.

Milos Obrenovic again became prince of Serbia for a brief, autocratic period. Upon his death in 1860, he was succeeded by his son Michael, also ruling for a second time. In 1868 Michael was assassinated, and for the next twenty years Serbia was ruled by his cousin Milan, whose scandalous private life and inattention to state affairs led to widespread unrest. In 1889 Milan, who had been recognized by that time as the king of Serbia, attempted to regain popular support by promulgating a new liberal constitution, but in 1893 his successor Alexander Obrenovic set the constitution aside and instituted an oppressive oligarchic rule. Disorders and plots multiplied toward the end of the century.

The first well-organized political parties came into existence during his reign. The liberals, who had been active since the assembly of 1858, were influential for most of the 1870s. Young conservatives who were known as progressives dominated affairs during much of the 1880s, but their close relationship with the palace caused them to lose ground after Milan's abdication in 1889. The new rising force became the Radical Party organized by Nikola Pasic, who remained its leader until his death in 1926. Ideologically the radicals had been inspired by Sviatozar Markovic, the first Serbian Socialist; the radicals claimed to represent the interests of the peasants and were in favor of local government, reform of the bureaucracy, and reforms favoring the needy.

The latter part of the nineteenth century was a period of international unrest throughout the Balkans. Serbia declared war on Turkey in support of the Bosnian peasant uprisings in 1876 and was rewarded by the Congress of Berlin, which recognized its complete independence from the Ottoman Empire. Serbia's internal weakness, however, enabled Austria to gain considerable influence over Serbian foreign affairs and trade. In 1882 Serbia was declared a kingdom, but neither its international prestige nor its internal affairs improved. By 1905 Austrian influence increased to the point where 90 percent of Serbian exports and 60 percent of its imports were controlled by the Austro-Hungarian Dual Monarchy.

In 1903 opposition to Obrenovic rule culminated in the brutal assassination of Alexander and his wife. The parliament elected Peter Karadjordjevic to the throne. An intelligent ruler, he revived and further liberalized the constitution of 1889. He reorganized the country's finances and reasserted Serbian independence of action from Austria. In 1905 the Serbs began trade negotiations with Bulgaria and planned to shift Serbian munitions orders from Austria to France. The Austrians tried to bring the Serbs to heel by placing a prohibitive tariff on all Serbian livestock. The so-called pig war of 1906 threatened disaster, for pigs were Serbia's main export. The Serbs succeeded in finding other markets, but the pig war reinforced hostility toward the Dual Monarchy among Serbian peasants.

This hostility had its counterpart in Austrian fear and mistrust of Serbia's expansionist policies. The foreign policy of the Radical Party governments that ruled Serbia under the constitutional Karadjordjevic monarchy after 1903 was based on the slogan "Serbia must expand or die." Expansionist efforts were directed toward the south into Macedonia and west toward the Adriatic through Bosnia and Hercegovina. These aims brought Serbia into direct conflict with the Austro-Hungarian Empire and Bulgaria. The Austrians were particularly anxious because of the rapprochement that took place just after the turn of the century between Serbia and Habsburg-controlled Croatia.

A serious crisis was created in October 1908 when the Austrian government annexed Bosnia and Hercegovina, ostensibly to frustrate Serbian plans to move into the two provinces. This unilateral move produced intense resentment in both Serbia and Montenegro. Serbia received encouragement—but no military support—from Russia. The British government also supported Serbia's diplomatic protests. Germany staunchly defended Austria's right to the territory. Thus were drawn the major outlines of the competing alliances that were to evolve into World War I.

Deprived of Bosnia and access to the Adriatic, Serbian hopes for expansion came to center on Macedonia, then part of the Ottoman Empire. In the 1890s a number of anti-Turk secret societies developed in Macedonia, chief of which was the Internal Macedonian Revolutionary Organization (Vatreshna Makedonska Revolutsionna Organizatsa—IMRO). Violent pressure groups representing Greek, Serbian, and Bulgarian interests also proliferated and kept the region in constant turmoil. From 1911 to 1912 various alliances were formed between Bulgaria, Greece, Serbia, and Montenegro, marking a temporary triumph over centuries of disunion and distrust. In 1912 the quick victory of the Balkan allies over Turkey, in the first Balkan War, led to a dispute between Serbia and Bulgaria over the sharing of Macedonia, which the war had freed from Ottoman rule. During June and July of 1913, supported by Greece, Montenegro, and Romania, Serbia defeated the Bulgarians. By the subsequent Treaty of Bucharest the Serbs acquired a much larger share of Macedonia—extending almost to the southern boundary granted the new state of Yugoslavia after World War I. The simultaneous creation of the independent state of Albania, however, frustrated Serbia's plans to reach the Adriatic (see fig. 5).

Serbian successes in the Balkan wars acted as an impetus for the other Slav peoples within the Austro-Hungarian Dual Monarchy,

Figure 5. Expansion of Serbia, 1804–1914

and the Austrian government decided to eliminate the Serbian threat. Therefore, when Archduke Franz-Ferdinand, heir to the Habsburg throne, and his consort, the Duchess of Hohenberg, were assassinated in Sarajevo (Bosnia) on June 28, 1914, by a young Bosnian, Gavrilo Princep, a member of a secret pro-Serbian terrorist group, the Austrian government presented Serbia with an ultimatum whose terms were so harsh as to preclude acceptance by the Serbs. The Serbian government suggested international arbitration of the question, but Austria declared war on July 28, 1914. Within a week Germany had aligned with Austria, while Britain, France, and Russia came to Serbia's defense. The war was destined to end Habsburg hegemony over the Balkans and to forge a Yugoslav state.

Bosnia and Hercegovina

Serbian groups settled the region of present-day Bosnia and

Hercegovina during the seventh century, but the area was separated from Serbia in the tenth century and experienced a different history. Bosnia or Bosna (from the Bosna River) appears to have originated as a small principality in the mountainous region of the upper reaches of the Bosna and Vrbas rivers. The name Hercegovina originated in the fifteenth century when a powerful Bosnian noble, Stephen Vuksic, gained control of lands in the southern part of Bosnia and took the title of Herzog, the German equivalent of duke, from which came the name of the region.

Situated on the dividing line between the areas of Roman Catholic and Eastern Orthodox religious influence, Bosnia and Hercegovina suffered from constant internal turmoil from the tenth through the fifteenth centuries. This situation was complicated by the introduction from Bulgaria of an ascetic heretical Christian cult—Bogomilism—during the twelfth century. It gained widespread popular adherence as a protest against the proselytism of both existing major religions. Many Bosnian nobles and a large portion of the peasantry persisted in the heresy despite repeated attempts by both the Catholic and Eastern Orthodox churches to crush the cult. The chaos caused by this religious struggle laid the country open to the Ottoman Turks after they again defeated the Serbs in 1459. By 1463 the Turks controlled Bosnia and twenty years later gained control of Hercegovina; many Bogomil nobles and peasants accepted the Islamic religion of their conquerors.

The Islamized nobles were allowed to retain their lands and their feudal privileges, and the peasants who accepted Islam were granted land free from feudal obligations. The Christian nobles were killed and Christian peasants subjected to oppressive rule. Early in the nineteenth century the Christian peasants revolted against the Islamic nobility in a series of uprisings that were bloodily suppressed. In 1850 the Turkish government itself put down the Bosnian aristocracy and established a centrally controlled Turkish administration. The Christian serfs continued to rebel against the new administration, and by 1875 both Bosnia and Hercegovina were in a state of general revolt. The following year Serbia and Montenegro declared war on Turkey in support of the insurrection. In 1877 Russia entered the war against Turkey in order to increase its influence among the Balkan Slavs. The Russian army defeated the Turks in January 1878, and the Treaty of San Stefano, which the Russians dictated in March 1878, provided for the recognition of an autonomous government in Bosnia and Hercegovina.

The Habsburg and British governments, fearing the growing influence of Russia in the Balkans, called the Congress of Berlin in July 1878, which revised the basic terms of the Treaty of San Stefano. The congress placed Bosnia and Hercegovina temporarily under the administration of Austria-Hungary, and in 1908 the Austro-Hungarian Dual Monarchy unilaterally annexed the two provinces.

Under Austro-Hungarian control the Bosnians were not permitted any degree of self-rule. Individuals from other parts of the

17

Dual Monarchy were brought in to administer the area. Material conditions in Bosnia and Hercegovina improved considerably, but the peasants were still subject to the basic features of the old feudal system. Nationalist tendencies developed among the people as a result of influences from neighboring Serbia and Croatia. In 1914 the population was divided. Many of the Catholics wished to retain their ties with the monarchy; the Eastern Orthodox Serbs wanted to unite with Serbia; and the Muslims were divided on the issue, some fearing both proposals. Revolutionary sentiments were widespread, particularly among the youth, and it was a young Bosnian who assassinated Archduke Franz-Ferdinand.

The Montenegrins

In medieval times the area north of Lake Scutari was known as Duklja, or Zeta. In the twelfth century it came under the rule of Stephan Nemanja of Serbia, but after his death Serbian power dwindled, and the region was ruled by a succession of local rulers.

After the Turkish victory over Serbia in the late fourteenth century the region, which had come to be known as Montenegro, the Venetian variant of the Italian word for black mountain, became a refuge for Serbs who refused to live under the Ottomans. Although Montenegro repeatedly suffered attacks by Turkish and other external forces over a period of some four centuries, it was never fully subdued. The constant struggles of the Montenegrins, particularly those with raiding Turks and Albanians, resulted in the development of the Montenegrin reputation for bellicosity.

In the early sixteenth century Montenegro became a type of theocracy with *vladike* (Eastern Orthodox bishops) exercising both temporal and spiritual control. The *vladike* were elected by local assemblies until 1697 when succession was restricted to the family of Danilo Patrovic Njegus. Since the *vladike* were celibates, the line passed from uncle to nephew. The Njegus family ruled Montenegro as bishop-princes for more than 150 years. Under the successive *vladike* the territory doubled in size.

In 1851 the offices of bishop and prince were separated, but the Njegus family continued to rule. Nicholas I became the prince in 1860 and remained ruler of Montenegro until the outbreak of World War I.

The 1878 Treaty of Berlin greatly increased the size of Montenegro and granted formal recognition of the country as a princedom. Nicholas I established a parliamentary constitution in 1905 and took the title of king in 1910. At the outbreak of World War I he went into exile. An opposition political movement, known as the Montenegrin Committee, was formed in Geneva and began to press for the incorporation of Montenegro into a union of all South Slavs. In 1918 Nicholas' rule was ended, and Montenegro became part of the new South Slav state.

The Macedonians

Long an area of contention and competition between the powers that figured prominently in the history of the Balkans, the territory covered by the historical-geographic term Macedonia has been divided among the states of Yugoslavia, Bulgaria, and Greece. Strategically located and ethnographically complex, Macedonia typifies the Balkan problem of conflicting interests and rival peoples.

Slav tribes settled in the region, an area considerably larger than Yugoslavia's Macedonian republic, in the seventh century, at which time the territory was under the control of the Byzantine Empire. During the ninth century much of Macedonia was incorporated by the Bulgars (also South Slavs) into the first Bulgarian Empire. In the latter half of the tenth century the region again came under Byzantine domination, which was troubled by repeated uprisings of the Macedonian Slavs.

During the fourteenth century most of Macedonia was conquered by the Serb ruler Stephen Dusan, who set up his capital at Skopje. After the death of Dusan the Serbian empire disintegrated, and following the historic Battle of Kosovo in 1389, the major part of Macedonia came under Ottoman control and remained so until the twentieth century

As Bulgarian nationalism developed in the nineteenth century, the Bulgarians, after much controversy, were successful in gaining Turkish approval for a separate Bulgarian Orthodox Church (the exarchate). Since the authority of the Exarchate covered most of Macedonia and part of Serbia as well as Bulgaria, the church became a means of extending Bulgar influence, a fact particularly resented by the Serbs.

Rivalry between Serbs, Bulgars, Greeks, and Turks was increased in the late nineteenth century. Russian troops invaded Turkey in 1877 and dictated terms of the Treaty of San Stefano, providing for a greatly enlarged, autonomous Bulgaria that was to include most of Macedonia. But the Treaty of San Stefano was quickly nullified by the Treaty of Berlin—a great disappointment to almost all elements of the Balkan population. The Treaty of Berlin returned Macedonia to the Ottomans, established an independent but greatly reduced Bulgaria, and allowed Austrian forces to occupy Bosnia and Hercegovina. Along with renewed Turkish control of Macedonia, the Austrian presence in Bosnia and Hercegovina came as a bitter blow to Serbian aspirations. The result was to increase Serbian and Bulgarian rivalry in Macedonia, and Bulgaria continued to use the Treaty of San Stefano as a basis for its claims to the area.

Bulgarian, Serbian, and Greek organizations launched intensive propaganda campaigns in Macedonia to strengthen their particular claims. Even Romania entered the contest, basing its claim on the Vlach population scattered throughout the Macedonian area. In 1896 the underground independence movement, IMRO, was organized within Macedonia. Torn between the competing forces, the

Macedonian peasants responded to the organization's slogan "Macedonia for the Macedonians."

Competition over Macedonia eventually led to the Balkan wars of 1912–13. Montenegro, Serbia, Greece, and Bulgaria joined together in a successful campaign to drive the Turks from Macedonia. Once this goal was achieved, however, the victors were unable to reach an agreement on the division of the territory, and Bulgaria attacked the Greek and Serbian forces in Macedonia. Montenegro, Romania, and Turkey joined with Greece and Serbia to defeat Bulgaria. A peace treaty, signed in Bucharest in 1913, ceded north and central Macedonia to Serbia, granted the southern region to Greece, and provided for a small extension of the Montenegro frontier. Bulgaria retained a small portion of eastern Macedonia. The areas of former Macedonia that came under Serbian control in 1913 were included within the Serbian territory under the Yugoslav kingdom, and were then given the status of a republic in post-World War II Yugoslavia.

The Yugoslav Movement and World War I

In the late 1800s Germany's Prince Otto von Bismarck predicted that "some damned foolish thing in the Balkans" would trigger the next European war. The assassination of Archduke Franz-Ferdinand on June 28, 1914, resulted in a series of foolish things. The Austrians issued an ultimatum to Serbia that would have resulted in Austria's absorption of Serbia. Germany announced its support of Austria; Russia, its support of Serbia. On July 28 Austria attacked Serbia, and within days World War I was under way.

The military campaign against Serbia proved more difficult than the Austrian-Hungarian general staff had expected. The Serbs resisted successfully, and the Balkan front soon reached a stalemate. The military balance changed only in 1915 when Bulgaria joined the Central Powers. Under joint German-Austrian-Bulgarian pressure the Serbian defenses collapsed. Belgrade fell on October 9, 1915, and by November it became clear that Serbia faced defeat. The army began a long retreat toward the Adriatic, finally reaching the Island of Corfu in January 1916; Corfu remained the seat of the Serbian government until the end of the war. The army was transferred to northern Greece and placed under the command of a French general on the Salonika front. When the French offensive started in 1918, the army played an important role in the defeat of Bulgaria and in the liberation of Serbia from the remaining German, Austrian, and Bulgarian forces.

The defeat of 1915 did not put an end to the many plans for the creation of a new South Slav state. The Yugoslav idea had strong roots and had been expressed several times since the late 1700s; even Karadjordje had expressed it in letters presented to Napoleon and to the Austrian emperor. During the nineteenth century, despite many conflicts provoked by both the Greater Serbian and Greater Croatian nationalists, the Yugoslav idea was kept alive by movements

Statue of Prince Mihajlo; National Theater and National Museum in background, Belgrade

such as that founded by Strossmayer. Ironically Yugoslavism appeared as a Croatian program, an answer to both Magyarization and Greater Serbianism. In fact the Serbs were among the last ones officially to endorse the Yugoslav idea. It was only in December 1914 that Serbia's Alexander called for the destruction of Austria-Hungary and the unification of the Serbs, Croats, and Slovenes into a single state.

In 1915 Ante Trumbic, representing the South Slavs of the Dual Monarchy, organized in London a Yugoslav Committee whose aim was to fight for the creation of a Yugoslav state in which the Serbs, the Croats, and the Slovenes would be equal partners. Serbian Premier Nikola Pasic's government was more eager to unify the South Slavs under Serbian leadership than to help create a federal state, and relations between the Yugoslav Committee and the Serbs were therefore rather uneasy. After the fall of tsarist Russia in 1917, Pasic realized that an intransigent position would isolate him diplomatically, and he gradually shifted his position toward more moderate lines. On July 20, 1917, his government and the Yugoslav Committee issued the Declaration of Corfu, calling for the creation of an independent kingdom of Serbs, Croats, and Slovenes; it was to be a constitutional and democratic monarchy, guaranteeing freedom of religion and the use of both the Latin and Cyrillic alphabets. Muslims were to enjoy the same rights as Christians; the

Karadjordje house, represented by Alexander, was to become the hereditary dynasty of the new kingdom.

The Declaration of Corfu did not settle the main problem of the future state; would it be a federal one as the committee wanted it to be, or a centralized one as desired by Pasic? The issue, which proved to be the centerpiece of interwar Yugoslav politics, was postponed for consideration by a constituent assembly to be convened after the war. Montenegro readily accepted the declaration. The Allies were thus presented with a united South Slav front.

The Allies had never regarded the Serbian demands with great sympathy and for military reasons were far more concerned with Italy. Still neutral, the Italians promised to join the allied camp if France, Britain, and Russia would accept Italy's territorial demands in central and southeast Europe. Convinced that Italian intervention would tip the balance in their favor, the Allies on April 26, 1915, secretly signed the Treaty of London, which granted Italy territorial concessions at the expense of Austria-Hungary, Albania, and Turkey. Some of this territory (Dalmatia, Istria, and western Slovenia) was inhabited by a large number of Slavs—lands that were supposed to become part of the future state of Yugoslavia. The treaty was kept secret, but some of its provisions became known to the Slavs. The growing fear of an Italian invasion to lay claim to vast sections of the South Slav lands provided a new impetus to the notion of a South Slav union. Thus the subsequent forming of the union was motivated at least in part by efforts to avoid subjugation by yet another alien power and not exclusively by any deep sense of commitment to the creation of a single state of South Slavs.

In Austria, Emperor Charles made a last effort on October 16, 1918, to save his empire by agreeing to reorganize it on a federal basis, but his attempt failed to attract popular support. As armistice neared, the Slavs proclaimed their secession from the empire on October 29, 1918. A Croatian, Serbian, and Slovene National Council was created in Zagreb with the main task of proceeding to unification. In Bosnia and Hercegovina local assemblies adopted a similar program. In November Montenegro renounced its sovereignty and joined the union of the other Slavic lands, and on December 1, 1918, Alexander officially proclaimed in Belgrade the formation of the Kingdom of Serbs, Croats, and Slovenes.

The new state faced a difficult diplomatic situation. It claimed much more territory than the Allies were willing to grant because some of the area had been promised to other powers such as Italy. From Albania, the Yugoslavs demanded the Scutari area; from Hungary—Backa, Baranja, Prekomurje, and Medjumurje; from Bulgaria—a strip of land running from the Danube to the Greek border; from Austria—Lower Styria and parts of Carinthia; from Romania—half of the Banat, formerly under Hungary but which the Allies had promised to Bucharest in 1916. Finally Italian and Yugoslav interests clashed over Istria and Dalmatia (see fig. 6).

The treaties of Saint-Germain, Neuilly, Trianon, and Rappallo

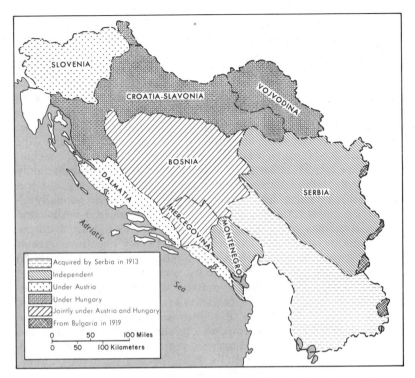

Source: Based on information from Gordon C. McDonald et al., *Yugoslavia: A Country Study*, Washington, 1973, p. 44.

Figure 6. South Slav Territories at the Formation of the Yugoslav State

resolved most of these territorial disputes and met most of the Yugoslav demands; but they did not get the Scutari area and the claimed parts of Styria, Carinthia, Istria, and Fiume. On the Dalmatian Coast Zadar remained an Italian enclave until after World War II. Some 720,000 Yugoslavs remained outside the new state while more than 1 million non-Slavs (mostly Germans, Romanians, and Hungarians) were included in it.

The Yugoslav Kingdom, 1918–41

Economic Developments

With about 11,984,000 inhabitants in 1918, the new state ranked tenth in Europe as far as population was concerned; in size it ranked twelfth. Natural resources were relatively abundant, especially the reserves of nonferrous minerals. On the eve of World War II Yugoslavia was the major European producer of bauxite, lead, chromium, and antimony and ranked second in the output of zinc, copper, and mercury. The reserves of coal were large but of low

23

quality; those of iron were scarce as were those of oil and natural gas, but hydrological energy was in great supply. Most of the population was active in farming. The percentage of workers in industry remained small throughout the interwar years, accounting for only 11 percent in 1931, and industry accounted for only 18.9 percent of the national income, compared to the 46 percent provided by agriculture.

Yugoslavia had inherited territories characterized by uneven levels of development. Slovenia, Croatia, and Vojvodina—the former Austro-Hungarian lands—were more advanced than Serbia. In 1918 Serbia, Montenegro, and Bosnia and Hercegovina had only 15 percent of the industrial enterprises in the kingdom, and this trend did not change during the entire period. Slovenia annually invested 2.5 times more capital in its industry than did Serbia and twenty-five times more than Montenegro, and its industrial output was four times greater than Serbia's and twenty-two times greater than Montenegro's. Only the mining industry progressed faster in Serbia than in the former Habsburg territories, but this was not enough to change the general pattern. Most of the industries remained concentrated in the northern and northwestern provinces, and the central government did little to change this uneven economic distribution to help develop the backward south and southeast. Throughout the interwar years Yugoslavia was heavily dependent on foreign capital. By 1937 the external debt had skyrocketed, and Swiss, British, German, French, and American capital held commanding positions in the economy, especially in the mining industry.

The land distribution pattern was different from province to province; in Serbia medium-sized holdings (five to twenty hectares) represented over 39 percent of all holdings, while the large estates (100 to 200 hectares) accounted for only 0.02 percent. In Croatia the first category was much smaller (almost 28 percent), and the large estates were more numerous. In some areas (Bosnia and Hercegovina and Montenegro) an almost feudal system remained in existence; in others (Croatia and Vojvodina) the peasants' land was heavily mortgaged. Agrarian reform was deemed absolutely necessary if progress were to be achieved in the rural areas and if agriculture were to become an efficient sector of the economy.

Steps toward agricultural reform were taken even before the official proclamation of Yugoslavia; in November 1918 the Zagreb National Council declared that in the new state everyone should be entitled to own enough land to ensure a reasonable living. The council abolished "all feudal relationships which still exist" and all "privileges which resulted from the feudal relationship." It also promised to expropriate with indemnity all the large estates and give the land to the peasants.

In Serbia the agrarian reform was not such a burning issue because the land problem had been solved by the reforms of Milos Obrenovic. The Serbian peasants had been owners of their land since

1833, and feudalism had disappeared together with the Turkish lords. The reform was badly needed in the newly acquired territories of Macedonia, however, as well as in independent but socially conservative Montenegro.

On January 6, 1919, Alexander's *Manifesto* made known the basic principles of the reform: "I wish that we immediately begin with a just solution of the agrarian question and that serfdom and large estates be abolished. In both cases the land will be distributed among the poor peasants and the former owners will be justly compensated. Every Serb, Croat, and Slovene should be full owner of his land. In our free state there can and will be only free landholders." On February 25 the government issued the Interim Decree on the Preparation for Agrarian Reform.

Because of the extreme variety of local conditions as well as inadequate preparation and personnel, the implementation of the reform took several years. Conflicting interests postponed for some time the definition of a large estate, thus making expropriation difficult. In Dalmatia, Banat, and Vojvodina more difficulties were created by the fact that many landlords were foreigners (Italians, Hungarians, and Germans) who claimed protection by outside powers. Legally the reform was considered to have come to an end in 1931 with the "Law on Liquidation of the Agrarian Reform," but for all practical purposes the reform was not completed in several areas until 1940.

Despite its defects and delays, the reform brought revolutionary changes. It liberated the peasantry from centuries-old feudal relations and created a large class of free landholders. About 500,000 peasant families were granted land, and Yugoslavia became a country of small and medium-sized farms (77 percent of the arable land). Most specialists agree that, as a result, the condition of the peasantry improved. Agricultural yields fell, however. From a strictly economic point of view, the large estate had been more efficient and productive than the small, fragmented peasant holdings, but socially the reform had been not only necessary but also unavoidable.

The Great Depression of the 1930s had devastating effects on all the agricultural East European countries, and Yugoslavia did not escape its impact. Nevertheless, the entire economy, including agriculture, recovered after the mid-1930s, and thanks to the war preparation going on all over Europe, the country even increased its exports.

In 1941 Yugoslavia was still far behind the industrial nations of Western Europe, but its economy was not a stagnant one. Belgrade tripled its population in twenty years, reaching 300,000 inhabitants, and Zagreb doubled in size to 200,000. The illiteracy rate dropped from 51.5 percent in 1921 to 44.6 percent in 1931. Per capita income, while still low, nevertheless was growing at an annual rate of 1.7 percent. Yugoslavia had a more progressive pattern than many other Central European countries. Despite many failures and disappointments, the country was moving both economically and socially toward progress and modernization.

From Democracy to Dictatorship (1918–34)

The new state had brought together five peoples (Croats, Slovenes, Serbs, Montenegrins, and Macedonians) of three different religions (Catholic, Orthodox, and Muslim), living in eight historical provinces (Croatia, Slovenia, Dalmatia, Vojvodina, Bosnia and Hercegovina, Serbia, Montenegro, and Macedonia), speaking three different languages (Serbo-Croatian, Slovenian, and Macedonian), and using two alphabets (Latin and Cyrillic) (see Peoples of Yugoslavia, ch. 2). The people and the languages were closely related, but in many areas the historical legacy had created more differences than similarities.

The mosaic-like political organization of the new state was reflected in the Constituent Assembly elected in November 1919. It included fifteen parties varying in size from one to ninety-two delegates. Each party—indeed each delegate—represented a narrowly defined set of regional, ethnic, religious, or socioeconomic groups, and none enjoyed broad social or political support. These parties drafted and lobbied for a multitude of proposals for organizing the new state, and with few exceptions the proposals reflected each group's particularistic orientation. For example, the Croatian Republican Party (formerly the Croatian Peasant Party) won the third largest number of votes in the election and controlled the fourth largest bloc of delegates in the assembly, yet it refused to participate in any proposed compromise solution and instead clung to its simplistic plan for the creation of a loose confederation of otherwise autonomous republics.

It was on such a diverse reality that the Constituent Assembly imposed a centralist constitution, adopted 223 to 194 on January 28, 1921. The constitution, known as the Vidovdan constitution, represented the point of view of the Radical Party led by Pasic and was opposed from the outset by the Croatian Republican Party led by Stjepan Radic and Vlatko Macek. The Serbs imposed a policy of strict centralization that the Croats opposed; most of the time the Republican Party refused to collaborate in ruling the country, making both the constitution and the parliamentary system unworkable. It was only in 1925 that Radic was convinced to join the government, but in 1928 he was killed in parliament by a Montenegrin deputy whom he had offended personally.

This bloody incident, in which four other Croats lost their lives, convinced King Alexander of the need for a stronger, more stable government. He first appointed a Slovene premier but then issued a royal decree in January 1929 by which he abolished the Vidovdan constitution and introduced his personal dictatorship: political parties were abolished, individual rights were limited, local councils were abolished, and the freedoms of speech, press, and association were curtailed. The former historic provinces were reconstructed into nine *banovine* (regions), and the name of the country was changed to the Kingdom of Yugoslavia. All powers were assumed by the king, to whom the ministers became solely responsible.

Alexander supposedly was moved by patriotic feelings and by a desire to put an end to the inefficient party system, but his dictatorship had more negative than positive results. The Croats became even more suspicious of Belgrade's intentions, and the leaders of the extreme separatist group, the *ustase* (see Glossary), fled the country, seeking help from Italy, Hungary, Bulgaria, and later Germany for their fascistic and anti-Yugoslav activities. In September 1931 the king officially put an end to his personal dictatorship and issued a new constitution. Some degree of parliamentary activity was permitted again, but most of the former authoritarian laws remained in force, giving Alexander control over the entire political system. In practice his dictatorship weakened the Serbian political parties while strengthening the non-Serbian ones. The Croatian Republican Party, the Slovenian Populist Party, and the Yugoslav Muslim Organization attracted many voters and became important factors in the political life of the 1930s.

Alexander's foreign policy was directed first of all toward securing the results of the Versailles treaties. He encouraged rapprochement with the victors of 1918 and tried to oppose the revisionist powers, i.e., those defeated in 1918 who wished to revise the treaties. In 1920 and 1922 Yugoslavia signed treaties of alliance with Romania and Czechoslovakia, both directed against Hungary. This system of alliances, backed by France with which Alexander signed a treaty of friendship in 1927, led to the creation of the Little Entente in 1933.

In the Balkans the revisionist power was Bulgaria, and Yugoslavia joined Romania, Greece, and Turkey in an attempt to make Bulgaria respect the status quo. Yugoslav-Bulgarian relations were centered not so much on the territories lost by Sofia after the war as on the Macedonian question. The terrorist group IMRO had its headquarters in Sofia, and Alexander tried repeatedly to convince Bulgaria's King Boris to curb IMRO's activities. In the early 1930s Yugoslav-Bulgarian relations improved, but in February 1934 Sofia refused to join the Balkan Entente created by Romania, Greece, Turkey, and Yugoslavia. The pact was designed to guarantee the existing borders against an attack by any Balkan state, but it did not include provisions for an attack by non-Balkan powers.

Alexander's most difficult diplomatic relations were those with Italy, which the Yugoslavs then considered their main enemy. The king tried to come to an understanding with the fascist state, but Italian dictator Benito Mussolini consistently refused to improve his relations with Belgrade, throwing his support to the Croatian *ustase*.

The Regency (1934-41)

On October 9, 1934, on his arrival in Marseille, France, the king was assassinated by members of IMRO, who reportedly were in the pay of the *ustase*. Peter II Karadjordjevic was only eleven years old when his father was assassinated, and in accordance with Alexander's will, his cousin, Prince Paul, was appointed regent. Elections were held in May 1935, and a new government was formed under the premiership of Milan Stojadinovic, the leader of a large coalition of Serbian radicals, Slovene populists, and Muslims. Stojadinovic embarked on a new foreign policy, moving closer to Italy and Germany and rejecting a 1937 French offer of a mutual assistance pact. The same year Yugoslavia signed treaties with Bulgaria and Italy. Mussolini pledged to respect Yugoslavia's territorial integrity and not to tolerate any anti-Yugoslav activities in Italy, a clause particularly important because *ustase* were operating mostly from Italian territory and under Mussolini's protection. In return for these promises, which the Fascists never actually respected, Yugoslavia accepted Italy's claims in Albania.

Stojadinovic, whom Italy's Foreign Minister Galeazzo Ciano called a Fascist "by virtue of his conception of authority of the state and of life," also tried to improve relations with Hitler, with whom he had talks in 1937. Unpopular at home, Stojadinovic was replaced in 1939 by Dragisa Cvetcovic. The most important achievement of the new prime minister was to come to an agreement with the Croatian Republican Party, signed on August 26, 1939. The opening paragraph declared that "Yugoslavia is the best guarantee of the independence and progress of the Serbs, Croats, and Slovenes." Croatia, Dalmatia, and seven other districts having predominantly Croatian populations were united into a new province that was given a separate legislature and extensive autonomy in fiscal and administrative matters. Macek became vice prime minister, and a new Cvetcovic-Macek government was formed to lead a country more stable internally but facing an extremely dangerous external situation.

In June 1939 Prince Paul visited Berlin, and Hitler wasted no time in expressing his dissatisfaction with Yugoslavia's foreign policy. Hitler suggested a withdrawal from the League of Nations as well as adherence to the Anticomintern Pact that had been concluded in 1937 by Germany, Japan, and Italy. The Yugoslavs refused, but after the beginning of World War II in September their chances of remaining neutral diminished considerably. With the defeat of France in May 1940, Yugoslavia was left at the mercy of the Axis Powers. An attempt at establishing closer relations with the Soviet Union failed, mainly because Stalin and Hitler were temporary allies. When Italy attacked Greece, the Yugoslav government did what it could to help its ally, hoping that the British would send troops to the Balkans as they had done in World War I. The British had enough problems defending themselves, however, and the Yugoslavs were left alone when Hitler invited them for new talks in Salzburg in February 1941. Cvetcovic and his foreign minister were asked again to join the Anticomintern Pact, and having practically no other alternative Prince Paul was forced to accept what amounted to an ultimatum. On March 25 in Vienna, the Yugoslav prime minister signed the protocol making his country a member of the Nazi camp.

In Belgrade the news of the event evoked a strong reaction by the public and the army. On March 26–27 a group of officers staged a coup, arrested the government, deposed the regent, and proclaimed Peter II king. General of the Army Dusan Simovic as the new prime minister declared that his government would respect "the protocol signed on the 25th of this month in Vienna," but he added that Yugoslavia "will insist in the most determined fashion on not being drawn into the present conflict." On April 6, without any declaration of war, the Axis Powers attacked Yugoslavia.

The War: Occupation and Resistance

The royal army was ill prepared for war; its thirty divisions were no match for the fifty-two German, Italian, and Hungarian invading divisions, of which two-fifths were armored and fully motorized. The plans of the Yugoslav general staff were outdated. They focused solely on the possibility of an attack from the north; the plans called for a gradual retreat toward the central part of the country and toward Greece and assumed that the army would be able to organize a prolonged resistance in the mountainous areas and that the link with Greece and the vital port of Salonika would be kept open.

These plans proved to be wrong. The war started with a massive air strike against Belgrade on April 6 and a land attack from Bulgaria into Macedonia on April 7. German forces converged on Belgrade from both north and south, while other divisions entered Croatia from Austria and Hungary, advancing toward Zagreb. The Italians attacked Slovenia and the entire Dalmatian Coast. On April 15 the Yugoslav Supreme Command was captured near Sarajevo, and on April 17 Yugoslavia surrendered unconditionally.

The country was partitioned among the Axis Powers except for Croatia, which became an "independent" state (see fig. 7). Germany annexed northern Slovenia and placed Serbia and the Banat under its direct military authority. In Serbia the Germans used General Milan Nedic, a former minister of war, to form a quisling government to handle everyday administration. Italy was awarded southern Slovenia, including Ljubljana, Dalmatia, and the Gulf of Kotor region; its vassal kingdom of Albania was given most of the Kosovo area. Montenegro was placed under Italian administration. Bulgaria received southeastern Macedonia, eastern Serbia, and the remaining part of Kosovo. Hungary got most of Vojvodina.

An independent state of Croatia had been proclaimed by the *ustase* just hours before the entry of the Germans into Zagreb, and Ante Pavelic was flown in from Italy a few days later to become its leader (*poglavnik*). Most of Dalmatia remained outside the puppet state, but Bosnia and Hercegovina were included in its borders. Almost one-third of the estimated 6,300,000 inhabitants were Serbs, and from the beginning the *ustase* adopted an anti-Serb policy of

Source: Based on information from *Documents on German Foreign Policy, 1919-1945*, Arlington, Virginia, 1976.

Figure 7. Partition of Yugoslavia, 1941

massacres, expulsions, and forced conversions to Catholicism. Concentration camps were established for Serbs, Jews, and Croatian democrats. Although independent in theory, the country was divided into two military zones—one German, another Italian—and placed under joint military occupation. For all practical purposes the Croatian government and its army (the Domobrans) were under German and Italian control. The Italian duke of Spoleto was proclaimed king under the name of Tomislav II, but he never set foot on Croatian soil, and during the entire war the puppet state remained under Pavelic's fascist control.

In Serbia a group of officers of the former Yugoslav Royal Army, led by Colonel Draza Mihailovic, refused to surrender and established a center of resistance in the hills of Ravna Gora in western Serbia. Calling his command post the Cetnik Detachments of the Yugoslav Army of the Fatherland, Mihailovic began taking steps for the organization of a future resistance movement such as registering men willing to fight and collecting arms and ammunition. (For many centuries the name *cetnik* had designated the anti-Ottoman guerrilla fighters.) His plans did not call for an immediate uprising because he thought that such a move would bring ruthless German repression upon the Serbs. Loyal to the king and strongly anticommunist, Mihailovic became the representative in Serbia of the exiled royal government, which in 1942 appointed him minister of war.

Cetnik groups were formed in many parts of Yugoslavia, and in theory at least many of them accepted Mihailovic as their leader. Convinced that he was the main representative of the internal resistance, the British began supplying him with military equipment and sent a liaison officer to his headquarters. Fairly soon, however, the Allies realized that the Cetniks were not really interested in fighting the Germans, and that many times they were in fact collaborating with the occupying armies and the quisling government of General Nedic.

If the Cetniks adopted a passive tactic, waiting for the Germans to be defeated by others, the Communist Party of Yugoslavia (CPY) began organizing an active resistance, especially after the German invasion of the Soviet Union. The CPY had been outlawed since 1921 and during the entire interwar period had strictly reflected Moscow's views, sometimes even at the expense of Yugoslavia's national interests. In 1937 Josip Broz Tito, who had fought in the Austro-Hungarian army in World War I until wounded and captured, and who then fought in the Soviet Red Army in the Russian Revolution, was appointed general secretary of the party by the Comintern. After the fall of Yugoslavia in 1941 the CPY adopted a rather prudent attitude, avoiding an open confrontation with Hitler, who was after all Stalin's ally. It was only after June 1941 that the Communists started organizing their Partisan (see Glossary) detachments and called for a national antifascist uprising. In July fighting broke out in Serbia, Montenegro, Slovania, and Bosnia and Hercegovina.

The two resistance movements thus adopted totally different tactics and soon became involved in a long and bloody civil war. In September Tito and Mihailovic met for the first time in a futile attempt to establish some sort of collaboration against the common enemy. Their great ideological differences made the two leaders even more suspicious of each other, and while Mihailovic persisted in his rejection of useless attacks on the Germans, Tito expressed again his determination to wage a total war. Any chance of collaboration disappeared in November 1941 when the Cetniks tried without success to overrun the Partisan headquarters.

By the end of 1941 the general revolt that had broken out in Serbia had been put down, and the Partisans were forced out of Serbia; they retreated into Bosnia where the army was renamed the National Army of Liberation and the Partisan Detachments of Yugoslavia. In November 1942 Tito summoned a conference of representatives from throughout Yugoslavia. This body proclaimed itself the Anti-Fascist Council for the National Liberation of Yugoslavia (Anti-fasistiko Vijece Narodnog Oslobodjenja Jugoslavije—AVNOJ). The Council represented all the democratic and antifascist Yugoslav parties, and a former speaker of the prewar parliament was elected as its president. Although there was considerable local autonomy, the Council was totally controlled by Tito and provided the Partisans with a useful political national organism.

Until the summer of 1943 the Partisans survived militarily with great difficulties; in February 1943 they managed to escape from Bosnia into Montenegro over the Neretva River; in May they moved back into Bosnia, again escaping an enemy encirclement at Sutjeska Gorge and the combined but disorganized pressure of the Germans, Italians, *ustase*, and Cetniks. The surrender of Italy in June 1943 dramatically changed the entire situation. The Partisans were able to secure most of the Italian war matériel left by the retreating army, and after June 1943 the Partisans established themselves as the dominant force in the territories formerly occupied by Italy.

Mihailovic's unwillingness to fight the Germans put him at odds with the Allies. By the end of 1943 most of the military aid formerly sent to the Cetniks was diverted to the Partisans, and in the spring of 1944 the British liaison officers were withdrawn from the Cetnik headquarters.

In November 1943 Tito took new steps toward the creation of a national government under his leadership; the second AVNOJ congress, held at Jajce, transformed the Council into a legislature and administrative body, a sort of provisional government known as the Council of National Liberation with Tito as prime minister. The Council decided that "the question of the king and of the monarchy" would be settled by the people after the liberation of the whole country and that Yugoslavia would be recreated as a federal state. It was at this meeting that Tito was awarded the military rank of Marshal of Yugoslavia.

Mihailovic tried to counter the Partisan's increasing influence with his own congress of Serbian, Croatian, and Slovenian representatives at Bar in June 1944, but the odds were more and more against him. At their Tehran meeting in December 1943, Winston Churchill, Franklin Roosevelt, and Stalin had decided to switch their support from the Cetniks to the Partisans, and in the spring of 1944, under strong British pressure, the royal government of King Peter declared its willingness to collaborate with the Council of National Liberation. In June Peter's prime minister, Ivan Subasic, met with Tito on the island of Vis and signed an agreement that paved the way for the final accords, which were signed in December in Belgrade. In September Peter broadcast an appeal to Yugoslavs asking them to respect the understanding with the Partisans. As a result many Yugoslavs who until then had been loyal to the government-in-exile switched their allegiance to the Council of National Liberation.

The Tito-Subasic agreement was supposed to provide the legal basis for the creation of a new and democratic Yugoslavia, and Tito repeatedly declared that his forces did not intend to impose their ideology upon the country. A regency was to be created until a popular referendum would decide the fate of the monarchy. The Council of National Liberation was enlarged with members of the prewar parliament, and an election of a constituent assembly was

Marshal Tito in Yugoslav mountains, World War II
Courtesy Embassy of Yugoslavia, Washington

called for in the near future to decide about the basic reforms needed by the Yugoslav society.

The Partisan position was strengthened even more during the last months of 1944. In September Tito's units established contact with the Soviet Red Army advancing from Romania, and Tito flew to Moscow for talks with Stalin. On October 20, 1944, Belgrade was liberated by Soviet troops and the communist provisional government moved into the liberated capital. The Yalta Conference of February 1945 endorsed the Tito-Subasic accords, and on March 6, 1945, a new provisional government was created with Tito as prime minister and Subasic as foreign minister. The five members of the democratic parties were soon forced to resign, one after another, and when Subasic departed in October the government was under Tito's complete control.

The end of the war also meant the end of the Cetniks and of the Croatian puppet state. After the fall of Italy, Dalmatia was theoretically integrated into Croatia, but most of its territory was controlled by the Partisans. When the defeat of Germany became evident, some *ustase* tried to overthrow Pavelic, but the conspiracy was discovered, and its leaders were executed. On May 6, 1945, Pavelic fled from Zagreb while his army and many terrified civilians crossed the Austrian border hoping to get protection from the Allies. Their surrender was not accepted, and the British forced back into Yugoslavia approximately 250,000 Croats, many of whom were immediately executed by the Partisans. The Cetniks had a similar fate. Mihailovic was captured, put on trial, and executed as a traitor.

The Communists, still preferring to be known as the National Liberation Front rather than the Communist Party in order to avoid provoking opposition from the Western Allies, entered vigorously into preparation for the November elections. Communism was carefully kept out of the campaign. The National Liberation Committee organized a nationwide political movement known as the People's Front (Narodni Front), which included individual members of many of the old political parties. Under strong communist control the People's Front served as a means of splintering and weakening the noncommunist parties. Edvard Kardelj, the leading theoretician of Yugoslav communism, asserted, "There is no doubt that the form of such a political organization as the People's Front greatly eases the breaking up of the remnants of the old reactionary parties with our masses, who are accustomed to political organization and who are politically active."

The People's Front conducted an extensive preelectoral propaganda campaign and appealed for a republican, federal, democratic Yugoslavia. Opposition newspapers were suppressed, and the fractionalized opposition political parties rapidly deteriorated under continual government pressure. In the end, parties opposed to the People's Front decided not to participate in the elections, and voters were offered a list consisting only of candidates of the People's

Partisan armored column near end of World War II
Courtesy Embassy of Yugoslavia, Washington

Front. The outcome of the election was a foregone conclusion and overwhelmingly in favor of Tito and the Communists.

On November 29, 1945, the Constituent Assembly was convoked. It abolished the monarchy and proclaimed the Federal People's Republic of Yugoslavia (Federativna Narodna Republika Jugoslavija). In December the British and French governments extended recognition to the Tito regime, and the United States indicated its intention of doing so. On January 31, 1946, the assembly unanimously approved the new constitution, patterned closely after the 1936 Constitution of the Soviet Union. On April 18 the United States formally recognized the new republic.

The constitution of 1946 established six constituent republics corresponding to traditional divisions of the area: Serbia, Croatia, Slovenia, Bosnia and Hercegovina, Montenegro, and Macedonia. An autonomous province, Vojvodina, and an autonomous region, Kosovo-Metohija (Kosmet), were included in Serbia (see fig. 1). Federalism was largely theoretical, as the powers of the republics were subordinated to the central government in all matters of importance, and in those limited areas left to the republics, close supervision was exercised by the central government.

On the national level government authority was centered in the cabinet headed by Tito and included the heads of the various ministries. A bicameral parliament, the Federal Assembly, consisted

35

of the Federal Chamber (Savezni Vijece) and the Chamber of Nationalities (Vijece Narodni). In practice the assembly functioned under the direction of the cabinet and did not initiate policy.

Assemblies also existed in each of the republics; the bodies on the republic and local levels, however, each called a People's Committee, were most important. These bodies existed on a hierarchical scale from the republic committee to committees for each district and village. For cities there were overall committees and, under these, local units. These lower level organizations were largely a sham, however. Tito and his colleagues were intent upon replicating the Stalinist model, and this called for central control by an all-powerful party. Eventually, however, the Stalinist model proved unsuitable and was rejected, and the regional and lower level governmental bodies achieved new and enhanced powers and responsibilities that they retained in mid-1981 (see The Process of Government, ch. 4).

Communist Yugoslavia

The Orthodox Years

The war had devastating effects on the country. Of the almost 16 million prewar Yugoslavs, 1.7 million—11 percent of the entire population—had lost their lives, the highest percentage of human casualties in Europe after Poland. Most of the fallen had been young people (average age—twenty-two). Among the professional groups the intellectuals and the skilled workers had been severely affected. Most of the cities were in ruins; one-sixth of the housing had been destroyed, and 25 percent of the population was homeless. An estimated 80 percent of the harvesting equipment was out of operation, and 53 percent of the cattle, 67 percent of the horses, and 40 percent of the carts and wagons had been lost. The communications system was badly damaged, and only 50 percent of the railways and 23 percent of the locomotives were operational. In the industrial sector, which in general had been under direct German control, the situation was no better. Production fell dramatically compared to the prewar figures; it dropped to 40 percent in the textile industry, to under 20 percent in metals, and to between 40 percent and 50 percent in food processing. Yugoslavia was faced with a real danger of mass starvation, which was avoided in 1946 and 1947 mainly through the generous aid provided by the United Nations Relief and Rehabilitation Administration.

Despite former assurances that he would not seek to impose communism on Yugoslavia, Tito wasted no time in restructuring the country along the most orthodox Stalinist pattern; no foreign observer could have detected in 1945 any trace of "national communism" in his approach to "building Socialism." A highly centralized, one-party system was forced upon the country with the Politburo of the CPY the center of power. The economic influence and power of the former middle class was broken through a series of sweeping confiscatory measures. As Tito declared to his biographer, Vladimir Dedijer, "the most dangerous thing for us now would be to stop at half way."

The property of the collaborators, enemies, and war profiteers had been confiscated in November 1944, before the end of the war. These categories were defined in an extremely vague way, and almost 80 percent of the industrial enterprises, banks, and wholesale trade facilities passed into the state's hands. Two other laws (December 1946 and April 1948) completed the process of nationalization, leaving practically no privately owned establishments in what was called the industries of "national importance."

Similar changes were introduced into the rural areas. An agrarian reform had been enacted in August 1945 limiting the size of holdings to twenty-five to thirty-five hectares and confiscating the rest without compensation (see Land Tenure and Agrarian Reform, ch. 3). The confiscated land was distributed to peasants, whose debts were also canceled. At the same time, following the rigid Stalinist model, the party engaged in an active policy of forcing the new landowners into cooperatives. To help mechanize the socialist sector in 1946 the CPY created the first state-owned tractor stations. The peasants resisted the creation of collective farms (*kolkhozes*), and by 1948 when the break with Stalin occurred, only 6.2 percent of the arable land had been collectivized.

The ambitions of the new regime were set very high. Milovan Djilas—at this time one of Tito's closest associates—claimed that Yugoslavia would catch up with Britain in per capita production in about ten years. To learn how to plan such a fast growth, Boris Kidric, the chairman of the Economic Council, was sent to Moscow to study the methods of Soviet central planning. Under his supervision, the first five-year plan (1947-52) called for an ambitious and unrealistic policy of industrialization based on the Soviet dogma that heavy industry must be given absolute priority. Huge investments were made in long-term projects including steel plants and hydroelectrical and thermoelectrical power stations. The gross industrial output was supposed to increase five times, and the CPY did everything it could, at least on paper, to respect Lenin's dictum that communism means industrialization plus electrification.

To enforce the "dictatorship of the proletariat" the party embarked on a policy of fierce repression, striking all opponents, from former collaborators to former "fellow travelers," who had cooperated with Tito in the past but were now questioning his policy. It is not possible to establish the exact number of people arrested and/or eliminated during this period by the Department for the Protection of the People; but in 1951 Aleksandar Rankovic, in charge of the security service and secret police, admitted that in 1949 (a rather mild year compared to the 1945-48 period) 41 percent of the arrests had been unjustified and 23 percent had been for crimes of "minor importance." He further admitted that the courts had "converted ordinary crimes into political offenses" and that many defendants had been deprived wrongly of their liberty.

Much of the party's wrath fell on churches because of their long and close association with ethnic divisiveness in Yugoslavia. The Serbian Orthodox Church, the persecution it suffered at the hands of the Nazis and the *ustase* notwithstanding, suffered from government policies. The church lost land, and schools, convents, and monasteries were closed; clergy were harassed as they attempted to visit parishes and attend to church matters. The Roman Catholic Church of Croatia had welcomed the creation of the *ustasa* state, and the Catholic archbishop, Alojzije Stepinac, had only half-heartedly voiced opposition to the vicious practices of the *ustase*. After 1942 he began denouncing more openly the *ustasa* atrocities against the Serbs, but he continued nevertheless to defend the existence of the puppet state, even calling it the fulfillment of "dreams of centuries." When the Partisans came to power he made no secret of his anticommunist convictions and continuously denounced the persecution that he asserted the Catholics were subjected to by the secret police. This defiant attitude led to his arrest in 1946; charged with treason, the archbishop was sentenced to sixteen years of hard labor (see Religion, ch. 2).

Tito's territorial disputes with the Western powers pushed him even more into Stalin's arms. In May 1945 the Partisans had taken Klagenfurt in Austria and had entered Trieste, which the AVNOJ congress of 1943 had claimed for Yugoslavia. In June strong Anglo-American pressure forced them to evacuate the Austrian town and to withdraw from Trieste. Trieste and a narrow strip of territory known as Zone A remained under Allied control, while the Partisans maintained their authority over the rest of Istria, which was known as Zone B. Yugoslavia continued to claim the entire peninsula including the port of Trieste, while the West favored its transfer to Italy. The Trieste issue embittered Yugoslav-Western relations for many years, and it was only in 1954 that an Anglo-American-Italian-Yugoslav treaty closed the matter by accepting the status quo along the lines of the 1945 partition.

Greece was another area of confrontation with the West. Greek Communists, who were waging a bloody civil war, had since 1944 enjoyed Tito's support, and throughout 1946 and 1947 Tito channeled large quantities of weapons and ammunition to them. A military mission was sent to help the insurgents, and in August 1947 the Balkan communist countries—Yugoslavia, Bulgaria, and Albania—formally established a Joint Balkan Staff to deal with Greek matters.

At the United Nations (UN) Yugoslavia actively endorsed all Soviet initiatives and in 1947 joined the Soviet condemnation of the Marshall Plan. Domestically as well as externally the Yugoslavs behaved from 1945 to 1948 like enthusiastic followers of the Soviet Union, and the newly created Communist Information Bureau (Cominform) rewarded them by establishing its headquarters in Belgrade. For most of the outside world, as well as for most Yugoslavs, the break of 1948 came as a total surprise.

The Break with Stalin

The roots of the conflict were nevertheless extensive, involving both political and economic aspects. Despite the heavy indoctrination—Djilas, for example, in 1944 viewed the Soviet government as "something greater than the leadership of my own party"—Partisan-Soviet relations had their ups and downs. On the one hand Stalin remembered Tito's reluctance to agree to the policy of a popular front in 1942, as well as the exasperating demands for military supplies made by the Partisans throughout the war. On the other hand Tito could not forget that the Soviets had sent a mission to Mihailovic as late as 1944, that they had provided practically no aid to the Partisans during the war, and that they had failed to support his claims over Trieste.

Belgrade gradually became disenchanted with Soviet economic policy toward its allies. The Soviet Union was supposed to have been the main supplier of capital for the reconstruction of the economy, and in 1946 it indeed promised loans of US$300 million; by 1948 the Soviets had supplied only 6 percent of the promised credits. By then all but the most fanatic admirers of Soviet policy had concluded that at least from an economic point of view Moscow was as egotistic as any great power and had no real intentions of helping Yugoslavia become an advanced industrial country. About 50 percent of the Yugoslav exports to the Soviet Union were raw materials for which the Soviets paid with outdated and expensive Soviet equipment. In 1946 the Yugoslavs reluctantly agreed to the creation of joint companies, another way to subordinate the economy to long-range Soviet plans. The paradox of the Soviet-Yugoslav relations in 1948 was that while Tito was eager to apply as soon as possible the Soviet pattern of industrialization and rapid modernizatrion, Moscow did whatever it could to prevent him from doing so in an effort to keep Yugoslavia at the level of a raw material-producing and agricultural country.

But the economic policy was not the only arena in which the two countries were moving in different directions. Politically, Stalin became sharply annoyed with Tito's initiatives in Balkan affairs and with his reluctance to adhere blindly to Moscow's line. The Soviets were particularly unhappy with tentative plans for a Yugoslav-Bulgarian federation; Tito and Georgi Dimitrov, the chief of the Bulgarian Communists, had discussed such a possibility even before the end of the war, and in 1944 Stalin seems to have agreed in principle to the projected federation. In 1947 Bulgaria and Yugoslavia signed a treaty of friendship paving the way for a customs union, and Tito declared on the occasion, apparently without consulting the Soviets, that "we will establish a cooperation so general and so close that federation will be a mere formality." At the same time, Dimitrov expressed hopes that a federation of the socialist countries would be possible sometime in the future "guided by our own interests."

This was offensive to Moscow, and in late January 1948 *Pravda* strongly denied that Eastern Europe needed any kind of federation or even a customs union. Stalin abruptly summoned the Yugoslav and Bulgarian leaders to Moscow. Dimitrov obeyed the call but Tito, sensing trouble, sent in his place Edvard Kardelj, probably his closest associate, and Vladamir Bakaric, the leader of the party in Croatia. To the stunned Yugoslav delegation, which also included Djilas, who already was in Moscow, Stalin and Soviet Foreign Minister Viacheslav Molotov harshly presented the Soviet grievances: there were problems the Yugoslavs and the Soviets were approaching differently, which were "inadmissible either from the party or the state point of view"; Moscow had not been consulted about the federation plan, nor about the intention of sending two army divisions to Albania; and the Yugoslavs were meddling in the Greek civil war without taking into consideration the Soviet position. Then, Stalin ordered the confused Yugoslavs and Bulgarians to proceed with plans for the federation. As a sign of good faith, Kardelj was forced to sign an agreement binding his government to consult with Moscow on any problem of foreign policy. "The trouble is," Stalin told a humiliated Dimitrov, "that you are taking a line different from ours."

The Yugoslavs left Moscow without having been able to get the economic and military aid they had hoped to receive. Although Djilas was still confident (after the meeting he cabled Belgrade— "there is no need to doubt for a moment the great love Comrade Stalin bears to our entire party, the Central Committee and particularly Comrade Tito"), a crisis of confidence was clearly emerging between the two parties. The Soviets decided to postpone the renewal of the Yugoslav-Soviet economic treaty, and Tito's pictures were removed from public places in various East European capitals. At this point the Yugoslavs decided to discuss the entire issue in the CPY's Central Committee meeting of early March, and the conflict rapidly moved toward its climax. The Central Committee chose to ignore Stalin's order to proceed immediately with the federation with Bulgaria, fearing that the repentant Bulgarians might be used as Trojan horses to weaken Yugoslavia. Later in the month the Soviets recalled their military and civil advisers and specialists from Yugoslavia because they were "surrounded by unfriendliness and treated with hostility."

From March 20 to May 22 Yugoslav and Soviet leaders exchanged several letters spelling out their respective positions and making it clear that the possibility of a compromise was getting smaller and smaller. The Soviet interpretation was clearly expressed in its note of March 27: the CPY was undemocratic and lacked self-criticism and a spirit of class struggle; capitalism had not been checked seriously enough, and the initiative of the masses was opposed; the Yugoslavs continued to exaggerate the role of the Partisans in the liberation of the country while playing down the role of the Soviet Red Army; and the government was penetrated by British spies and the party was doing nothing to have them removed. Furthermore, the Soviets charged, their civil and military advisers were not given accurate information regarding the economic and military situation of Yugoslavia.

Tito tried for a while to preserve at least the appearance of friendship and sent a message in early April mentioning the "unbreakable bonds" linking the two countries. He invited Moscow to send representatives to see for themselves how misinformed Stalin was about the conditions in Yugoslavia. But he boldly added, "No matter how much each of us loves the land of socialism [the Soviet Union] he can in no case love his country less." The letter also insisted that "we are developing socialism in our country in somewhat different forms," a notion totally unacceptable to Stalin.

The Soviets rejected the invitation to visit Yugoslavia and suggested in return that the entire dispute be presented to the Cominform. At the same time, Moscow leveled new accusations against the Yugoslavs, such as having slipped into deviationism and having adopted an anti-Soviet attitude.

Tito refused to attend the Cominform meeting, which took place in Bucharest at the end of June. On June 28, Saint Vitus' Day (Vidovdan), a day on which many important things had happened in Serbian history, the Cominform passed a resolution declaring that the CPY had placed itself outside the "united communist front" and had broken its internationalist traditions by taking "the road to nationalism." The "healthy elements" within the party were called "to compel their present leaders to recognize their mistakes openly . . . to break with nationalism and return to internationalism. Should the present leaders of the Yugoslav Communist Party prove incapable of doing this, their job is to replace them and to advance a new internationalist leadership of the party. The Information Bureau does not doubt that the CPY will be able to fulfill this honorable task."

For most Yugoslavs as well as for the Western world, Tito's expulsion from the Soviet bloc came as a complete surprise. It is still difficult to understand Stalin's motivations, but there is no doubt that it was he who forced the break upon the reluctant Yugoslavs. In 1948 the Soviet dictator had reached the zenith of his power, but his newly acquired world influence was encountering many challenges; the Cold War was being vigorously waged by both sides, and the Berlin blockade had put even more strains on East-West relations, which were apparently moving toward a confrontation. Stalin was not inclined to tolerate even the slightest initiative among his satellites, and it was natural for him to want to replace a leader—appointed by him in 1937 anyway—once his loyalty was questioned. Stalin seems to have provoked the conflict confident that an alternative leadership would be easy to find. In doing this he seriously misjudged Tito's popularity and his grip over the CPY. The Cominform appeal to rebellion was not followed, and Yugoslavia was forced to depart the "brotherly camp" and pursue its own different way.

The Yugoslav Way

When the Fifth Party Congress of the CPY met in Belgrade in July 1948—the first congress to be convened since 1928—most of the "Cominformists," such as Andrija Hebrang and Stefan Zujovic, and some 14,000 confused and less important party members were already in jail. The congress dealt only occasionally with the Cominform resolution and chose to leave the door open by avoiding personal attacks on Stalin. The crowd chanted such old slogans as "Long live the Leader and Teacher of the Progressive Humanity, Comrade Stalin," and Tito closed the last session with the words "Long live the Great Soviet Union with the genius Stalin at its head." Official propaganda adopted the explanation that the conflict was the result of a misunderstanding and that the party would continue to carry on the teachings of Marxism and build a socialism similar to the one existing in the Soviet Union.

The attitude of the Soviet bloc was universally negative, and the Yugoslavs soon felt the effects of political and economic pressure. Several of the East European governments began hunting "Titoists," staging trials, and conducting purges and executions. Koci Hoxe in Albania, Lazslo Rajk in Hungary, and Traiko Kostov in Bulgaria were executed in 1949. The friendship treaties were abolished unilaterally in an attempt to isolate Yugoslavia politically, while economic relations came to an almost complete halt. At the time 57 percent of Yugoslavia's imports and 52 percent of its exports were with the communist countries of Eastern Europe, and the blockade had serious repercussions on the economy. The first Five-Year Plan had been based on the assumption of good trade relations with the "brotherly countries," and the entire planning therefore had to be redone. When in February 1949 the Soviet Union and its satellite countries formed the Council for Mutual Economic Assistance (Comecon), the Yugoslavs were told that they could join only if they would change their policies. Isolated, facing hostile powers from both East and West, the CPY was forced by necessity and not by conviction to rethink the whole strategy of "building socialism" in its own and original way.

The new course was not obvious from the beginning. Quite the contrary, the party sought to neutralize the Cominform accusations by practicing an even more orthodox domestic and foreign policy. At the UN, for example, Yugoslav diplomats were unconditionally supportive of Soviet initiatives. At home, party documents tried to mobilize the masses for the fulfillment of "the basic tasks stipulated in the Five-year Plan." Collectivization was supposed to go on "with more boldness and increased tempo," and pressure was put on the peasants to force them onto collective farms, the numbers of which jumped from 779 in 1947 to 6,964 in 1950. As late as 1952 Tito was still asserting that "without the victory of the socialist sector in our villages there can be no ultimate victory of socialism in our country." Nevertheless, because of the peasants' passive resistance, collectivization made slow progress, and at its height only about one-fifth of the cultivated land was organized into collective farms.

By 1950 it had become obvious to the Yugoslav leadership that just continuing to follow the Stalinist pattern was not going to put the country on the road of modernization. "One day, it must have been in the spring of 1950," recalls Djilas, "it occurred to me that we Yugoslav communists were now in a position to start creating Marx's free association of producers. The factories would be left in their hands with the sole proviso that they should pay a tax for military and other State needs that remain essential." It is not very clear how this idealistic and highly theoretical approach was explained to the party but Djilas, Kardelj, and Kidric were apparently able to convince Tito that self-management was to be Yugoslavia's answer to the Soviet pattern. The Basic Law on Workers' Self-Management was introduced to the parliament by Tito, who presented it as the first step toward building the right kind of socialism (see Role of Government, ch. 3).

The law put a theoretical end to the state's ownership of the means of production, entrusting what was now called "social property" to the workers of each enterprise. A council of fifteen to 120 members was to be elected by the workers in such enterprises and invested with extensive powers. According to the law the council ". . .approves the basic plans and annual balance sheet . . . [and] adopts conclusions regarding the management of the enterprise and the fulfillment of the economic plans." It also elected a board of management but not the director, who continued to be appointed by the state. The party remained in firm control of the economy through such levers as central planning. Even if their rights have been considerably enlarged by socialist standards, the workers had practically no real power to influence the decisionmaking process as long as the party and its representatives had a practical monopoly over such questions as drafting the plans, concluding contracts, allocating assets, and deciding investment policy and prices.

The law on self-management was adopted at a time when the economy was in great trouble. The Soviet blockade had reduced foreign trade to 35 percent of the 1948 level; industrial production was falling; the harvest of 1950, because of a severe drought and peasant resistance to collectivization, was disastrous, and the national income was well below the 1948 level. It was evident that formal self-management alone was not enough to revive the economy and assure the country's economic survival. The CPY, while maintaining its power monopoly, had to create a more practical model of development in which the rights given the workers would not be meaningless. In order to be efficient, self-management had to be part of more general reforms involving both the economic and political institutions of the country.

Such reforms were gradually introduced from 1950 to 1953, slowly but fundamentally distancing Yugoslavia from the Soviet pattern of development. The special privileges of the new ruling class were abolished in the fall of 1950, and the State Central Commission and the Federal Planning Commission were abolished in February and April 1951. The same year, consumer rationing was practically eliminated while price formation of consumer goods was made free. A new law restricted the scope of the federal budget, and more important than anything else, the Law on the Planned Management of the National Economy of December 1951 abandoned the Soviet system of central planning and took the first steps toward creating a market-oriented economy.

The law put a practical end to the command, centralized economy, the "social plans" changing from compulsory to indicative. The state stopped directing the microeconomic planning, limiting its functions to the macroeconomic. Through investment policy and the so-called basic propositions, the state was still able to control the general development of the country, but for the first time the workers' councils were given real economic power. Enterprises were allowed to write their own production plan and to decide about the nature, quantity, and quality of output and the selling of the products. As a result the enterprises became unavoidably market oriented.

Early 1950 brought important changes in the agricultural sector as well. The process was slow, the CPY bending only gradually and reluctantly to the evident failure of the collectivization experiment. The Machine Tractor Stations were closed in 1950 and compulsory deliveries abolished in 1951; but the decision to put an end to the collectives was taken only in 1953 when the parliament adopted the decree on Property Relations and Reorganization of the Peasant Work Cooperatives. The peasants were allowed to leave the cooperatives and take with them the equipment and the title to the land they had been forced to give up when the collective had been created. The closing of a collective was to be decided by the simple vote of its members; those collectives operating in the red were automatically abolished. As a result of the law, most of the peasants returned to the private sector. In just a few months, fewer than 2,000 collective farms were still in existence with a working force of only 192,582 peasants on less than 10 percent of the arable land. In order to prevent the creation of larger holdings and a new class of large landowners, the Law on Agricultural Land Fund of May 1953 generally restricted the maximum holding to ten to fifteen hectares, a size far below the maximum of thirty-five hectares allowed by the agrarian reform of 1945.

The CPY had finally admitted the failure of Soviet-style agriculture and the importance of the individual peasant. As a party leader declared after the law was introduced, from now on the only role of the state should be "to see that our peasants, no matter to which sector they belong, become modern agriculturists."

The reform of the economic structure was only one aspect of the fundamental change Yugoslavia was undergoing; the other one was the reform of the political structure—the rethinking of the role of the party and of the state. Contrary to the Stalinist theory of the strengthening of the state, the Yugoslavs adopted the theory, as Kardelj put it in 1952, "of the withering away of the state and with it of any party system." The first institutions to be reformed according to this new, unorthodox approach were the people's committees of the local governments, which were allowed a larger degree of autonomy, including the power to decide their own budgets and social plans. Six months later, in November 1952, the Sixth Congress of the CPY tackled the most difficult problem: the place of the party in a society based on self-management and economic decentralization. As expected, the resolution and the new statute placed the emphasis on its "conscious role" instead of on the formerly "leading role." The congress determined that the "basic duty and role of the communists is not and cannot be the direct operative manager and commander in economic, state and social life"; the party should inspire the general policy but not get involved in the day-to-day administration of the country. The principle of the separation of state and party was adopted, and party organizations within the state apparatus were abolished. As a symbol of its new decentralized character the Communist Party of Yugoslavia changed its name to the League of Communists of Yugoslavia (LCY). These changes were embodied in the Constitutional Law of January 1953, which partially replaced the former constitution of 1946.

As a result of these economic and political reforms as well as of the continuously growing Western aid, the Yugoslav economy was finally able to escape stagnation after 1953 (in 1953 national income rose by 18 percent) and to embark on a boom that lasted almost without interruption until the mid-1960s.

The limits of political and economic democratization were nevertheless clear; as Djilas put it later ". . . it is hardly possible to change the present system . . . Only crumbs from the tables and illusions have been left to the workers. Without universal freedom not even workers' management can become free."

The idealistic Montenegrin—who had been expelled from the LCY in 1954 for his criticism of the new ruling class—was not the only one to think that the reforms had not gone far enough and that they had just replaced a brutal and inefficient dictatorship with a more sophisticated one. Moreover the reforms failed to satisfy the demands of the different national groups, and by 1967 the Croatian problem had surfaced again.

It began as a linguistic movement aimed at obtaining recognition of Croatian as a separate language to be used in Croatia exclusively and by federal authorities in parallel with Serbian, but it escalated rapidly into bolder economic and political demands. The reforms of 1965–66 had tried to solve some of the more pressing economic problems, but the results were not clear. Within the LCY itself an influential group had opposed the new course and the further withering away of the central authority, favoring instead a return to a more centralized form of government. Nevertheless a new package of economic measures had been presented to the parliament giving the republics more financial authority to deal with a decentralized and free market (see Role of Government, ch. 3). But the Croats (as well as the Slovenes) continued to express their dissatisfaction with the allocation of central government funds. The federal government agreed to make significant concessions and increased the powers of the republics, especially in the disputed problem of allocations for development from the Federal Investment Fund. In April 1970 the republics were officially proclaimed sovereign units bound only by "an institutionalized agreement" among themselves (see The Constitutional Order, ch. 4).

While proceeding substantially in this direction, Tito sharply spoke against nationalism (see Glossary) and promised to take "administrative measures" against it if necessary. He even used the threat of a Soviet invasion to warn that "others would immediateiy be present if there were disorder." Student demonstrations in Zagreb as well as the sympathetic attitude of the Croatian leadership for the students' now clearly nationalist demands convinced Tito that he had to act swiftly in order to preserve the achievement of his regime. The leaders of the Croatian party were purged; over 400 students were arrested; and the Matica Hrvatska—a cultural institution that had started the whole movement with its cultural nationalism—was suspended. Croatian nationalism continued to manifest itself mostly outside Croatia, carried on by the large Croatian communities living in the West.

The Policy of Nonalignment

The break with Stalin opened the unexpected possibility of improving relations with the West despite the Trieste problem, which remained a cause of friction until 1954. Western aid was essential for the survival of the economy, and the Yugoslavs presented a formal request for aid in foodstuffs to the United States in October 1950. By 1952 Western aid, mostly American and British, had been made available, and the West had replaced the Comecon countries as the main trade partner of Yugoslavia. The United States also supplanted the Soviets as the main arms supplier, and a military aid section was added to the American embassy in Belgrade.

Further reorientation was obvious in Tito's foreign policy. In 1953 he visited London, his first visit outside the communist world since the war, and Churchill used the occasion to make the startling declaration that "should our ally, Yugoslavia, be attacked, we would fight and die with you." The same month Stalin, to whom Churchill had in 1943 offered a 50 percent influence in Yugoslavia, died, and only four months later the new Soviet leadership confidentially expressed its desire to exchange ambassadors and "normalize" Soviet-Yugoslav relations. The contacts improved rapidly after the emergence of Nikita Khrushchev as the general secretary of the Communist Party of the Soviet Union. In May 1955, Khrushchev,

*Prime Minister Jawaharlal Nehru of India and
President Gamal Abdul Nasser are
President Tito's guests at Brioni in 1956.
Courtesy Embassy of Yugoslavia, Washington*

Soviet Premier Nikolai Bulganin, and an imposing Soviet delegation arrived in Belgrade, publicly apologizing for the mistakes of 1948 and putting the entire blame on "the enemies of the people, Beria and Abakumov, the contemptible agents of imperialism." Stalin's name was not mentioned, but the so-called Belgrade Declaration of June 2, 1955, gave complete satisfaction to the Yugoslavs. It pledged "mutual respect and non-interference in internal affairs for any reason, whether of economic, political, or ideological reason, since questions of the internal structure, differences of social systems, and differences of concrete forms of developing socialism are exclusively a matter for the people of the different countries."

By signing the Belgrade Declaration the Soviets were apparently accepting the existence of different ways of building socialism. The Yugoslavs soon discovered, however, that their relations with Moscow would follow a tortuous line, dependent in great part on Soviet world strategy and on events the Yugoslavs could neither influence nor control. Despite Tito's undoubted delight with Khrushchev's secret speech of March 1956 in which he sharply criticized Stalin and with the abolition of the Cominform in April 1956, Soviet-Yugoslav relations were chilled by Soviet intervention against the Hungarian revolution in November 1956 and by the Kremlin's resumed attacks in 1957 on "revisionism . . . under the pretext of national peculiarities." The chill lasted for three years, but despite improved relations in the 1960s the Yugoslavs and the Soviets found themselves in disagreement almost as often as they were in agreement. They adopted, for independent reasons, the same position in the Arab-Israeli conflict, particularly during the June 1967 War, but they reached the point of an almost open confrontation in 1968 when Tito sided enthusiastically with the reformist Czechoslovak movement and strongly condemned Soviet intervention against it.

Relations with both East and West had clear limits for a communist but nevertheless non-Soviet country, and the need for new directions became obvious. The rise of the Third World provided Tito with an alternative, a golden opportunity for asserting independence and emerging as a world leader equally distanced from the East as well as from the West.

Tito began to cultivate close ties with India and Egypt at about the time that sweeping reforms were changing the pattern of internal Yugoslav development. An embassy was opened in New Delhi in 1950, and friendly relations were established with Gamal Abdul Nasser in 1953. In 1955 Tito visited both India and Egypt, and for the first time he described the nonaligned nations as Yugoslavia's "true allies and . . . greatest friends." The next year the three leaders met again, this time on the Yugoslav island of Brioni, and the joint communiqué of the meeting endorsed the principle of the nonaligned movement, which the Bandung Conference of African and Asian nations had drafted in 1955. The communiqué called for peaceful coexistence, the end of power bloc policy, creation of a world security system, and disarmament. The first summit of the nonaligned countries met in Belgrade in 1961, further enhancing Tito's prestige as an influential world leader (see Foreign Policy, ch. 4).

Tito's Last Years

The Yugoslavs seem to have a special love for constitutions; they change them frequently (1946, 1953, 1963, 1974), and the constitutions are among the longest in the world. When the 1974 Constitution was adopted by parliament, the hundreds of pages dealt not only with matters of principle but also with some very specific problems as well. Yugoslav constitutions have been an expression of political principles, economic policies, moral commitments, and judicial realities. The Constitution promulgated on February 21, 1974, purports to reflect the structural changes the society had gone through since 1963 and at the same time to provide that the Yugoslav way will be continued and developed (see The Development of the Contemporary Political Order, ch. 4). The Constitution reemphasizes the importance of self-management and provides a complicated legal basis for its protection. Self-management was extended to such social services as health and education, indicating the state's willingness to transfer some of these costly operations to the local communities and keep the state's involvement at a minimum. Republics and local governments came to exercise considerable influence over economic matters.

Politically the Constitution seeks to reorganize the socialist parliamentary system and make it more representative. Under its very complicated provisions, a delegate system was introduced, meaning that the candidates are selected through a lengthy process involving several levels of approval. Only "respectable" candidates may be included on the list, and they must be accepted by the Socialist Alliance of the Working People of Yugoslavia (SAWPY—see Glossary).

A few weeks after the adoption of the Constitution, the LCY held its Tenth Party Congress (see The League of Communists, ch. 4). The major theme of the congress as outlined in the speeches of the various party leaders, and particularly by Tito, was that although decentralization through self-management was essential and would proceed, the paramount role of the LCY was equally essential as the coordinator and unifier of economic as well as political affairs.

Shortly before his death in 1979, Kardelj completed a book that was published in English under the title *Democracy and Socialism*. (The translation of the title from Serbo-Croatian is *The Direction of Development of the Political System of Socialist Self-management*.) The book consists of Kardelj's efforts to prove that self-management is far superior to any bourgeois multiparty system and that "socialism is not conceivable without democracy," even if it can only be "democracy in socialism." The 1974 Constitution, various legislative acts of the late 1970s, Kardelj's book, and Tito's speeches to the Tenth Party Congress collectively indicated that the Yugoslav leadership was increasingly concerned with the piling up of internal and external problems and was somehow trying to return to a firmer policy. Low productivity, growing inflation, and the unrest of the intellectuals and of the nationalities were sources of a potential internal crisis. Externally the worsening of East-West relations after the signing of the Helsinki Final Act in 1975 and the discord within the nonaligned movement challenged some of Tito's former policies. He remained generally committed to the principles of nonalignment, the North-South dialogue, and "progressive" causes in general; but relations with Moscow never really improved, and the 1970s marked an even wider gap between the positions of the two countries. Tito unconditionally supported the anti-Soviet Eurocommunist parties, and in 1978 he welcomed Hua Guofeng, Chairman of the Communist Party of China, to Belgrade in an effort to establish a rapprochement with China. Despite the anticapitalist rhetoric the country remained heavily dependent economically on the West, while trade relations with the Comecon countries were carefully watched to avoid an excessive dependency.

His long and in general successful reign persuaded Tito that he had a historic mission to fulfill; in 1963 he declared that "I am responsible before history and before the people for the proper course of development of this country. So . . . people should understand and remember that it cannot be otherwise." Although he avoided the political excesses of some of his Balkan neighbors, a personality cult of sorts did emerge. Until his death in May 1980, Tito kept his country on a moderate course, and as far as the South Slavs are concerned, represented possibly the most progressive period they had experienced during their turbulent history.

* * *

For an English-language presentation of Yugoslav history in a general southeast European context, the interested reader might consult Robert Wolff's *The Balkans in Our Time*. Among the many histories of Yugoslavia, Stephen Clissold's *A Short History of Yugoslavia* and Vladimir Dedijer's *History of Yugoslavia* are among the more useful. Jozo Tomasevich's *Peasants, Politics, and Economic Change in Yugoslavia* and *War and Revolution in Yugoslavia: 1941–45: The Cetniks* are excellent presentations of the economic, political and military problems facing Yugoslavia from its creation to the end of World War II.

The bibliography on Tito's Yugoslavia is immense; aspects of Belgrade's position are set forth in Dedijer's *Tito Speaks* and *The Battle Stalin Lost*; Milovan Djilas' *Tito: The Story from Inside* is a fascinating though not always balanced biography of the Yugoslav leader by the famous dissident. For excellent general presentations George Hoffman and Fred Neal's *Yugoslavia and the New Communism*, Dennison Rusinow's *The Yugoslav Experiment*, and Sir Duncan Wilson's *Tito's Yugoslavia* merit careful attention. (For further information see Bibliography.)

Chapter 2. The Society and Its Environment

Folk dancers

FEW EUROPEAN STATES can match Yugoslavia in sheer ethnic diversity: six major "nations" and a plethora of minority groups are central to the country's social and cultural life. In the early 1980s the country was a study in contrasts with the 1919–41 interwar kingdom. The major ethnic groups persisted, but the communist-led forces that liberated Yugoslavia from the Nazis had—literally— remade the social and political face of the country. Serbs had held almost exclusive sway in the kingdom; their preponderance frustrated the aspirations of the non-Serbian majority for autonomy and self-rule as surely as had Habsburg and Ottoman hegemony. The overweening Serbian dominance fueled nationalistic animosities to such an extent that World War II brought not only the Nazi onslaught but also civil war.

Socialist Yugoslavia remained a country of profound ethnic cleavages, where history's legacy was one of cultural diversity accompanied by deep-seated socioeconomic disparities. Government, nonetheless, conformed more closely to a federal model than any the southern Slavs had known previously. The communist regime, only too aware of what thwarted nationalist aspirations had cost Yugoslavia, was assiduously evenhanded in dealing with the "national question." There were perennial points of contention and periodic outbreaks of unrest; ethnicity seemed at times a lens through which Yugoslavs viewed the universe. But the process of government— however uneven—was not paralyzed by ethnically based hostilities. Socialist Yugoslavia was a multinational state in which officialdom was at pains to include the country's constituent peoples in social and political life.

Affluence and poverty split along ethnic lines: Croatia, Slovenia, Vojvodina, and Serbia proper were prosperous relative to Kosovo, Montenegro, Macedonia, and Bosnia and Hercegovina (see fig. 1). The economic disparities between the developed and the less developed regions were central in socialist era ethnic relations. The proper policy to follow in developing the poorer regions was a constant topic of debate: what should be the role of federal and republican governments in development policy; how much should the affluent be obliged to contribute to the development effort; should development priorities (and a host of issues related to social equity) or economic efficiency dictate investment policy? The questions resurfaced in a variety of guises, and after thirty-odd years of socialist development, little was certain except that the problems of the less developed regions had proved far more persistent than anyone might have anticipated.

Beyond ethnic diversity Yugoslav society itself had become a dramatically changed and highly differentiated one. Interwar Yugoslavia was largely rural and peasant, impoverished and illiterate.

53

The elite was not simply privileged, but an exceptionally narrow segment of society; the middle orders—a group of middling farmers, substantial numbers of educators and professionals, a prosperous petite bourgeoisie—were virtually nonexistent. The elite's wealth—except for a few industrialists, financiers, and merchants—lay less in controlling the economy than in monopolizing the government apparatus and a tax system that was almost hopelessly inequitable. The elite in communist Yugoslavia remained privileged, but it was magnitudes more diverse than its interwar counterpart. Increasing industrialization, a changing economy, and expanding educational opportunities generated scores of jobs for a new class of technical experts; cadres of engineers, scientists, and managers transformed the traditional elite.

The same changes revolutionized rural and urban life. Cities, for centuries the bastions of the urban elite and the small merchant class, expanded astronomically. Peasants migrated or commuted to take advantage of nonagricultural employment and educational opportunities. The tide of migrants taxed already strained urban services as well as limited employment opportunities, but at the same time it relieved, on a material level, some of the worst effects of chronic rural overpopulation. Traditional family life adapted to the periodic absence of a portion of the household or to having kin permanently resident in the city. Small, private family farms continued to play a significant role not just in agricultural production, but in rural society and the complex relations between city and countryside.

Geography and Population

In terms of geography and population, Yugoslavia is the largest Balkan nation. Its boundaries encompass approximately 255,892 square kilometers (although data are varied), making the country the seventh largest in Europe (excluding the Soviet Union). The preliminary report of the 1981 census indicated a population of 22,352,162, the eighth largest in Europe, again excluding the Soviet Union. Politically the country is divided into six republics and two autonomous provinces. Geographically it consists of the coastal and interior highlands and mountains and the Pannonian Plains in the north and northeast (see fig. 8). Demographically it contains numerous ethnic groups and the adherents of three major religions (see Peoples of Yugoslavia, this ch.).

Topography

The greater part of the country is hilly or mountainous; about 60 percent of the total land area consists of hills and ridges from 200 to 1,000 meters in elevation, and another 20 percent consists of high mountains and ranges over 1,000 meters high. Tall mountains are a dominant feature of the landscape in the south and southeast as well as in the northeast near the Austrian border.

Geological fault lines are widespread in the mountains south of the Sava and Danube rivers. These structural seams in the earth's crust periodically shift, causing earth tremors and occasional earthquakes. The most vulnerable region lies in the general area between Banja Luka and Skopje. An earthquake in Skopje in July 1963 killed over 1,000 people and demolished almost all of the city's buildings in three quick shocks that lasted only thirty seconds. As of mid-1981 the disaster remained the worst in the nation's history. Although the epicenter of the quake was at or near the city's center, the government rebuilt Skopje on the same spot, thus continuing over 2,000 years of urban life. In October 1969 an earthquake destroyed over 70 percent of the buildings in Banja Luka, but only nine people out of a population of over 70,000 were killed.

Coastal and Interior Highlands

The highland region is the most extensive and rugged area of the country. It extends in a northwest-southeast direction for about 960 kilometers from the Austrian to the Greek border. The west and northwest sections of this extensive region contain mountains resembling the higher Austrian Alps to the north, having sharp peaks and ridges. Interspersed among them are deep gorges and narrow valleys.

The Julian Alps, which occupy the westernmost corner of the country, are among the most rugged in Europe and contain many summits that exceed 1,800 meters. One peak, Triglav, has an elevation of 2,846 meters, the highest in the country. Eastward these mountains possess less well-defined ridges, and their crests decrease in height to about 1,000 meters in the vicinity of Maribor.

South of these mountains the rough terrain changes to hilly areas interspersed with flat valleys. Many of these valleys enlarge into basins whose elevations are generally less than 450 meters. One of the largest of these extended basin areas is located near Ljubljana. Farther to the south the rugged terrain extends into the limestone ranges of the Dinaric Alps. This region, frequently referred to as karst or karstland, is distinctive because of the underground drainage channels that have been formed by the long-term seepage of water down through the soluble limestone. This action leaves the surface dry and over the years has formed many large depressions in the high coastal plateaus.

The coastal area is studded with more than 600 offshore islands, most of which are rocky and hilly. The Dinaric chain consists of ridges that parallel the coast and range from 700 to over 2,200 meters in height. The flat depressions formed in the limestone hills vary considerably in size. Most are quite narrow, but some have been elongated to as much as sixty kilometers. The general surface configuration of the karst area is rocky, featuring many desolate cliffs that support little vegetation.

The east central part of the country is an extensive, dissected region with crests and ridges between 500 and 1,800 meters in elevation. In the north the foothills of the mountains merge with the

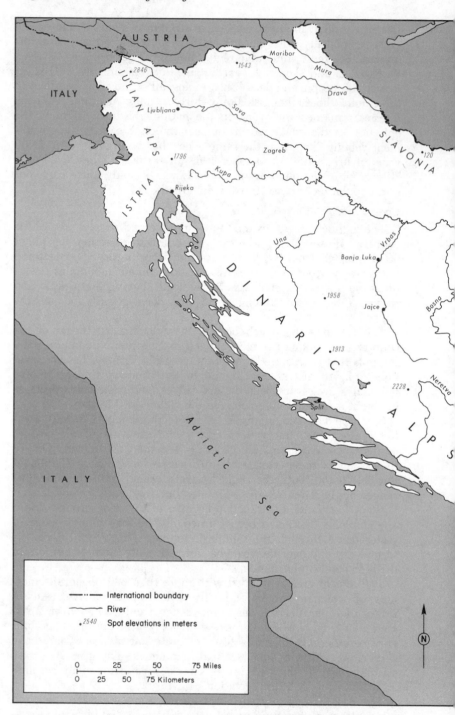

Figure 8. Topography and Drainage Systems

upland terraces of the Pannonian Plains; in the south there are karst-like uplands, and the ridges have greater ranges of elevation. The highest peaks are located in the interstream areas of the mountains near the Albanian border.

The highlands in the eastern section include several systems of rugged mountains and hill groups. Most of these are separated by broad valleys and fairly flat though narrow basins. Summits in most of the region are sharp-crested and rise between 600 and 1,200 meters. The highest and most rugged terrain in this section of the country is in the southern portion, west of Skopje and along the Bulgarian border.

Large areas of rolling hills are located in the vicinity of Skopje and Pristina. These hills, as well as those further to the north above the Nisava River, are marked by numerous corridors formed by low valleys and small narrow basins. In some places these valleys are connected by narrow defiles and rise rather abruptly into the steep slopes of the foothills of the nearby mountains.

Pannonian Plains

The Pannonian Plains are a southward extension of the Great Hungarian Plains (Pannonia) and consist of the valleys of the middle and lower Drava, the middle and lower Sava, the lower Tisa, and the middle Danube rivers. Occupying approximately 20 percent of the country's land area, this region extends about 480 kilometers northwest-southeast and has a maximum north-south width of about 200 kilometers. This region, the most fertile in the nation, is the area occupied by the ancient Pannonian Sea, which disappeared as the runoff from the surrounding mountains gradually filled it with rich alluvial deposits. It is a sedimentary region containing wide valley basins, alluvial plains, sandy dunes, and low, rolling hills covered with fertile loam.

In general the area is low and flat. Few elevations reach more than 100 meters above sea level. The major rivers are located on broad flood plains. The western portion of the plains rise to rolling hills that reach elevations of 150 meters or more. Between the Drava and Sava rivers a narrow ridge, averaging about 240 meters in height, extends to the southeast and bisects that portion of the plain lying to the west of the Danube River.

Drainage Systems

In the Pannonian Plains drainage is to the Black Sea through the Danube and its four large tributaries: the Drava, Tisa, Sava, and Morava. The Danube in some places has a width of over three kilometers and depths up to fifteen meters or more at high water. Large fluctuations between high and low water are typical. High water generally lasts from March or April until May or June; the low water period usually lasts from mid-July to late October.

The largest portion of the broad interior highlands area is drained by the Danube and the upper reaches of its right bank tributaries.

In the southeast the Vardar River and its tributaries drain that area into the Aegean Sea; the Neretva River is the principal source of drainage from this area into the Adriatic Sea.

Drainage on the western slopes of the karst area is provided by short rapid surface streams and underground drainage into the Adriatic. The bulk of the water collects in depressions among the limestone hills and seeps into underground channels. Occasionally the water emerges in springs, but most of it moves into the Adriatic below sea level, then rises to the surface of the sea.

Climate

Lying largely in the southern part of the northern temperate zone but subjected to cold continental air currents from the north, the country experiences a wide variety of climatic conditions. Most of the variations are determined by proximity to the coast and by altitude. Across most of the country cloudiness is greatest and humidity highest in the autumn and early winter months. Although surface winds are generally light and seasonal variation in precipitation is small, annual precipitation varies to a considerable degree from one part of the country to another.

In the narrow zone along the coast, the general characteristics of the Mediterranean climate prevail with mild rainy winters, short springs, fairly hot and dry summers, and long pleasant falls. July is the hottest month, but temperatures during the entire summer are remarkably steady and the sky clear. January is the coolest month, but it is still moderate.

Throughout the mountainous central, eastern, and northwestern sections of the country, the climate is influenced appreciably by the continental air movements of eastern and northern Europe and to a lesser degree by the Mediterranean air masses from the south and southeast. Snow accumulates over large areas in winter and lasts for long periods in the higher elevations. Precipitation varies widely, ranging from about 100 to over 190 centimeters annually and occurs mostly at the beginning of summer (see table 2, Appendix).

Snow and cold weather accompany north and northeasterly winds in the late fall and early winter. In the spring the country is warmed by south and southwesterly winds. In the more elevated areas cool summers and long snowy winters prevail. Valleys generally enjoy a more temperate climate than the mountain slopes and ridges.

Across the Pannonian Plains typical continental climate prevails. Winters are cold, temperatures reaching $-2°C$ and freezing sections of the large rivers and streams in the area. Snow cover is generally light but frequent. Summers are hot and often humid, and maximum temperatures are often near $37°C$. Although annual precipitation amounts to only fifty to seventy-five centimeters, it is well distributed.

Population

The preliminary results of the 1981 census reported a population of 22,352,162, an increase of about 1,827,000 from the 1971 census report. According to these initial data, 577,648 citizens resided outside the country as temporary workers, mostly in West European countries, a decline of almost 100,000 from the number working abroad in 1971.

During the decade between the censuses the total population grew at a rate between .08 percent and .09 percent per annum. This rate of growth concealed significant regional variations, however (see table 3, Appendix). In Vojvodina, for example, the population increased by about 4 percent during the intercensal period, whereas in Kosovo the increase was over 27 percent (see Albanians, this ch.).

In the mid-1970s life expectancy at birth was projected at sixty-nine years of age (about sixty-six for men, seventy-two for women). The male-female ratio was given as 100 to 105. As of mid-1981, data on these and related items of population dynamics were not available from the 1981 census.

In the mid-1960s, in order to move toward a controlled rate of growth, greater stress was placed upon influencing prospective parents, particularly newly married couples, to participate in family planning. On May 8, 1969, a liberalized General Law on Abortions was promulgated. On the same day, the government announced a new Resolution on Family Planning, which had been adopted on April 25 by the Federal Assembly, the highest organ of government. It urged further expansion of education in family planning for all who desired it and the use of modern contraceptive knowledge by those who wished to control the size of their families and emphasized the role of the social services and other national institutions in sex education and other preparations for planned parenthood.

Peoples of Yugoslavia

Overview

Yugoslavia of the early 1980s was the most ethnically diverse of the East European states. The 1981 census enumerated six "nations," (see Glossary) whose traditional territory lay primarily within Yugoslavia's post-1918 boundaries: Serbs, Croats, ethnic (Bosnian) Muslims, Slovenes, Montenegrins, and Macedonians. In addition the 1946, 1963, and 1974 constitutions along with the relevant amendments recognized various "nationalities" or national minorities: Albanians, Bulgarians, Czechs, Slovaks, Italians, Hungarians, Romanians, Ruthenians, Ukrainians, and Turks were the most prominent. Finally, there were several smaller ethnic groups, which represented less than 0.1 percent of the total population: Romany, Vlachs (remnants of the pre-Slavic settlers of the region), a fraction of the pre-World War II Sephardic Jewish community, Greeks, Poles, Russians, Austrians—to name a few (see fig. 9).

Communist Yugoslavia's constitutions from 1946 through 1974 guaranteed full equal rights for all ethnic groups. Republic/provincial constitutions also dealt with their own constituent nations

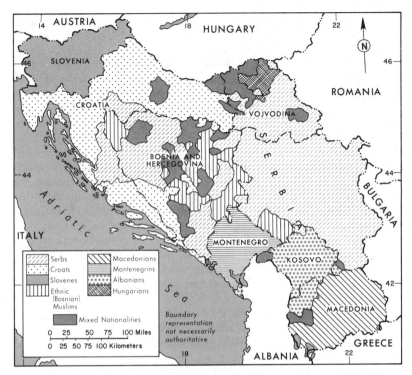

Figure 9. Peoples of Yugoslavia

and nationalities (see Glossary), but these documents carried out the basic principles of the 1974 Constitution (see The Constitutional Order, ch. 4). There were minor variations in republic/provincial legislation affecting minorities, but in general nationalities had the rights to which all citizens were entitled, i.e., the right to the use of their native language and participation in public life, government, and the armed forces.

Ethnic complexity reflected a degree of political, historical, linguistic, religious, and cultural diversity unparalleled in a single, twentieth-century, European nation-state. The country's diverse population encapsulated the vagaries of Balkan history since Roman times. The Theodosian line dividing the western Roman from the eastern Byzantine world cut through modern Yugoslavia. The country's population comprised three major religious creeds (Eastern Orthodox, Roman Catholic, Islam). Serbo-Croatian and Croato-Serbian represented both the Cyrillic and Latin alphabets. Even ignoring the differences in orthography, there was substantial linguistic diversity: Serbo-Croatian, Albanian, Slovenian, and Macedonian were all major languages. Hungarian, Turkish, Bulgarian, Romanian, Italian, Vlach, and Czechoslovak were among the most significant minority languages.

61

Yugoslavia's legal heritage includes antecedents from eight distinct juridical systems. Its political roots are scarcely less diverse. Slovenia and Dalmatia came from the Austrian portion of the Habsburg Empire; Croatia and Slavonia had semiautonomous status under Hungarian control. Vojvodina was under exclusively Magyar administration, and Bosnia and Hercegovina were under joint Austro-Hungarian rule. Serbia was under Ottoman rule for centuries before becoming sovereign in the nineteenth century; Montenegro held onto a slim independence despite Ottoman incursions. Macedonia remained under Ottoman rule until the 1912 and 1913 Balkan wars (see The Yugoslav Movement and World War I, ch. 1).

Much of contemporary society can be understood against the backdrop of ethnic and historical diversity. Ethnicity—inextricably linked to disparate political styles—was the defining force of interwar politics. Political parties appealing to voters in nationalistic (see Glossary) terms won; those relying on pan-Yugoslav sentiments or class allegiance lost. The myriad governments of the 1920s as well as the royal dictatorship proved notably ineffectual in curbing Serbian hegemony or Croatian obstructionism—the twin banes that plagued interwar government.

A unified Yugoslav state meant very different things to the various southern Slavs. Serbia wanted outlets to the Aegean and Adriatic—not a merger with the Roman Catholic Croats and Slovenes, tainted in any event by their long association with the Austro-Hungarian Empire. Censuses provide a telling glimpse of Belgrade's attitude toward the many peoples within Yugoslavia's borders: interwar censuses lumped Croats, Serbs, Bosnian Muslims, Montenegrins, and Macedonians into a single category—Serbo-Croat. Croat aspirations were ill-served by a union with the Serbian kingdom, which carried no guarantees for a federal sharing of power. Bosnian Muslims, having raised a "clientele strategy" to a high art in centuries of dealing with Ottoman and Habsburg rulers, had some small share in bureaucratic patronage positions. Slovenian parliamentary experience had been learned in roughly a century of maneuvering in the Vienna Reichsrat under Austrian domination. They were past masters at coalition government and managed (mostly through the Serbs' willingness to ally with them against the less tractable Croats) quite well in interwar coalitions.

Diverse political heritages and cultural traditions combined with wide divergences in economic development. Slovenes, Croats, some Serbs, Germans, Magyars (all north of the Danube and Sava rivers) were relatively well-off. The south—most of Serbia, Montenegro, Bosnia (short form for Bosnia and Hercegovina), and Macedonia—bore the full brunt of Ottoman rule and was often wretchedly impoverished. In 1921 more than half the population (over five years of age) was illiterate, but this rate ranged from less than 9 percent in Slovenia to over 80 percent in Macedonia (see table 4, Appendix). Public health services and transportation facilities reflected the same disparities.

Yugoslavia fell within weeks of the 1941 Nazi invasion of the country. World War II was also a civil conflict for the country. Parts of a dismembered Yugoslavia went to Italian-ruled Albania, to Bulgaria, Italy, and Germany. A puppet fascist regime ruled a much-enlarged Croatia. The war was bitter and internecine—it would scarcely have seemed to provide a more promising basis for a unified multinational Yugoslavia than the interwar kingdom had. The loss in human life was immense—over 10 percent of the population died. Beyond the numbers of dead there was a staggering level of physical destruction: more than 25 percent were without shelter at the war's end; over 70 percent of industrial capacity was destroyed.

Some observers suggest that the sheer level of loss blunted ethnic hostilities. Certainly the civil war made painfully clear how costly the Serbian domination of interwar government had been. The postwar communist regime has followed a policy of tailoring government appointments to reflect Yugoslavia's ethnic diversity. A "nationality key" governs top-ranking appointments—the federal Presidency, the top echelons of republic and federal administrative bodies, and those appointed by the Federal Assembly are carefully balanced among the constituent nations and nationalities.

There was a tendency for ethnic balance to decline among lower level civil servants. The location of the federal government in Belgrade meant that most low-ranking employees were Serbs. Because of the republics' increasing role in federal decisionmaking in the late 1960s–1970s, careerists were more and more in need of a constituency in their native republics to reach the upper echelons of the government bureaucracy. An excessively Belgrade-based career was a handicap to the upwardly mobile Croat, Slovene, ethnic Muslim, Albanian, or Macedonian.

Comparable trends emerged in the Yugoslav People's Army (YPA) and the League of Communists of Yugoslavia (LCY): the higher the position, the more closely appointments conformed to the "ethnic key." In the army the efforts to maintain ethnic balance within the high command broke down within the officer corps proper (see table 5, Appendix). The centuries-long military tradition of Serbia and Montenegro played a role in recruiting young men from those republics to a military career. Croats, Slovenes, and Hungarians were likely to find a military career less enticing than the economic opportunities afforded by the northern half of the country. Until the early 1970s Serbs and Montenegrins were slightly overrepresented in the ranks of generals as well—a reflection of their extensive involvement in the Partisans (see Glossary). Despite the importance of Partisan experience for a military career, the army's high command was scrupulously balanced to avoid even a hint of Serbian preponderance.

Serbs and Montenegrins were also slightly overrepresented in the LCY—again their high level of involvement in the Partisan forces gave them an edge. Croats, Slovenes, Albanians, and ethnic Muslims were all underrepresented. Serbs predominated in the ethnically mixed republics and autonomous provinces as well, though

the balance altered in the mid- to late 1970s. Albanians and Macedonians were concentrated in agriculture—an occupational group
traditionally underrepresented in East European communist parties. Until Aleksandar Rankovic's demise as head of the secret police
in 1966, the LCY's centralized administrative apparatus viewed
with suspicion Hungarians and Albanians clustered on Yugoslavia's
borders with those countries.

A Belgrade economist characterized Yugoslavia, with its prosperous north and impoverished south, as a country combining the
economies of India and the Federal Republic of Germany (West
Germany). Whatever the shortcomings of such an analogy, the
country's disparate levels of economic development have proved a
persistent problem for the regime. Since 1947 the federal government has designated Macedonia and Montenegro as less developed
regions (and thereby eligible for special investment funds). Kosovo
has been so designated since 1957; Bosnia's status varied, but parts
of the republic have received federal funds since 1947. In the early
1960s parts of Serbia and Croatia also received development funds.
Since then, however, federal funds have gone to Bosnia, Montenegro, Macedonia, and Kosovo.

Yugoslavia's less developed regions were characteristically regions
of small, fragmented land holdings, where most of the populace
earned a living in private agriculture. Per capita income in the 1970s
averaged roughly two-thirds the national rate. More than three-
fourths of all households earned less than the national average; in
Kosovo, 100 percent. By almost any socioeconomic criterion the less
developed regions trailed Yugoslavia's northern half. Life expectancy was lower; there were approximately two-thirds the physicians
per 1,000 inhabitants. Illiteracy rates were nearly six times those of
the prosperous northern regions (see table 6, Appendix).

Economic development policy was a consistent subject of debate
among the various republics and autonomous provinces. In general
the well-to-do republics objected to the portion of their income
siphoned off for investment in the less developed regions. In their
view development funds for the poorer regions were well and
good—if these investments generated a rate of return comparable to
the developed regions. Such a criterion was virtually impossible, of
course, for the infrastructure-poor south to meet. Alternatively the
developed regions (especially Croatia) argued that even they had
pockets of poverty, and it hardly made sense to ignore these areas in
favor of Bosnia, Montenegro, Macedonia, and Kosovo. The lesser
developed regions saw the gap between themselves and the
wealthier north persisting or widening. They argued for more funds
targeted for the south and a cut in their contributions to the federal
budget.

A variety of programs allocated investment funds to the less developed regions from the 1950s through the 1970s (Role of Government, ch. 3). Reforms during the 1970s gave enterprises in the developed regions more latitude in making their own investments in the

Young Yugoslav women

Yugoslav dancers

south, but the federal government remained the major channel for the south's development funds. By the mid-1970s the rough equivalent of 3 percent of the developed regions' gross material product (GMP—see Glossary) went to development—an amount equal to nearly 10 percent the less developed regions' GMP. In the 1970s Kosovo was the biggest gainer in transfer funds; with less than 20 percent of the population of less developed regions, it received one-third the federal investment funds (see table 7, Appendix).

Despite the substantial funds poured into the less developed regions, the gap between them and the country's wealthiest regions widened in the 1970s. Annual per capita income in Kosovo averaged 25 percent that of the nation as a whole, 15 percent that of Slovenia.

A variety of problems hampered development efforts in the south—limited transportation facilities, a disproportionate emphasis on heavy industry (with limited short-term returns), and wage scales favoring capital-intensive investments contributed to the south's disappointing economic performance. Perhaps the single most damaging factor, however, was the poorer regions' cripplingly high population growth rate. Between 1947 and 1966 Kosovo's national income grew by 320 percent—hardly less than Slovenia's 360 percent. Per capita, however, Slovenia's growth rate was 311 percent to Kosovo's 274 percent. The picture is one of general postwar economic growth—but the rank of the individual regions on a national income scale has changed little. Had the less developed regions maintained a population growth rate comparable to that of the developed north, Bosnia, Macedonia, and Montenegro would have had, by the mid-1970s, a per capita GMP equal to approximately 80 percent of the national average. Even Kosovo's rate would increase from one-third to half the Yugoslav average.

As of late 1981 Serbs remained the single largest nation, accounting for more than one-third of total population (see table 8, Appendix). They were followed by Croats (slightly less than 20 percent of total population) and varying percentages of ethnic Muslims, Slovenes, Albanians, Macedonians, Montenegrins, and others. Those registering as Yugoslavs more than quadrupled their share of total population—a dramatic increase some observers attributed to a rising number of interethnic marriages in the country. There was significant ethnic diversity within each republic/provincial population. Only Serbia proper (excluding its autonomous provinces, Kosovo and Vojvodina), Slovenia, and Montenegro were largely monoethnic. Croatia had a substantial Serb minority. Kosovo was primarily Albanian but contained Serb and Montenegrin minorities; in Vojvodina the Serb majority shared the stage with Hungarians and Croats. Macedonia had Turks and Albanians to complement the Macedonian majority. Bosnia and Hercegovina was the most ethnically mixed of the republics with Serbs, Croats, and ethnic Muslims the main groups.

Changing demographic patterns had an impact on Yugoslavia's ethnic map. The rate of natural increase declined from a high of

16.4 per 1,000 inhabitants in 1948 to an estimated eight per 1,000 in 1980. More important, population growth rates varied dramatically among major ethnic groups. The less developed south and parts of Montenegro and Bosnia far outstripped the developed north and west. Concerned observers in Slovenia, Serbia, and Croatia dubbed the demographic transformation the "White Plague." Since World War II the proportion of Serbs, Croats, and Slovenes declined relative to that of Macedonians, Albanians, and ethnic Muslims.

Between 1950 and 1980 Kosovo's rate of natural increase ranged from 50 to over 100 percent higher than the national average. Croatia's and Serbia's were below the national average by roughly the same percentage. Preliminary reports on the 1981 census indicated the birthrate for Yugoslavia's Albanians to be among the highest in Europe. Between 1971 and 1981 Kosovo's population grew by more than a quarter; Albanians accounted for most of the increase. Bosnia and Montenegro increased roughly 10 percent, and ethnic Muslims showed disproportionate gains; Macedonia increased by 16 percent. By contrast Serbia proper grew less than 8 percent, Croatia and Vojvodina by less than 5 percent. Live births provided an index of changing demographic trends; in the early 1980s they ranged from a low of 1.83 live births per woman in Serbia proper to 4.66 in Kosovo.

Serbs

Serbs, in the early 1980s, were the most dispersed of Yugoslavia's nations. Although concentrated in Serbia proper, they accounted for a substantial percentage of total population in Vojvodina, Kosovo, Bosnia, and Croatia. Serbs' distribution reflected many of the vicissitudes of Balkan history and played a pivotal role in the country's complex ethnic relations in the 1970s. Vojvodina presented few problems; Serbs constituted a clear and growing portion of that province's populace, while the Hungarian minority—through the combined effects of emigration and a low birthrate—declined.

In Croatia and Bosnia the situation was more complex. Serbs were a significant minority in Croatia; they were the single largest ethnic group in Bosnia but were outnumbered by an increasing margin by the combined total of Croats and ethnic Muslims. A concern for the fate of Serbs outside the republic proper conditioned Serbian reactions to efforts at decentralization. It was evident in Serbian nervousness at any possible Croat-ethnic Muslim alliance in Bosnia. Part of Serbian alarm at the resurgence of Croatian nationalist sentiment in the late 1960s-early 1970s was the memory of Serbian suffering at Croatian hands during World War II (see The War: Occupation and Resistance, ch. 1).

Kosovo—at the center of the medieval Serbian kingdom and the core of much of Serbian cultural heritage—was the Serbs' greatest concern in the early 1980s. Between 1961 and 1981 Serbs dropped from roughly 23 percent to slightly more than 13 percent of the province's population; at the same time, Albanians rose from two-thirds to over three-quarters of all inhabitants of Kosovo. In part the Albanian high birthrate accounted for the province's changing ethnic portrait; the exodus of Serbs from the province, however, was more worrisome to Serbian officialdom. There had been a trickle of Serbs, mostly white-collar workers, displaced by the growing Albanian presence in local industry and government administration from the late 1960s onward. At the time of the March–April 1981 Kosovo riots, the trickle became a stream, not just of former civil servants and intelligentsia, but of farmers apprehensive of the growing Albanian nationalist fervor (see Albanians, this ch.).

A series of nineteenth-century peasant revolts formed the basis of modern Serbian national consciousness. Serbs viewed themselves as a nation-at-arms; World War I culminated centuries of armed resistance against foreign overlords. They saw themselves as liberators of Croatia and Slovenia—nations that had proved unwilling or unable to defend themselves against Austria-Hungary and whose loyalty was suspect. Serbia's monumental losses in World War I reinforced its tendency to see the Yugoslav government as its own dearly won bailiwick. The per capita loss of fighting men was two-and-a-half times that of France and three times that of Britain and Italy. The army casualty rate was 40 percent of those under arms. Losses to battle and epidemic disease amounted to one-fifth the total population.

The kingdom's Serbian political elite were excessively centralist, accustomed to rule and disinclined to share the spoils of power. There were, on the eve of World War II, two Croatian and two Slovenian generals in the army; the rest—161 generals in all—were Serbs or Montenegrins. In 1941, of 1,500 military cadets, 1,300 were Serbs. Serbs dominated the civil bureaucracy as well; in 1939 they held 100 percent of the higher administrative posts in the office of the premier, 89 percent of those in the Ministry of the Interior, 82 percent of those in the foreign service, 96 percent in education, and 85 percent in justice.

Concern about the Serbian reaction to policies balancing participation in government by the various ethnic groups dominated Serbian-regime relations in the post-World War II era. Serbs were major participants in the Partisan liberation movement; their sufferings at the hands of Croatian Fascists appalled even the Nazis (see The War: Occupation and Resistance, ch. 1). Both circumstances led the communist regime to react vehemently against any sign of resurgent "greater Serbia hegemonism." Sentiments at all comparable to those of Serbs in the interwar kingdom drew sharp criticism from the authorities—as for example a 1980 offering by a Serbian poet in a Serbian Orthodox magazine complaining at the Serbs' sufferings in World War II, and as the poem's refrain noted, ". . . what has it all got us?" (see Religion, this ch.). By the same token, authorities feared an anti-Albanian backlash to the 1981 Kosovo riots. Serbs had the sense of having sacrificed much and gained little but increased demands by the intransigent Albanians; "greater Albanian hegemonism" was the Serbian complaint.

Croats

Despite substantial linguistic similarity and a common Slav background, Croatia's cultural traditions and political heritage contrasted dramatically with Serbia's. The Roman Catholic Church preserved Croatian national identity during the centuries of Venetian, Ottoman, and Austro-Hungarian rule. Despite the church's ultramontane loyalties and Latin liturgy it gave Croatia a literate clergy who both used Croatian as the language of pastoral work and preserved it as a literary tongue from the Counter-Reformation to the nineteenth century. Roman Catholicism imbued nineteenth-century Croatian nationalism with the cultural ethos of Western Europe. As with many Balkan peoples, language and religion acted as unifying forces linking educated and uneducated Croats alike.

Writers, scholars, commercial interests, well-to-do farmers, and timber producers spearheaded the nineteenth-century Croatian nationalist movement. Croatian nationalism, influenced by French revolutionary thought (through a brief period of Napoleonic rule), gained impetus from Hungary's aggressive Magyarization drive in the late nineteenth century (see The Croats, ch. 1). Hungarian insistence on Magyar as the language of public life alienated the growing intelligentsia. Transportation policy undermined Croatia's flourishing trade with the Dalmatian Coast and antagonized traders and large landowners. Agricultural policies and taxation impoverished the peasantry.

Croatian political leaders devoted their political energies to opposing whatever government was in power to counter the Magyarization drive. The same tactics underlay their participation in the interwar kingdom. The Croatian Peasant Party, the leading party, made occasional attempts to join whatever Serbian cabal might be in power, but its efforts were erratic, unpredictable, and, not surprisingly, unsuccessful (see The Yugoslav Kingdom, 1918–41, ch. 1). In the Croatian view the kingdom was no less "a prison of nations" than the Austro-Hungarian Empire had been. Serbian rule merely exploited Yugoslavia's advanced, European-oriented northern half for the "Balkan primitives" of the south.

Had there been any lingering doubt about Croatian disenchantment with Serb domination—they regarded the kingdom as little else—World War II dispelled it. Roughly half the population ruled by the Croatian puppet state were Serbs. The *ustase* (see Glossary) were vehemently Catholic, anti-Semitic, and anti-Serbian; their avowed policy was to convert one-third of the Serbs, deport another third, and "eliminate" the rest. The regime closed all Serbian Orthodox Primary Schools, outlawed the Cyrillic alphabet, and ordered Serbs to wear colored arm bands.

In the early 1980s Croats were Yugoslavia's second largest ethnic group. Although the economic reverses of the 1970s dealt harshly with the republic's economy, Croatia remained one of the most prosperous regions of Yugoslavia. Croatian nationalist sentiment intensified in the late 1960-early 1970s. The issues underlying the "Croatian crisis" were those frequently troubling multinational Yugoslavia—the authority of the federal government vis-à-vis that of individual republics and the extent of Serbian preponderance in government. Croats wanted greater control of republic finances, especially their own substantial foreign exchange earnings. President Josip Broz Tito's personal intervention resolved the immediate crisis; and a substantial portion of the 1970s constitutional reforms dealt with questions implicitly raised by the Croatian demands (see The Development of the Contemporary Political Order, ch. 4).

Beyond the issues themselves was the disturbing tendency for Croats to regard every social, economic, and political question as a reflection of nationalist sentiment. Issues focusing on banking and economic development policy generated more general and (apparently) popular concerns with possible Serbian dominance and manifestations of anti-Serbian feeling. Cyrillic roadsigns were defaced; there were Serb-Croat brawls. Matica Hrvatska, a Croatian cultural organization suppressed in 1972, multiplied its membership and demanded, among other things, separate Croatian membership in the United Nations (UN). Students at Zagreb University elected a Roman Catholic-nationalist student rector. Authorities found the prospect of a mass movement led by elements of a disenchanted Croatian intelligentsia profoundly disconcerting.

Occasional manifestations of what the authorities referred to as "nationalist hatred" surfaced in Croatia in the late 1970s–early 1980s. Émigré organizations dedicated to an independent Croatia engaged in a terrorist campaign mostly against Yugoslav diplomats. Professor Franjo Tudman, a historian and former Partisan general, gave a series of interviews to Croatian émigré journals and received a three-year sentence for "hostile propaganda" in 1981. In similar circumstances Vlado Gotavac, a Croatian writer, was charged with saying that Croats were subject to "political, social and cultural subjugation."

Slovenes

Situated at the point where the Balkan and Italian peninsulas meet the European continent, Slovenia is at the juncture of the Germanic, Latin, and Slav cultures. The Slovenes were among the least numerous and westernmost of the Slav peoples; their ethnic survival under nearly 600 years of German hegemony was a tribute to, if nothing else, sheer tenacity. The Slovenes were unique among the nations of the Austro-Hungarian Empire in lacking virtually any history as a sovereign state. Slovenia lacked an indigenous nobility and, until the nineteenth century, a significant petite bourgeoisie.

As with many of the East European Slavs, Slovene ethnic consciousness grew with the Reformation/Counter-Reformation emphasis on vernacular languages as vehicles for proselytization.

Awareness of their linguistic uniqueness laid the groundwork for a Slovene sense of cultural identity. Even in the late nineteenth century the lower ranking Roman Catholic clergy, Slav to the man, were critical in fostering ethnic identity among the mass of Slovenes as well as maintaining the Slovenian language in the face of Germanization efforts in the schools.

Intellectuals trained by the Catholic clergy spearheaded the movement for Slovene cultural identity in the nineteenth century. They were responsible for establishing Slovenian as a literary language. Theirs was explicitly an apolitical effort, however; even in the ferment of the 1840s the Austrian police reported the Slovenian provinces free of political malcontents. Only during the Balkan wars (1912, 1913) was there agitation for a political union outside the empire.

Slovenia was the most economically favored region in the interwar kingdom. Widespread primogeniture had limited the land fragmentation typical of the Balkans. Slovene peasants did not lack their share of distress in the 1920s and 1930s, but they were, as a group, middling farmers. The Roman Catholic clergy, which was active in Slovenian politico-economic affairs, was particularly so in the countryside. They organized credit and marketing cooperatives freeing Slovene families from the pernicious indebtedness that afflicted rural Yugoslavia.

Slovenian readiness to negotiate and compromise served them well in the interwar and post-World War II eras alike. Slovenes were, in fact, an indispensible ingredient in the parade of coalition governments of interwar Yugoslavia. The Habsburg tradition of local autonomy resulted in the Slovenes having a highly trained corps of administrators. Linguistic distinctiveness staved off Serbian bureaucrats who flooded into Croatia instead.

Even as the numerically insignificant Slovenes feared being engulfed by Germanic hordes under Habsburg rule, post-World War II demographic trends have been disquieting for contemporary Slovenes. The republic's portion of total population dropped from 8.8 percent in 1953 to 8 percent in 1981. Slovenia's rate of natural increase averaged roughly two-thirds that of the nation as a whole in the 1960s and 1970s.

Slovenes maintained a strong sense of cultural continuity into the 1970s. They remained profoundly Roman Catholic. Polls consistently found Slovenia to have the lowest percentage of atheists; more Slovenes than any other national group favored an increase in the clergy's activity in social affairs.

The region's general level of prosperity remained high throughout the socialist era; in the 1970s it ranked first or second among the republics in terms of average monthly income and first in percentage of the economically active population employed outside the private agricultural sector. It had the highest literacy rate, the lowest proportion of the population without any schooling, and the highest rate of participation in vocational educational programs.

Slovenia's concern with government policy and decentralization have been similar to Yugoslavia's other developed regions. In the nationalities crises of the early 1970s the Slovenian leadership was less unyielding than the Croatians. The growing realization in Slovenia that the republic relied on the south for raw materials and protected markets made for a certain community of interests with low income regions. Slovenia was center stage during the 1969 "roadway crisis." The dispute centered on the allocation of funds to road-building projects in Serbia and Croatia instead of the much-needed link between Ljubljana and Nova Gorica. The republic leadership protested vigorously, and the Slovene public voiced its disapproval in mass demonstrations.

Montenegrins

Montenegrins were numerically the smallest of the Yugoslav nations; their share in the population was a declining one. Politically and culturally their closest affinity lay with the Serbs; like them the Montenegrins were Orthodox believers, spoke Serbo-Croatian, and used the Cyrillic alphabet. In those events shaping modern Yugoslavia, Serbs and Montenegrins played comparable roles. Both defined cultural identity in terms of struggle against the Turk. Montenegro maintained a tenacious and tenuous hold on autonomy in the face of recurrent Ottoman incursions (see The Montenegrins, ch. 1). Traditional society was one of shifting alliances among warring clans, each made up of patrilineally related extended families withstanding the predations of both Turks and rival clans. It was a politically decentralized society where loyalty to one's kin, expressed in a commitment to family honor, was paramount. Warfare and raiding were endemic, personal courage and success in combat the preeminent male virtues. The extended family in its most traditional form existed well into the twentieth century; bride theft and blood feuds were, if not commonplace, by no means uncommon. In the mid-1970s a socialist observer could still complain that the "old patriarchal peasant-like mentality and consciousness" was obstructing the revolutionary changes in Montenegrin social life.

Montenegrins were merged with other "Serbo-Croats" in interwar censuses; and neither language nor religion permit them to be distinguished from Serbs. Nonetheless the best indications are that they played a significant role in, if nothing else, the army. Montenegrins were prominent in communist and Partisan organizations; they were subsequently disproportionately overrepresented in the higher reaches of officialdom. Some 15 percent of the leaders of federal administrative bodies were Montenegrins in the early 1970s—over three times their share of the Yugoslav population. In keeping with their long-standing military tradition and their Partisan record, they comprised nearly one-fifth of the generals of the YPA. Their representation in the officer corps, while less marked, was still greater than their proportion of total population.

The Montenegrin-Serb alliance has been, with few exceptions, close throughout the socialist era, and Montenegro has normally been a firm supporter of federal government policy. Montenegrin Communists, however, had a rate of expulsion from the LCY for pro-Soviet (or Cominform—Communist Information Bureau—see Glossary) sympathies following the country's 1948 break with Stalin far higher than other republics. One in six Montenegrin Communists was expelled in contrast with one in twenty Croats, one in twenty-three Bosnians, and one in thirty-one Macedonians (the Serbs never published their expulsion rates). In 1974 a group of Communists, largely Montenegrins, was accused of forming a secret pro-Soviet party. A 1969 Montenegrin decision to build a monument to the priest-bishops who ruled the country until 1851 precipitated protests by the Serbian Orthodox Church, which owned the proposed site. The Montenegrins countered by accusing the church of trying to deny their existence as a separate nation. The exchange led to a vehement campaign to encourage Montenegrin culture, which was followed, in the wake of the Croatian crisis, by a purge of the more extremist elements.

Montenegro benefited particularly from development policy: per capita investment has been higher than the national average and higher than the less developed regions' average as well. Industry grew dramatically following War War II; by the late 1970s fifty-seven of every 1,000 inhabitants worked in industry (nearly five times the 1952 rate). The number of persons engaged in agriculture accounted for 72 percent of the populace in 1948; but only 35 percent in 1971. Life expectancy by the early 1970s had risen some twenty years. Many of the problems typical of the less developed regions, nonetheless, were Montenegro's too. Small, fragmented family plots earning less than two-thirds the average income of agricultural workers dominated agriculture. Much investment was inordinately capital-intensive. The region suffered from low prices for its raw materials in the early 1970s, and development had left pockets of Montenegro poor and untouched.

Ethnic Muslims

Most (roughly 90 percent in the 1970s) of Yugoslavia's ethnic Muslims lived in Bosnia and Hercegovina. They comprised a growing portion of the republic's population. Their rapid increase was less a matter of natural increase than undercounting in earlier censuses when ethnic (Bosnian) Muslims were classed as Serbs, Croats, Serbo-Croats, or Yugoslavs.

Muslims, as a class, were disproportionately represented among the privileged under Ottoman rule. In the late nineteenth-early twentieth centuries (then under Austro-Hungarian hegemony) they accounted for 90 percent of all landowners with tenants and half the urban population. They suffered from the Turkish decline, and substantial numbers fled to Turkey. The 1918 land reform eroded the economic resources of those who remained. None of this had much impact on most ethnic Muslims, however, who were of the humbler strata of rural society. They were peasants eking out a living and facing many of the same constraints their Christian counterparts did: rural overpopulation and unfavorable terms of credit did not spare the Muslim peasant in the early twentieth century.

Ethnic Muslims were concentrated in the northwest regions of Bosnia. This pattern changed to one of Serbian-Muslim villages to the south and east and Croatian-Muslim ones westward toward Dalmatia. Even within ethnically mixed areas the rule was segregation into Serbian, Croatian, or Muslim neighborhoods.

The Muslim intelligentsia had an ambiguous relationship to interwar Yugoslavia's governments. They suffered from Serbia's hegemony and Belgrade's barely concealed view that Muslims were the chief impediment to Serbian dominance in Bosnia. Nonetheless the seemingly endless coalition cabinets of the 1920s relied on Muslim participation, and Muslim leaders exploited Serbian electoral weakness to their own advantage. Because Croats regarded them fundamentally as Croats of Islamic persuasion, Muslims suffered significantly less than Serbs in the Croatian fascist state. A number of prominent Muslim leaders were compromised by their complicity with the fascist government. Their most consistent enmity during World War II focused on the Serbian Cetniks (see Glossary).

Many Muslims entered the ranks of urban entrepreneurs, traders, and craftsmen after losing their landholdings in the interwar era. The postwar era found them underrepresented in the upper echelons of government and among artists, technical specialists, and enterprise managers. Limited surveys in the late 1960s found ethnic Muslims clustered in a variety of traditional crafts (goldsmithing and coppersmithing, for example) and modern services (auto, television, and radio repair).

Those of a religious bent benefited from the government's relatively benign tolerance toward organized religion as well as Yugoslavia's desire to impress Arab nations with a "showcase" Muslim community. The situation worsened in the late 1970s-early 1980s with stern warnings to Islamic leaders of the perils of pan-Islamic nationalism (see Religion, this ch.). Observers suggested that the regime's concern may have had less to do with Islamic fundamentalism, than with forestalling any Croat-Muslim coalescense to the disadvantage of Bosnia's minority Serbs.

Macedonians

The central government's recognition in 1945 of Macedonians' equal legal status with Yugoslavia's other nations was a benchmark in that region's long-standing discord. Neither the Greeks nor the Bulgarians recognized the Macedonians as a distinct ethnic group in the late 1970s. For the Bulgarians, Macedonian was simply a dialect of Bulgarian, and the region itself was part of Greater Bulgaria liberated in the Russo-Turkish War of 1878, only to be lost through the diplomatic chicanery of the great powers at the Congress of Berlin in 1878. Western Macedonia's divison between the Serbian kingdom and Greece was a major bone of contention in the first and second Balkan wars.

Bulgaria reluctantly renounced its claims to western Macedonia following World War II. Nonetheless that country sporadically asserted that Macedonians were not a separate nationality but a Bulgarian minority within Yugoslavia—a claim Belgrade found implicitly irredentist. The controversy waxed and waned in the 1950s and 1960s. Debate heated up in the late 1970s on the occasion of the centennial anniversary of the Treaty of San Stefano (1878–1978) and continued into the early 1980s in Skopje and Sofia publications (see The Macedonians, ch. 1).

Serbia's policy of aggressive centralization bred considerable discontent in the region in the interwar era. Much like the Croats, Macedonians found the overweening Serbian hegemony intolerable. Bulgarian troops entering Macedonia in 1941 were welcomed as liberators. Sofia Fascists soon pursued policies as offensive as Serbia's previous ones.

In general Macedonia benefited from Belgrade's post-World War II policies. The region's status as a separate republic gave the intelligentsia a separate state government apparatus, league of communists, and academic establishment. Given the salience of language and ethnic identity in Eastern Europe, the recognition of Macedonian as the republic's national language and the 1948 publication of its first grammar gave added credence to the Communists' commitment to a truly multinational Yugoslavia. The formation of the Macedonian Orthodox Church assuaged fears of Serbian domination in that quarter (see Religion, this ch.). The proportion of Macedonians in the army officer corps and the high command was at parity in the early 1970s.

Macedonia's reaction to central government development policy and the resurgent nationalism of the 1970s was more complex. The region's poverty in interwar Yugoslavia was extreme even for the Balkans. Serbs—the vast majority of the rural populace—gained their freedom only in the twentieth century, and then only to become sharecroppers under the most straitened circumstances. Like neighboring Kosovo it was an impoverished agricultural region. While Macedonians—leery of possible Serbian preponderance—favored decentralization in the 1960s, it was on the assumption that there would be continued efforts to funnel development funds to the region.

Albanians

Yugoslavia's largest national minority was its Albanian community, in 1981 numbering some 1.6 million, nearly 7 percent of the population. Most Albanians were concentrated in Kosovo where they constituted roughly 80 percent of the population; another quarter million resided in neighboring Macedonia and Montenegro. All told, an estimated one-third to one-half of all Albanians lived in

Yugoslavia—making them one of the largest potentially irredentist communities in the world.

Albanians were, in addition, Yugoslavia's largest non-Slav ethnic group, and Kosovo beyond a doubt was the country's poorest region. Poverty and ethnic distinctiveness added to astronomical population growth were hardly a felicitous combination for the Albanians. Kosovo itself was significant in the historical and cultural heritage of both Serbs and Albanians. For Serbs the region was the core of their medieval kingdom, the scene of their final defeat at the hands of the invading Turks in the 1389 Battle of Kosovo, and the location (at Pec) of the Serbian patriarchate's seat. For the Albanians, Pristina was a center of rising Albanian nationalism in the nineteenth and twentieth centuries.

Albanians, even more than other non-Serbs, were excluded from power in interwar Yugoslavia. Their poverty and almost complete inexperience in government made them unlikely allies for the dominant Serbs in any event. That they were not Slavs made their adherence to Islam seem more compromising, more "Turkish" to Serbs.

Albanians' lot improved dramatically following Rankovic's dismissal in 1966. Kosovo became an autonomous province in 1968; Albanians had extensive control of the local political administration, and cultural and educational organizations (see The Process of Government, ch. 4). Pristina University, founded in 1970, was Yugoslavia's third largest university by 1980. Its enrollment expanded nearly seven times in the decade and was transformed from being a disproportionately Serb student body to one predominantly Albanian.

Nonetheless Kosovo's per capita economic growth dropped further behind even the less developed regions and contributed to growing instability in the ethnically sensitive region. Kosovo in the 1970s was still a region of marginal family farms, accounting for nearly 90 percent of the arable land and comprising 70 percent of the republic's population in 1972. It was as well a region of massive social change. Urban growth far outstripped housing and services. The population explosion fed into rising under- and un-employment and rural overpopulation; 11 percent of the population was employed compared to 26 percent nationally. More than half the population was under nineteen years of age; one-third was in school. Women in secondary schools and universities grew from virtually nil in the early 1960s to nearly one-third of all enrollment in 1981. At the same time the authority of those who traditionally maintained order—family elders and religious leaders—declined. While the number of Albanians holding higher academic degrees rose, the preponderance of graduates in the liberal arts gave Kosovo little of the technical expertise it needed. Employment opportunities for Albanian speakers were limited in Serbo-Croatian regions. The dramatic increase in educated Albanians contributed less to an indigenous intelligentsia than to unemployed academics.

Farmer plowing field near Pristina, Kosovo
Courtesy WORLD BANK PHOTO (Yosef Hadar)

Nationalistic fervor along with the conflicting loyalties of Serbs, Montenegrins, and Albanians gave the regime considerable cause for disquiet. There was unrest among Albanians in 1968 and 1980; in 1981 poor living conditions at Pristina University sparked the most serious violence to date. Much about these disturbances caused grave concern to the authorities. Albanians wanted full status as a republic—a demand that would be difficult to negotiate with Serbs (see The Domestic Political Agenda, ch. 4). Moreover some demonstrators suggested that the proposed Kosovo republic ought to include Albanians in Macedonia and Montenegro too. Some extremists even voiced secessionist sentiment calling for a "Greater Albania."

Rioters included not only students, but workers, peasants, and even Communist Party members. Those sought in connection with the unrest, according to official sources, were hiding in villages, suggesting a measure of at least tacit popular support. Authorities also feared ethnic backlash and rising violence as Serb and Montenegrin farmers fearful for their safety barricaded their villages against possible Albanian incursions.

Social Groups

Society of the early 1980s was largely the creation of the post-World War II communist regime. A legacy of socioeconomic and

77

ethnic cleavages remained; nonetheless the social scene would have been hard for an observer from the interwar kingdom to recognize. The interwar society was overwhelmingly rural, agricultural, impoverished, if not absolutely destitute; a small middle level of professionals and government administrators were concentrated in a few urban centers. In the early 1980s all this had been transformed. There was a substantial nonagricultural labor force; peasants had become workers and had created a new category to describe the process of leaving the family farm for nonagricultural employment, the peasant-worker. The elite, still a privileged stratum, expanded to include not just bureaucrats, professionals, and military officers but a growing corps of technical experts and managers for the changing economy.

The mobility involved in the evolution of socialist Yugoslavia was enormous. Peasants still remained a goodly portion of the populace, but the sons and daughters of peasants were industrial workers, managers, teachers. People who began World War II as subsistence farmers and ended it under arms in the Partisans experienced almost unparalleled mobility. Tito, son of a Slovenian-Croatian peasant family, was unusual in the measure of his success, but not his career pattern.

Peasants

Despite rapid industrialization throughout the post-World War II era, peasant farmers remained a substantial portion of the population in the 1980s. Some 2.2 to 2.9 million individuals owned the small plots associated with private agriculture; peasants accounted for 95 percent of the agricultural labor force, and their holdings represented roughly 85 percent of all arable land. More than any other segment of society they inherited the legacy of Ottoman misrule, interwar neglect, and extreme overpopulation.

The impact of Ottoman rule on the agricultural south's social and economic development can hardly be overstated. "The centuries do not follow one another," an early twentieth-century traveler commented of the regions under Turkish control, "they co-exist." Ottoman rule split the rural populace into a dominant Muslim minority and a subservient Christian majority, but both suffered alike in the chaos surrounding the empire's decline. The sale of public offices (with tenure limited to a single year) and the erosion of centralized authority took their toll of the peasantry. Brigandage was widespread and contributed to the general instability of rural life. Prime agricultural land went unoccupied as those who could fled Ottoman rule, while those remaining behind clustered in villages; dispersed farmsteads invited pillage of the worst kind. Taxation undermined farmers' incentives to improve production. ("Why breed better horses?" a typical peasant replied to a traveler's query. "If they were good for anything, the government would take them. . . .") The combined effects of banditry and poor transport hampered commerce. Tariffs favored foreign imports, thus limiting local manufactures. Graft and corruption were a pervasive part of public life.

The rise of the Serbian kingdom, the switch from pastoralism to sedentary crop production, and the adoption of New World cultigens rapidly led to overpopulation. In Serbia, for example, the population tripled in the course of the nineteenth century as families streamed into regions liberated from Ottoman rule and chronic rural unrest. Nineteenth- and twentieth-century land reforms distributed many large estates to peasants, and land reclamation projects in the 1920s added roughly 20 percent to the cultivable land. Despite this, and even allowing for the labor-intensive technology in use, over 40 percent of the agricultural population was surplus in the interwar kingdom. In terms of overpopulation, Yugoslavia consistently outranked all other East European countries.

To rural overpopulation was added chronic indebtedness. In rural Yugoslavia the merchant-moneylender replaced the Muslim landlord as the main agent of peasant exploitation. In 1932 over one-third of all peasant households were in debt to a sum of nearly half the previous season's gross income. Periodic moratoriums on debt repayments and farm foreclosures gave occasional relief but by no means solved the small farmer's problems in obtaining reasonably priced credit. Taxation further impoverished the peasantry, who regularly footed half the tax bill and got in return perhaps 1 percent of budget allocations.

Small private holdings were the rule in agriculture in the 1970s. The communist regime abandoned early efforts at collectivization in the economic crises of the early 1950s. It was an effort, some observers suggest, to retain the support of the rural populace who had made up the ranks of the Partisans. Legislation in 1953 limited the amount of land private farmers could hold to ten to fifteen hectares. Most families were in little danger of exceeding this limit; farm size averaged 3.5 hectares per family in 1980. Added to this was a degree of extreme land fragmentation. A sample of farms in Kosovo in the 1970s found that the average family's holdings included some six plots of 0.6 hectare each. Nearly four-fifths of all farms were five hectares or less (see table 9, Appendix).

In growth and earnings private farms lagged behind the socialized agricultural sector. Private agricultural earnings were less than half (41 percent) the nonfarm sector in 1975. At the same time the private agricultural labor force declined by nearly one-third (1954–71). As the young (particularly men) left in search of industrial employment, the peasant labor force aged and "feminized." In the 1970s women accounted for an estimated 60 percent of private agriculture's labor.

The rural populace made do under these apparently dire circumstances because the family farm was less a means of livelihood than a base of operations. The farm was the peasant family's patrimony, the keystone of family resources, but hardly the sole support of the rural household. Balkan peasants have a long history in the wage labor market. They ventured everywhere from Anatolia to America as migrant workers while under Ottoman and Austro-Hungarian rule. Temporary or permanent migrant labor was a critical safety valve during the interwar era as well.

Yugoslavia's post-World War II industrialization with its concomitant improvement in transportation opened up new possibilities for off-farm employment closer to home. Peasants became commuters as well as migrant laborers. By 1970 nearly 1.5 million peasants (roughly one-quarter of the economically active rural population) were employed outside of agriculture. About half the rural population lived in households with at least one "peasant-worker." By the mid-1960s nonagricultural earnings exceeded rural families' farm income. Over time, peasants with larger and larger holdings have become involved in wage labor; again by the late 1960s even families with eight or more hectares earned one-third their income from nonagricultural activities.

The pattern of involvement in wage labor varied according to the family's resources. Well-to-do peasants able to muster the ready cash for travel expenses and work permits took advantage of the lucrative international labor market. Those from relatively poorer families stayed closer to home. The impact of occasional or semipermanent wage labor on rural life was pervasive. Everything from young women's trousseaux to home renovation relied on off-farm employment.

At the same time that the peasant-worker's wages have been an invaluable addition to family income, the family homestead has been a significant asset for the first generation industrial laborer. The family farm provided a portion of the worker's foodstuffs and a "safety net" in case of unemployment. Policymakers lamented the peasant-worker's tendency to be absent from work at times of peak agricultural labor and bemoaned the extent to which farms became mere "gardens" as workers directed their attention toward nonfarm employment. Nonetheless wage labor blunted the impact of rural overpopulation and land fragmentation on the peasant family; and the family plot made the transition to off-farm employment more secure for the peasant-worker.

Workers

The nonagricultural work force was almost entirely the creation of the post-World War II industrialization drive. In 1948 agriculture provided a livelihood for nearly three-quarters of the population; by the mid-1970s roughly two-thirds of those economically active found employment outside agriculture. From 1954 to 1975—when agriculture lost 1 to 2 million workers—industrial jobs grew at an average annual rate of 4.3 percent.

Early in the de-Stalinization campaign following Yugoslavia's expulsion from the Cominform, the government instituted a far-reaching program aimed at turning over control of state enterprises

The Society and Its Environment

(virtually all enterprises were state owned) to workers (see Communist Yugoslavia, ch. 1). Legislation culminating with the Associated Labor Act of 1976 elaborated the institutional arrangements whereby workers were to run their enterprises (see Role of Government, ch. 3). Self-management was the basic principle underlying workplace organization.

A complex organizational apparatus surrounded workers' participation in self-management. Each worker belonged to a Basic Organization of Associated Labor (BOAL) depending on his or her precise role in the production process. BOALs in turn elected workers' councils, which appointed a number of hierarchically organized bodies (translated variously as central workers' councils, management boards, and executive organs). These set wages, investment policy, and production goals. An enterprise director (or a managing board) appointed by the executive organ had responsibility for the day-to-day running of the enterprise.

The implementation of self-management, despite its profoundly egalitarian ideology, reflected the stratification of the industrial work force. Skilled and better educated workers participated disproportionately on workers' councils (see table 10, Appendix). From the mid-1950s to the mid-1970s skilled workers, roughly a third of enterprise employees, regularly garnered half the slots on workers' councils. The percentage of semiskilled or unskilled workers declined during the same period. Presidents of workers' councils also came disproportionately from the ranks of skilled workers or white-collar employees. Those with advanced educational degrees accounted for nearly two-thirds of all presidents of workers' councils. Participation on membership boards and executive organs revealed the same trends.

The enterprise director (and his professional and technical staff) wielded considerable influence. The director's ability to obtain and control the flow of information about business conditions and the overall enterprise operation put him in an advantageous position to affect decisions. Workers, skilled and unskilled alike, exercised more control over policies affecting working conditions and wage payments—matters they found most salient. Over time, workers have focused increasingly on these issues, leaving investment and production decisions and the daily running of the enterprise to the director and technical experts.

Actual patterns of authority and decisionmaking showed significant variation. Workers' councils were most effective in smaller enterprises, in those with an urban, skilled labor force. Peasant workers or the unskilled were often unaware of their rights under self-management and were more liable to be manipulated by technical experts and managerial employees.

In particular cases, the interests of management and skilled and unskilled workers often diverged. Policies geared toward enhancing the enterprise's efficiency and competitiveness conflicted with higher wages and job security for workers. Whatever the actual logistics of self-management in specific cases, workers' control meant that the enterprise responded to market conditions differently than its capitalist counterpart. Economic downturns meant not layoffs as much as a reduction in investments or, less frequently, wages. An enterprise can reduce its labor force only with the consent of workers, which normally meant finding them alternative employment or providing new job training. One author, for example, describes an electrical factory reducing its work force by giving the laid-off workers an interest-free loan to establish another plant.

Between 1958 and 1978 there were approximately 3,000 strikes in Yugoslav enterprises. Strikes began in the late 1950s in Slovenia and spread over the next decade southward through Croatia and Serbia, then to Bosnia and finally to Macedonia, Montenegro, and Kosovo. Most strikes occurred in the developed regions. Wages and failure to comply with the norms of self-management were the most frequent complaints that sent workers out on strike. Workers objected to management's failure to communicate adequately about decisions affecting enterprise affairs.

The general pattern for strikes revealed much about the operation of the workplace. Strikers were most frequently unskilled workers; in the late 1960s four-fifths of all strikes involved only unskilled workers, and nearly three-quarters of all strikers were unskilled workers (see table 11, Appendix). Strikers directed their discontent not at workers' councils, nominally in control of the workplace, but at enterprise directors, local government bodies, and executive organs—those perceived as making the decisions most responsible for workers' discontent.

Although the right-to-strike was not formally recognized in labor legislation, the authorities' approach to labor unrest was pragmatic. Officials viewed strikes as an indication of inadequate implementation of self-management. Workers' lack of education or lack of experience were often cited causes of work stoppages. Officials insisted managers' and experts' subversion of self-management caused strikes. Denunciations of "bureaucratism" and "technocratism" began almost with self-management's inception and continued into the 1980s. Distribution of personal income, the criteria for income distribution, and labor relations in the self-managed firm were the most frequent complaints strikers had in the early 1980s.

The growing dichotomy between workers and the managerial elite was central to workplace dynamics. Work stoppages and official excoriations of "technocratism" reflected the changing role of formal expertise within the enterprise. Management favored hiring and promoting in terms of formal educational qualifications rather than training workers for advanced positions. Hiring individuals holding higher educational degrees increased dramatically in the 1960s and 1970s and contributed to the growing stratification of the work force.

Increasing inequality in incomes was part of the same process.

Early post-World War II income distribution was highly egalitarian—a dramatic contrast with interwar Yugoslavia where rentiers, entrepreneurs, and professionals—5 percent of the population—received more than a quarter of national income. By 1951 white-collar workers' incomes exceeded those of skilled blue-collar workers by only 25 percent. Since then, however, the trend has been toward increasing income differentials between skilled and unskilled, professional and manual or clerical workers (see table 12, Appendix). From the early 1950s through the early 1970s the spread between the lowest and the highest incomes rose from 1:1.25 to 1:8.00. Not only did professionals substantially out-earn everyone else, but the most highly skilled blue-collar workers averaged roughly two-and-a-half times the wages of their unskilled counterparts—a differential that exceeded the disparity between skilled and unskilled workers in Britain, France, and West Germany. These trends continued through the 1970s with differences in regional and industry wage scales growing, until in 1980 the highest paid skilled workers earned nearly four times the wages of the lowest paid unskilled employees.

Women played a significant role in the Partisans—they comprised 100,000 of a total 800,000 in the force—and in the Anti-Fascist Council for the National Liberation of Yugoslavia (Anti-fasistiko Vijece Narodnog Oslobodjenja Jugoslavije—AVNOJ) where they numbered over 2 million—but their participation in the post-World War II transformation of society was anything but equal. Earlier interwar legislation aimed only at protecting women's subservient status within the patriarchal family; the communist regime, however, repeatedly guaranteed full equal rights and a wide range of protective legislation for pregnant women and working mothers. Woman's participation in the labor force lagged behind the improvements in her juridical status. Women in the 1970s were slightly more than one-third the total labor force—a percentage that had (except for a statistical anomaly in the 1948 figures) remained roughly constant since 1931.

Women faced a number of handicaps, especially in leaving private agriculture and entering the expanding social sector. In education and level of skill they lagged behind their male counterparts. Even in 1971 after decades of compulsory education and a dramatic increase in female enrollments, over 20 percent of women over ten years of age were illiterate, compared with less than 8 percent of men. Women were consistently in the less skilled segments of the work force—those hit hardest during economic downturns. Women's education and employment trailed men's especially in the less developed regions—a reflection of both those regions' straitened economic circumstances and their Islamic heritage (see table 13, Appendix).

Women's employment grew in the 1960s and 1970s as the service sector expanded. Between 1970 and 1974 women were nearly half of all first-time job holders; female employment grew at double the rate for males. Women concentrated in the conventional fields of female employment: public services, retail trade, and light manufacturing. In the so-called noneconomic activities of public services and social welfare, women made up nearly 60 percent of all employees by mid-decade (see table 14, Appendix). Similarly, in trade and catering they constituted one-half of the employees.

Intelligentsia

By convention Marxists subdivide the intelligentsia into its creative (writers, artists, journalists), professional (lawyers, doctors, educators, civil servants, professional politicians, leaders of mass organizations, communist officials), and technical (engineers, scientists, often enterprise managers) segments. The intelligentsia was pivotal in the massive changes Yugoslavia underwent in the nineteenth and twentieth centuries. The coalescence of a dissatisfied intelligentsia and an oppressed peasantry more than once transformed the Balkans. Insofar as one might speak of the intelligentsia as an elite within a self-managing society, it is the social group that has undergone—both in personnel and in structure—dramatic changes since 1941.

In interwar Yugoslavia, despite the prevalence of revolving-door cabinets, the ruling elite was a minute group of some fifty to sixty educated and politically experienced individuals. A larger "middle stratum" concentrated in urban or semiurban centers served as an administrative elite. Government service—following the requisite educational background, i.e., secondary or university schooling—was virtually the only employment for the ambitious individual.

There were significant ideological, political, religious, and ethnic differences within this elite, but the extent to which they represented a small fraction of the population they ruled can hardly be exaggerated. The elite were overwhelmingly Serbs; most Croatian intelligentsia and the minute number of educated Macedonians and Albanians were excluded. Their disaffection at having virtually the only avenue of upward mobility—government service—closed to them contributed much to the endemic separatist and nationalist sentiment of the era. Beyond this, in a country where perhaps half the citizenry could read and less than 10 percent lived in cities, the urban and educated elite was indeed at the top of a very steep social pyramid. The intelligentsia stood at the apex of a society that was overwhelmingly peasant, rural, and uneducated; they were without rival—no rising industrial bourgeoisie threatened the hegemony of the state bureaucracy.

Social mobility was limited; the elite was drawn from the sons of those families in the narrow middle and upper strata: large landowners and a handful of industrialists, financiers, civil servants, and military officers. There was mobility between the middle and upper social groups, if only because the governmental apparatus expanded following World War I. Moreover there was significant upward mobility for the three-generation span that included the Serbian struggle for independence from Ottoman rule. Grandfather, peasant;

Opera House, Zagreb

father, middle-level civil servant; son, upper echelon civil servant was not an atypical family history for the fortunate few in the interwar elite.

In 1948 the Communist Party of Yugoslavia (after 1952 the League of Communists of Yugoslavia—LCY) could hardly have been more different. Forged in the Partisan and AVNOJ war experience, a small remnant of the prewar membership remained in the middle and upper ranks of the leadership. These were largely intellectuals, students, and some workers—an ambiguous category including professional cadres like Tito and Rankovic. Beyond this, however, the party had become, in the course of the war, one of

85

peasants and workers. It was notably rural; Belgrade, the bastion of the previous elite, was strikingly underrepresented: 95 percent of the communist elite in 1945 was not from the nation's capital.

Partisan service or, for a few, pre-1941 membership in the Communist Party was the prerequisite to a successful elite career. In the late 1960s when those in the LCY with pre-1941 service (retired and active) accounted for less than half a percent of the total membership, they still represented over 15 percent of those in leading positions in the LCY and society at large. Over three-fourths of pre-1944 members pursued professional political or military careers following World War II.

With a few notable exceptions those who took power following the war were the sons of peasants and workers. This pattern persisted through the 1960s, when more than half of those in top leadership positions had fathers who had been workers or peasants. The degree of three-generation social mobility was even more pronounced. More than 75 percent of Yugoslavia's top leaders had grandfathers who were workers or peasants. The same pattern of occupational mobility—intra- and inter-generational upward mobility—described the country's professional classes as a whole. In 1960 nearly one-third of all white-collar workers had been peasants themselves in 1946, and nearly three-quarters came from peasant or worker families.

As the Partisan generation aged, education reinstated itself as the conventional entrée to a professional career. By the late 1960s-early 1970s roughly nine-tenths of those occupying highly qualified professional positions did so on the basis of their formal educational credentials. Older employees upgrading their job qualifications through continuing education were part of this trend. So too were younger professionals who had been full-time students. Expanding higher education facilities, largely open admissions, and substantial public financing for education all contributed to intergenerational mobility. In the early 1950s roughly a third of all university students came from peasant-worker backgrounds; by the end of the decade nearly half did. Even in the mid-1960s nearly two-thirds of the students enrolled in the universities of Belgrade, Zagreb, and Sarajevo had parents with eight years or less of schooling. As the numbers of those with formal educational training increased and they became more firmly ensconced in the privileged strata, intergenerational mobility declined. There were still significant numbers of young peasants entering the urban-industrial labor force; a mid-1970s survey of workers under twenty-five years of age found approximately a quarter of their fathers were private farmers. At the same time the chances that workers' or peasants' children would be university students declined relative to that of the offspring of professionals.

Similar trends were apparent in the social background of the LCY membership. When the Communists assumed power, half the members were peasants; another 30 percent were workers. By the late 1960s more than 40 percent of the LCY membership professionals were white-collar employees; peasants' proportion had fallen to less than 1 percent. Administrators, intelligentsia, managers, and technical experts were all overrepresented relative to their share of total population.

The rise of a substantial technical intelligentsia was a major social development in socialist Yugoslavia. It was an occupational group that enjoyed considerable popular prestige; Yugoslavs surveyed in the late 1960s ranked mechanical engineering as the most prestigious occupation. Even given high wages and readily available employment in Western Europe the technical intelligentsia was underrepresented among Yugoslav migrant workers (see Migration, this ch.).

The relationship between the regime and the technical intelligentsia was complex. On the one hand government policies fostering greater educational opportunities and economic development were critical in the emergence of those with technical or managerial expertise. The LCY has been at pains to cultivate a loyal, highly trained technical intelligentsia. The relationship between the experts and those who favor "democratic centralism" was stormy. The technical elite have been supporters of enterprise autonomy, and they have waxed and waned in official favor or disfavor. In the mid-1960s LCY members began commenting on the experts' "petty bourgeois mentality." "Technocrats" became the new class enemy guilty of subverting self-management and constituting a new elite.

The regime's relationship with the creative intelligentsia was likewise complex. Intellectuals of the nineteenth and early twentieth centuries were catalysts in the rising nationalism of the peoples within the Austro-Hungarian and Ottoman empires. Slav writers and journalists articulated and publicized popular aspirations. Socialist Yugoslavia's creative intelligentsia contained two distinct strains: a group committed to the traditional nationalistic concerns and another of humanistically oriented Marxists.

The traditional intelligentsia have been consistently at odds with the government's efforts to control nationalism. The regime has been preoccupied with the possibility that the traditional intelligentsia might strike a responsive cord with the general populace. The banning of Matica Hrvatska in 1972 for its role in resurgent Croatian nationalism reflected that concern (see Croats, this ch.). So too did legal action against dissident Serbian and Croatian writers in 1981. Albanians were the most manifestly disaffected intellectuals in the early 1980s. Disillusioned Albanian intelligentsia, educated largely in the humanities and facing limited employment possibilities, played a major role in the Kosovo region's 1981 unrest.

Marxists critical of LCY policies or their implementation were the other major group of dissident intelligentsia. Milovan Djilas, former Partisan and high-ranking communist official, was best known to Westerners. His series of articles in the early 1950s critical of the privileges communist officials enjoyed and calling for more democratic government led to his imprisonment; his 1980 biography of Tito stirred up considerable comment. Djilas was part of a highly developed tradition of dissidence among Yugoslav Socialists.

From the 1950s through the 1970s more than half a dozen critical journals were published at one time or another. The most prominent of these was *Praxis*, published in Serbo-Croatian and in an international edition (with articles in French, German, and English) from 1964 through mid-1974. *Praxis* focused on Marx as a humanist philosopher and a variety of issues of general interest to philosophers, literary critics, and social scientists. It recognized ideological differences within Yugoslav Marxism that the regime might have preferred to ignore, though the *Praxis* editorial staff and contributors—*praxisovci*, as they were commonly called—were careful not to challenge the basic legitimacy of one-party rule. At its peak the international edition included articles by scholars of world renown—Marxists and non-Marxists alike.

The relationship between the *praxisovci* and officialdom was always uneasy. As early as 1965 officials criticized *Praxis'* "alchemistic mixture of abstract eternal truths about humanity and freedom," in the absence of much cognizance of "the objective laws of social life." The Croatian crisis of 1970–71 left the journal's Croatian contributors—all outspoken critics of nationalism—unscathed. Things were more difficult for the Serbian *praxisovci*; the running battle between them and the League of Communists of Serbia (LCS) figured in the journal's ultimate demise. The "Belgrade 8"—all on the Philosophy Faculty of Belgrade University and all associated with *Praxis* and/or the Serbian critical journal, *Filosofia*—were a cause célèbre throughout the 1970s into mid-1981. There was a long and hard-fought battle over the dismissal of the eight professors that involved the LCS, the university's Philosophy Faculty, the LCS University Committee, and students in Zagreb and Belgrade. The Serbian parliament finally dismissed the eight by legislative fiat—a move that drew angered protest from a wide variety of sources. It undermined the long-standing autonomy of the university that had been the 1930s training ground for a host of prominent communist leaders.

In 1980–81 the Serbian parliament deprived the remaining "Belgrade 7" (one *praxisovci* had taken other employment) of the 60 percent of their salaries they had been receiving since the 1975 ban on their teaching activities. A number of intellectuals called for a new independent journal, *Javnost (Public Life)*, to publish Yugoslav socialist and nonsocialist authors. Authorities turned down the request to publish it in November 1980. Concurrently West European and Yugoslav *praxisovci* announced plans for a new international edition of *Praxis*. The regime feared any rapprochement among members of Yugoslavia's diverse creative intelligentsia. In addition they found the continued widespread support for the *praxisovci* among Belgrade University students disturbing.

Students were a perennial source of concern for the regime. Like the *praxisovci* they were often committed Marxists critical of persistent inequality under socialism—"dinar socialism." They were, however, far more demanding than their elders in agitating for reform. Students, often in the Korcula summer institute, pushed the *praxisovci* to more and more radical critiques of Yugoslav socialism. The authorities' most serious cause for alarm was student unrest in 1968 at various universities around the country, in 1981 at Pristina University and in 1971 at Zagreb University. In Pristina the incidents were highly tinged with nationalist sentiment, although often phrased as a critique of Yugoslav inequity in contrast with Albanian egalitarianism (see Albanians, this ch.). Zagreb student complaints were largely nationalistic, although here again the threat of the November 1971 student strike focused on the currency issue (see Croats, this ch.). In the 1968 Belgrade student riots—which set the stage for all subsequent student unrest—it was difficult for officialdom to find a similar hint of nationalism, because students in Zagreb, Ljubljana, and Sarajevo protested in solidarity. The students' main objection was to the "embourgeoisement" of Yugoslav socialism, the perceived failure of self-management to create an egalitarian society. Authorities explicitly feared that student discontent might spread to workers, generating mass unrest. It was another facet of the intelligentsia-masses linkage that was historically such a volatile combination in Balkan politics.

Family Organization

Society, despite the massive changes of the socialist era, remained oriented to family and kin. The rights and duties kin bore toward one another were defined with a rigor that a North American observer would find unusual. The Basic Law on Relations Between Parents and Children in 1962, for example, defined the material support legally due one's parents, children, siblings, grandparents, and so forth. Kin were obliged to support their needy or incapacitated relatives; the law specified the order in which one was entitled to aid and assistance from both lineal and collateral relatives. Family and relatives were a central focus of an individual's solidarity and loyalty.

The *zadruga*, a kin-based corporate group holding property in common, was the basis of rural social organization throughout the Balkans. The rights and obligations of *zadruga* members were enshrined in customary and formal law from the feudal era onwards. Throughout rural Croatia, Serbia, Montenegro, Hercegovina, Macedonia, Kosovo, and much of Bosnia, the *zadruga*, as a formally constituted kin group, persisted until well after World War II. Its most common form was a group of patrilineally related males, their spouses, and children who owned and farmed land in common.

Zadruga persisted amidst "the cultural flux of Balkan history" because membership in a corporate group conferred clear advantages on the individual peasant family. The *zadruga* was essential to the success with which the Balkan peasantry endured wars and foreign rule, exploited pioneer lands, switched from pastoralism to agriculture, and took advantage of seasonal off-farm employment. Its precise configuration varied throughout the past five centuries in response to the highly uncertain political-economic-ecological conditions of the Balkans. The *zadruga* permitted the peasantry to maintain a sense of cultural identity during the centuries of foreign domination; it was a bulwark against the predations of state and bandit alike. The hearth was the focus of family loyalties, a meeting place for all major family decisions and the locus of religious ceremony. Religion—so influential in preserving Slav culture under Ottoman rule—centered on the individual *zadruga* rather than the parish church (see Religion, this ch.). Each *zadruga* had a patron saint (the practice extended to ethnic Muslims) and the saint's day celebration (*slava*) was the high point of the ritual calendar.

Large multifamily households had significant advantages—particularly in rural areas—well into the twentieth century. A substantial adult labor force permitted the extended family to specialize and engage in a variety of subsidiary operations to supplement agricultural income. It limited the burden of agricultural labor at peak seasons, permitted men to engage in politics, and gave women time for handicrafts. An extended family's wealth virtually always outstripped that of two to three nuclear households of comparable size. Beyond the advantages of a ready pool of labor, the extended family was, in a sense, a self-contained social security system for the peasant household. It was a haven for the orphaned, the widowed, the infirm, and the elderly. It smoothed the curves in the individual farming family's labor supply—young couples could rely on the assistance of teenagers and grandparents with the necessary agricultural and domestic tasks a single nuclear family would be hard pressed to accomplish.

The extended family's composition changed in response to increasing life expectancy in the twentieth century. The number of generations in a given household increased from two to three or even four, while the number of collateral relatives—brothers, cousins, second cousins—decreased. Patriarchal authority—often onerous within the traditional *zadruga*—was more so when a parent might expect to live significantly longer. Increased longevity lengthened the period of time an adult might be subject to parental authority. The wars of the twentieth century along with expanding urbanization and nonagricultural employment following World War II contributed to a decline in the extended family's joint ownership of property.

The extended family became a cooperative rather than a formally corporate kin group. Family loyalty and general feeling of responsibility toward kin persisted. Individuals relied on relatives for mutual aid and support in a wide variety of social and economic contexts. Families underwrote much of the cost of urbanization and industrialization throughout the 1960s and 1970s, with relatives providing urban housing for students from the countryside and employment advice and assistance for the recent rural-urban migrant (see Migration and Urbanization, this ch.). Migrants maintained reciprocal ties with their kin in the country, periodically offering assistance with agricultural tasks; for example, a mid-1970s study found that roughly 40 percent of the factory workers surveyed spent their vacations helping out on the family farm. Even among the country's technical and managerial elite, kinship figured in the relationship between commune and enterprise and reinforced local and familial loyalties.

Fictive kinship in the form of godparenthood crosscut the strongly familial focus of Slav social relations. With marriage it was the means *zadruga* had at their disposal to establish alliances with other kin groups. The institution took on the corporate character typical of traditional Slav kinship. Although Orthodox canon law does not specify that godparenthood can be heritable, traditionally the godparent-godchild relationship formed a permanent link between the two *zadruga*, one that was inherited patrilineally. The relationship implied feelings of deep mutual respect between the two groups; a godfather normally presided not only over the infant's christening, but also his or her first birthday and his wedding.

Even Muslim Slavs adopted the practice; although fictive kinship was less elaborate among ethnic Muslims, godparents sponsored the cutting of the dried umbilical cord (five to seven days after the child's birth) and his first hair cutting. There were few specific obligations attached to the relationship beyond a generalized expectation of friendship and assistance. Often godparenthood formed a link between Muslim and non-Muslim or reinforced that between Muslim kin. In all cases the tie was between individuals implying no relationship or obligation between the larger kin groups.

In socialist Yugoslavia fictive kinship persisted as a tie between individuals rather than kin groups. In the urban setting, parents' coworkers were increasingly chosen as godparents. Alternatively a city dweller may have chosen someone in the countryside as a child's godparent, and the peasant, a friend or relative who had migrated to the city.

As urban growth increased, large and extended families declined. From the 1948 through the 1981 censuses average family size dropped from 4.37 to 3.67. The decline was steepest in the developed regions. In Kosovo approximately three-quarters of all households had five or more members in the early 1970s, and over a quarter had ten or more members. Focusing on household composition rather than simple size, as late as 1953 roughly one-third of all households were extended families. The percentage of extended families dropped precipitously by the early 1970s, a measure of the advantages of smaller domestic groups in the urban setting. Approximately three-fourths of all urban households were nuclear families—a percentage that held constant in developed and less developed regions alike. The persistence of extended households in the countryside, albeit as a minority, was striking. Looking at data for central Serbia from the

1528, 1863, and 1961 censuses, anthropologist E.A. Hammel found virtually no significant difference in the proportion of all households that were nuclear or extended. In the early 1970s nearly one-quarter of all rural households remained extended families.

Migration and Urbanization

Migration

The most notable post-World War II migration trend was the waves of Yugoslavs seeking temporary or semipermanent employment as guestworkers (*Gastarbeiter*) abroad. This movement began extralegally in the 1950s, and when emigration restrictions were eased in the 1960s, the response was far beyond the authorities' expectations. Estimates of the number of Yugoslav *Gastarbeiter* in the 1970s and early 1980s varied, but whatever the precise magnitudes involved, every count of Yugoslav *Gastarbeiter* suggested that employment outside the country played an immensely important role in many workers' lives. In the early 1970s roughly 20 percent of the total labor force was employed abroad. Yugoslavia's rate of emigration was second only to Portugal's among European countries. At the movement's peak in 1973 some 1.1 million workers and dependents were living abroad. Estimates of Yugoslav workers employed abroad in the late 1970s-early 1980s—after the mid-1970s recession had sent many guestworkers back home—still ranged from 675,000 to 800,000.

In the early 1970s the main centers of emigration were not Yugoslavia's poorer regions but the economically developed north and west. Croatia, northeast Slovenia, east Vojvodina, and northeast Serbia contributed a disproportionate percentage of all emigrants. In preliminary results of the 1981 census Serbia proper, Montenegro, and Kosovo had all made gains in the number of their workers temporarily employed abroad. The number of Croatian *Gastarbeiter* declined by 40 percent leading to speculation that many were becoming permanently resident abroad.

Emigration began in Yugoslav cities among workers who were generally older, skilled, and male and attracted by higher wages in West European countries. By the mid-1970s the emigration process had spread to rural areas and included farmers, unskilled laborers, and women. Overall in the 1970s emigrants were more likely than the populace as a whole to have completed elementary school and vocational training. Among *Gastarbeiter* in Western Europe, Yugoslavs were consistently the most highly skilled. Forty percent of all emigrants were employed before taking a job—a figure that left out those leaving the country immediately after completing schooling and training and so obscuring the extent to which the *Gastarbeiter* came from the most productive strata of the labor force.

The departure of skilled workers was especially acute in Croatia where, in the early 1970s, skilled workers were one-third of all emigrants. The skilled worker's penchant for foreign employment was implicated in slowdowns in the growth of a variety of industries. In tourism, shortages of trained caterers and waiters were frequently dire. Waiters would work a single season on the Dalmation Coast, then emigrate to Austria or France. Seaside hotels became accustomed to training a new staff each season or employing their own *Gastarbeiter* from Poland or Czechoslovakia.

The drain of skilled workers was a snowballing process. Guestworkers returned home on vacation and broadcast the advantages of foreign employment to family and friends, thus leading more and more workers to emigrate. One group of fifteen welders and technicians left a Croatian shipyard en masse on hearing the virtues of work abroad touted by returning friends.

Approximately one-third of all emigrants were women—a percentage that corresponded to their share of the domestic labor force. Striking disparities in the rate at which women emigrated from various regions reflected the country's cultural diversity. Slightly more than 40 percent of all emigrants from Vojvodina and Slovenia were women, as were over a third of those from Serbia proper and Croatia. Women participated in emigration least in Kosovo, where they accounted for less than 5 percent of all emigrants (and nearly 20 percent of the provincial labor force).

Emigration from rural areas offered a pressure valve for continuing problems with agrarian overpopulation. Guestworkers from rural areas have been less skilled than their urban counterparts; their departure, given the prevalence of extended families to take up the slack in farm chores, has not been as disruptive as that of skilled urban workers. Families can continue to farm while emigrants' earnings permit the purchase of modern agricultural equipment. In areas with ready access to tourist spots families have intensified fruit and vegetable production, improved their livestock and dairy herds, and upgraded their vineyards.

The single most common item for which foreign earnings were spent—that for which nearly half of all workers sought employment outside the country—was housing. Those who planned to spend their earnings improving their farms remained a minority even among rural migrants. Those who planned to go into private crafts were a small fraction of the *Gastarbeiter* population.

Most emigrants from rural regions regarded foreign work experience as part of the transition to urban, nonagricultural employment. The farm and the extended family remained for them a haven in case of prolonged unemployment. Investment in private crafts was hedged with uncertainties about that sector's future in socialist Yugoslavia. Many emigrants purchased trucks or cars and went into hauling and transport on their return to the country, but there was a distinct limit to the number of truckers and taxi drivers the economy could absorb. Further, where private trucking firms began to compete with the social sector (as they did in the late 1960s in Croatia and Bosnia), government regulations limited their scope severely. In a single instance—after overcoming significant obstacles—some

Gastarbeiter managed to set up a tile factory with their families. Socialist officialdom was on the horns of the dilemma about the proper policy toward such efforts. On the one hand the authorities wished to encourage investment, but on the other hand they feared that handing an increasing share of economic activity to private hands raised the specter of "re-emergent capitalism."

The sheer numbers of Yugoslav workers in West European countries complicated foreign relations. Government efforts to have host countries recruit in the lesser developed regions, an attempt both to stem the tide of skilled personnel emigrating and to relieve unemployment in those areas where it was most acute, met with limited success. So too did the drive to entice West European employers of *Gastarbeiter* to locate factories in Yugoslavia.

In the late 1970s-early 1980s Yugoslavia concluded bilateral agreements with most West European countries employing Yugoslav guestworkers. The agreements covered a variety of rights and benefits for Yugoslavs while working abroad, such as unemployment compensation, vocational training, and the right to organize. Education of workers' children was a particularly salient issue. Host countries were at a loss to devise educational programs adapted to Yugoslavia's multinational labor force. Non-Serbo-Croatian speakers objected to instruction in that language; Serbs protested the use of the Latin alphabet, Croats that of the Cyrillic.

The return of Yugoslav guestworkers in the mid-to-late 1970s posed a variety of problems. As with emigration statistics, the precise number of returnees was not known, but between 1974 and 1980 some 300,000 to 400,000 *Gastarbeiter* returned to the country. Unskilled workers accounted for roughly 80 percent of all returnees. They added to the press on domestic employment created by people leaving agriculture and by the population's natural increase.

Returning emigrants have faced a measure of resentment; the feeling seemed to be that there was something less than an unflagging commitment to socialism in a worker who left the country to amass capitalist wealth. Beyond this, authorities feared guestworkers' exposure to émigré nationalist groups. These groups originated with the emigration of (primarily) Cetniks and *ustase* following World War II and, more recently, the Croatian crisis of 1970–71 (see Croats, this ch.). The émigrés included Serbs, Croats, and Macedonians, and their organizations ranged in their political platforms from advocates of pluralistic democracy to outright terrorists; most were vehemently nationalist and separatist. Émigré journals were readily accessible at the main disembarking points for *Gastarbeiter* or at places where they tended to congregate. The journals exposed migrants to nationalistic and anticommunist editorials. The Yugoslav government monitored *Gastarbeiter* contacts with émigré groups. At least two Croats and two Serbs were tried (in three cases found guilty) on charges stemming from their possession of émigré journals or remarks they had made critical of the government. Sentences ranged from eighteen months to five years.

Domestic migration has been massive since the end of World War II; according to the 1961 census one in every three Yugoslavs had migrated to a current residence. Much of this was the movement of peasants to the cities that played such a large part in the country's urbanization. While domestic migration involved a substantial portion of the populace, individuals tended to move short distances, and migration was overwhelmingly intrarepublic. In the thirty-year period from 1945 through 1975 over 80 percent of all Yugoslavs who migrated did so within a single republic.

Ethnicity was central in defining migration patterns. The flow of Albanians and Macedonians from the low-income southern region was curtailed by cultural and linguistic barriers. Ethnicity defined the pattern of what limited interrepublic migration there was. Croats left Bosnia for Croatia; Serbs departed Kosovo for Serbia proper. The 1976–80 social plan called for greater interrepublic migration to help alleviate unemployment in the south, but to little avail.

Urbanization

Yugoslavia's diverse ethnic heritage defined the country's urbanization. Larger urban settlements often had their antecedents in the Roman era when major overland trade routes (linking Adriatic ports with the east) passed through the region. Slovenia and much of Croatia had a tradition of small, dispersed cities and towns scattered throughout the countryside. These were trading, religious, or political centers dating from the Middle Ages. Dalmatian coastal cities grew as seaports for the lucrative Adriatic trade. In regions under Ottoman rule, urban settlements were essentially alien enclaves existing for the empire's military garrisons and civil bureaucracy. Until the twentieth century, Montenegro and Macedonia were almost entirely rural. Belgrade, at the conflux of the Danube and Sava rivers, was a strategic prize, sought after and held in turn by Huns, Romans, Byzantines, Bulgars, Magyars, Serbs, Magyars (again), Turks, and finally Serbs. An urban geographer can find in Yugoslav settlements those patterned after Roman (and subsequently Habsburg) gridirons, along with scattered hamlets, nucleated villages, and the remnants of large Turkish estates.

Massive urbanization was a post–World War II phenomenon. At war's end nearly 80 percent of the populace lived in the countryside; between that time and 1970 some 4.5 million Yugoslavs (a number equivalent to nearly 20 percent of the country's 1981 population) migrated to cities. The urban population grew by 80 percent between 1953 and 1971. Yet in the early 1970s Yugoslavia still ranked as one of the least urbanized European countries. Twenty-eight percent of the population was urban in 1961; cities grew in the 1960s and 1970s, but in the mid-1970s little more than one-third of all Yugoslavs lived in urban centers.

In the early 1970s roughly one-half to two-thirds the population of republic capitals, i.e., most of the largest cities, had been born elsewhere. Only 30 percent of Belgrade's population was native to the city. Over half of the city-bound migrants came not from towns or smaller urban centers but the countryside itself. Yugoslavia had a first generation urban population whose experience with city life was often scant indeed. (Anthropologist Andrei Simic describes a 1960s Belgrade migrant who routinely unplugged his refrigerator during the winter months; who, after all, was his reasoning, would want a cold drink when the weather was cold?)

Rural-urban migration for the peasant often began with a stint as a laborer in a nearby town; a commuter gradually progressed to semipermanent or permanent employment in the republic capital. A family's husbands and brothers tended to migrate prior to its sisters and wives. The assistance of kin was critical in an individual's migration history. Yugoslavs adapted new patterns of reciprocity to the traditional obligations kin had toward one another. City dwellers—even second-generation urbanites—maintained their ties with their rural kin. In a study of Belgrade, Simic found even natives or long-term residents were able to list 150 to 300 kin; often more than half of these relatives still lived in the countryside, and equally often the urban migrant had maintained contact with rural kin over decades and generations (see Family Organization, this ch.).

The distribution of small towns and cities throughout the countryside and government policies aimed at locating factories outside the largest urban centers blurred conventional dichotomies. Rural and urban, agricultural and nonagricultural tended to merge in socialist Yugoslavia. In the late 1960s-early 1970s nearly one-third of the "urban" population were also agriculturalists. At the same time the number of erstwhile peasants commuting to work in cities was increasing. In the early 1970s approximately 40 percent of the nonagricultural population lived outside cities—a figure that rose to nearly 60 percent in Bosnia and Slovenia and 50 percent in Croatia and Kosovo. Commuting was a Yugoslav way of life.

Six large cities (Belgrade, Zagreb, Skopje, Sarajevo, Ljubljana, and Novi Sad) all having populations of more than 150,000 inhabitants dominated urbanization. Belgrade and its surrounding suburbs accounted for 90 percent of all urban growth in Serbia in the 1960s; Zagreb's population increase was greater than that of all other Croatian regions. Likewise Titograd and Skopje each absorbed nearly two-thirds of their respective republics' population increase. Only Slovenia with a tradition of smaller dispersed cities broke the pattern. Ljubljana represented less than 30 percent of Slovania's total population growth. In 1981 the six largest cities represented nearly 20 percent of total population. Beyond this, however, the landscape was one of small towns and villages. The urban populace was distributed among, at one end of the urban scale, republic/provincial capitals, and at the other, numerous hamlets and small cities. In the 1970s nearly 60 percent of all Yugoslavs lived in settlements of less than 2,000 people.

Housing was in short supply in the face of the expanding urban

Open market, Belgrade

growth. Housing construction for 1971–81 was roughly that projected for the 1976–80 social plan. While the urban population grew
in the decade, housing construction in cities dropped. Urban centers
received 10,000 fewer housing units in 1978 than in 1975—a decline
that was sharpest in the six largest cities. In Slovenia this drop was
part of that republic's effort to foster "polycentric" urban growth.
Overall, however, the drop reflected a shortage of building materials, rising construction costs, and difficulties in implementing self-
managed housing.

Finding housing was a major problem for the rural-urban
migrant. Single male migrants frequently resorted to the dormitory
housing that many enterprises maintained for their workers.
Migrants from other cities or towns fared better in the housing
search than rural-urban migrants; their success was a function of
greater experience with the urban milieu and their generally higher
educational or professional qualifications. Quality of housing improved with length of residence, and the acquisition of adequate
housing was a mark of a migrant's success.

Both investment in housing in the social sector and housing conditions themselves varied according to a region's socioeconomic development (see table 16, Appendix). The disparities in investment between the developed and the less developed regions were substantial. Both in per capita and absolute terms, Croatia, Slovenia, and Serbia proper led Kosovo, Macedonia, and Montenegro. In per capita spending Slovenia led, more than tripling low-ranking Kosovo's rate of investment in housing in the social sector.

Religion

There were in Yugoslavia in the early 1980s some forty recognized religious communities. Most believers were Roman Catholics (Slovenes and Croats), Orthodox (Serbs, Montenegrins, and Macedonians), or Muslims (Bosnians, Albanians). A very rough estimate of the membership of each creed in the early 1970s would be: 30 percent Roman Catholics, 35 percent Serbian and Macedonian Orthodox, and 12 percent Muslim (see fig. 10). There were as well small pockets of Protestants in Vojvodina and Slavonia, scattered groups of Greek or Uniate Catholics, a few members of the Old Catholic Church, and a remnant of Yugoslavia's pre-World War II Jewish community. Finally, there were numerous small groups that did not conform to the common ethnic-religious pattern, e.g., Catholic Serbs on the Montenegrin coast and Catholic Albanians in Kosovo.

Religion has been a critical component in cultural and ethnic identity since the ninth-century conversion of many Slavs to Christianity. It was, however, a matter of family-based religious practice wherein doctrinal orthodoxy of any sort played a minor role. The Balkans—even before the Turkish onslaught—were at the fringe of the Christian world. From the perspective of Rome or Constantinople alike the region was the frontier, rife with heresies, its clergy largely uneducated and often poorly linked with general church organization, and a faithful too often in the throes of superstition. Travelers' accounts through the nineteenth century attest to an ignorance of even the most rudimentary dogma and doctrine. There were reports of clergy in rural Bosnia who were unaware of the schism between the eastern and western Christian churches, ignorant of the Ten Commandments, and unable to recite the simplest prayers.

Religion was traditionally a family affair; religious observances meshed with and reinforced the familial orientation of Balkan social life. Religion among the largely peasant rural populace focused on family well-being and survival. Bosnian families would have their male children both baptized and circumcised. Albanian *zadruga* would have a portion of the family profess Christianity, the rest Islam, and the religion of the *zadruga* head corresponded to whomever held power. Ottoman rule, by limiting the building of churches, reinforced the family orientation of Slav religious practice.

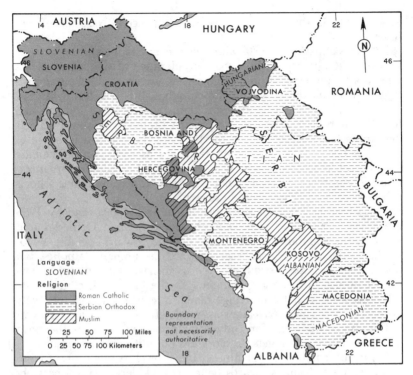

Figure 10. Principal Languages and Religions

From the Counter-Reformation onward, however, both Orthodoxy and Roman Catholicism played central roles in rising Slav nationalism. Both religions had, beyond substantial doctrinal similarity, a number of points in common. In both churches the lower ranking clergy resisted the denationalizing efforts of their hierarchies (the Italian Vatican in the case of the Catholics and, until the late nineteenth century, the Greek Phanariots in that of the Serbian Orthodox). In the case of the Bosnian Muslims, religion was the defining element in ethnic identity. Their national consciousness developed in response to nineteenth-century Ottoman efforts to modernize, which the Bosnians opposed.

Religion's long-standing association with nationalism colored church-state relations into the early 1980s. A 1936 article by Tito suggested that Communists would do well to ignore the philosophical and theological differences separating themselves from religious adherents and concentrate on bettering "the hell on this earth, whose flames engulf believers and non-believers alike." The article long served as a justification for a pragmatic, tolerant approach to religion. Communist officials were at pains to point out that Marxist atheism was not antireligious. In their view religion would wither away, even as the bourgeois nationalist state would, with the progress

99

of socialism. In the meantime a policy of "peaceful coexistence" was in order.

At the same time, the Communists came to power in circumstances that allowed little scope for tolerance of opposition forces and made blunting ethnic animosities paramount. Communists sought to break the power of the churches; this was less a Marxist commitment to "scientific atheism" than the belief that religion had fed the nationalistic hatreds that devastated Yugoslavia. Their determination was not simply to eliminate the political leverage of churches but to undermine their influence as well. The immediate post-World War II era was a difficult one for religious organizations. There were trials of major religious leaders, religious schools were closed, and clergy were harassed.

The situation eased considerably in the mid-1950s, and by 1959 the government could positively praise the Serbian Orthodox and the Muslim communities for their attitude toward socialist Yugoslavia. Officials were less effusive toward the Roman Catholics, but noted that they too recognized "the usefulness of maintaining normal relations with the government." In the late 1970s church-state relations were, if not a marriage made in heaven, at least relatively even. The top Yugoslav leadership made efforts to include believers within the framework for consensual decisionmaking in the post-Tito era. There was a general emphasis on unity and consensus.

Points of contention remained. Local-level communist officials were often less benign towards believers and clergy. Hardliners objected to the (in their view) relaxed official attitude toward the "opiate of the masses." Usually government judgments about religious activity reflected the general domestic situation; the churches' lot was easier as long as affairs in multinational Yugoslavia ran smoothly. Thus, for example, there was a period of unease associated with the general crackdown in Serbia and Croatia in the early 1970s. The issues affecting church-state relations varied from one religion to another, but the most persistent general concerns were children's right to religious instruction, discrimination against believers in public life, and the interdict against "political activity" on the part of clergy.

By 1980 all republics had enacted laws governing religious communities in keeping with the provisions of the 1974 Constitution (which reconfirmed the provisions of the 1963 constitution affecting religion). The particulars of the republics' laws varied, but in essence they guaranteed freedom of religion, recognized the separation of church and state, and acknowledged that the state might provide financial assistance to religious institutions (though this was not mandated). Anything akin to stirring up nationalistic hatreds in religious guise was, of course, strictly prohibited, as was the clergy's involvement in political activity; the definition of "political activity" remained a subject of interpretation.

Legislation permitted all religious communities to establish a press; most had done so by the 1960s; the Serbian Orthodox,

Islamic, and Roman Catholic communities all published a variety of periodicals. Religious groups had campaigned for access to television, but this was denied. The legislation prohibited social activity on the part of clergy, a catchall category that included soccer clubs, dancing groups, and almost any youth activity not strictly religious. A provision in the Croatian draft legislation would have prohibited economic activity as well, but the popular outcry there, where the Roman Catholic Church is active in social services, led to the measure's removal from the final law.

Religious instruction for the faithful remained limited, although a Macedonian proposal limiting religious education to those over eighteen years of age was revised because the public objected so vigorously. In general, children themselves and both parents had to consent for religious instruction to be granted. Public school teachers scheduling activities to conflict with religious instruction or ridiculing those students who attend have hampered the legislation's implementation.

Nearly forty seminaries and theological faculties were in operation in the 1970s and remained largely free from government intervention. The religious press published some thirty-odd periodicals. Discrimination against religious adherents was a perennial problem; those in the army officer corps, government service, or teaching were vulnerable. The extent to which local officialdom pursued antireligious policies varied considerably, and vigorous complaints by religious leaders often brought redress.

Roman Catholicism

The Roman Catholic Church remained without doubt the most comprehensively organized single religious community in Yugoslavia in the early 1980s. Catholic publications comprised more than two-thirds of the religious press; their readership dwarfed that of all other groups; and more than 80 percent of the country's theological faculties and seminaries were Roman Catholic. In part because of the hierarchy's ultramontane loyalties and, paradoxically, because of the church's intimate association with Croatian nationalism, Roman Catholicism's relationship to communist, multinational Yugoslavia was more difficult than that of other religious communities.

The Croats' Catholicism was part of their sense of being European and Western, while the Serbs were Byzantine and Eastern. Croats were accustomed, from the Austro-Hungarian Empire, to being part of the majority religion. More than this they saw themselves (for centuries) as the easternmost outpost of Christianity, defenders of the Holy Faith against the predations of infidel Muslim and schismatic Byzantine alike.

Catholic Croats formed a unified sociopolitical community in the interwar kingdom. Catholicism was a central element in their political style, although it combined with anticlericalism in a way that made Croats view their neighboring Slovenes as priest-ridden.

Stjepan Radic, charismatic leader of the Croatian Peasant Party in the 1920s, would open political rallies with "Praise be to Jesus, down with the clergy."

By contrast clergy played a prominent role in Slovenian interwar politics. Catholic clergy had been critical in the nineteenth-century agrarian reform movement. Catholicism was linked to Slovenian nationalism, but it neither foreclosed Slovenian participation in the Serb-dominated kingdom nor fed into a sense of cultural superiority as Catholicism seemed to. Catholicism was pastoral and pragmatic in Slovenia. At least the lower ranking Slovenian clergy were active in the Partisans; the Catholic church in Slovenia fared concomitantly better under communist rule than its Croatian counterpart.

Catholicism's association with the Croatian fascist state and its connection with nationalistic sentiment meant hard times early in the post-World War II era. The deportation of thousands of Serbs, the wholesale slaughter of others, a program of forced (if selective) conversion of Orthodox to Roman Catholicism, policies that ranged from ethnocide to genocide by a fascist regime claiming that its "whole work is based on fidelity to the church and the Catholic faith . . ." could hardly fail to have a deleterious impact on church-state relations—the Catholic hierarchy's disavowal of *ustasa* policies notwithstanding.

The 1946 trial of Alojzije Stepinac, archbishop of Zagreb during World War II, set the tone of relations between the Catholic church and the communist regime. The regime accused the archbishop of supporting the Croatian fascist state and encouraging *ustasa* resistance after the communist takeover. The issues and evidence surrounding the trial were complex, and as of mid-1981 the entire court transcripts had not been published. The trial itself and Stepinac's sentence to sixteen years at hard labor (he was released and permitted to live in his native village in 1951) along with the Vatican's subsequent naming him a cardinal (1952) blighted Vatican-Yugoslav relations at least until the cardinal's death in 1960. Arguments about Stepinac's guilt or innocence continued into the 1980s.

Throughout the 1950s relations between the regime and the church were strained. Nonetheless the 1953 Law on the Status of Religious Communities guaranteed freedom of religion and marked the beginning of a gradual improvement in church-state relations. The regime permitted Cardinal Stepinac to be buried from the Zagreb cathedral with the full honors due an archbishop—a gesture that did much to dissipate the bitterness surrounding his trial and imprisonment.

The situation of the Roman Catholic Church improved further in the 1960s. In 1966 the government and the Vatican signed the Protocol of Discussions between the Representatives of the Socialist Federal Republic of Yugoslavia and Representative of the Holy See. The protocol recognized the Vatican's jurisdiction (within the limits of Yugoslav law) in the ecclesiastical affairs of the Roman Catholic

Church, guaranteed the rights of believers to practice their faith (again within the law's limits), and acknowledged the government's prohibitions on political activity on the clergy's part.

Except for a brief period during the Croatian crisis early in the decade, relations between the Catholic community and the government were even throughout the 1970s. A 1980 meeting between Pope John Paul II and Yugoslav President Cvijetin Mijatovic confirmed the success with which the 1966 protocol had been implemented. A new round of polemics in early 1981 took observers by surprise. This exchange began with a sharp attack on the Croatian Roman Catholic Church for its "oppositional and nationalistic activities," and escalated to include renewed charges against the Catholic hierarchy for its complicity with the World War II Croatian fascist state. In part officialdom was concerned that the Catholics of Croatia not project "the Polish situation upon our social reality."

The authorities also took strong exception to an October 1980 petition for amnesty for political prisoners that was signed by (among others) two Croatian Catholic priests. Archbishop Franjo Kuharic of Zagreb demanded that political prisoners be allowed to see a priest. Thereafter the Yugoslav Bishops' Conference in May 1981 entered the fray to complain about discrimination against believers.

Serbian Orthodox Church

Orthodoxy played a role in defining Serbian consciousness comparable to that of Roman Catholicism in Croatia. Establishing an autocephalous church including all Serbs (or all those viewed as Serbs) was part and parcel of national liberation. The Orthodox church in Montenegro had maintained a substantial measure of independence throughout Ottoman rule, and temporal and ecclesiastical rule were largely combined in the region (see The Montenegrins, ch. 1). Orthodox faithful in Macedonia were under control of the Orthodox Church of Greece until 1872, when the faithful in western Macedonia affiliated with the exarchate of Bulgaria. The Ottomans saw the Orthodox church as a hotbed of seditious discontent throughout their reign. They abolished the Serbian patriarchate in 1766 because of the hierarchy's continued involvement in uprisings, and the 1832 reestablishment of the patriarchate was a benchmark in the struggle for independence.

The Serbian Orthodox Church of the interwar kingdom united a variety of churches previously administratively autonomous and acquired jurisdiction over the bishoprics (eparchies) of western Macedonia. Its policy aimed at creating a strong and centralized hierarchy. Further, in the church's view it was the protector of Serbian national heritage. Serbian hegemony and the church's well-being were integral, and a threat to one was tantamount to an attack on the other.

The church was decimated in World War II both in Serbia under

Nazi control and in Croatia under the puppet fascist regime. The Nazis rapidly interned a number of bishops and metropolitans and curtailed the movements of those who remained at liberty. The strain on church organization was made worse by the influx of Serbian refugees from Croatia. The Orthodox followers suffered in the *ustase's* systematic campaign to "Croatize" the state. Nearly two-thirds of all Orthodox priests were deported, and most of those who remained were killed in *ustasa* pogroms. Perhaps one-quarter of all churches and monasteries were destroyed. Orthodox faithful were subject to forced conversion to Roman Catholicism (the Catholic hierarchy protested), though significantly anyone who might remotely be construed as a Serbian leader, i.e., anyone who was not a peasant—was not permitted to convert.

While Roman Catholicism was suspect because of its connection with the *ustase*, the Serbian Orthodox Church came under scrutiny because of its association with Serbian nationalism. The Communists feared the resurgence of the "Greater Serbia hegemony" that had inflamed ethnic tensions in the interwar era. The Orthodox members fell victim to the regime's general effort to limit religion's influence in social life and to make the country a federation of equal nationalities. Vicar-Bishop Varnava Nastic was tried in 1946 and found guilty of "weakening the military and economic strength of Yugoslavia, of helping terrorist bands, and of hostile propaganda." Like the Catholic clergy, Orthodox priests faced considerable harassment early in the socialist era.

The Serbian Orthodox hierarchy fought a running battle with non-Serbs within the church until the mid-1960s. Although autonomy for other nationalities was ostensibly the question, a number of related issues were at play. The furor over priests' associations and the efforts of Macedonian and Montenegrin clergy for a more democratic church structure intensified the hierarchy's fears of civil control of church matters. The Holy Episcopal Sabor (the assembly of bishops that governs the Serbian Orthodox Church) adopted a 1947 constitution that strengthened the hierarchy's authority, as did a series of 1967 amendments.

Macedonia was the most persistent problem for the hierarchy until the late 1950s. The region had been under the control of the Bulgarian fascist state during World War II, and the war disrupted normal relations between the Serbian patriarchate in Belgrade and the Macedonian dioceses (see The War: Occupation and Resistance, ch. 1). Most of the Serbian clergy were deported; the Orthodox priests remaining were either pro-Bulgar or Macedonian nationalists active in the Partisans. By the war's end the clergy were accustomed to running church affairs with autonomy. The clergy met in 1945 and declared the formation of an independent Macedonian Orthodox Church. The Serbian Orthodox hierarchy held off recognizing the church until 1959 when, under considerable government pressure, Patriarch German consecrated a Macedonian bishop. The

Macedonian synod declared itself an autocephalous Orthodox church in 1967.

Just as officials periodically accuse Roman Catholic Croats of harboring pro-*ustasa* sentiments, they denounce the Orthodox Serbs for their "Cetnik spirit." In late 1980 authorities claimed that an Orthodox priest had sung nationalistic songs at a christening. Earlier that year officials condemned a Serbian poem eulogizing the Serbs' Orthodox faith and the sufferings they had endured for it (see Serbs, this ch.). Officials found the poem indicative of the disturbing extent to which the Orthodox faithful were still imbued with nationalism and dissatisfied with the church's position in socialist Yugoslavia.

Islam

Bosnia and Hercegovina and present-day Albania were unique within European parts of the Ottoman Empire in witnessing large-scale conversion to Islam. Not only did most of the urban-artisanal population convert, but a substantial portion of the rural populace did so as well. A significant free Muslim peasantry existed along with the majority population, Christian serfs. Conversion was the price of free landholder status. The unification of Yugoslavia in 1919 brought together three distinct Muslim communities: ethnic (Bosnian) Muslims from Bosnia, Albanians from Kosovo, and a small Turkish minority in eastern Serbia (see Ethnic Muslims, this ch.). Estimates of the number of "Muslims by faith" in the early 1980s ranged from 3.5 million to 4 million.

In 1930 the country's diverse Muslim groups united under the authority of a single ulama (religious scholar), the Rais-ul Ulama in Belgrade, who was responsible for enforcing the Islamic religious and legal prescriptions and administering the affairs of the Muslim community. The Supreme Council, the highest governing body of the Muslim community, elected the Rais-ul Ulama. The council was composed of representatives from Bosnia, Serbia, Macedonia, and Montenegro. Two groups of Muslim scholars (one in Sarajevo, the other in Skopje) assisted the Rais-ul Ulama in religious matters.

The Muslim community followed the Sunnite doctrine and practice introduced by the Turks in the fifteenth century. Popular practice, however, was strongly influenced by the customs and beliefs of the surrounding Christian populace and varied from community to community. Bosnian Muslim women enjoyed more privileges than their counterparts in most Middle Eastern Islamic communities.

Relations between the Muslim community and the communist regime were, for most of the post-World War II era, even. By and large imams (religious leaders) kept a low profile during World War II. Authorities tried and sentenced to death the mufti of Zagreb on charges of inciting Muslims to murder Serbs. Aside from this there were few of the trials that plagued high-ranking clergy in the Orthodox and Roman Catholic communities. The regime commonly used its own Muslim community as a link with Arab countries.

Throughout the 1960s and 1970s Yugoslav Muslims studied in centers of Islamic learning abroad.

In the 1979–80 period Muslim-state relations took a turn for the worse. Tito threatened stern measures to deal with the "undermining activities of some clericalist circles." Most observers were persuaded his remarks were directed at a Muslim community too enthralled (in the regime's view) with the Islamic revolution of Iran's Ayatollah Ruhollah Khomeini. "Pan-Islamic nationalism," commented Hamdija Pozderac, 1979 representative in the LCY Central Committee (the only ethnic Muslim), abused "faith for political purposes." Ulama Ahmed Smaljlovic, spiritual head of the Muslim community, was quick to disavow a connection with "any worldwide Islamic tendency."

Education

Education in the 1980s offered a dramatic contrast to the interwar kingdom. Primary schooling in the kingdom had been a four-year cycle, and while enrollments more than doubled between 1919 and 1940, there were still a quarter of a million Yugoslav children who attended no school on the eve of World War II. Muslim parents remained suspicious of education for women, and schools were inaccessible to a goodly portion of the rural populace. Illiteracy averaged roughly 40 percent of the population over ten years of age in the late 1930s, but even this figure masked glaring disparities between regions. While more than three-quarters of all Slovenes and Croats could read and write, only 10 percent of Kosovo's Albanians could. Education was highly centralized, and instruction was in Serbo-Croatian. Macedonians and Croatians in particular resented Belgrade's hegemony in this arena. Support for the *ustase* was widespread among Croatian teachers within the Serb-dominated system.

Education, not surprisingly, occupied a prominent place in government planning and spending throughout the socialist era. In the late 1970s the education budget amounted to roughly 6 percent of national income. The 1958 General Law on Education increased the primary education cycle to eight years and made attendance compulsory for children from seven to fifteen years of age. Between 1945 and 1978 the proportion of children enrolled in elementary school rose from 40 percent to some 95 percent of the school-age population. Female enrollment increased until girls accounted for roughly 47 percent of primary school students and 45 percent of all secondary students. The increase in education facilities and enrollments was particularly marked in the less developed regions. In Kosovo, for example, the number of primary school students grew nearly ten times between the end of World War II and the mid-1970s. Instruction was in the native language of the majority of the students (with a complex formula for dealing with ethnically mixed areas).

The growth in secondary and higher eductaion was equally impressive. From 1947 through 1978 the number of students in secondary schools rose by more than 650 percent; in the late 1970s approximately 90 percent of all students completing elementary school continued their education. The number of postsecondary educational institutions—less than forty in 1947—was in the hundreds in 1976. Further, the dispersion of these schools in smaller cities and towns (40 percent were outside the main cities) alleviated the glaring inequity in educational resources between city and countryside. Overall enrollment increased more than twenty times, that of women nearly forty times.

A series of reforms culminating in a 1974 resolution by the Tenth Party Congress (calling for yet further changes) revamped the interwar educational system. The "Resolution on the Tasks of the LCY in the Socialist Self-Managed Transformation of Education" set forth guidelines for the organization and administration of a decentralized educational system. The thrust of the reforms has been to entrust educational policy, provision of school services, expansion of the school system, general policy, personnel decisions, and financing to "self-managed communities of interest for education" (SCI-E). The SCI-E are formed from local BOALs and other self-managed organizations. Their precise configuration varied from preschool to primary educational institutions to those of higher education; all conform to the specific republic/provincial legislation on education. SCI-Es for postprimary schools focused on a specific educational center, university, or program. Student participation was structured into the organization; in all postprimary institutions the SCI-E included student representatives—frequently in high-ranking positions. A student was associate rector of the University of Zagreb in 1978, and a number of others served as associate deans of their respective institutions.

Postprimary education was nothing if not complex; it included a highly developed system of vocational training that could and usually did lead to entry into special two-year vocationally or professionally oriented colleges. There was as well the standard secondary school that prepared students for university education. Finally there were a multitude of workers' and people's universities geared toward continuing adult education.

The 1970s reforms made extensive revisions of the secondary school curriculum. The first two years of postprimary education were to have a core of courses common to all institutions. The reforms standardized subject matter and integrated it more closely to the needs of the workplace. The changes also upgraded studies of Marxist-Leninist theory, self-management, and civil defense.

The reforms dealt with a number of pressing problems. Despite the highly developed vocational education system, conventional secondary school followed by university training remained the most common career path for socially mobile students. Because university admissions were largely open, many students used a two-year advanced training course as a springboard to college entrance. Critics insisted that the short-cycle, vocationally oriented higher education was inadequate both as job training and preparation for advanced academic study. Dropout rates remained high. In Slovenia, certainly the most wealthy republic, in the early 1970s less than half of all entering students completed their first year of advanced study, and only 12 percent of students earned their degrees within a standard five-year period. Dropout rates were high in elementary school as well, and despite the massive growth in enrollment, illiteracy (15 percent in 1971) remained the highest among countries with comparable school attendance rates. Through the core curriculum the reforms aimed at eliminating the dualism between academic and vocational education. Finally a number of measures not fully implemented in late 1980 attempted to smooth the student's transition from school to workplace.

Health and Social Welfare

Malaria, typhus, typhoid, syphilis, dysentery, and trachoma were endemic in interwar Yugoslavia. The kingdom had Europe's highest death rate from tuberculosis—a direct reflection of generally poor nutrition and sanitation and woefully inadequate health care. Health care was largely the prerogative of city dwellers; there was one physician per 750 inhabitants in urban centers, but the rate was nearly twenty times that in the countryside. The expansion of health care in the socialist era has been perforce extreme. By the late 1970s the endemic infectious diseases that had ravaged the population were reduced to individual cases. The number of physicians tripled between the 1950s and the late 1970s; the number of medical faculties quadrupled. By the early 1970s there was one doctor per 934 inhabitants (versus nearly one per 12,000 in the interwar era). Crude mortality rates dropped from twenty deaths per 1,000 inhabitants (1920) to 8.7 (1975).

There remained problems, but the general improvement in health care and delivery of health services was dramatic. The disparity between rural and urban servies persisted; rural health care positions went unfilled even though there was a dearth of urban vacancies. In Greater Serbia in the early 1970s, for example, there were over 200 medical positions unfilled, although between 1965 and 1970 one-third of all medical graduates went abroad in search of work. Even focusing on general practitioners (the physicians most likely to serve in the countryside) and on a developed republic, Croatia, the patient load per physician ranged from 1,500 to 9,500.

Medical students in Yugoslavia came disproportionately from urban, professional families. A late 1960s survey of students at the Zagreb University Medical Faculty found that children of professionals (who represented less than 15 percent of those finishing primary school) were nearly two-thirds of the faculty's total enrollment. The urban bias was equally pronounced. A mid-1970s study at Belgrade University found that only 5 percent of fifth-year medical students came from rural areas—37 percent were from

Belgrade itself. Although medical students paid no tuition, they did have to pay their living expenses. A well-to-do family that could bankroll five years of room and board or one that was resident in a city with a medical faculty was an asset for the aspiring medical student. Medical students from urban areas were also least likely to serve in the countryside. Local communes or enterprises frequently paid a stipend to medical students with the stipulation that they repay the grant with service in the local area. This arrangement had limited success in altering the long-term imbalance in rural-urban health services.

The difference in health care was most marked between the developed and the less developed regions. Kosovo's ratio of physicians to population was, in the early 1970s, less than half the national average, as was the number of hospital beds available (see table 17, Appendix). While health care improved dramatically in all regions—the ratio of physicians to population increased roughly five times in Kosovo, Macedonia, Montenegro, and Bosnia between 1950 and 1973—the relative differences between the affluent and the poor regions altered very little.

In the late 1970s the country's infant mortality rate—one of Europe's highest—reflected in part the continuing inequality in health care. Nationally infant mortality was 36.5 per 1,000 live births, but the republic/provincial rates ranged from a low of 19.3 in Slovenia to a high of 69.2 in Kosovo (see table 18, Appendix). In the less developed regions mortality among children under five years of age was two to seven times higher than the national average.

Republic and provincial constitutions (in keeping with the provisions of the federal Constitution) ennumerated the rights of citizens to health care. All citizens are entitled to treatment of infectious diseases and mental illnesses likely to endanger themselves or their environment and to general health education. Pregnant women, infants, and preschoolers should receive complete medical care. Children are to get preventive care and treatment until the age of fifteen years (twenty-six years in the case of students).

The communist regime established a general health insurance program in 1945. Early coverage was spotty for a substantial portion of the population—private farmers and their families were not covered until 1959. Overall coverage rose from one-quarter of the population in 1952 to more than three-quarters in 1978, although disparities in the benefits private farmers and workers received persisted into the 1970s. As with the availability of health care in general, peasant families in poorer regions fared worse than other segments of the population. In the early 1970s the agricultural population overall used health care facilities approximately one-fourth as frequently as workers (see table 19, Appendix).

"Self-managed communities of interest for health care" organized health care. Like comparable organizations in education the communities represented both the users and the employees of health care facilities (see Education, this ch.). A council of delegates formed from the health facility's workers' council and local citizens and another from the local enterprises contributing taxes to the facility comprised a given "community of interest for health." In general each commune had a health center, although there was provision for cooperative use of facilities through agreements between various communes. Changes in communities of interest for health in the 1970s attempted to give workers greater influence in the running of health facilities and limit that of "technocrats and bureaucrats" (see Workers, this ch.; Intelligentsia, this ch.). The changes also aimed at making health organizations more responsive to the needs of the local population and less subject to the dictates of physicians and health professionals.

Retirement and disability pensions in the late 1970s covered all employed and nonagricultural self-employed workers. Measures were being implemented or were under consideration to extend benefits to private farmers often in exchange for the sale of their land to an agricultural cooperative. Retirement age was sixty years (with at least twenty years of service) for men and fifty-five years (with at least fifteen years of service) for women. Legislation in the early 1970s (hotly debated throughout the decade) made retirement mandatory. Workers were entitled to disability insurance only after one-third the length of time on the job that a retirement pension required. A preliminary draft of the Law on Basic Rights Under Old Age and Disability Insurance, completed in late 1980, proposed a variety of changes in the years of service requirements and the calculation of pensions.

* * *

There is voluminous English-language literature on Yugoslavia. Duncan Wilson's *Tito's Yugoslavia*, Dennison Rusinow's *The Yugoslav Experiment*, Bogdan Denitch's *The Legitimation of a Revolution*, and Gary K. Bertsch's *Values and Community in Multinational Yugoslavia* offer a portrait of the massive social changes since World War II. Offering more detailed analyses of ethnic relations are: "Yugoslavia: Unity Out of Diversity?" by David A. Dyker; "Converts and Consanguinity: The Social Organization of Moslem Slavs in Western Bosnia," by William G. Lockwood; and *The Ohrid Seminar on Minorities*, edited by Boris Visinski. *Opinion-Making Elites in Yugoslavia* (Allen H. Barton et al., eds.); "Market Socialism and Class Structure," by Frank Parkin; "Workers' Councils and Political Stratification," by Sidney Verba and Goldie Shabad; and "The Pink Yo-Yo," by E.A. Hammel all examine social trends in the post-World War II era.

"Social Mobility and the Durability of Family Ties," by E.A. Hammel and Charles Yarbrough; "Economic Change, Social Mobility, and Kinship in Serbia" and "The Zadruga as Process," both by E.A. Hammel; and *Communal Families in the Balkans*, edited by Robert F. Byrnes, analyze social organization and kinship. Samuel L. Sharp's "Ethnicity and Migration in Yugoslavia" and Ivo Baucic's "Regional Differences in Yugoslav External Migration" examine migration trends. Andrei Simic's *The Peasant Urbanites* looks at the process of adaptation for rural-urban migrants.

Stella Alexander's *Church and State in Yugoslavia since 1945* describes the relations between the regime and the Serbian Orthodox and the Roman Catholic churches. K.F. Cviic's "Yugoslavia's Moslem Problem" looks at the Islamic community. Robert Berg et al. in *Health Care in Yugoslavia and the United States* outlines the nature of self-managed health care. Frederick D. Kinzer in "Educational Reforms in Yugoslavia" does the same for the school system. (For further information see Bibliography.)

Chapter 3. The Economy

Woman working in factory

ECONOMIES IN COMMUNIST countries differ markedly from those in the rest of the world. Although Yugoslavia started to develop during the late 1940s according to the Soviet pattern, abrupt changes made by officials in the 1950s and subsequent amendments made the politico-economic system unique. An attempt was made to blend the strengths of both the communist and capitalist systems with the added, distinctive feature of workers' control of management of businesses and the economy. This was the first attempt in a large country to achieve workers' self-management. Trial and error was necessary; change has been continuous as institutions and policies have been altered in the search for those most effective.

Economic growth has been remarkable under the Yugoslav system, transforming an agrarian nation of the 1940s to an industrial one in the 1980s. The country moved up in the ranks of developing nations to middle-income status. Per capita gross national product was US$2,430 in 1979, and in several economic measurements Yugoslavia was approaching the level of some countries of Western Europe. Industrialization has been the engine of growth, but growth was accompanied by periodic high inflation and balance of payments problems.

The late 1970s was such a period, requiring stabilization efforts into the 1980s. In 1981 inflation and unemployment remained high, real wages had declined, and imports on which the economy depended had been reduced, further hobbling and disrupting adjustment efforts. In early 1981 economic dissatisfactions contributed to serious disturbances in Kosovo, the poorest province. The rest of the country was better off, but there was pressure on officials and workers to improve, through economic measures or institutional changes if need be, the management and efficiency of the economy.

Role of Government

Government became very active in economic affairs when the Communist Party of Yugoslavia (CPY) emerged in full control of the country after World War II. The most immediate concern was repair of the extensive damage the war caused. In 1945 a major land reform program was instituted, and collectivization of agriculture began soon afterwards. Nationalization of mining, industry, banking, transportation, and most trade followed. A central planning agency was established, and the first five-year plan (1947–51) drafted. The government rapidly adopted the Soviet economic model.

In the Soviet model the economy was organized vertically with a command structure from the top down. The central authorities attempted to make all economic decisions—setting quotas for production units that were almost completely state owned, directing the flow of materials through the economy, establishing prices for nearly everything including labor and capital, and controlling investment and consumption. Much of this was incorporated in annual and five-year plans that had the force of law. Market forces exerted no influence on production, consumption, or investment. The system was effective in mobilizing resources and channeling them to priority areas. It worked in Yugoslavia where war damage was quickly repaired and large investments were begun in industry.

After World War II many economists in Eastern Europe questioned the appropriateness of the Soviet economic model for the conditions in their countries, but by the late 1940s all of the East European states had adopted it. Stalin, the leader of the Soviet Union until 1953, tolerated little opposition or independence. Josip Broz Tito and those around him were independent, taking a separate line from the Soviet Union on several issues including some economic ones (see The Break with Stalin, ch. 1). In June 1948 the Communist Information Bureau (Cominform—see Glossary) expelled Yugoslavia. The communist countries instituted a boycott—abrogating treaties and trade agreements, canceling loans, and severing nearly all foreign trade with Yugoslavia. The impact on the economy was severe, causing a decline in gross national product (GNP) and making the first plan obsolete.

The break with the Soviet Union and other communist countries resulted in a reevaluation of economic doctrines and policies. Peasant resistance had thwarted the collectivization drives of the late 1940s. In the early 1950s collectives were allowed to disband, and most did. A large part of agriculture has since remained in the private sector (see Agriculture, this ch.). Except for private farming, however, the means of production remained socially owned (see Glossary). By the late 1970s the socialized sector accounted for about 85 percent of gross domestic product (GDP) and over half of total employment. Yugoslav leaders also rethought their position in the world in the face of the hostility from other communist countries. Financial and military assistance was sought and obtained from several noncommunist industrialized countries, and Yugoslavia began forging a new foreign policy and relationships with various parts of the world (see Foreign Policy, ch. 4). Although relations were later reestablished with communist countries and substantial trade developed, Yugoslavs were reluctant to become overly dependent on any one group of countries.

The reevaluation also sent leaders back to Marx to find aid in building a communist society. Many Yugoslavs, in common with other Communists, have believed that the original Soviet economic model with its subsequent modifications was not a workers' paradise. It has been frequently called state capitalism or etatism, in which the state exploits the worker.

The Beginning of Workers' Self-Management

In 1950 Yugoslavia began building a new and unique economic order based on workers' self-management. its first step was essentially workers' participation, through workers' councils, in the management of the firm where they were employed. The workers had little impact at first because of their inexperience and, more important, because most enterprise managers were appointed by and responsible to the government. The concept of workers' self-management implied, however, a considerably different set of operating conditions than existed in the early 1950s. Only gradually were the central controls of the Soviet model relaxed.

In the early 1950s, rationing of consumer goods, compulsory deliveries of agricultural products, and centralized distribution of raw materials and finished goods were abolished, and a partial role for the market in allocating goods was accepted. Enterprises generally gained the freedom to determine what they would make, where they would buy, to whom they would sell, and what prices they would charge. The incomes of employees became largely dependent on the earnings of their enterprises, and enterprise earnings became more dependent on their competitive ability in the market. A variety of charges and taxes, however, limited the amount of funds available to enterprises for income distribution and investment.

In 1951 the role of planning changed to become one that indicated goals in the economy (indicative plans) instead of the mandatory targets formerly imposed under the centralized command structure. The economy operated under a series of annual plans until the second five-year plan (1957-61) was drafted. Under the annual plans a high rate of savings and investment was maintained. The 1957-61 plan was fairly ambitious, but the investments that preceded it permitted a rapid expansion of output; the plan was declared fulfilled in 1960, a year ahead of schedule. The third five-year plan (1961-65) was more ambitious, but it was abandoned after a couple of years because a poor harvest and a stabilization program made the plan goals unattainable.

In the early 1960s the economy faced growing inflationary pressure and balance of payments problems. These contributed to a national debate about the role of government and enterprises and of plans and the market in economic growth and development policy. In 1961 a series of measures, hastily drafted and implemented, opened the economy by replacing a system of multiple exchange rates with a single (although devalued) rate, reduced tariffs and quantitative restrictions on imports, restructured financial markets, and reduced government control over wage determination in order to increase enterprises' financial interest in productivity. The continuing economic difficulties and the failure of these reforms intensified the debate about the role of government.

The debate, concentrated within the government and the League of Communists of Yugoslavia (LCY—formerly the Communist Party of Yugoslavia), largely concerned more centralized state control versus more scope for market forces and enterprise autonomy. The forces for liberalization won, and in 1964 resolutions were adopted by the Federal Assembly and the LCY endorsing major economic reforms. Implementation occurred between 1964 and 1967; most of the changes became amendments to the 1963 constitution.

The wide-ranging reforms were often referred to as market socialism. They included administrative upward price adjustments to bring them more in line with world prices, progressive removal of price controls, devaluation, currency reform, reduced controls on imports and exports, and lower customs duties and export subsidies. Major changes in the banking system resulted in greater independence of action and a broader range of activity. Significant reductions in taxes and other changes contributed to greater enterprise autonomy and transferred the main responsibility for the use of investment funds from the state to banks and enterprises. The objectives of the reforms were to reduce government's role in general and to transfer to republics, provinces, and lower administrative levels most of what remained; to encourage enterprise efficiency and raise quality of output (partly through closer integration with the world economy); and to distribute the benefits of economic growth through increases in consumption. The latter was intended to raise the standard of living as well as to provide incentives to workers to increase productivity and to lower production costs. The reforms were the zenith of the trend toward reliance on supply and demand to guide production and investment even though there were still many imperfections in the market, such as continuing government intervention.

The fourth five-year plan (1966–70) was drafted during the beginnings of the reforms. Annual plans were discontinued, and the five-year plan became a broad guide for the basic direction and general conditions of economic activity to be incorporated in the decisions of enterprises and various levels of government. Stagnation in 1966 and 1967 resulting from the reforms caused a reduction of the broad goals in the plan and a failure to meet some of the output targets.

The economic reforms of the mid-1960s created additional problems as well as exacerbating older ones. The government lost a large degree of control over aggregate demand, and what policy measures remained were used ineffectively. Enterprises raised wages faster than productivity and obtained credit from banks and local governments for increased inventories and fixed assets. Taxes and other pressures pushed enterprises toward a capital-intensive approach in investments. The results included growing inflation, increasing unemployment, a slowing of economic growth, and a need for larger investments to achieve an additional unit of growth, an increase of imports while expansion of exports slowed, and a perceived concentration of power in banks, enterprise managers and their technical staffs, and large trade firms at the expense of workers' self-management. Although enterprise workers established and controlled their own managerial staffs, the growing complexity of operations permitted managers to exert considerable influence on an enterprise's decisions. Moreover disparities in development and income in the various regions had not changed appreciably.

The profound and highly emotional cleavages between the various nations and nationalities (see Glossary) that make up Yugoslavia have a long history (see Peoples of Yugoslavia, ch. 2). In 1945 the CPY adopted as one of its goals the elimination of the great economic disparities between the various republics and what later became autonomous provinces. Until 1963 the General (Federal) Investment Fund directly financed major investments including those in the regions designated as underdeveloped. The reforms of the mid-1960s established the Fund for Accelerated Development of Underdeveloped Republics and Autonomous Provinces, financed by a charge on enterprise assets. The Fund for Accelerated Development provided long-term, low-interest loans or grants for development projects that tended to be large and capital intensive, such as those in mining, mineral processing, and heavy industry.

Self-Management in the 1970s

Partially in response to the problems that followed the 1965 economic reforms, a series of measures were adopted to alter the functioning of the economy and improve the mechanisms of workers' self-management. In 1971 constitutional amendments started the modifications. The 1974 Constitution consolidated the earlier changes and introduced others to provide a comprehensive and consistent framework for revision of the system of economic management. All during the 1970s individual measures were instituted pertaining to portions of the economy; the effects of many were not clear, statistically or otherwise, by 1981.

The 1976 Law on Associated Labor defined many of the elements of self-management organizations. The primary purpose of the law and other changes was to give the decisionmaking power—without autonomous intermediaries (or a sharing of power such as participation in management)—to individuals directly affected by the decisions. The primary building block was the Basic Organization of Associated Labor (BOAL), defined as the smallest indivisible entity, alone or within an enterprise, that produced an output that was or could be marketed. BOALs are legal persons with elected councils, their own balance sheets and accounts, and their own plans. Each BOAL had the right to withdraw from larger organizations unless that would jeopardize the survival of other BOALs. One or more BOALs may form an enterprise (also called a working organization), which is a legal person and has its own accounts and management organs. Enterprises can form with others a Complex Organization of Associated Labor (COAL), which is a legal person and has its own workers' council and management. COALs provide for vertical and horizontal integration to improve cooperation and specialization between component units. An enterprise usually may be a member of more than one COAL in order to benefit from such specific management functions as joint production planning and joint marketing. These worker organizations elect delegates that represent them in the country's political organizations (see The Constitutional Order, ch. 4).

Yugoslavia has introduced a bewildering array of terms often for common entities, although many of the new terms have specific legal meanings. Thus government consists of sociopolitical communities that are organized from the commune (*opstina*) level to the federal government. Sociopolitical organizations are largely those of the LCY, the Socialist Alliance of the Working People of Yugoslavia (SAWPY—see Glossary), and the trade unions (see The Process of Government, ch. 4). "Communities of Interest" are established by law or by BOALs when cooperation is required to provide such services as railroads, telephone, education, health, and science, or to create other economic, social or infrastructural organizations. Communities of interest usually consist of suppliers of services and their users organized with equal rights in an assembly that is the self-management unit setting the scope and cost of services. There are numerous other definitions, such as those concerning workers, working people, banks, and various cooperation arrangements between private individuals and between individuals and social sector units.

The effects of the changes in the 1970s were to decentralize decisionmaking. The BOALs were enhanced as well as government at the commune level and then the republics, while the federal government was limited to relatively few functions. Part of the innovation to make the revision of the system work was the introduction of "social compacts" concluded between organizations of associated labor, communities of interest, economic chambers in government, and sociopolitical communities. Examples of the kind of relations in social compacts were criteria for distribution of income, foreign trade relations, employment policy, designation of priority activities, and the basis for formation of price policy. Social compacts frequently state policy objectives for topics of broad interest, such as plans, income distribution, employment, and prices, but their goals were enforceable only by persuasion.

Reinforcing the social compacts are Self-Management Agreements (SMA) concluded between self-management organizations in the social sector. SMAs are binding contracts enforceable through the courts in case a party fails to fulfill its obligations. SMAs are used to regulate a wide range of relationships from the funding of organizations of associated labor and communities of interest to the distribution of joint income, sharing of risks, and allocation of income to wages and investment. Social compacts and SMAs have substituted for direct action by government and have been the mechanism for introducing such measures as price controls and incomes policy, for example. Plans of an enterprise or SMA have to be approved by each of the BOALs involved before becoming valid.

Planning by federal agencies during the 1960s suffered from little input from below and few means to encourage adherence to the plans. Enterprises and banks paid little attention to the plans. Thus a different approach to planning was incorporated into the changes in self-management during the 1970s, which also reflected a strong belief that planning remained necessary to guide development and avoid waste of scarce resources. Nor did the new system of economic management reject the use of the market to achieve efficiency in the allocation of resources. Instead an effort was made to combine the advantages of market signals and planned development.

A radically new system of planning, established by law in 1976, was a response to the failures of purely indicative planning. Each organization that will be affected by the plans must draft its plan for its own operations. BOALs and enterprises prepare micro plans while macro planning is conducted within and between sociopolitical communities (social plans). Planning is conducted simultaneously at all levels, there being no hierarchy through which plans pass for approval. The numerous individual plans are then modified through discussions with all affected parties, and the results are made into binding social compacts and SMAs. The exchange of information and planning process is continuous, with annual assessments and adjustments for changing conditions. A firm timetable is set, which if not met because of unresolvable conflicts, permits sociopolitical communities or other government bodies to issue temporary rulings.

Planning starts with the issuance by federal authorities of a law stating the time period of the plan, the timetable for major steps, and minimum indicators that must be prepared. Although production and social planning start separately, they become united in the harmonization at the various levels of government. The planning procedures oblige planning units (enterprises and political entities) to consider broad objectives and the trade-offs necessary to meet goals. Participation in the planning and forced attention to a broad perspective are expected to enlist workers' support and dedication to plan goals.

The confusing complexity of the new planning system held potential long-run benefits. The compulsory and exhaustive exchange of information would facilitate reaching a rational choice in decisions. The consensus approach ensured that all interests were represented but that the choice among alternate solutions was the expressed preference of many economic units. In particular the process helped planning coordination between republics, a problem in earlier plans. The new system also attempted to achieve an equilibrium solution based on expressed consumer preference, rather than the trial and error method of the market or the assumed preference required in central planning.

As of mid-1981 the new planning system had not been in operation long enough nor were adequate statistical data available for an evaluation. Some problems had appeared, however. The planning cycle is long, requiring two to three years. The system will also be difficult to adjust if underlying economic circumstances change from that on which the plan was drafted. The dependence of the country on foreign trade increased the probability of unforeseen events. Moreover the continued strong economic and political position of communes and republics has perpetuated the local orientation of investment and production and made difficult nationwide solutions of such problems as the country's energy balance (see Energy, this ch.). A waste of scarce foreign exchange reportedly occurred in 1981, for example. An effort was made to allocate foreign exchange to the units that earned it, including subcontractors and suppliers of raw materials. This led to complaints from some enterprises that they did not receive their share. In addition it tended to result in a separate balance of payments for each of the republics and autonomous provinces. In 1981 some republics imported refined petroleum products at greater cost than if crude oil had been imported and refined in the nation's underused refineries.

The new self-management organizations and planning system were logical developments in the unique path the Yugoslavs have taken in economic management and were an ingenious way to handle the nationalities issue. It resulted at times in hard bargaining and some compromises that may not have been the optimum economic solution. The system provided safeguards; the federal government could and did issue temporary rulings to resolve conflicts or to cope with situations that were not being dealt with effectively through the normal mechanisms. In June 1981, for example, the federal government stepped in to attempt to control prices (see Banking and Inflation, this ch.).

Fiscal Policy

The decentralization process since the 1960s has reduced the role of the federal government and fiscal policy in management of the economy. In the late 1970s federal expenditures were only about one-fifth of the total for the public sector. The federal government's direct primary role was maintaining the armed forces and central administration. Moreover federal expenditures were inflexible relative to revenues—more than one-half was for defense and another one-third was for administration and pensions (see table 20, Appendix). In 1980 federal expenditures jumped sharply because of defense spending, aid to Montenegro after an earthquake, and increased pension payments that were indexed to the cost of living.

Since the mid-1970s, the federal budget has shown sharp changes as activities were shifted to lower levels of government and communities of interest with corresponding adjustments of revenue sources. In 1978, for example, responsibility for some food subsidies was transferred to the republics, and responsibility for export subsidies to Communities of Interest for Foreign Economic Relations (CIFER). In June 1981 additional funds were needed to stimulate exports, and the federal government assigned a portion of its share of import fees to CIFERs while proposing that other levels of government cut spending to contribute the remaining required funds. In another example the federal budget's share of customs duties was expected to rise from 40 percent in 1980 to about 67 percent in 1981.

Other indirect taxes, largely a sales tax, provided revenue to both federal and lower levels of government, the shares of which were also subject to change. The republics collected income taxes from individuals and enterprises, as well as applying additional levies for various purposes, resulting in different rates of taxation from republic to republic. The republics contributed a portion of these revenues to the federal budget; the share of republic contributions in total federal revenues shifted quickly in the late 1970s. Some of the funds received from the republics were transfer payments for such specific purposes as earthquake aid, budget support for social services in Kosovo, and financing for the Fund for Accelerated Development of the Underdeveloped Republics and the Autonomous Province of Kosovo.

Financing development of the underdeveloped regions—a government goal since 1945—continued to be a contentious issue in the 1980s (see The Process of Government, ch. 4). Controversy existed over the amount of aid, the way it was financed, and its effectiveness. In absolute terms rapid growth had occurred in the underdeveloped regions, particularly Kosovo (the poorest), as the result of substantial investments. Much of the investment, such as that in Kosovo, went into electric power plants and mining, however, which were capital intensive and afforded relatively little employment. Moreover the underdeveloped regions tended to have high birthrates, causing per capita income to approach only slowly the Yugoslav average, and unemployment remained high (see Peoples of Yugoslavia, ch. 2). After hard and difficult bargaining between republics, it was agreed that 1.83 percent of the country's gross social product (see Glossary) would be used to finance development in the underdeveloped regions during the 1981–85 plan—an amount that could total the equivalent of about US$7.3 billion. The developed republics would contribute about half to the Fund for Accelerated Development, and the rest would be in the form of direct investments by individual enterprises from the various republics.

The federal government may incur surpluses or deficits, but they were usually small and unintentional (autonomous and cyclical factors) rather than a method to influence economic activity. The federal deficit reached a record high of 2.25 percent of gross social product in 1976; by 1979 it was down to 0.75 percent of gross social product. In 1980 the deficit reached 22 billion dinars (for value of the dinar—see Glossary), the highest absolute deficit, which amounted to 1.25 percent of gross social product. This increased deficit had little effect on the economy because the more important expansionary elements of wage payments and fixed investments fell in real terms.

The bulk of public sector revenues and expenditures are outside of the federal budget (see table 21, Appendix). In the late 1970s about 600 sociopolitical entities (other than those at the federal level) accounted for slightly less than one-fourth of public sector expenditures. Communities of interest and various funds that provided such services as education, welfare, health, and social security accounted for over half of public sector expenditures. The communities and users of their services voted on the level of taxation and contributions that mainly finance the services. The communities and sociopolitical units below the federal level were expected to maintain balanced accounts; an unexpected surplus or deficit was supposed to be corrected in the next quarter.

Problem of Workers' Self-Management

The extensive revisions of self-management organizations during the 1970s were intended to adjust for economic deficiencies perceived to have been caused by the 1965 reforms, to add to workers' decisionmaking power, and to correct for long-term economic problems. The revisions had contradictory tendencies. By furthering the decentralization process and adding to the number of economic agents, local and republic intervention was not appreciably modified nor was central management strengthened. The LCY was expected to exert stronger influences to counteract centrifugal forces and forge consensus to achieve national goals.

By 1981 inflation, unemployment, and balance of payments constraints still plagued the economy. Tools for regulating aggregate demand remained weak. Self-management organizations continued a high level of investment but were slow to complete projects, unnecessarily tying up investable funds. Self-management organizations tended toward capital-intensive investments, and efforts to expand job creation were only partially successful. External developments combined with domestic factors to increase the constraints arising from the shortage of foreign exchange (see Foreign Trade and Balance of Payments, this ch.).

In the early 1980s various Yugoslav officials and economists offered their solutions for the country's problems. Some believed that the institutional arrangements were sufficient if more effort were made to make them work. Others noted such particular institutional problems as the tendency toward regionalization in investment, production, and marketing, suggesting that institutional changes might be needed to improve economic management. Some economists argued that the economic problems could be remedied by structural adjustments, policy shifts, and other economic means. There was broad agreement, however, that in the 1980s the economy faced serious difficulties, but it was not clear whether major modifications in the role of government and of self-management institutions would follow.

Workers being transported from city to work site, Split
Courtesy International Labor Organization

Growth and Structure of the Economy

Since 1945 Yugoslavia's economic goals have been rapid growth, transformation of a predominantly agrarian nation into a modern, diversified one with strong links to the world economy, and equality of income between individuals and between regions. Remarkable success has been achieved for several of the goals. In 1938 the country lagged some 30 percent behind the world average in per capita income. As a result of a rate of growth nearly double that of the world average, by 1977 per capita income was over 30 percent above the world average, and the economy had indeed been transformed. Industrial production surpassed that of agriculture in the early 1960s, and by 1981 the economy was approaching that of some West European countries in terms of diversification and modernity. Considerably less success was achieved in reducing income inequalities.

The growth was the more notable because of the severe shocks the economy suffered during the 1940s. The battles of World War II resulted in the deaths of over 10 percent of all Yugoslavs, destruction of about 40 percent of industry, and serious disruption of the transportation system; in addition some 3.5 million people were left homeless. Extensive reconstruction was necessary. The break with the Soviet Union in 1948 caused trade with communist countries, which amounted to 56 percent of the total in 1947, to cease by 1950 as did development credits that had been extended. The Yugoslavs also greatly increased defense spending. Between 1948 and 1952 there was almost no economic growth.

The period of adjustment after the break with other communist countries lasted into the early 1950s, but thereafter the economy grew rapidly. Between 1954 and 1974 real gross material product (GMP—see Glossary) grew at an average of 7.2 percent a year and real personal incomes in the modern, socialized sector by 5.8 percent a year. Rapid industrialization fueled significant economic growth. Gross industrial output increased an average of 9.5 percent a year as a result of a high level of investment that averaged about 30 percent of GMP in the early years. Investments in real fixed assets grew an average of 8.7 percent a year. At the same time there occurred a healthy diversification and growth of exports that averaged 8.5 percent a year. The openness of the economy helped efficiency and competitiveness in domestic industry.

When Yugoslavia adopted the Soviet model in 1945, it also began to use Soviet statistical procedures and national accounts. The primary difference between the communist methodology and that used in most of the world and standardized by the United Nations relates to productive and nonproductive activities. The broadest economic measure in communist practice is GMP (also called social product), the value added at market prices of the productive economic sectors. Productive sectors consist of those that contribute directly (including trade and transport) to the production of commodities. Thus GMP excludes such services as public administration, defense, finance, education, health, and housing, which are included in the familiar GNP and GDP. GDP is roughly 15 percent higher than GMP. Yugoslav statistical agencies also computed GNP according to standardized procedures that were available for some years. Where possible, GNP or GDP will be used in this chapter because of their greater familiarity to most readers.

Foreign economists have additional problems with some Yugoslav statistical measures. Over the years substantial changes occurred in relative prices. Thus a number of statistics show considerable variation depending on the base year of prices. Agriculture, for example, accounted for only 23 percent of GMP in the low farm prices of 1952 but 38 percent in 1966 prices. The other difficulties are technical and primarily concern statisticians attempting precise measurements, particularly for comparisons between Yugoslavia and other nations.

In spite of the high performance of the economy over two decades, there were disquieting signs. Economists discerned cyclical patterns related to rapid growth and then periods of adjustment. More importantly, since the 1950s there has been an appreciable slow up in most economic indicators. The slow up showed up by decades and other time spans, but the 1965 economic reform is often used as the dividing point. Thus the average growth rate of GMP was 8.4 percent a year between 1954 and 1965 compared with 6.4 percent a year between 1965 and 1974; over the same years the average rate of gross industrial output fell from 12.2 to 7.7 percent a year; that for industrial employment, from 6.6 to 3.3 percent; social sector employment, from 5.9 to 2.9 percent; exports, from 11.7 to 5.6 percent; and fixed investments, from 9.2 to 8.2 percent a year. In contrast the rate of growth of imports fell much less than exports, and inflation accelerated greatly.

There were many causes for these changes, some of which were intentional, such as allocating a greater share of income to consumption. The nature of investments and inefficiencies in implementation, however, required increasing sums to yield an additional unit of social product, and some government policies discouraged job creation. Investable funds tended to be confined within regions, and access varied greatly between enterprises. The process of decentralization reduced the tools for economic management and coordinated efforts; planning, resource allocation, and policy formation became largely regional, i.e., republic and provincial functions. The result was an excess demand on resources, growing inflation, and balance of payments problems. The domestic situation was the cause of inflation until 1973 when international prices, particularly for oil, added external factors. A worsening employment situation and balance of payments problems had been masked by a substantial migration of Yugoslav workers abroad who sent home a large flow of foreign exchange in the form of private remittances (see Labor, this ch.).

The 1976–80 five-year plan was drafted to adjust for these problems under the new system of planning. In addition an economic recession in Western Europe in the mid-1970s limited Yugoslav export possibilities and forced many of the workers abroad to return home (see Migration, ch. 2). The planners anticipated relatively high growth while making structural adjustments in the economy. GMP was projected to increase at an average rate of 7 percent a year; exports, 8 percent a year; and imports, 4.5 percent a year. The strategy projected a rapid shift to export production, while import dependency was to be reduced by expanding domestic production of intermediate materials and capital equipment. This shift was ambitious, exceeding the experience between 1965 and 1975.

Between 1976 and 1980 substantial economic growth was achieved. In 1976 social product increased only 3.9 percent because of the balance of payments constraints and a stabilization program. Successful reduction in 1976 of the balance of payments deficit resulted in more expansionary policies and growth of social product by 8 percent in 1977 and nearly 7 percent in 1978 and 1979. By late 1979 increasing inflation and balance of payments difficulties required a return to stabilization measures; social product increased only 2.5 to 3 percent in 1980. For the plan period, real growth was about 5.8 percent a year.

The main source of growth in the 1976–80 five-year plan was industrial production, which increased an average of 7 percent a year between 1976 and 1979. In 1980, however, it increased only about 4 percent as shortages of raw and intermediate materials and energy disrupted the productive process. The 1976–80 plan placed stress on production of items to provide import substitution, but output fell short of the targets. In contrast production of consumer goods and some other nonpriority sectors grew faster than expected because of the high level of domestic demand. Agricultural output probably increased only 1.6 percent a year between 1976 and 1980 (compared with planned growth of 4 percent a year), and unfavorable weather caused marked fluctuations.

The apparent weakness of the 1976–80 plan proved real. In earlier years a considerable import dependency, particularly on intermediate materials and capital goods, had developed that continued in the early 1980s. In 1976 and 1980 deep cuts were made in imports, sharply restricting economic growth. Although imports fluctuated widely from year to year, their growth between 1975 and 1980 was below the 4.5 percent a year planned. Export growth was substantially less than planned, increasing about 4.6 percent a year compared with 8 percent in the plan. An important part of the expansion of exports occurred in 1980 when they rose about 9 percent. The slow growth of exports was compounded by deteriorating terms of trade, especially the sharp rise in imported crude oil prices that began in 1979. By 1980 the balance of payments constrained economic growth as the limitation of imports disrupted industrial production (see Foreign Trade and Balance of Payments, this ch.).

Between 1976 and 1980 fixed investments substantially exceeded the plan, increasing almost 9.5 percent a year. Gross fixed investment as a share of GDP rose from 28 percent in 1975 to nearly 32 percent in 1979. The sectors of energy, raw materials, and intermediate goods received priority as planned, but output fell short of targets in some instances as completion of projects fell behind schedule. Nonpriority sectors also made substantial investments. The high investment helped job creation; social sector employment increased about 4 percent a year compared with the planned 3.5 percent a year. Nonetheless unemployment increased. The high level of investment resulted in an excessive number of uncompleted projects which, according to press reports of a speech by the president of the Federal Executive Council amounted to 597 billion dinars by 1981 (about one-half of total GMP in 1980) and thus contributed to inflation.

By 1980 inflation and balance of payments difficulties were severe. Authorities instituted a stabilization program that included a decline in fixed investments in real terms, a sharp cut in imports while promoting exports, devaluation of the dinar in terms of the United States dollar that amounted to about 28 percent over the year, and an effective incomes policy that reduced real net earnings in the social sector by 7 to 8 percent. Despite the curtailment of economic activity and other measures, prices continued to rise— the inflation rate reaching 30 percent instead of the 17 percent planned—partly because of rising international prices compounded by the effects of devaluation. By 1981, the start of a new five-year plan, the economy had serious problems that threatened to limit economic growth for some years in the future and would require difficult adjustments (see The 1981–85 Plan, this ch.).

One of the serious problems was the continuing regional disparities in incomes and employment opportunities. By the late 1970s per capita income in Kosovo was less than one-third that of the national average while that of the other underdeveloped regions, the republics of Bosnia and Hercegovina, Macedonia, and Montenegro, was about two-thirds (see fig. 1). Per capita income in the most developed republic, Slovenia, was more than seven times that of the province of Kosovo. In addition unemployment was substantially higher in the underdeveloped regions, but labor mobility was limited by cultural and linguistic factors (see Migration, ch. 2). The riots in Kosovo in 1980, in which economic frustrations were a major grievance, were another reminder to officials of the urgency of solving the regional problems.

By 1981 the structure of the economy was approaching that of industrialized countries of Western Europe. Since the mid-1960s the main trend had been the continuing decline in the importance of agriculture. Its share of GDP had fallen from 19 percent in 1968 to 13 percent in 1979 (see fig. 11). Industry's contribution had risen and amounted to 37 percent. The service sectors, specifically miscellaneous services and transportation and communications, had grown

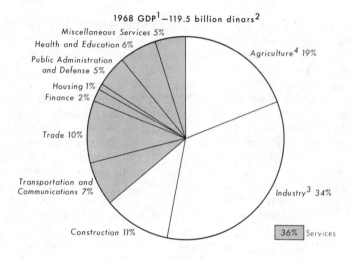

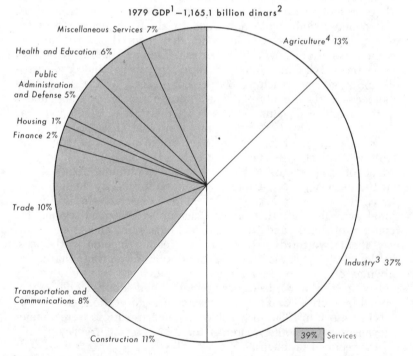

[1] At factor cost in current prices.
[2] For value of the dinar—see Glossary.
[3] Includes mining, manufacturing, and utilities.
[4] Includes forestry and fishing.

Source: Based on information from the Organisation for Economic Co-operation and
Development, *Economic Survey, Yugoslavia*, Paris, May 1981, p. 50.

Figure 11. Gross Domestic Product, by Sector, 1968 and 1979

more rapidly than the average for the economy, and services accounted for 39 percent of GDP.

Labor

Several economists consider the slow creation of jobs one of the most serious defects in Yugoslavia's development policy. Although employment in the social sector expanded at an average rate of about 4 percent a year since 1954, this was insufficient for the supply of workers seeking employment. Since the mid-1970s officials and self-management organizations have taken steps with some success to enlarge employment opportunities. Nonetheless unemployment had increased by 1981.

The basic problem has been to create jobs not only for the natural increase in the working-age population but also for the large migration of private farmers to the urban centers in search of higher incomes and modern amenities. Yugoslav statistics, unfortunately, do not show the number of private farmers but only include them in a residual figure. Labor force data primarily pertain to the socialized sector (see table 22, Appendix). Thus the exact number of farmers that have left agriculture was unknown but the influx was large— exceeding 1 million between 1968 and 1980 and perhaps approaching 2 million.

For several years following the 1965 economic reforms, the employment problem was solved by migration of workers abroad. Immediately after the reforms, slow economic growth and the emphasis on efficiency reduced the expansion of domestic employment opportunities at the same time that a large number of new workers entered the labor force. Exit requirements were liberalized, allowing an increasing number of Yugoslavs to leave for work in Western Europe, which was experiencing a labor shortage. The exodus peaked about 1973, when an estimated 1.1 million Yugoslavs were working abroad (12 percent of the labor force), nearly half of them in the Federal Republic of Germany (West Germany). The migration of workers provided a safety valve, and their remittances became a very important source of foreign exchange.

After 1973, recession and increasing domestic employment problems in the host countries resulted in a substantial return of foreign workers to their home countries. The 1981 Yugoslav census indicated 577,650 workers abroad, suggesting the net return of workers since 1973 may have averaged over 70,000 a year. The returning workers added to the pressures from the natural increase of the population and rural migration on the socialized sector to create additional jobs.

Between 1975 and 1980 socialized sector employment increased an average of 4 percent a year compared with a planned 3.5 percent a year. The high rate of investment plus official policies contributed to the growth. Employment targets have been included in social compacts to encourage greater employment. Self-management organizations complied. Some economists have argued that worker control would tend to minimize employment, but investigations suggested that enterprises tended to overemploy rather than underemploy workers. New organizations have been devised to encourage private enterprise activities as a means of expanding employment, although the ceiling of five hired workers still applied. By 1980, tax policy, lack of access to credit, and other inhibitors had kept the expansion of private nonfarm activity considerably below that planned. Employment in private, nonfarm businesses amounted to 2 percent of total paid employment in 1980.

Although economists have mustered data supporting the argument that workers' self-management did not inherently preclude full employment, the Yugoslav system had some features that tended to restrict expansion of employment. The tax system inflated the cost of labor relative to other factors in production by the way it was assessed. Fringe benefits to individuals, such as housing, and to groups, such as recreation facilities, were financed from enterprise profits, and these added to labor costs. Moreover the cost of capital was artificially low, and part of the return to capital was paid out in the form of workers' income. Mobility of capital and labor was restricted between republics, and entry of new firms or bankruptcy of failing ones was infrequent. In the 1970s authorities introduced some measures to reduce the bias toward capital, but more remained to be done in the 1980s to stimulate full employment.

In spite of the better-than-planned growth of employment, unemployment increased in the 1970s. Between 1975 and 1980 those registered for employment increased by nearly 250,000 workers, reaching 785,000 in 1980 or an unemployment rate of 13 to 14 percent. The upward trend of real unemployment was confirmed by the rapid increase among those registering for employment of persons seeking their first job. Yugoslav unemployment data and the unemployment rate need to be interpreted, however. Some of those registering for employment (generally assumed at about 40 percent) already had jobs or were students. In addition the unemployment rate was computed essentially against socialized sector employment. Thus both measures tended to overstate unemployment particularly when compared with other nations, such as the United States' unemployment statistics.

Unemployment was regionalized. High population and labor force growth rates and the flight of individuals from the agricultural sector in the less developed regions caused much greater unemployment. In 1978 the unemployment rate in Slovenia, the most developed republic, was 1.5 percent compared with nearly 27 percent in Kosovo, the poorest region. Projections into the 1980s indicated a reduction but still considerable unemployment. The severity of the problem would depend not only on expanding job opportunities but also increasing the mobility of labor and raising incomes of private farmers to reduce the exodus from farms.

Industry

After World War II the new communist leaders chose industrialization as the vehicle for rapid economic growth and raising income levels for the population. Since the early 1950s more than half of investments in fixed assets have been channeled into industry. By 1979 industry, including mining, was the most important sector of the economy, contributing 37 percent of GDP and employing 23 percent of the labor force. The expanding industrial establishment as well as the rest of the economy consumed greater amounts of energy. The sharp jumps in crude oil prices during the 1970s considerably complicated the country's energy balance and the balance of payments.

Energy

In 1975 domestic sources supplied two-thirds of the primary energy consumed. Coal accounted for 63 percent of the domestic supply of energy; petroleum, 19 percent; natural gas, 8 percent; hydroelectric power, 9 percent; and firewood the remainder. Imported crude oil supplied about 28 percent of the primary energy consumed, and some coking coal accounted for the remainder of imported energy. The energy pattern had probably changed in only minor ways by 1981.

Coal deposits were large and widely dispersed, located in the northern, central, and southern regions of the country. Coal reserves were estimated at about 22 billion tons, equivalent to several hundred years of supply at current extraction rates. More than half of the reserves were located in Kosovo. The bulk of the coal was lignite; there was some brown coal and almost no hard coal. The low caloric content of nearly all of the coal made it suitable mainly for generating electric power at close-by thermal plants. There were about fifty mines, but four accounted for over half of output. In the 1970s substantial investments were made in mining and processing facilities, and production rose from 27 million tons in 1970 to 47 million tons in 1980, between 8 and 11 million tons short of the 1980 target under the five-year plan (see table 23, Appendix).

Small deposits of crude oil had been discovered over the years, and there were on the order of 45 million tons of proven reserves, enough to last little more than a decade. More than thirty fields were located in the Pannonian Plains. Prospects were considered good for additional finds, and exploration was under way in several parts of the country, including offshore in the Adriatic Sea. Production increased slowly—from 2.7 million tons in 1969 to 4.1 million tons in 1979 and 4.2 million tons in 1980. Crude oil consumption increased rapidly after the mid-1960s, at double the rate for all primary energy sources, because of increased vehicle traffic, growth of petrochemical industries, and construction of some electric plants fired by petroleum products. After 1973 efforts were made to reduce oil consumption because of its escalating cost; by the late 1970s domestic oil production supplied only about one-quarter of consumption.

Crude oil imports in 1979 amounted to 11.8 million tons, less than half of which was supplied by the Soviet Union. Soviet oil was shipped by barge up the Danube River. The remainder came from the Middle East, primarily Iran and Iraq, to Adriatic ports. The war between Iran and Iraq that began in 1980 disrupted supplies, and Yugoslavia bought more oil from Libya. In 1979 an oil terminal on Krk Island in the north Adriatic and a pipeline (capacity 20 million tons a year) to Hungary and Czechoslovakia were completed as a joint effort. Spurs led from this pipeline to distribute Yugoslavia's purchases of imported crude to most of the country's six refineries (see fig. 12). In 1980 domestic refining capacity was over 25 million tons a year, substantially above the 16 to 18 million tons of crude usually available annually for processing. By the early 1980s refining capacity was scheduled to reach 32 million tons a year as expansion of existing facilities and a new refinery at Skopje were completed. Critics charged that each republic seemed to think it had to have its own refinery regardless of economic considerations. Imbalances during a year often required small imports or exports of refined products.

Natural gas is an increasingly important energy source and industrial raw material in Yugoslavia, as elsewhere in the world, partly reflecting its lower price. Gas, associated with crude oil and in separate fields, has been found in the Pannonian Plains and in the Adriatic area. Proven reserves would last about thirty years at 1979 extraction rates. Prospects reportedly were good for additional discoveries, and exploration was continuing. In 1981 transportation of gas remained essentially by pipeline. In the late 1970s two important connections were made via Austria and via Hungary to gas pipelines from the Soviet Union. Yugoslavia also was a participant in a proposed natural gas pipeline from Algeria to southern Europe via Tunisia and Italy with possible completion around the mid-1980s.

Natural gas production and consumption has been restrained by the lack of distribution facilities. Few plants or areas had access to natural gas before the 1970s, so most were unprepared to use it. In the 1970s pipelines for distributing gas were expanded substantially, and production of domestic gas gradually increased, reaching 1.9 billion cubic meters in 1978. The tie-in with the gas line from the Soviet Union in 1979 required a cutback of domestic production to 1.8 billion cubic meters of gas. Imports from the Soviet Union amounted to about 1 billion cubic meters, less than the agreed import of 3 billion cubic meters, because of the lack of distribution pipelines, particularly in Serbia, and the necessary conversion investments by potential consumers. Since the mid-1950s some 2,800 kilometers of pipelines for distribution of gas were completed, but an assured supply of 7 billion cubic meters of gas from domestic and foreign sources by 1985 required an approximate doubling of the pipeline network in the early 1980s for this available energy to be used. Republics varied in their responses to the national energy plans.

Hydroelectric power was another important primary energy source. Numerous sites have been identified for possible hydroelectric generation that have a production potential totaling about 64 billion kilowatt-hours. In 1980 several such plants were in operation and had a capacity of about 6,200 megawatts and a production of about 28 billion kilowatt-hours. Approximately 40 to 45 percent of the hydro potential was being used. Eleven additional hydro stations were under construction, reflecting official policy since the 1950s to rely on domestic energy sources as much as possible.

The country also has uranium deposits that were to be developed to fuel nuclear power plants. The first nuclear power plant, located at Krsko in Slovenia, was completed and expected to start operations in late 1981. Its installed capacity was 664 megawatts, and it is expected to produce about 4.4 billion kilowatt-hours of electricity a year in full operation. The plant, built in cooperation with Westinghouse, took three years longer than scheduled and had a cost overrun of 80 percent. The United States will provide nuclear fuel until Yugoslavia's own production becomes available. Long-term plans called for ten more nuclear power plants to go into production after 1990.

The bulk of primary energy was consumed in generation of electricity; the remainder was used for heating, in operation of the transportation system, and as industrial materials in manufacturing. At the end of World War II electricity supplied by small local generators was available primarily in larger urban centers. Since then an integrated system has been developed to meet the rapid increase of consumption required by industrialization and the extension of service to most parts of the country has been accompanied by an increased use of appliances. Between 1950 and 1980 installed capacity rose from 673 to 13,093 megawatts (an average annual increase of 10.4 percent) and generation from 2.408 to about 59 billion kilowatt-hours (an average annual increase of 11.3 percent). Per capita consumption rose from about 139 kilowatt-hours in 1950 to about 2,500 kilowatt-hours in 1980. Although per capita consumption in Yugoslavia had increased, it still lagged behind many countries of Western Europe and the Soviet Union. In spite of the rapid growth, generation of electricity was not meeting demand.

In 1980 the electric power grid had interconnections between almost all generating units, consuming centers, and bordering countries. Yugoslavia both imported and exported electricity at various times with the West European system and was extending links to its communist neighbors. The grid was under constant expansion. Nearly half of generating capacity consisted of hydro facilities that were heavily dependent on rainfall and river flows. Only a small part had adequate storage capacity to assure a steady water flow and capacity generation year-round. In the late 1970s water flow had been higher than normal, permitting hydrogenerators to produce

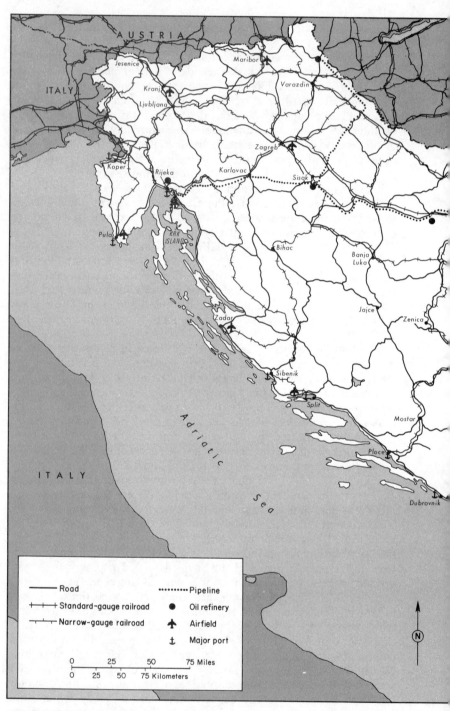

Figure 12. Transportation, 1981

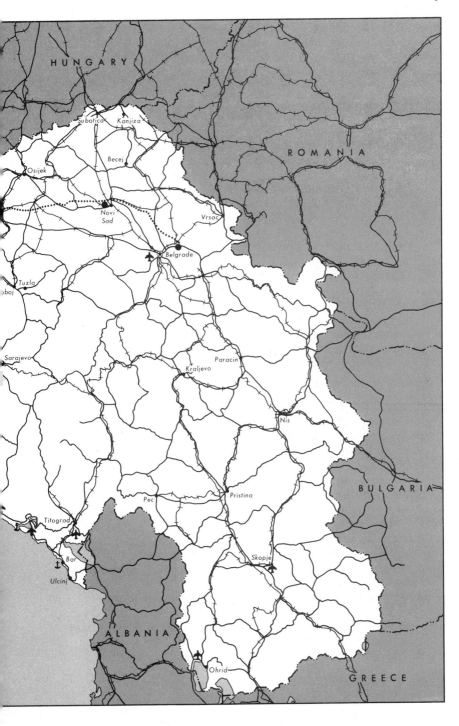

more than anticipated. Coal-fired thermal generators supplied about 40 percent of the electricity, and petroleum fuels and natural gas fueled about 10 to 15 percent of the electricity, depending on need. In 1978 manufacturing and mining consumed 58 percent of the electricity available, households 30 percent, and all other users the remainder.

There were several reasons why the electricity supply failed to keep up with demand. The decentralized system allowed republics, banks, and enterprises priorities other than national goals. Thus the channeling and scheduling of investment funds varied. In the 1976–80 five-year plan little more than 60 percent of the goals in installed capacity, transmission lines, and necessary auxiliaries were accomplished. The failure to meet the production targets for coal and a necessary slowing of oil imports also affected electrical production. During the 1970s user charges for electricity were kept low, encouraging consumption and reducing funds of electrical enterprises for investment.

The favorable water flow during the late 1970s kept electric power generation from falling further behind consumer demand. Nonetheless there were shortages at times that required reduced voltages and other economy measures. In December 1980 an excess of consumption caused the frequency and voltage to drop to a point where the disconnect linkage to the West European system opened, and the Yugoslav system broke down. Three-quarters of the consumers were without electricity. The outage was temporary, but it pointed up the lack of reserve capacity and the narrow energy balance of the country.

Critics charged that the country lacked an adequate energy policy. Yugoslav officials had promoted development of domestic energy resources and conservation of imported fuels through price increases, odd-even days for gasoline purchases, reduced allotments, shortening the periods of heating, and other measures. A 2 percent reduction of oil consumption in 1981 was anticipated, including a 6 percent drop of imported petroleum after a 10 percent decline in 1980. By March 1981, however, press reports indicated that several republics and provinces were not providing the agreed foreign exchange to import crude petroleum, and some even were importing refined products for their own use at a higher cost than imported crude refined domestically. These were problems of the decentralized economy.

Federal officials were trying to balance the country's energy needs based on energy studies. By 1985 coal production was planned to increase to 82 million tons, domestic crude oil extraction to 5 million tons, and installed electric generation capacity to 21,500 megawatts. This was an ambitious program that would be difficult to implement. Failure to achieve even parts of the goal would cause strains in the energy supply to the economy.

Mining

Yugoslavia possesses an abundance of mineral deposits and remains

Electric rail cars
Courtesy WORLD BANK PHOTO (Yosef Hadar)

Highway in Skopje
Courtesy WORLD BANK PHOTO (Yosef Hadar)

a significant world producer of mercury, magnesite, lead, zinc, copper, bauxite, and antimony. In 1980 proven iron ore reserves amounted to over 900 million tons and supplied most of the requirements of the domestic iron and steel industry. Small amounts of other metals were produced, largely as by-products from processing other ores, and included nickel, platinum, palladium, bismuth, cadmium, chromite, germanium, gold, manganese, selenium, and silver. Mining of nonmetallic minerals included limestone, asbestos, gypsum, mica, rock salt, quartzite, sand, and clays. Deposits of phosphate rock were being evaluated for commercial extraction to supply fertilizer materials. In 1981 exploration for minerals deposits was continuing in many parts of the country (see table 23, Appendix).

Manufacturing

Although Yugoslavia was predominantly an agrarian nation at the end of World War II, a start had been made on industrialization. Besides traditional industries (food processing, wood and timber products, and building materials), crude oil extraction, mining and processing of copper, zinc, and bauxite; steel, chemical, and textile industries; and electric power had been established during the interwar (1919–41) period, mostly by foreign investors. It was known that important additional natural resources were available for exploitation. At the war's end, the country was ready for industrial expansion regardless of the political complexion of the new government.

When the Communists assumed control in 1945, they immediately began adopting the Soviet economic model that emphasized development of industry, particularly heavy industry. The extensive war damage to industrial equipment was quickly repaired, helped by international assistance. By 1948 the official index of industrial production was 50 percent above that of 1939. Meanwhile the state had nationalized most of the economy including industrial facilities.

The Soviet economic model centralized nearly all economic decisions and included almost complete control of economic variables. Thus consumption and investment were controlled by plan, as was the allocation of investment funds for development. Yugoslavia started with this system in 1945 and began channeling the major share of fixed investment to industry out of a very high rate of savings. The introduction of workers' self-management in 1950 and other measures that decentralized economic decisionmaking only partly diluted central control over the allocation of investment funds and development policy.

Since 1945 development policy has remained consistent in stressing industrialization—including education, vocational training, and incentives to workers—as the means to modernize the economy. In 1981 the primary focus continued to be on expansion of the energy base, exploitation of other natural resources, and development of basic industries which included metallurgy and capital equipment. Emphasis did vacillate between the priority branches because of specific circumstances, but the focus remained on heavy industry. The development policy achieved its basic purpose. By the early 1960s industry surpassed agriculture in its contribution to social product, and by 1978 the value added by industry was more than three times that contributed by agriculture.

The consistent policy, supported by large investment allocations and a flow of workers from rural areas, caused industrial output to lead the economy in its expansion. The official index of industrial production increased by 8.5 percent a year between 1949 and 1979. Some economists, pointing out deficiencies in the methodology of the index, calculated the growth rate of industrial expansion some 20 percent lower and close to rates achieved by other rapidly industrializing countries. Even with qualifications, Yugoslavia achieved a notably high rate of industrial growth—supported by statistical evidence and observation over time.

One incidental measure of industrial growth not available in statistics is the supply of locally manufactured equipment to the country's defense forces. This expanded from clothing and other minor items, for example, to aircraft, submarines, surface vessels, and a wide range of infantry weapons by the late 1970s (see Missions and Organization, ch. 5). One basic reason for industrialization was to develop the country's defense capabilities. The break with the Soviet Union in 1948 increased official attention on an economic structure that would contribute to defending the state's independence.

Between 1949 and 1979 the fastest growing industrial branches (as reflected in the official indices of industrial production) were oil and gas extraction, manufacturing of electrical machinery, transport equipment, chemicals, electric power, and oil refining. These were essentially priority branches that started from low levels of production. Other priority branches that were more developed in the late 1940s—such as coal mining, ferrous and nonferrous mining and processing, and metal manufacturing—expanded output significantly, but growth rates were considerably lower. Several nonpriority branches, such as furniture, paper, and extraction of construction materials as well as the traditional food and beverage industries, expanded faster than the industrial average.

Three decades of concentrated investments resulted in an impressive expansion in the range and depth of industrial output. The aluminum industry, for example, expanded from one of essentially extracting and exporting bauxite to one increasingly capable of producing aluminum ingots and manufactured products. Manufacturing increasingly supplied the domestic market with a wide range of consumer goods, including frozen foods, cars, refrigerators, and television sets, and a growing amount of machinery and equipment for additional expansion.

The structure of industry changed markedly from that dominated by food processing in the 1940s. In 1978 the value added by industry (in 1975 prices) amounted to the equivalent of about US$11.7 billion, of which food processing contributed 15 percent; textiles and clothing, 14 percent; machinery and transport equipment, 21 percent; chemical, 8 percent; and other manufacturing (in which metal fabrication was most important), 42 percent. The structure of Yugoslav industry was approaching that of West European countries.

The government, at various levels, used many tools to influence the pace and direction of industrial growth. Until the mid-1960s the federal government directly allocated a substantial amount of the investment funds. Since then recourse has been more toward such indirect measures as credit, tax incentives, and commercial policies. Innovations and adoption of advanced technology were encouraged by various means, including joint ventures with noncommunist industrial firms. The Yugoslav law on foreign investment requires 51 percent Yugoslav ownership but otherwise leaves most matters to be worked out between the participants in the joint venture. The flow of foreign investment has not been as large as hoped, but by 1980 several joint ventures had been formed. One of current significance was participation by a large international chemical firm in a large petrochemical complex at the crude oil terminal of Krk Island.

The focus on energy and the development of basic industries resulted in an industrial structure consisting of a small number of large facilities with heavy capital costs and offering relatively few jobs. In 1977 basic industries (primarily energy, ferrous and nonferrous metallurgy, chemicals, and paper) accounted for 56 percent of fixed assets in the socialized sector, contributed 32 percent of value added, but employed only 21 percent of the workers in the socialized sector. Small-scale industry in Yugoslavia was usually defined as firms that employ fewer than 125 workers. In the social sector there were a relatively large number of such industrial facilities (perhaps 4,000), but they contributed around 10 percent of value added by industry. In addition there was a small private industry—basically artisans and handicrafts. Limited data suggested that small organizations were generally efficient and provided valuable supplements to production in larger plants. In the 1970s officials encouraged private individuals to form industrial cooperatives through various incentives.

Although the index of industrial production sustained a high rate of growth between 1945 and 1980, there was a significant slowing of the rate of increase, which attracted the attention of economists both Yugoslav and foreign. The slowing was perceptible by the early 1960s, but several economists have used the economic reforms of 1965 as the beginning of a new period. Between 1948 and 1965 the official index of industrial production increased by 9.9 percent a year compared with a rate of 7.1 percent a year between 1965 and 1978.

Several reasons have been advanced for the slowing of the rate of growth in industrial output, all of which probably contributed but none of which appeared paramount. For several years after the war, industrial production rose quickly because only simple reconstruction was needed in some industries to raise production; economies of scale were easily achieved in the transition from artisans and work-shops to mechanized factories, and greater education and skills in the labor force contributed to productivity. Higher technology also played a part.

As effects of these positive factors diminished, negative forces assumed more prominence in affecting industrial output. By the 1960s the easily exploited resources and areas of the economy had been largely developed. Additions to industrial output required larger investments and became more difficult to accomplish—extending cost estimates and completion times. Overall coordination and management of development and of individual projects became increasingly necessary even though decentralization of economic decisionmaking was the trend. Efficiency in investments and production, although a sought-for goal, was often difficult to achieve for a variety of reasons.

Institutional factors affected efficiency of production and invest-ment. Capital was less mobile than assumed, for example. Private capital was encouraged to establish entities that would produce parts, products, or services needed by the economy, but investors would lose control of their assets and hence have been reluctant to invest. Units of associated labor were encouraged and expected to invest in other aspects of production and areas, particularly the less developed republics and provinces. Since such investments resulted in creation of organizations of associated labor that could decide to become independent, by 1981 there had been less of a flow of capital to the underdeveloped regions than expected.

During the 1970s the growing influence of the regional govern-ments resulted in greater intervention in economic matters. For ex-ample, there were an excessive number of slaughterhouses—there was one in almost every locality, and most were small, antiquated, and lost money—but closing them would create unemployment and problems for farmers. Despite an excess of crude oil refining capac-ity in 1980, the industries' importance in the economies of most regions meant that even more refineries were being installed. At the same time, investments in coal mining and expansion of electric gen-erating and transmission were substantially behind schedule, con-tributing to a shortage of electricity. In addition natural gas supplies were available to help the country's energy balance, but construc-tion of pipelines for distribution had fallen considerably below the plans. Moreover producers that incurred continuing losses were sup-posed to be liquidated, but few were. Reasons were usually found to finance the losses.

The iron and steel industry provided in a single industry an exam-ple of many of the problems that existed in varying degrees in other industries. During the 1960s and 1970s consumption of iron and steel products grew rapidly, usually faster than industrial produc-tion itself because its output supplied the growing fabricating in-dustries that produced finished products. The main consumers were metal manufacturing (consuming over half of output), construction, and defense industries. Production lagged behind consumption, thus requiring growing imports to meet needs. In the early 1960s domestic production supplied about 90 percent of requirements, but it was substantially lower by 1980; in 1980 some projections indicated a continuing decline in self-sufficiency at least to the mid-1980s.

The iron and steel industry consisted of about a half-dozen independent plants, essentially one in each republic, with a total capacity in 1981 of about 4.3 million tons of crude steel and 5.5 million tons of other products. This meant that the units were too small to achieve economies of scale. Expansion and addition of new facilities had been almost continuous, but construction schedules frequently were not met and cost overruns were high. The planning and designing of units tended to be oriented toward regional markets, and as a result there was insufficient coordination between plants. The result was excess capacity for some products and not enough of others. Many facilities were underutilized because of lack of familiarity with some of the imported technology, irregular supply of inputs, and failure to install subcomponents in time to avoid bottlenecks. Underutilization was an important contributor to the inability of the domestic industry to meet consumption needs.

Inefficiencies required frequent price increases for steel products, including a 20 percent increase in late 1980 and a proposed increase of 14 percent in 1981. In 1980 some mills complained that they had been unable for years to make the necessary investments in ore mining to maintain sufficient supplies for the plants because of the prices enforced on their products. At the same time, Yugoslav journalists claimed that domestic steel products were 20 to 70 percent more expensive than those imported, depending on which mill was used for price comparison. In 1981 the iron and steel complex in Serbia reportedly was to be the recipient of the twenty-second financial rescue operation in recent years in order to keep it from defaulting on its foreign and domestic debts incurred in varous expansion programs.

Many of the iron and steel plants were set up to use domestic iron ore, but the mines had not been expanded fast enough to meet needs. Other plants required imported ore and steel scrap to operate. Where coke or coking coal was used, it also had to be imported. It was normal and economical for an industry of this size to import some semifinished and finished steel products to provide the varieties required by consumers, but such imports increased as the domestic industry fell behind consumption. Nonetheless the domestic industry had capacity for nearly 900,000 tons of specific products for which there was no market, either locally or in foreign countries. In 1979 about 1 million tons of iron ore, 3 million tons of coking coal, 345,000 tons of scrap, and nearly 2 million tons of semifinished and finished steel products were imported; the total value of these imports was nearly US$1 billion, compared with exports of steel products of about US$100 million. In the late 1970s and early 1980s the import needs of the iron and steel industry were a serious drain on the country's foreign exchange resources in spite of the potential of domestic sources.

By 1981, when foreign exchange was short and imports were being limited, steel producers and consumers found it difficult to arrange production plans. Estimated consumption requirements were about 5.7 million tons of iron and steel products, but substantial increases over 1979 would be required in imports of ore, coking coal, scrap, and semifinished and finished products to meet these consumption needs. Bargaining between producers and consumers was reflected in numerous press articles; finding the necessary foreign exchange for the expanded level of imports proved difficult. Although the production planning had started in September 1980, by April 1981 the problem of foreign exchange, and therefore production, had not been settled, and some steel mills were announcing reduced production programs because of the lack of imported materials. It was uncertain that the industry would be able to supply even 4 million tons of steel products.

Yugoslav observers candidly acknowledged the lack of coordination among iron and steel plants in constructing facilities and developing raw material supplies and the excessive costs resulting from underutilization of expensive imported equipment and technology. Moreover they were aware that the situation for iron and steel would deteriorate further by 1985 if planned expansions were carried through because costs would increase. Some writers proposed studies and plans on a national basis to develop the raw material supplies and balanced production at the various stages of production of steel products so that equipment would be used as near the optimum level as possible. They pointed out that the more difficult the situation, such as the shortage of foreign exchange that would probably last for some time, the more important efficiency became, and that by 1981 financial losses at some mills had already drained considerably income from fellow workers in other industries in the region.

The iron and steel industry represented perhaps the worst case in Yugoslav industry, but a few others, such as chemicals, exhibited some of the same problems. Other branches—such as electrical engineering and motor vehicles, both closely linked to international firms—appeared better organized and more efficient. Since the 1960s, industry has become exposed to foreign competition as the economy has been freed, and many firms have proved an ability to compete at home and abroad. In the 1980s efficiency will become even more important in all branches of industry if exports are to grow; otherwise the balance of payments constraint will retard industrial growth.

Agriculture

Between the early 1950s and the late 1970s, agricultural output increased about three times as fast as the population, lessening the country's dependence on imports. By the late 1970s Yugoslavia was only a small net importer of agricultural products. Except in years of adverse weather, the country had become generally self-sufficient in cereals and was usually an exporter of meat and live animals. Domestic production was deficient in dairy products, eggs, vegetable oils, and high-protein livestock feed; imports of tropical fruits and coffee were necessary to meet the increasing demand for those commodities. Between the early 1950s and the mid-1970s, the average daily caloric intake increased by over 850 calories, leveling off above 3,500 calories a day since then, a high level. Starch and fats contributed most of the calories, but in the 1970s the consumption pattern shifted toward livestock products, high-quality fruits and vegetables, and processed foods. The effect was to increase the net import deficit in agricultural products by the late 1970s.

Although agricultural output had increased about two and one-half times between 1947 and 1977, the average rate of growth was only about 3 percent a year between 1968 and 1978 while domestic food consumption increased at about 4 percent a year. During the 1976–80 five-year plan, the agricultural sector expanded an average of only about 1.6 percent a year instead of the planned rate of 4 percent a year—partly because of unfavorable weather. Agriculture's relative importance in GDP steadily diminished after World War II as other sectors grew more rapidly. In 1979 agriculture contributed about 13 percent of GDP and employed between 26 and 31 percent of the labor force.

Increasingly during the 1970s, officials recognized that agriculture needed more attention. Employment objectives for the economy were not being met, partly because private farmers left their small plots to seek higher incomes in other sectors. Moreover, domestic demand, exceeding the growth of agricultural output, and changing dietary preferences combined to increase imports and diminish exports of agricultural products. By 1981 authorities viewed agricultural development as critical to easing the balance of payments constraint and to renewed high growth in the rest of the economy.

Land Use

The territory of Yugoslavia totals nearly 25.6 million hectares. Forests occupied almost 9.2 million hectares or approximately 36 percent of the total area. In 1978 total agricultural land amounted to 14.4 million hectares (56 percent), 4.3 million hectares of which were mostly highland pastures suitable only for grazing. Over 9.9 million hectares were cultivated, consisting of cropped areas (7.2 million hectares), orchards (476,000 hectares), vineyards (247,000 hectares), and meadows (2 million hectares). In 1978 the cropped area contained 4.4 million hectares of grains; 904,000 hectares of fodder crops; 651,000 hectares of vegetables; 540,000 hectares of industrial crops; and 670,000 hectares of fallow or untilled acreage. The remainder of the total area consisted of mountainous terrain, urban development, and rivers, lakes, and marshes.

Until the early 1960s the amount of agricultural land, especially the cultivated acreage, was expanding. Increasingly, however, it was marginal land that was brought under cultivation. In 1960 or shortly thereafter, the amount of agricultural land peaked at about 15 million hectares (10.3 million hectares of cultivated land). Since then the amount of agricultural land has been slowly declining, largely because of urbanization and industrial development. The decline in the cultivated area was somewhat more rapid because some of the more marginal cultivated plots were returned to livestock grazing.

Although agricultural activity exists throughout the country, the most productive and highly developed is that in the fertile plains of Vojvodina and Croatia, which produce over half the country's grains and three-quarters of the sugar beets. In the hilly areas of Serbia, Slovenia, and Bosnia, cropping and livestock rearing are usually combined. Raising livestock predominates in the mountainous west and south (see fig. 8). The Mediterranean climate near the Adriatic Coast permits cultivation of grapes, olives, and citrus fruits. Further south in Macedonia, tobacco, cotton, and rice are grown.

In 1978 over 60 percent of the cropped area was planted in grains, largely wheat and corn. The grain acreage peaked in the early 1960s and has since been declining because of government policies and changing dietary habits. In 1978 the grain acreage amounted to 4.4 million hectares, about 1.2 million hectares less than in 1960. The decline in grain acreage was partially compensated for by an expansion of the area planted in vegetables, fodder, and such industrial crops as sugar beets. There was also a small increase in tree crops (orchards) since 1960 and a smaller decline in vineyards.

The bulk of the country's agricultural land depends on rain for moisture, causing substantial variations in production from year to year. In 1978 only about 145,000 hectares were irrigated, approximately 1.5 percent of the cultivated land. Between 1955 and 1978 the irrigated acreage increased by 47,000 hectares or an average of slightly more than 2,000 hectares per year. Most of the irrigated land was located in Macedonia and Kosovo, where intensive vegetable gardening had developed. Socialized farming accounted for a disproportionate share of the irrigated fields and had most of such modern equipment as sprinkler systems. Much of the irrigation on private farms was traditional gravity feed, which was usually inefficient and often antiquated.

Estimates of the country's potential for irrigation exceeded 3 million hectares. In some regions irrigation would only supplement rainfall, but it would permit intensive cultivation in other regions now too arid for cropping. Large-scale expansion of irrigation offered significant increases in productivity, but large irrigation systems would be costly. Officials appeared cautious about rapid expansion of irrigation. The country also had about 1.2 million hectares of land in need of drainage systems for full realization of the crop production potential. Croatia, Slovenia, and Montenegro had

147

the most serious drainage problems. Drainage systems could raise production appreciably, but detailed studies would have to establish those that would be the most cost-effective.

Land Tenure and Agrarian Reform

In 1918 when the country was formed, it was an agrarian nation in which owner-operated small farms were the norm. Nonetheless because of its diverse ethnic groups and land tenure systems stemming from foreign rule, considerable variation in nationality of ownership and size of landholdings existed. Strong backing for land reforms pushed through one such measure in 1919. Serbia and Montenegro were unaffected because small peasant-operated farms were traditional. The targets were the other areas that had had the most pronounced effects of the Austrian, Hungarian, and Turkish control. Implementation of land reform progressed slowly because of various local problems, but by the late 1930s ownership of nearly 25 percent of the agricultural land had been transferred to about 30 percent of the peasants. Although the reform corrected the worst inequities in landownership, reduced the number of landless to about 150,000, and created an independent peasantry, landholdings were neither equalized nor made economic.

When Tito and his colleagues assumed power in 1945, they were confronted not only with the tremendous task of rebuilding the war-devastated agricultural sector but also numerous endemic social and economic problems, such as the small size of holdings, rural over-population, and a low level of agricultural technology. The initial solution was to adopt the Soviet economic model, which included collectivization of agriculture. In 1945 an agrarian reform law began the process of establishing a socialized agricultural sector, which was to be the principal vehicle for the expansion of output and the improvement of agricultural technology.

The 1945 land reform provided for expropriation, in many circumstances without compensation, of all land exceeding the varying limits set for different kinds of owners. The upper limit of private holdings was twenty-five to thirty-five hectares, depending on region. By 1946 some 1.2 million hectares of farmland and several hundred thousand hectares of forests had entered the public land pool, over 40 percent of which came from confiscation of property belonging to German nationals who had fled or had been forced to leave the country. Just over half the land expropriated was distributed without charge to landless or land-poor peasants, many of whom had been Partisans (see Glossary) during World War II. Of the remaining public land, nearly half was turned over to state forestry agencies and the rest used to create state farms on the Soviet pattern.

In 1946 the government moved a step further toward collectivized agriculture through a law governing cooperatives. The peasants were receptive to cooperatives partly because of a long tradition in Croatia and Serbia of ownership, farming, and profit sharing on a communal basis. Cooperatives had been established during the late 1800s, and the number increased rapidly during the 1920s and 1930s. Most were credit cooperatives, but others were formed for such activities as marketing or distribution of inputs. The destruction and disruptions of World War II broke up many of the existing cooperatives.

The 1946 law and subsequent legislation established essentially two forms of cooperatives. The general cooperative, which older cooperatives became, were basically agencies of the government in the purchase of agricultural produce through a system of compulsory deliveries at low, government-set prices and the distribution of inputs and other goods needed by rural households. The other major form of cooperative contained the features of the general cooperative, but land and equipment were pooled and fields worked collectively. The government favored the latter type; general cooperatives were usually associations for credit and marketing and perhaps included some joint activities such as in the use of machinery, but few involved collective efforts in farm operations. Some cooperatives held title to the land, which by law could not be returned to private ownership.

Although joining cooperatives was legally voluntary, considerable pressures were exerted on farmers to join. Nonetheless cooperatives expanded slowly until the government launched an intensive collectivization drive after the break with the Soviet Union in 1948. In 1950 the number of cooperatives peaked at about 16,000, and socialized agriculture held just over one-third of the agricultural land. The momentum of the collectivization drive slackened in 1950, mainly because of strong peasant resistance. Farmers slaughtered livestock and endured privations in preference to joining cooperatives and, particularly, the collective farms. Moreover many existing cooperatives had problems of varying severity. The situation in the countryside became chaotic in 1950 when one of the worst droughts in the country's history occurred.

In the early 1950s officials reviewed collectivization of agriculture while beginning the introduction of workers' self-management in the economy. Modifications affecting farmers included dissolving machine tractor stations, distributing equipment to cooperatives, abolishing compulsory deliveries of farm produce, and fixing more realistic prices for such commodities. An increasing volume of applications to resign from cooperatives led to a 1953 law governing cooperatives. Members were allowed to withdraw and disband many collective farms, and most did except in Vojvodina, where a number remained because a substantial part of their land had come from public holdings and could not be turned over to withdrawing members. In 1953 the legal ceiling for private landholdings, which was still in effect in 1981, was reduced to ten hectares (in special cases to fifteen hectares), partly because many members withdrawing from cooperatives had relatively large holdings. Some 276,000 hectares were taken under this reform measure; the land was not distributed to private farmers but became part of the public land pool to endow state and collective farms. The legal concept of social property reflected an attempt to reconcile the legal right of socialized agricultural institutions to use the land without actually owning it.

By 1953 officials were implicitly acknowledging the error of wholesale adoption of Soviet collectivization but not abandoning the goal of socialized agriculture. They shifted to more voluntary and flexible methods and organizations. Meanwhile they conceded to the peasants' desire to remain independent by permitting withdrawal from collective farms and accepting a large private sector in agriculture. The normal ten-hectare limit on private ownership, however, largely precluded the use of hired labor or large machinery except under cooperative arrangements. Yugoslav agriculture became even more dominated by many small-scale farmers.

Since the early 1950s official policy has accepted the two-sector approach but strongly favored socialized agriculture. The bulk of investments, inputs, and technical personnel have been channeled to state farms and cooperatives. In the late 1970s socialized farming employed about 5 percent of the agricultural labor force, controlled 16 percent of the cultivated land, but accounted for 27 percent of the country's agricultural output and about half of the marketed supplies of staple commodities. Because of its favored position and substantial holdings of the most fertile land, socialized agricultural production increased an average of 10.9 percent a year between 1954 and 1972 compared with an average increase of 2.9 percent a year by private farming over the same period.

At the beginning of 1978 there were 2,704 socially owned farms. They controlled nearly 1.6 million hectares compared with 921,000 hectares in 1954. Socialized agriculture consisted primarily of reorganized state farms along with a few collective farms, research institutes, and numerous cooperative associations. In the 1960s and 1970s state farms were encouraged to branch out into processing and marketing, becoming agrobusinesses, or in Yugoslav terms—*agrokombinats*. In the late 1970s about 100 of these agroindustrial complexes, all of which had over 5,000 hectares (and some over 100,000 hectares), farmed over 60 percent of the cultivated land in the socialized sector. One of the large combines, which started out in farming, employed 2,700 workers, but farming accounted for only 25 percent of its activities by 1980; about 70 percent of its activity was food processing, and 5 percent was trade. The agrobusinesses were responsible for all or nearly all of the processing of agricultural commodities.

During the 1970s the forms of agricultural organizations changed, and their number increased along with the constitutional and legal changes made in self-management organizations in other sectors of the economy. The agrobusinesses, being vertically integrated enterprises, consisted of several BOALs plus additional intermediate organizations. Agrobusinesses were encouraged and expected to form relationships with farms in their vicinity. The relationship might be simple, short-term contracts with individuals for purchase or sale of commodities; more complex arrangements with a group of farmers could entail the supply of such services as credit and machinery time and, often, long-term contracts for purchase and sale of commodities needed by each other; or even a partial integration with a group of farmers organized into a cooperative whereby the members had a voice in management of the agrobusiness.

In the 1970s under the Law on Associated Labor, the forms and status of cooperatives changed. Individuals, including farmers, who owned a means of production were encouraged to form cooperatives or singly or as a group to arrange cooperation agreements with social enterprises such as agrobusiness. The intent was two-fold: to permit workers in the private sector to form self-management associations and to link the private and socialized sectors more closely. In 1976 basic cooperatives achieved status as a legal person for the first time, securing rights comparable with those of social enterprises. The various forms of cooperation arrangements contained inducements for peasants to join—such as farmers retaining title to their land, gaining access to credit, inputs, and technical services from agrobusinesses to which they usually sold their produce under prices set about planting time, and by the late 1970s participating in social sector health and pension programs. The disadvantages included reduced flexibility compared with individual farmers and some reduction of prices paid for farmers' produce because of overhead costs of the cooperation organizations.

The independent peasants appeared cautious about joining the various cooperative associations. Critics also claimed that the agrobusinesses often did little to stimulate cooperation organizations, preferring instead to rely on short-term purchase and sale contracts with individuals rather than becoming involved in profit sharing and management arrangements. Moreover standardization of terminology appeared to be lacking, and sharp shifts appeared in statistics in the late 1970s, making it difficult to discern the changes taking place. At the beginning of 1980 there were just over 2,000 agricultural cooperation organizations of all kinds (525 of which were listed as cooperatives) with perhaps 250,000 to 300,000 members participating. The bulk of the associated farmers formed cooperation organizations based on long-term contractual arrangements with agrobusinesses rather than the more restrictive farm cooperatives.

During the 1970s official policy acknowledged the considerable potential in the private sector and the need to raise its productivity. In fact the ability of the independent small farmer to increase yields over the years (although much more slowly than the socialized sector) in spite of being starved for inputs, credit, and technical services was remarkable and saved agriculture from becoming a problem in earlier years. By the late 1970s the number of private farmers was variously estimated at between 2.2 to 2.6 million, controlling

84 percent of the cultivated land, accounting for 73 percent of the gross social product produced by agriculture in 1979, and constituting 95 percent of the agricultural labor force. In the 1980s private farming remained the dominant sector by many measures.

The task of upgrading the technology and productivity of private farming was difficult. In the late 1970s the average private farm was about 3.5 hectares (or slightly less) and consisted of several separate plots. The extreme fragmentation as well as the small average size of farms greatly inhibited the application of modern techniques; moreover just developing the organizations and infrastructure to reach the widely dispersed farming communities was a task of substantial magnitude. More than half of the income of private farm households came from nonfarm activities. The size of farms varied in different parts of the country. Private farms in Vojvodina and Croatia tended to be larger, and many achieved yields nearing those of state farms. In more isolated and particularly upland areas, private farms tended toward the subsistence level. Farmers' incomes in the less developed regions were low, near the poverty level of the equivalent of about US$430 a year in 1980.

Low incomes and the lack of amenities caused many farmers to seek nonfarm employment, particularly the young. The exodus has been substantial over the years, amounting to more than 1 million people between 1968 and 1978. The remaining private farm population grew older. By 1980 over 600,000 hectares of farmland was not being cultivated, presumably because the owners had become too old or had left for employment in urban areas. Socialized agriculture did lease and purchase some land from private farmers but was restricted in such activities by inadequate funds.

In the 1970s encouraging results were achieved in the linking of socialized and private farming through the various forms of cooperation. Between 1973 and 1978, for example, the private farm area devoted to such major crops as corn, wheat, and sugar beets, grown under cooperation arrangements with the socialized sector, increased by 37 percent, and much greater cooperation was accomplished in livestock. In another example labor productivity on private farms increased by nearly 7 percent a year between 1973 and 1978 as a result of a substantial increase in the use of machinery, fertilizers, and improved seeds obtained in part through cooperative arrangements with the socialized sector. In 1980 and 1981, however, criticism mounted that agriculture was not achieving the plan goals, particularly in private farming. Unfavorable weather was partly to blame, but low levels of investment, slow organization of private farmers, and reluctance of agrobusinesses to expand cooperation with peasants were cited as major problems to be solved. In mid-1981 it remained to be seen whether the self-management and cooperation organizations would be sufficient to raise yields and productivity in the private sector toward those achieved on state farms, but it was clear that private farm productivity had to be increased if the country's agricultural potential was to be realized.

Cropping Patterns and Production

Climatic conditions permitted cultivation of a wide variety of crops. Even in localized areas, the cropping alternatives were usually numerous. Cropping was guided in part by planning in the socialized agricultural units, the republics, and by national entities for the economy's various needs. The cooperation arrangements and purchase contracts between socialized agricultural and private farmers further facilitated planning and the distribution process. Most of the extensive private sector depended largely on relative prices, tradition, and weather expectations for making cropping decisions.

There are two markets for agricultural produce—the official or socialized market and the informal peasant markets. The official market with authorized purchases and set prices accounted for about 40 to 50 percent of total sales of agricultural products. In the official market the government set purchase prices and guaranteed minimum prices for important products such as cereals and meat. Minimum prices, but not guaranteed, were set for a number of commodities, such as milk, sugar beets, tobacco, and other industrial crops to be processed, based on costs of production in the socialized sector. The official prices, announced at the beginning of the growing season, influenced planting decisions in both the socialized and private sectors. In the late 1970s, for example, relative prices favored wheat compared with sugar beets, causing the area planted in sugar beets to decline below that necessary fully to utilize processing capacity in 1980 even though refiners offered to pay nearly 30 percent more than the minimum price. Prices for some commodities, mostly those highly perishable, and products sold in peasant markets were largely uncontrolled. The government at the federal or republic level also sometimes paid premiums to encourage planting and production of basic commodities.

The most important crop, grown in most parts of the country, was corn. Before World War II it was the basic bread grain, but 80 percent of the corn was used for livestock feed by 1980 and little for direct human consumption. Between 1975 and 1979 corn production alone accounted for 15 percent of total agricultural output and 59 percent of grain production. In the past half-century between 2 and 2.6 million hectares were devoted to corn; since 1975 corn acreage ranged between 2.1 and 2.4 million hectares. Corn production amounted to 10.1 million tons in 1979 and averaged 9.2 million tons between 1976 and 1979. Yields on large, modern state farms were among the highest in the world, but over 80 percent of corn output came from private farms where yields were usually much lower, in part because of cultivation under unsuitable conditions and lack of high-yield seeds and other inputs. A significant amount of corn was sold in isolated peasant markets above official prices to peasants requiring livestock feed, although less than one-fifth of the corn produced was marketed. Socialized agriculture sold

153

about 55 percent of its output, but private farmers used nearly 90 percent of their output to feed their own livestock. Vojvodina, Serbia proper (excludes autonomous provinces of Vojvodina and Kosovo), and Croatia were the major production areas.

Wheat was the other major crop, and it was grown in many parts of the country. Between 1975 and 1979 wheat acreage ranged between 1.5 and 1.7 million hectares, and production, 4.4 to 6 million tons (4.5 million tons in 1979). In 1981 planned production of grains was 18 million tons, of which wheat would account for 6 million tons; corn, 11 million tons; and all other grains, 1 million tons. Wheat acreage has been slowly declining, but yields trended upwards to keep output close to consumption requirements except in years of unfavorable weather. Wheat is the basic bread grain, although some has been used for livestock feed when other fodder was unavailable. Complaints in the press indicated that many farmers failed to use cornstalks and other roughage for livestock feed as effectively as farmers in France and other parts of Western Europe, so that when feed imports had to be curtailed in the late 1970s, some peasants substituted wheat, reducing their surplus for marketing.

Cropping and production of other produce was much less widespread. Production of grains other than corn and wheat altogether amounted to little more than 5 percent of total grain output. In 1979 potatoes occupied 296,000 hectares with production of 2.6 million tons; sugar beets, 140,000 hectares with production of 5.9 million tons; sunflowers, 257,000 hectares with seed production of 525,000 tons; and tobacco, 140,000 hectares with production of 56,000 tons. Outputs of major fruits were 1.3 million tons of grapes; 516,000 tons of plums; and 434,000 tons of apples. The country had a substantial wine and liquor industry based on its agricultural products. Tobacco was exported, up to about one-third of the crop in good years, after meeting domestic requirements.

Yields for most crops have risen significantly since the early 1960s, largely reflecting introduction of high-yield seeds and increased use of fertilizer and modern practices. The gains have been much greater in the socialized sector than in private farming. The draft plan for agricultural development for 1981–85 anticipated that agriculture would expand at about 4 percent a year—6 percent a year in socialized farming and 4 percent a year by private farmers. Observers have questioned the ability of the socialized sector to achieve the planned rate of growth because it has reached a level of development at which substantially greater yields would be difficult to achieve. Conversely the goals for the private sector appeared to observers more attainable. They argued that the potential for increased production from individual farmers is quite large if the necessary investments and policy measures are implemented that would result in greater use of fertilizers and improved seeds.

Livestock

Raising of livestock has become the most important aspect of

Alfalfa being stored in silos on dairy farm
Courtesy of U.S. Department of Agriculture

farming; its share of total agricultural production increased from about one-third after World War II to well over one-half by the mid-1970s in response to rising incomes and the demand for more meat in the diet. Exports of meat and live animals have also provided valuable foreign exchange, and officials hope to expand such exports in the 1980s.

Two severe constraints had to be overcome for fuller exploitation of the country's livestock potential. Supplies of feed had to be increased and the quality of animals improved. Reducing both of the constraints was complicated by the concentration of animal husbandry in the private sector, often in isolated upland regions. In

1979 nearly 90 percent of the livestock by weight was privately owned and a higher percentage in terms of numbers alone.

Pigs were the most numerous of the farm animals (except for chickens) and the most important source of meat. The number of pigs increased from 4.1 million in 1949 to 7.7 million in 1979, accompanied by a substantial increase in the body weight as improved varieties were introduced. The amount of pork produced for meat consumption amounted to almost 500,000 tons in 1979. The number of cattle increased from 5.3 million in 1949 to 5.5 million in 1979, but the increase of body weight approached nearly three-fold, reflecting a substantial upgrading of the herds for both meat and milk production. The country had relatively good veterinary services, although outlying areas had less access than major agricultural centers. Beef production was 338,000 tons in 1979.

Sheep, concentrated in upland and mountain areas where natural grazing land existed, were raised more for wool than meat. The number of sheep declined from nearly 11.7 million in 1949 to 7.3 million in 1979. Meat from lamb and mutton amounted to 62,000 tons in 1979. Macedonia, Serbia proper, and Bosnia and Hercegovina were the major sheep raising regions.

Commercial poultry farming expanded rapidly in the 1960s as it did in many places in the world. The number of poultry increased from 19.4 million in 1949 to 61.5 million in 1979 while body weight also increased three-fold, resulting from concentrated feed. Consumption of chickens rose from very modest levels to become an important protein source in the 1970s. In 1979 production of poultry meat amounted to 253,000 tons. Commercial chicken farms were located in all of the republics and provinces, but the most important producers were Croatia, Serbia proper, Vojvodina, Slovenia, and Bosnia and Hercegovina.

Per capita consumption of meat increased rapidly, by 37 percent between 1971 and 1979. In the latter year it amounted to 52 kilograms per person. Animals are slaughtered throughout the country; an unofficial count indicated perhaps 1,500 slaughterhouses, most of which were small, inefficient, and operated at a loss. A 1978 law established standards for processing meat for export that only a few could meet. Observers expected slaughtering eventually to become concentrated in the efficient and more hygienic processing units.

The rise of consumption and the shortage of feed have hurt exports. In 1980 exports of meat products and livestock amounted to US$361 million (137,700 tons). The most important product was baby beef, largely exported to Greece and in smaller amounts to Italy, Iran, and Iraq. Other important livestock exports were horses and canned pork. Baby beef and piglets had been important exports to Western Europe, but agricultural policy of the European Economic Community (EEC) in the late 1970s imposed a levy on Yugoslav meat exports that made it difficult to market such products. Yugoslav officials anticipated reduced sales in the early 1980s to all EEC countries, which also included Greece. In 1980 imports of livestock products and feed were at about the same level as exports of livestock products.

The most important constraint that inhibited growth of meat and dairy production was a shortage of feed. Alfalfa, clover, and corn were the main supplements to natural pastures. Journalists noted that France obtained much more feed from corn and its stalks than Yugoslavia did. By 1981 officials were attempting to expand the supply of livestock feed, including silage from cornstalks, through a variety of programs. Although plants to process concentrated feed had been constructed during the 1970s, the country depended on imports in 1981 for high-protein additives such as fish meal from Peru and soybean cake from China and the United States. The country appeared to have a comparative advantage in livestock products, partly because of the low incomes of many of the private farmers. It will be difficult, however, for officials to implement programs in the 1980s to improve the quality of animals and the supply of feed in order to meet the increasing domestic demand and to attain the hoped-for exports, considering the concentration in the private sector and the dispersed and isolated nature of most livestock activity.

Fishing

In spite of the long, indented Adriatic coastline and numerous rivers and lakes, the fishing industry was underdeveloped and of minor economic importance. One of the basic causes was that fish had not become a part of the diet, except in localized areas, until modern refrigeration was introduced. Even though annual per capita consumption of fish doubled between 1952 and 1977, in the latter year it only amounted to 2.5 kilograms. The other fundamental deficiency was that the industry lacked dynamism in upgrading its fishing equipment, extending its activities, and marketing its product.

Although the fishing industry has been expanding, its progress has been much slower than planned, particularly in the late 1970s. An ambitious program was adopted in 1977 for implementation by 1980, but by 1980 it was uncertain that it could be attained even by 1985. A major shortfall was undertaking long-distance fishing in collaboration with developing countries. In 1978 the total fish catch amounted to 63,000 tons, consisting of 37,000 tons from salt water (almost entirely from the Adriatic) and 26,000 tons from fresh water. The goal for 1980 was 135,000 tons of saltwater fish alone.

Officials wanted to increase the fish catch to help the balance of payments. In 1979 the country imported 28,000 tons of fish products for human consumption, mainly frozen fish, worth about US$23 million. In the same year fish exports, largely canned, were 24,000 tons, worth nearly US$39 million. In 1979, however, 82,000 tons of fish meal costing about US$40 million were imported for concentrated livestock feed as well as larger amounts of soybean cake. Development of the fishing industry could eliminate the payments for imported protein additives used in livestock feed.

Forestry

The country had large forest areas, surpassing a number of countries in Europe. In 1978 official statistics showed 9.2 million hectares of woodland, 6.3 million of which was publicly owned. Bosnia and Hercegovina had 2.4 million hectares of forests, Croatia 2.1 million hectares, Serbia proper 1.8 million hectares, and Slovenia 1 million hectares. Improvements in forest management have been steady since World War II and included an extensive and expanded afforestation program. Afforestation rose from about 19,000 hectares in 1958 to 43,000 hectares in 1978, the bulk of which in the 1970s was conifers. Timber cutting increased from 13.3 million cubic meters in 1958 to 19.7 million cubic meters in 1978, the bulk of which was in public forests. Broad-leaved trees were the main source of timber, although cutting of conifers was increasing, reflecting the emphasis in the afforestation program. Lack of roads and facilities hampered cutting and management in some of the country's valuable virgin forests lying in isolated mountainous areas.

Banking and Inflation

In the 1970s the banking system was restructured in response to deficiencies that emerged in the 1960s. Reforms in the 1960s had been partly based on the belief that government had intervened excessively in the allocation of resources, and that such decisions were best left to those most affected—the workers. By the mid-1960s the federal role in investment financing was greatly reduced. Self-financing by enterprises proved limited, however. Banks played an increasing role, channeling household savings to finance enterprise investments. By 1970 bank financing of total fixed investments approached one-half, and it was about 48 percent in 1980.

The reforms in the 1960s did not produce the desired results. Regional barriers restrained mobility of capital. For political reasons duplications of factories and facilities continued to be built in each republic. Excess demand for credit forced banks to ration it. By the early 1970s Yugoslavs saw the banks as exercising too great an influence although some economists argued the opposite point—that banks were too liberal in granting credit and not rigorous enough in evaluating projects, thus contributing to inflation and questionable investments.

All during the 1970s measures were introduced affecting the financial structure. Laws in 1976 and 1977 specifically dealt with the banking system and credit operations. The National Bank of Yugoslavia along with eight national banks in the republics and autonomous provinces constituted the country's central bank (commonly called the National Bank). It had most of the normal central bank functions, such as currency issue, extension of credit to banks and governments, and regulation of credit, other banks, and foreign exchange transactions. It had available various tools, such as reserve requirements, rediscount facilities, and purchase and sales on the foreign exchange market. The central bank had little control over interest rates, however. For major decisions—those affecting republic or province—a consensus among the nine banks was required.

Banks were the predominant financial institutions (accounting for about 65 percent of total financial assets in the mid-1970s), although there were investment loan funds, insurance firms, and savings institutions including the Post Office Savings Bank, which provided easy access through many branches for most of the population. A 1977 law formalized a reorganization of banks that had begun in the early 1970s. Three different categories of banks were established called internal banks, basic banks, and associated banks. In mid-1979 there were 160 basic banks and nine associated banks. The number of internal banks was unknown. In addition the Yugoslav Bank for International Cooperation was created in the late 1970s to provide a variety of services in foreign trade, including insurance and export credits for commodities and overseas construction contracts.

Internal banks are the financial counterpart to BOALs. One or more BOALs, enterprises, communities of interest, or other self-management organizations in the social sector (but not governments) may establish an internal bank to meet the banking needs of its founders. An internal bank keeps accounts and makes payments for its founders but may not extend credit. Internal banks maintain deposits in basic banks to effect transactions beyond the circle of founders, but deposits are not kept with the central bank and regulations are minimal. Internal banks were established to handle the greatly increased transactions and accounts resulting from the division of enterprises into BOALs so that BOALs would not have to turn to larger banks for services and credit. Internal banks are the financial decentralization that corresponds to BOALs on the production side.

Basic and associated banks perform the usual banking services, including financing trade and investments. Basic banks are formed by BOALs, internal banks, enterprises, communities of interest, and other social legal organizations (except governments). The founders have equal voice in management of basic banks regardless of the amount of funds contributed, and they usually have unlimited liability for the bank's obligations. Basic banks can unite to form an associated bank to handle such large transactions as major investments and foreign borrowing. In several instances, branches of the former commercial banks became basic banks that joined to become an associated bank using the same name it had as a commercial bank. The former branches operated with considerable autonomy in their locality as basic banks. Although a few banks operated throughout the country, many remained regional or smaller in their operations.

Banks were not formed to make a profit but to perform services, primarily for the members who retained favored access over nonmembers. By pooling resources of self-management associations, banks in theory could provide liquidity and investments to those in need without an autonomous intermediary. In fact, however, banks have been more important in channeling household savings to investments by self-management organizations. Since the mid-1960s banks have for the most part set interest rates. They have been low and usually negative in an inflationary situation, particularly in the 1970s when founders were the main borrowers as well as in control of management. Interest rates neither reflected the cost of money nor played much of a role in investment decisions. Banks did not carry out settlement of transactions; a separate nonfinancial, service agency maintained accounts for banks, making the necessary entries for payments.

The trend toward decentralization since the 1960s largely stripped the federal government of fiscal policy and dismantled other means of controlling aggregate demand. Monetary policy remained the basic tool. Several economists believed that the central bank had sufficient means to exert greater control over expansion of the money supply than were actually used. Part of the problem lay in the contradictory responsibilities assigned to the central bank—namely monetary stability and supplying the credit needs of the economy and government. Credit needs usually took precedence except when the highest Yugoslav leaders agreed that stabilization was a priority goal. The result was increasing inflation from 1965 onward.

Many factors affect the growth and control of inflation besides monetary policy. The Yugoslav price system has undergone various degrees of liberalization since the complete control exercised in the late 1940s, but it has never been wholly free of intervention by various levels of government, and considerable influence remained in 1980. Since the 1965 reforms an effort has been made to keep domestic prices close to world market prices, but some lagged more than others. In the 1970s the principle was established that when government intervention kept prices too low, that body was responsible for compensating the producing units. This was one of several measures enacted in the 1970s to force greater discipline in the economy and reduce the demand for credit.

In 1975 a law concerning payments between enterprises was introduced to control the growth of interenterprise credit that was outside of the banking system. Inefficient producers or those with cash flow problems often resorted to nonpayment of obligations to banks and suppliers, which had a snowball effect, particularly in times of credit contraction. Three times between 1971 and 1974 the large indebtedness of enterprises had to be converted into long-term credits or written off. Enterprises also failed to pay suppliers, thus extracting a form of credit. By late 1975 this interenterprise debt had reached 60 percent of the social sector GMP. This huge indebtedness was settled in various ways, including sanctions against enterprises that were unable to meet their obligations. Three hundred enterprises were undergoing liquidation in 1976, but because the system largely precluded lay-off of workers, most of the failing

Beach at Dubrovnik
Courtesy WORLD BANK PHOTO (Hilda Bijur)

enterprises were probably merged with more efficient producers. Since 1976 buyers have been required to settle obligations in fifteen days or provide the seller with a bill of exchange guaranteed by a bank; the bills of exchange can be discounted. The change did not rule out growth of interenterprise indebtedness, but it forced such credits into banking channels where they became subject to a degree of control.

A 1976 law stipulated the method by which enterprises computed income. The most important feature was that goods had to be sold and legal payment received to enter income computation. The intent was to stop the practice of including in the calculation of income the production of goods that were unmarketable or that had been sold to an enterprise that would not pay. In the same year, annual revaluation of fixed assets on which the legal depreciation rate applied became mandatory; previously, fixed assets had been revalued every five years. This measure was to ensure a higher savings rate by enterprises to increase the funds at their disposal.

A stabilization program in 1976 cut the increase of the cost of living from 25 percent in 1975 to 11.6 percent in 1976, but more expansionary policies in the next few years saw the inflation rate rise again. The cost-of-living index rose 15 percent in 1977, fell to 14 percent in 1978, and reached 20.4 percent in 1979. In 1980 the index rose 30 percent, compared to a planned increase of 17 percent.

Retail prices increased 39 percent when measured from December 1979 to December 1980. Domestic factors accounted for most of the inflation after 1975, but rising international prices, particularly for crude oil, also became important after 1978.

By 1981 increasing inflation indicated that the many reforms had not effectively dampened excessive demand. Yugoslav officials and economists noted many different problems with little agreement that one was more important. The problems included overly regionalistic approaches, underused industrial capacity, excessive investment, failure to complete projects on time, wage increases above that of productivity, failure to comply with social compacts on wage and price increases, and too great a share of investment going into nonproductive activities. In 1980 the federal government was more active, providing firm guidelines that were incorporated into social compacts to limit the increase of wages and salaries; the effect was to reduce real earnings in the social sector by 7 to 8 percent. In 1981 the federal government, in agreement with republics, imposed a 7 percent ceiling on price increases for goods and 5 percent for services during the year as a temporary palliative to slow the rise of prices. By 1981 there was wide agreement that inflation had to be controlled and that the 1981–85 plan would have to sacrifice some economic growth to achieve price stability.

Foreign Trade and Balance of Payments

Since World War II foreign trade has been important to the economy, primarily because of the need for imports. In the early years, most manufactured goods, including equipment for industrialization, had to be imported. As the domestic industrial base expanded, the import dependency shifted toward raw and semi-finished materials. In 1979 the ratio of imports to GDP was 21 percent, about the same as in 1965. Exports expanded and diversified along with the rest of the economy, but there was not a close relationship between economic growth and exports. For most of Yugoslavia's industry, exports were a minor part of activities, and rapid economic growth tended to diminish efforts to export. The ratio of exports to GDP generally declined, from 16 percent in 1965 to 10 percent in 1979. Balance of payments difficulties have been a recurrent problem, causing frequent policy shifts and a growing foreign indebtedness.

Until the early 1960s, Yugoslavia retained many of the features of the communist foreign trade system first established in the late 1940s. One feature was the separation of domestic prices from those in other countries through a variety of buffers. An implicit system of multiple exchange rates provided one of the buffers and also incentives for exports. Between 1954 and 1965, exports increased by an average of 11.7 percent a year, a rate higher than that of the economy as a whole. By 1965 foreign trade was liberalized; many of the interventions were abolished or reduced. The goal was alignment of domestic prices with international prices, integration of the country into the world economy, and eventually convertibility for the dinar. These goals still guided policy in the early 1980s.

In the late 1970s several laws altered the administrative structure for foreign trade. Communities of Interest for Foreign Economic Relations (CIFERs) were formed at the federal, republic, and province levels to bring together the earners and users of foreign exchange to plan and guide foreign economic activities. Among other duties, CIFERs are responsible for drafting regional and national balance of payments plans, allocating and regulating foreign borrowing rights, administering the export incentive program, and allocating and monitoring the use of foreign exchange. The changes were gradually effected during 1978, and before the CIFERs were fully staffed and functioning they were given the task of allocating foreign exchange during a period of shortage that apparently exceeded their capabilities.

Under the Yugoslav system the BOALs earning foreign exchange had rights to it. This included subsidiary suppliers down the line, who contributed to some degree to the export of goods and services. Retention rights were to be spelled out in self-management agreements between suppliers. Those that did not need or had excess foreign exchange would sell it to their regional CIFER to be purchased by an importer in need of exchange for an approved commodity. In a period of foreign exchange shortage, complaints have been voiced by suppliers of an unfair division. Complaints have also been voiced that suppliers were profiting from sales of unneeded foreign exchange, in effect introducing a variety of implicit foreign exchange rates. The system also tended to regionalize the balance of payments although there was some pooling of foreign exchange for needs of the federal government and regions that lacked sufficient foreign exchange earning power for necessary and planned imports.

Although foreign trade was liberalized after the mid-1960s, commercial policy was an important adjunct of economic development policy. During the 1970s exports were encouraged through subsidized credit and general and selective incentives, including retention rights to foreign exchange. Data were unavailable on changes introduced by CIFERs for export promotion. Imports were restricted in a number of ways, including some quotas and the necessity to procure a certification that domestic suppliers were not available. In 1979 the average, effective tariff rate on imports was about 22 percent, but this fell in 1980 when an import surcharge was abolished. Customs duties tended to be higher for finished goods than for raw and semi-finished materials, although after 1976 more protection was given to raw materials to encourage production while duties on machinery and equipment were lowered somewhat.

Foreign exchange shortages have imposed cuts in imports, such as in 1976 and 1980. Although the value of imports rose from US$14 billion in 1979 to US$15.1 billion in 1980, the volume decreased by more than 10 percent. A rise of over 70 percent in imported oil and gas prices was an important factor, adding US$1.2 billion to the import bill even though the volume was 5 to 6 percent less. In 1980 oil and gas imports cost US$3.1 billion, about one-fifth of total imports (see table 24, Appendix). Imports of raw and semifinished materials (including oil and gas) amounted to 62 percent of total imports, compared with 31 percent for finished manufactures (primarily machinery) and 7 percent for food and agricultural commodities. The reduced volume of imports created problems throughout the economy and particularly in industry.

The country's exports were diversified for its stage of development. In 1980 finished manufactured articles accounted for 45 percent of total exports. Other important categories were: semifinished materials, 22 percent; chemicals, 11 percent; agricultural materials, 11 percent; and raw materials, 7 percent. The total value of exports amounted to almost US$9 billion, a 32 percent nominal increase over 1979 resulting from the balance of payments pressures and successful efforts to increase exports (see table 25, Appendix).

Although exports increased sharply in 1980, their expansion has been substantially lower than imports since 1965 and a major factor contributing to the country's balance of payments constraints. Economists attributed the sluggish growth to several causes. Perhaps most important was the nature of exports for most Yugoslav enterprises, which focused primarily on production for the home market and only secondarily devoted attention to the potential export market. In addition official policy that encouraged additional processing for the greater value-added restricted growth of exports of raw materials, partly minerals and metals, to Western Europe. During the 1970s Yugoslavia had some success increasing exports of heavy electrical equipment, transport equipment, wood products such as furniture, and selected items of clothing and footwear to Western Europe but less success in other products compared with other developing countries. Specific policies adopted by the EEC may have restrained Yugoslav exports to these countries as the Yugoslavs claimed, but it would not explain the inability to increase exports to the rest of Western Europe. Yugoslavia had more success expanding exports to Eastern Europe, particularly after the mid-1970s, and to developing countries over a wide range of manufactured goods.

Most of Yugoslavia's foreign trade is with industrialized countries. Those in the Organisation for Economic Co-operation and Development (OECD), which included nearly all of the major noncommunist industrial powers, accounted for 53 percent of imports and 37 percent of exports in 1980. The bulk of that trade was with EEC countries (see table 26, Appendix). Trade with the United States only amounted to US$1 billion of imports and US$400 million of exports. In the 1970s trade with communist countries, primarily the

Soviet Union and Eastern Europe, grew substantially, and in several years after 1974 these countries were the largest market for Yugoslav exports. Trade with developing countries remained relatively minor in spite of the rise in value of oil imports.

The slow growth of exports has caused a worsening balance of payments situation for the country. Several times during the 1970s (in 1972, 1975–76, and 1979–81) balance of payments constraints forced a slowdown in domestic activities. Once the immediate situation eased, however, officials returned to the expansionary policies of the past. The 1976–80 five-year plan attempted structural adjustments to reduce permanently the import dependency and to expand exports, but it was far less successful than planned. By mid-1979 Yugoslavia again faced a very difficult situation in its international payments, one that could persist for several years.

Although the trade balance was critical to the long-term balance of payments, services also played an important role. In fact after 1977 the inflow of service payments (but not on a net basis) exceeded the value of exports. The most important inflow was remittances from workers abroad, reaching over US$4 billion in 1980. In spite of a declining number of workers in foreign countries, remittances continued to rise during the 1970s, but officials anticipated a drop in the 1980s. Tourism and transportation services were also important foreign exchange earners. Yugoslav contractors have won an increasing number of overseas construction contracts that added to the inflow of payments. The outflow of service payments was also growing, particularly personal remittances. Interest on the country's foreign debt increased from US$820 million in 1979 to nearly US$1.3 billion in 1980. Net service receipts in 1980 amounted to 62 percent of the trade deficit (see table 27, Appendix).

In most years of the 1970s and every year since 1976 the current balance of goods and services was in deficit. The size of the deficit was increasing, amounting to US$1 billion in 1975 and US$3.7 billion in 1979. The Yugoslavs have received long-term credits for development as well as other international assistance from governments and institutions. The World Bank (see Glossary) has been a major lender, financing a variety of projects in the economy. Increasingly in the late 1970s, however, the country has had to resort to commercial borrowing at world interest rates. Gross medium- and long-term capital flows averaged US$2.6 billion between 1976 and 1979; they rose to perhaps US$3.6 billion in 1980. Short-term borrowing was erratic but increased by nearly US$300 million in 1980. The country's external medium- and long-term debt exceeded US$13 billion, and the short-term debt was about US$650 million at the end of 1980. Debt servicing (interest and principal) amounted to over US$3.2 billion in 1980, about 20 percent of exchange earnings from exports of goods and services. The situation was precarious; at the beginning of 1981 official foreign exchange reserves were sufficient to pay for only about one month of imports of goods and services.

The 1981–85 Plan

The outlines of the 1981–85 five-year plan available in mid-1981 reflected the seriousness of the internal and external economic situation. Officials were forced to break with traditional thinking and scale down the pace of development in order to make adjustments in the economy. Some of the target annual growth rates (in real terms) over the five years included: social product, 4.5 percent; agriculture, 4.5 percent; industry, 5 percent; fixed investments, 1.5 percent; imports, 1 percent; and exports, 8 percent. By reducing domestic demand and shifting resources to exports, the plan expected to bring the rate of inflation and the deficit in the balance of payments to manageable proportions by 1985.

Although targets have been substantially reduced compared with earlier plans, the 1981–85 plan was ambitious in several respects under present conditions. Holding imports to a 1 percent increase a year (in real terms), if successful, will require delicate management so as not to disrupt industrial production and not to starve it of necessary equipment for technical advances. Expanding exports by 8 percent a year could prove difficult if economic conditions in OECD countries stagnate because the world situation has a pronounced impact on Yugoslavia's foreign sales. Moreover a complicated policy mix will be required to encourage enterprises to think permanently in terms of foreign markets. Reducing demand by cutting government consumption in half and fixed investments even more will require a degree of discipline hard to achieve in the country's decentralized management structure. The plan also called for a 40 percent reduction in personal consumption and nearly a 50 percent reduction in real disposable income, as well as substantially lower fringe benefits for social sector employees. The changes in workers' organizations during the 1970s were intended to introduce them to the trade-offs necessary for economic growth.

The Yugoslavs were proud of and worked to make their system of workers' self-management effective, not hesitating to criticize their own creations and make frequent changes. In 1981 efforts were still ongoing to staff and make effective the changes introduced during the 1970s. The plan period to 1985 could well be a severe test of the dedication to self-management and building a unified nation. A united effort and skillful economic management will be required to bring the country's economic problems under control. The 1981–85 plan requires belt tightening by nearly everybody. Major miscalculations or lack of cooperation by self-management organizations would likely impinge on real incomes and consumption. If such should happen, the reaction of the population, or at least parts of it, is open to question, for the rapid economic expansion and rising standards of living over the past three decades had presented such a problem only for brief periods.

*   *   *

Widespread interest in Yugoslavia's economic system has produced numerous books and articles. A basic study is *Yugoslavia, Self-Management Socialism and the Challenges of Development,* written by Martin Schrenk and a team from the World Bank. Other recent books include John H. Moore's *Growth With Self-Management: Yugoslav Industrialization, 1952–1975;* Ellen Turkish Comisso's *Workers' Control under Plan and Market: Implications of Yugoslav Self-Management;* Jaroslav Vanek's *The Labor-Managed Economy;* and Branko Horvat's *The Yugoslav Economic System: The First Labor Managed Economy in the Making.* Briefer studies include Laura D'Andrea Tyson's *The Yugoslav Economic System and Its Performance in the 1970s* and OECD's annual surveys *Yugoslavia.* The Yugoslav government publishes statistical data annually in *Statistical Pocket-Book of Yugoslavia* (in English) and in the more comprehensive *Statisticki Godisnjak Jugoslavije,* which in a separate volume provides an English translation for the tables. (For further information see Bibliography.)

Chapter 4. Government and Politics

Josip Broz Tito—May 1892 to May 1980

THE STRUCTURE OF GOVERNMENT and the character of politics in contemporary Yugoslavia have been shaped in large part by conflicts arising out of the coincidence of ethnic and religious divisions in the population with differences in the level of economic development of the regions, and by the simultaneous commitment of the communist political leadership to maintaining national unity and constructing the "self-managed" social order called for by the official ideology. Each of these factors is reflected in both the formal, constitutional system of government and the actual process of political decisionmaking. Nationality conflict and interregional economic conflicts have driven Yugoslav political development and, especially, the development of formal institutions and organizations, in the direction of decentralization. The dual commitments of the party, however, have led it to play a changing role in Yugoslav politics. At times it has pursued policies that reinforced the centrifugal impetus of nationality and regional conflict, and at these times the society has been plunged into conflict and even crisis. But at other times the party has been a strong, integrative force; and when it has, Yugoslav government and politics have been stable.

For most of the 1970s the integrative power of the party was largely a product of the personal authority and activity of President Josip Broz Tito and the cohesiveness of the older generation of political leaders he gathered around him in the highest organs of the state and party. The deaths of Edvard Kardelj in February 1979 and Tito in May 1980, however, marked the beginning of a period during which that generation of leaders will be disappearing from the scene. The generation coming to power in the early 1980s lacked the long, common experience of underground revolutionary activity, wartime resistance and revolution, and resistance to Soviet domination that unified these older leaders. The continuing stability of the system in the post-Tito period, therefore, will depend on the ability of the new leaders to maintain political unity despite the nationality differences, regional economic conflicts, and personal political ambitions that divide them.

The Development of the Contemporary Political Order

Constitutions play several roles in Yugoslav politics. They are intended by the leadership to provide normative guidelines for the ongoing development of the political order. As one parliamentary functionary involved in the drafting of the most recent reform put it during an interview conducted in December 1980, constitutions in Yugoslavia "reflect our hopes for the future." At the same time, however, this functionary pointed out that "we make a constitution for real life, that is why it is not very general or abstract, [why it is]

171

more concrete and more detailed." Constitutions and constitutional reforms in Yugoslavia thus also codify practices that have emerged in the period since the previous reform and are used by the leadership to bring old organizational and institutional formulas no longer appropriate to these practices into line with them. In addition to these practical roles, constitutions in Yugoslavia also serve important symbolic functions.

Constitutional reform has provided the communist political leadership with an important mechanism for responding to the pressures inherent in a multinational society. Since the establishment of the state in 1918, the structure of government, the procedural provisions for decisionmaking, and even the delineation and status of the territorial units of government themselves have been subjects of political conflict and have complicated the drafting of constitutions. The communist political leadership has manipulated one or more of these elements in the successive constitutions it has prepared since coming to power in an effort to mitigate inter-nationality conflict by fulfilling as many of the national (see Glossary) aspirations of each group as is compatible with survival of Yugoslavia as a unified state and maintenance of control over the state by the League of Communists of Yugoslavia (LCY). The constitutional reforms adopted since 1966 have granted progressively greater autonomous power and authority to the republics and provinces and expanded their role in the federal decisionmaking process. They have also incorporated important concessions to the distinct ethnic identities of the population in each region, including the granting of a full range of linguistic and cultural rights. (As used herein, region means the six republics and the two autonomous provinces; see fig. 1.) Moreover the formal political order in each region is defined by a separate republic or provincial constitution that emphasizes the distinct national identity of the region and the attributes of full statehood enjoyed by it.

The symbolic importance of constitutions—both federal and regional—in Yugoslav politics has also made them the continuing focus of political struggle. At each stage, constitutional reform has reflected the political balance in the party leadership between center and region; between supporters of more authoritarian and more liberal visions of society; and between supporters of more radical, ideologically motivated change and pragmatists. Thus while the 1946 constitution reflected the wholesale adoption of Stalinist formulas for the organization of the state, the Fundamental Law—in effect, a new constitution—adopted in 1953 reflected the establishment of a more liberal, anti-Stalinist leadership in the party. Following soon after the momentous Sixth Party Congress in 1952, at which that leadership—largely under the inspiration of Milovan Djilas—officially renounced direct party control over society in favor of a more distinct separation between the party as an organization and the government and significantly decentralized the party itself, the 1953 constitutional reform increased the power and authority of the federal and local governments and introduced partial guarantees of individual civil liberties.

The mid-1950s was a period of partial recentralization in the party. The reforms of 1952–53 had introduced substantial confusion among the rank-and-file members and resulted in a significant weakening of the organizational coherence of the party and its influence over society. Beginning in mid-1953, therefore, Tito and other members of the leadership began to have second thoughts about the pace of reform. They initiated a series of measures designed to restore party discipline and affirm the continuing political power and authority of the party, including the January 1954 condemnation of Djilas for deviationism. This recentralization of power did not, however, deter the leadership from continuing to construct a more liberal political order through constitutional reform.

The drafting of an entirely new constitution began in the late 1950s and was completed in 1962. Formally promulgated in 1963, the new constitution introduced important changes in the organization and operation of the political system. The Federal Assembly, or parliament, was completely reorganized. Created in 1946 as a bicameral body with a Federal Chamber and a Chamber of Nationalities modeled on the Soviet Union's Supreme Soviet, the Federal Assembly was reorganized in 1953. The Chamber of Nationalities became a component part of the Federal Chamber; its members were to participate in the Federal Chamber on an equal basis, but they also retained the authority to convene separately to discuss and, if necessary, veto any legislation affecting the nations (see Glossary) and nationalities of Yugoslavia. In its place as the second house of parliament, the 1953 reform created a Chamber of Producers, composed of direct representatives of the working class employed in the various sectors of the economy, introducing an element of corporatism into the system of political representation. The 1963 constitution applied this corporatist-like principle of representation far more comprehensively to the federal parliament. It divided the Federal Assembly into five chambers: a Federal Chamber, having general competence; an Economic Chamber, which was the former Chamber of Producers under a new name; an Education-Cultural Chamber and a Social-Health Chamber, each composed of representatives of workers in their respective sectors; and an Organizational-Political Chamber, composed of representatives of workers in administrative positions in the economy and society including, of course, political workers. The Chamber of Nationalities was retained as a component part of the Federal Chamber.

The structure of the Assembly reflected the belief of those who drafted the constitution that Yugoslavia had overcome the divisions of nationality and was on the road to establishing a truly socialist order determined by the common class interests of workers. Inherent in this structure was the recognition that workers who were engaged in the same economic activity in each region might share particular interests that differed from those of workers engaged in another activity. But those who drafted the constitution were confident that these could be mediated by the Federal Chamber, which shared the decisionmaking authority of each of the specialized chambers in an arrangement that made the Assembly an effectively bicameral parliament.

The 1963 constitution also altered the status and organization of the Federal Executive Council (the executive agency of the government). The president of the republic (Tito) was no longer also president of the council. Instead, the president of the republic nominated a candidate for president of the council who in turn nominated the other members of the council. The council as a whole was then elected by the Federal Chamber of the Assembly. These changes broke the direct political link between the party and the government and established the council as a classic parliamentary government. At this time the council and the Assembly began to take a far more active role in the preparation and debate of federal policies. Although the LCY continued to determine the agenda of government activity and the broad outlines of policy, the constitutional reform of 1963 created institutional channels of access for a broad range of self-managing (see Glossary) interests to participate in and influence the formulation of federal policies.

The 1963 constitution was the product of a confident and, by and large, united leadership. Its preparation was overseen by members of the then-dominant liberal coalition in the party leadership, including Kardelj, the party's chief theoretician, and Vladimir Bakaric, the Croatian party chief. It was written with the assistance of liberal legal scholars and political scientists such as Jovan Djordjevic, the Western-trained Serbian legal scholar who headed the most important of the working groups that actually drafted the constitution. The liberal proclivities of its authors were clearly evident in the extensive human and civil rights provisions and the unprecedented, for communist systems, introduction of a system of constitutional courts to protect those rights.

There were, however, those among the leadership who opposed the liberalization of the political system advanced by this coalition. The most prominent opponent of liberalization was then party secretary Aleksandar Rankovic. As secretary for organizational affairs and de facto head of the secret police, Rankovic was perfectly placed to ensure the preservation of an informal, centralized system of command and influence inside the party itself, despite the formal decentralization that had taken place since 1953, and to extend that system into other, ostensibly self-managing, nonparty organizations. Nevertheless he did not actively oppose the constitutional reforms advocated by the liberals, probably because of a belief that the formal institutions of the state were not as important for the determination of policy as the informal organizationl network he commanded. His only intervention in the drafting process came in the final stages when he secured the creation of an office of vice president of the republic, which he could then occupy, thereby giving formal sanction to his informal status as heir apparent to Tito.

Debate over the economic reforms of the early 1960s and over a major economic reform of 1965 revealed clearly the deep political divisions between the liberal majority in the party leadership, led by Kardelj and Bakaric, and the conservative "opposition" led by Rankovic. The debate over establishing a modified market economy revealed the mutually reinforcing character of conflicts based on regional economic interests, ideological differences, and ultimately nationality. The 1965 decision to establish a modified market economy linked the conflict between regional economic interests to the ideological conflict between "conservatives," who viewed centralized allocation as the most appropriate means of achieving redistribution and equalization of wealth to which the party was committed, and "liberals," who acknowledged that the operation of a market system would at first encourage greater investment in the already-developed regions but argued that this would lead later to investment in, and the development of, the underdeveloped regions.

This conflict, in turn, was linked to a broader conflict between two visions of the role of the party in society. Those in favor of centralized allocation tended also to favor direct party control, characteristic of the pre-1952 period, while those in favor of reliance on the market tended to favor the less coercive vision of the party embodied in the decisions of the Sixth Party Congress. Not surprisingly, the leaders of the lesser developed regions mostly were numbered among the "conservatives," while the "liberals" came primarily from the more developed regions. The fact that the republics and provinces are generally viewed as "national homelands" and that their populations historically have been mutually antagonistic only made the apparent conflict between the commitments to redistribution and economic reform even more difficult to resolve.

The central leadership was in fact divided between the so-called liberal and conservative elements for most of the 1950s and early 1960s. During this time Tito played a central role in determining party policy. Although he supported measures aimed at decentralization of the economy and reduction of the state's role in the self-managing economy, he continued to support the more authoritative and centralistic vision of the party held by the leaders who opposed those reforms. With his support, the liberal majority in the leadership was powerful enough to win the adoption of specific reform measures, including the 1963 constitution and the 1965 establishment of a "socialist market economy." But the liberals could not effectively implement those measures or turn real power over to the institutions of the state as long as their opponents retained control over party personnel policies and the instruments of coercion and continued to enjoy Tito's support. Indeed, until the conservative opposition was defeated, the party leadership continued to decide the most important issues—meaning the potentially most explosive ones—behind closed doors and to impose the solutions they devised on the formal decisionmaking bodies of the state.

By 1966 the conflict between the liberal majority and the conservative opposition had assumed the dimensions of what Tito himself called "a struggle for power" within the LCY. The liberals defeated Rankovic and his supporters only when a set of fortuitous circumstances allowed them to collect evidence of widespread abuses by the secret police under Rankovic's control. These included wiretapping and surveillance of members of the leadership, including Tito himself, which had suppressed open discussion and planted mistrust in the party heirarchy. The impact of these revelations was enormous. Tito remarked to the Central Committee assembled to oust Rankovic and his supporters in July 1966 that he was reminded "a little of what it was like at one time under Stalin."

The combined impact of the economic reforms and the sharp curtailment of secret police activity that followed the ouster of Rankovic transformed political life in Yugoslavia. The autonomous decisionmaking power of self-managing enterprises were expanded, and they, as well as all other organizations and institutions, enjoyed greater latitude for activity free from direct control from the center or police surveillance. This permitted the rapid emergence of social forces that heretofore had been repressed (see Peoples of Yugoslavia, ch. 2). Changes in the internal organization and operation of the LCY itself increased the political significance of self-management enterprises.

As organizational secretary of the party, Rankovic had controlled from Belgrade appointments of cadres to middle and lower level positions in the regional party apparatuses. After his ouster the central leadership, composed in large part of individuals whose political bases lay in the regions, transferred much of this power—as well as authority over the regional security police organizations—to the regional party organizations The power of the regional leaderships vis-à-vis the center was significantly enhanced. At the same time, however, the liberal coalition, now squarely in control at the center, adopted a system for the election by secret ballot of the members of local party organizations. These local party organizations in turn rapidly assumed increased powers. They began to nominate candidates for positions to which individuals had previously been appointed, and a rapid democratization of inner-party life ensued. As a result party leaders at all levels increasingly became subject to pressures from the members who elected them.

The effects of these organizational and procedural modifications were reinforced by changes in party membership. New members were being enrolled from among the ranks of workers and managers with experience in self-management. Older members with more conservative orientations were being expelled or were resigning. Democratization of party elections, therefore, made possible the election of lower and mid-level party functionaries who had little if any prior experience in party work. These new functionaries and

President Tito in his office
Courtesy Embassy of
Yugoslavia, Washington

the new general membership were unwilling to accept restraints on free discussion within the party that were absent outside of it. Indeed, the LCY decisionmaking process quickly became characterized by open debate and disagreement—even within the central and regional leaderships.

Democratization of party life was paralleled by democratization of political life in general. Prior to 1966 the party had usurped much of the authority and responsibility of parliamentary bodies and other social institutions. Party functionaries no longer were permitted to hold positions in the republic or federal administrations at the same time, and the professional staffs of these bodies no longer were permitted to perform party functions. These were assumed by the specialized services of the central party organs. Paradoxically, this resulted in an increase in the number of cadres working in the central party apparatus at a time when the independent power and authority of the central party was on the decline.

The withdrawal of direct party supervision over the operation of state institutions permitted these institutions increasing autonomy. Already rooted in local territorial and functional constituencies, the federal and republican parliaments quickly became arenas for the expression of conflicting local interest. Rather than providing an institutional "transmission belt" for the implementation of party policies, the parliamentary system rapidly was transformed into a channel for the expression of local and popular demands on the government and the party.

The post-Rankovic period was characterized by the general organizational expansion of society. The provisions of the 1963 constitution guaranteeing individual liberties gained new life. Small groups of citizens undertook organized social and economic activities free from close party or police supervision. The communications media expanded dramatically with the establishment or expansion of regional newspapers and periodicals and radio and television stations, especially in the languages of the national minorities. All these institutions and organizations—as well as self-managing economic enterprises—enjoyed greater autonomy from direct police and party supervision than ever before. With this autonomy came greater freedom of expression, and the public media soon became the site of political debates even more wide-ranging and unrestricted than those taking place at the same time in the party.

Having renounced simple repression as a tool for the regulation of political conflict and having permitted the rise of relatively autonomous social forces, the communist leaders now faced the task of reconciling conflicting social forces not fully under their control. This was made more difficult by the fact that all but the very highest party leaders, such as Tito, Kardelj, and Bakaric, were becoming increasingly dependent on the support of the broader party membership in their respective republics and provinces, and especially dependent on the middle and lower level party cadres who staffed major social and political institutions and were key actors in party elections. Without their support it would be impossible for any regional party leader to implement policy and difficult for him to retain his position. The party masses in each of the regions, in turn, were now coming more strongly under the influence of social forces and institutions outside the party. This influence was difficult to break—even through the manipulation of party personnel policies—and it made individual Communists more difficult to mobilize on behalf of party policy.

The constellation of social and political forces that emerged in the post-Rankovic period proved the assumptions of the liberal party leadership about the relative strength of nationality and class interests to have been badly mistaken. The late 1960s saw an exponential increase in the frequency and intensity of political conflicts linking ethnic, regional, and economic issues and dividing the country and its communist political leadership into distinct ethnoterritorial blocs. Milestones in the escalation of these tensions were marked by the conflict in late 1966 between Bosnia (Bosnia and Hercegovina) and the other republics over the federal government's division of funding for aid to the underdeveloped regions. Bosnia called the Chamber of Nationalities of the Federal Assembly into substantive session for the first time in its history in order to reverse the decision. This set in motion once again the process of constitutional reform: the highly nationalistic "Declaration on the Name and Position of the Croatian Literary Language" adopted by a group of Croatian cultural organizations in March 1967, and the equally provocative response by Serbian writers broke a long-standing truce imposed by the party leadership in the 1950s on the explosive question of Serb-Croat relations. In the fall of 1968 there occurred a series of major nationalist (see Glossary) demonstrations by Albanians in Kosovo and northwestern Macedonia, which included demands for the separation of ethnically Albanian territories from Yugoslavia and their attachment to Albania. There followed in August 1969 a series of political protests and demonstrations in Slovenia, prompted by the apparent denial by the Federal Executive Council of funding for road-building projects in that republic, but which rapidly escalated to include nationalist and separatist demands and placed the question of relations between the regions and the federation on the political agenda. While these conflicts were the most dramatic manifestations of rising levels of hostility, they were by no means the only ones. Indeed, the society as a whole experienced a dramatic resurgence of conflict during this period, dominated by the national question. And these conflicts hastened the rapid "federalization" of the party that had begun with the ouster of Rankovic and gave rise to the genuine "federalization" of power and authority in the state.

The party leadership agreed in November 1967 that, in keeping with the statute adopted at the Eighth Party Congress in 1964, the next LCY congress would be convened after the republican party congresses. Although the 1964 statute had preserved the political primacy of the all-Yugoslav congress, the leadership now decided that the LCY congress was to develop "a synthesis of the results of the congresses of the Leagues of Communists of the republics" and establish this synthesis as a guideline for the central leadership. Moreover in mid-1968 they restructured the central party organs. A fifty-member Presidium was established as the main leadership organ, to be composed of an equal number of members elected by the party congress in each republic, rather than appointed by the center. These changes meant that the members of central party organs—with a few important exceptions—would owe their allegiance to the republican and provincial organizations that had placed them there, not to their colleagues at the center. This altered the nature of the decisionmaking process within the political elite. It very rapidly came to be the case that "important decisions no longer were made at the federal summit but rather [by] direct contacts among representatives of the republics—in the form of bilateral and multi-lateral interpersonal visits and discussions of republican State and Party delegations." By the time of the Ninth Party Congress in March 1969, there no longer existed an independent "party center" other than President Tito, "who all the more frequently received delegations of the republics for political discussions and in this way created a platform for political decisions."

Federalization of the party was accompanied by the simultaneously increasing influence of republic and provincial representatives

179

in the government and parliament. The Bosnian initiative in 1966 resulted in the adoption in 1967 of a series of amendments that enlarged the role of the Chamber of Nationalities, and thereby the republics and provinces represented in it, in the federal decision-making process. The chamber was now required to meet separately to consider social plans, all bills affecting the revenue of the regions, and all matters heretofore in the independent jurisdiction of the Federal Chamber, making it in all but formal organization a separate chamber of the Assembly.

As the Chamber of Nationalities expanded its domain of competence and became more a creature of the republics, the need for the government to achieve interrepublican agreement on federal policy prior to its submission to the parliament also increased. Consequently the Federal Executive Council introduced the practice of holding "consultative meetings" with representatives of the executive councils of the republics and provinces to determine the position to be taken by the federal government on the "more important socioeconomic questions." These meetings quickly assumed such importance that "not a single more significant issue could be presented to the council before it had been discussed at a consultative meeting." This practice became institutionalized after 1969 with the establishment of a Coordinating Commission within the council, composed of representatives of the federal, republican, and provincial executive councils.

The increased control of the republics over federal policymaking sharply reduced the ability of the government to make decisions. During 1967 and 1968 enormous problems began to build up in the economy as the federal government, which still retained important monetary, fiscal, and taxing powers required to implement policy, was prevented from acting because of disagreement among the republics over the substance of the policy to be pursued in each area. The increasingly important role of banks in the economy in general, the investment policies of banks and governments, the foreign currency exchange systems, and tax policies all became the subjects of interrepublican bargaining and conflict (see Role of Government, ch. 3). At the same time growing economic problems were generating increasing dissatisfaction in the population.

In June 1968 Belgrade University students staged a week-long strike. The strike focused on the problems of growing unemployment, increasing economic inequality and materialism, and the frustrations of the younger generation over the logjam in career advancement caused by the near monoply of executive and professional positions enjoyed by the cadres of the revolution, who were still only middle-aged and sometimes poorly qualified. The strike received support from the provincial campuses of that university, and from the students of other universities, including Sarajevo and Zagreb universities. The student demonstrators' socialist orientation toward these problems was little consolation to the political leadership faced with the task of solving them.

The outside threat posed by the Soviet invasion of Czechoslovakia in August 1968 served to calm internal Yugoslav quarreling—but not completely. Throughout 1967 and 1968 and into 1969, the Croatian language issue simmered. Nationalists on both sides of the issue continued to exploit the freedom of action that came with the post-Rankovic democratization of society (see Peoples of Yugoslavia, ch. 2). The same issues raised by the "declaration" continued to be raised by Croat writers at conferences and meetings, and they continued to be answered by their Serb counterparts. These exchanges simply remained off the front pages of the major newspapers. In the fall of 1968 large-scale riots broke out among the Albanian populations of several cities in Kosovo and northwestern Macedonia.

One of the more moderate demands of the Albanian demonstrators was for elevation of Kosovo's status within the Yugoslav federation to that of a socialist republic. This demand was at least partially accommodated in another series of constitutional amendments adopted in December 1968. The appellation "Socialist" was added to that of "Autonomous Province" for both Vojvodina and Kosovo, and the basic legal order of each of these regions was now to be established by a constitution separate from that for the Republic of Serbia. In addition ethnic groups with the official status of nationalities or "national minorities" (Albanians and Hungarians among them) were granted the same rights—including the use of their native languages in public institutions—as the "nations" of Yugoslavia. Both socialist autonomous provinces, however, remained constituent units of the Republic of Serbia.

These changes were adopted largely in order to continue the process started by the 1967 amendments—that is, to strengthen the control of the republics and provinces over the federal decisionmaking process. They elevated the Chamber of Nationalities to a fully independent body and made it, instead of the Federal Chamber, the chamber of general competence. All federal legislation now had to be approved by the Chamber of Nationalities.

These changes led to public discussion in Yugoslavia of whether one country could be considered a "confederation." Officially this view was rejected because the amendments had not altered the rules for decisionmaking within the chamber. It continued to make decisions on the basis of a majority vote of all its members. A realistic Yugoslav analyst, however, viewed the operation of the Federal Assembly quite differently. The author of an empirical study of the operation of the Assembly acknowledged in 1969 that it was "hardly likely" that delegates in the chamber would act independently of the other delegates from their republic or province, and he pointed out that they were also likely to be under the strong influence of their respective regional leaderships.

The inability of the party and government to forge interrepublican agreements on specific policy issues led by default to increased activity on the part of the reorganized federal parliament. Following the 1967 elections, debates and discussions both in the committees of the

Assembly and on the floor of the chambers themselves became increasingly lively. Not only the volume, but also the scope of Assembly work increased. The increased activity of the Chamber of Nationalities suggested to some foreign observers at that time that Yugoslavia was moving in the direction of parliamentarism, but hindsight suggests that it would have been more accurate to suggest that the Yugoslav state was moving toward *immobilisme*. The 1967 and 1968 amendments rendered the parliament—through the Chamber of Nationalities—susceptible to the same stalemating forces that were affecting the party and government.

By late 1968 and early 1969 the need for authoritative political leadership, immune from particularistic pressures and able to provide sober judgment, was clear. It also was clear that such leadership could be provided only by a revitalized central party organ. On the eve of the Ninth Party Congress in March 1969, however, it seemed unlikely that such an organ would be created. As the leadership had decided earlier, each of the regional party organizations had convened its own congress in advance of the federal one and had elected a certain number of its members to serve on the central organs of the LCY. Those elected to membership on the central Presidium—which was supposed to serve as an authoritative, policy-making body for the entire party—generally were not the most authoritative and powerful members of the republican organizations. Those members were elected instead to positions within their own republican party organizations. If the Ninth Party Congress had unfolded as planned, that is, had these personnel assignments simply been "verified," there no longer would have been any central party organ with even a pretense to authority over the regional organizations. Moreover there apparently would have been no formal executive body at the center of the party. The small Secretariat of the Presidium envisaged in July 1968 had been eliminated from the draft party statutes submitted to the congress. Precisely because of this, Tito acted on his own initiative to construct a more authoritative central party organ.

Immediately prior to the congress, Tito held a series of private "consultations" with the leaders of the republican party organizations. Despite certain "reservations" expressed by several of the regional leaderships, it was agreed to create a new Executive Bureau of the Presidium, composed of "leading comrades" from all of the regions. This step was necessary, Tito later explained to the congress, because "the new central leadership must be stronger in composition in order to be able to ensure the unity of the League of Communists and its authority." The fifty-two-member Presidium elected by the republican, provincial, and Yugoslav People's Army (YPA) party organizations was too large and its members were too strongly subordinated to their republican and provincial constituencies to do the job. It was necessary also "because the League of Communists needs continuity. Some of us already have gotten on considerably in years, and in the highest leadership continuity has to be ensured, the experience of the older must be transferred to the younger." Consequently the new Executive Bureau of the Presidium would include "some younger comrades" and be composed of "two outstanding leaders from each republic and one from [each of] the autonomous provinces . . . together with the President of the LCY."

Tito's action required the republican party leaderships to decide in advance of the federal congress both the kind of role they wished to see this new body play and who would be selected to serve on it. The role envisaged for the new Executive Bureau varied from republic to republic and, as a result, so did the nature of the members selected to serve on it. Both the Croatian and Bosnian parties selected their two most powerful leaders to serve on the Executive Bureau—their party presidents and secretaries. The Macedonian party—the League of Communists of Macedonia—selected its president and a Macedonian who had spent his entire career in the federal party. The Slovenian, Serbian, and Montenegrin parties selected neither their presidents nor their secretaries. These parties selected individuals associated primarily with the federal party apparatus rather than the republics. The only exception was the selection by the Slovenian party of then relatively unknown Stane Dolanc to accompany Kardelj into the Executive Bureau.

Clearly the new Executive Bureau was better suited than the full Presidium to fulfill the role of an integrative, leading organ for the LCY. It was smaller; it immediately enjoyed enormous prestige as the apparent institutional successor to Tito; its members were released from other responsibilities and could focus on the solution of divisive political problems; and it was to make decisions as an independent, collegial body, taking into account the interests of all the republics and provinces. But political realities prevented the bureau from providing the unifying force for which it had been created. Membership was determined not from the center, but by nomination of the regional party organizations. Members could not simultaneously hold positions in their respective republican and provincial party organizations because the bureau, which was to meet at least weekly to discuss and dispose of political problems, required them to remain in Belgrade. This severely restricted the ability of even the most powerful bureau members to influence, let alone control, the course of events within their own republics, and required the politically less powerful members to be at least as responsive to their respective regional party organizations as to the views of their colleagues on the bureau. Moreover the responsibilities of the bureau were so broad that almost every divisive issue fell within its domain. As a result other institutions and organizations that in the past had acted to control conflicts within their own territories or organizations began to defer action until the issue had been discussed in the Executive Bureau. Consequently the bureau rapidly became overworked, and conflicts often reached serious proportions before they could be resolved.

183

Only a few months after the creation of the bureau, an interregional conflict of crisis proportions broke out over a Federal Executive Council decision not to include a Slovenian road-building project as part of a package of such proposals for funding by the World Bank (see Glossary). News of the council's decision provoked angry demonstrations in the affected Slovenian communities. In a matter of days demonstrations spread across Slovenia. The demands raised at the demonstrations escalated and widened to include nationalist-separatist demands. Official Slovenian governmental bodies joined in the protest, and the Slovenian party leadership became caught between its inclination to support the central decision and defend Yugoslav political integrity on the one hand, and the obvious need to demonstrate its responsiveness to, and thereby defuse the outrage of what was its constituency, on the other. Matters rapidly worsened, however, as leaderships of the other republics began to pass judgment on the events in Slovenia. While the Croatian republican leadership openly supported the demonstrators' claims that the decision had not been made according to the prevailing rule of interregional consensus, the Macedonian leadership condemned the protests and called for immediate action by the central party leadership to establish order.

By the time the Executive Bureau convened in August, it was clear that the Federal Executive Council had, in fact, observed all established rules of decisionmaking and that the failure in this case lay with the Slovenian regional leadership for having failed to support the council's decisions by explaining matters to its constitutents. The bureau issued a low-key condemnation of the Slovenian events and simply urged the federal and regional governments to coordinate their actions more closely so as to avoid such "communications failures" in the future. The damage to interregional relationships was already done, however. In the course of the crisis, heated criticism of the relationship between center and region had been raised, and pointed questions about the division of authority between the federation and the regions had been put forward, all with the apparent sanction of the Slovenian regional leadership. And these questions were underlined by the continuing inability of the government to reach decisions in areas ostensibly in the autonomous jurisdiction of the federation in the face of ongoing interregional conflicts in the consultative bodies of the council and in the committees of the Chamber of Nationalities.

The interregional deadlock in the federal decisionmaking process prompted two distinct reactions in the leadership. The Croatian party leadership apparently decided late in 1969 to pursue the solution of pressing economic problems on a republic rather than federal basis. This strategy was unveiled at a January 1970 Croatian Central Committee meeting at which then Croatian party president Savka Dabcevic-Kucar launched an all-out attack against "unitarism"— the insistence on central power at the expense of the republics and provinces. She proclaimed that regional nationalism of the sort that had provoked recent crises was no longer the main obstacle to progress. Rather that obstacle was now unitarism; and she subtly equated unitarism with Serbian nationalism—historically associated with a strong centralized Yugoslav state and hostile to the weakening of that state to accommodate the national aspirations of the other Yugoslav peoples. Despite certain reservations expressed by Bakaric, she argued that the Croatian party had cut chauvinistic, Croatian political nationalism off at its roots and that its main organizational base—the historical Croatian cultural organization, the Matica Hrvatska—represented a potential partner, rather than an enemy, in the struggle to resolve Croatian social and economic problems.

This meeting marked the beginning of a concerted assault by the Croatian leadership on the powers of the federation. They attempted to reduce those powers not by a direct attack on the federation itself, but rather by pushing through changes in federal cadres policies and decisionmaking processes intended to strengthen the ability of a single republic to prevent the federation from taking any action to which it was opposed. They won a partial victory in April when the central party Presidium accepted the principles of unanimity in federal decisionmaking (officially called the "harmonization" of views), regional parity in federal representation, and regional control over appointments to federal positions. And they won again in the fall when Tito proposed the creation of a new collective state presidency composed of "the best people from the republics" to serve as an arena for high-level resolution of interregional conflicts over federal policy.

By suggesting the creation of a state presidency, Tito was in a sense recommending the separation of party and state that had been anticipated on the eve of the Ninth Party Congress almost two years earlier. In effect he was attempting to ease interregional conflicts by resuming the process of reform. But by now the Croation leadership had committed itself to a solution based on maximizing the autonomy of that republic in all areas, and the idea of an authoritative federal institution independent of regional influences or control was seen by them not as a concession to reform but as an attempt to recentralize power.

Creation of the collective Presidency did suggest an attempt to concentrate power at the center, for Tito asserted that "the most outstanding people of the League of Communists will be in it." Since 1966 the party leadership had remained organizationally distinct from the state administration. Although still deeply involved in governmental policymaking, the party formally exercised its leadership through organs subject to the effective control of the regional party leaderships. Overlapping membership between the party Presidium and the collective Presidency would represent a return to earlier practices and, to the extent that either body enjoyed real power rather than influence, concentrate power in the hands of those individuals who were members of both.

By reducing the supervisory role of formal party organs, overlapping membership between the Presidency and Presidium might reduce regional control over the exercise of central power, but only if those who held positions in both bodies ceased to act as representatives of regional interests, and this appeared unlikely. Nonetheless Tito reported that "when discussions about this reorganization began, there arose certain complaints in some places, a certain disorientation. It began to be said that this will be a kind of directorate, and similar [things]." He dismissed these as "stupidities" (*gluposti*). But they were much more than that. They reflected a fundamental division between the Croatian party leadership and, to a lesser extent, the Slovenian leadership, and those of the other regions, which precluded the kind of interregional and republic-federal cooperation that would be necessary if the new presidency were to function as an integrative institution. Moreover, because implementation of this proposal required a new round of constitutional reforms, it opened the entire political order of the Yugoslav state to legitimate change. It provided the Croatian leadership with an opportunity to break the deadlock over federal policy by amending the constitution to remove entirely areas of contention from the competence of the federation.

The process by which the new series of amendments were drafted took the form of complex interregional negotiations focused on redefining the relationships between the republics (and provinces) and the federation, on reducing the independent power and functions of the federation, and on reorganizing federal institutions and prescribing new rules for decisionmaking in them. A less controversial element in these negotiations was discussion of the continuation of the economic reforms of the mid-1960s. These discussions focused on expanding the autonomous power of self-managing economic enterprises and extending the principle of self-management to additional spheres of social life. There was comparatively little conflict over the formulation of constitutional amendments dealing with the latter issues. Almost all public attention was focused on the more directly political amendments, although the changes embodied in the amendments concerning self-management would later assume vastly increased importance.

The process of drafting the amendments unfolded on two levels. The first consisted of discussions among constitutional and legal experts representing their respective republics and provinces. Although there were serious differences in views among these individuals, their discussions proceeded relatively quickly and smoothly. Their task was to record, not to reconcile divergent views. Reconciliation of conflicting views was to occur at another, higher level of the process among a group of politically powerful representatives of the republics and provinces. At this level disputes over the organization of state institutions became linked to current political conflicts between the regions over specific federal policies. This made the reconciliation of opposing views on either set of issues still more difficult.

In effect, the conflicts then paralyzing the political process were translated into the language of constitutional reforms and reproduced in the amendment process.

Both the policy disputes dividing the regional leaderships and differences over constitutional formulas for the organization and operation of the state became even more difficult to resolve because the constitutional amendment process also opened the door to public discussion of issues that heretofore had been excluded from the public domain. Unlike the period of the Croatian "Declaration" and the Serbian "Proposal," the regional party leaderships now either were unwilling or unable to enforce the boundaries of these discussions. As a result nationalist forces throughout Yugoslavia could use discussions of constitutional questions and later discussions of draft amendments to the federal and republican constitutions to offer highly provocative counterproposals and to raise highly explosive issues.

Although there was a resurgence of nationalist unrest throughout the country, it was most pronounced in Croatia. Nationalist forces there—both Croat and Serb—were well-organized and politically active. The Croatian nationalist leadership appeared to enjoy widespread popular support and was able to exert enormous political pressure on the party leadership. At the same time the party leadership of that republic was divided over how to react to these forces. As a result nationalist unrest in Croatia reached crisis proportions during 1971. The Matica Hrvatska expanded its membership and increased its nationalistic activities dramatically, as did the Serbian cultural organization in that republic, Prosvjeta. An organized group of student nationalists with close links to the Matica leadership seized control of Croatian student organizations and transformed the universities into hotbeds of nationalist activity. Incidents of nationality confrontation, conflict, and even violence in everyday life were occurring with greater frequency and were reported in the increasingly nationalistic press with a certain amount of glee.

Early in March draft texts of the constitutional amendments prepared in response to the proposal to establish a collective Presidency were submitted to the central Presidium for discussion and approval. In his report to the Presidium as chairman of the Coordinating Commission responsible for drafting the amendments, Kardelj acknowledged that negotiations over the amendments dealing with the political order had been characterized by sharply divergent views and intense conflicts among the representatives of the republics and provinces. The solutions finally adopted in these amendments reduced the independent powers of central institutions to a minimum. Specific procedural and organizational changes were adopted to ensure the participation of representatives of all the republics and provinces in the formulation of federal policy in areas that required interregional consensus. These changes made the regional leaderships politically responsible for the day-to-day operation of the federation. Even the independent authority of the

Chamber of Nationalities was reduced in favor of direct representation of the regional leaderships in the formulation of proposals for federal policy in the Federal Executive Council.

These amendments reflected almost complete acceptance of the Croatian leadership's positions on the future organization of the Yugoslav community. Consequently the central leadership and the leaderships of the other republics and provinces expected that their adoption would quiet nationalist unrest in Croatia and contribute to the resolution of oustanding interregional policy disputes. Instead, however, submission of the draft amendments to public scrutiny was followed by still sharper interregional conflict and yet more intense inter-nationality conflicts not only Croatia, but throughout the country.

Adoption of the federal amendments in June 1971 necessitated the amendment of each of the regional constitutions. Nationalist forces in Croatia, led by the Matica Hrvatska, used the public debate over the Croatian constitution to propose their own formulas for defining and organizing the Croatian republic. These amounted to nothing less than an open bid to break the party's monopoly on political power and in effect to remove Croatia from the federation in all but name. Increasingly radical demands by the Matica Hrvastka and the nationalist Croatian student leaders, and the apparent inability or unwillingness of Dabcevic-Kucar and her allies to control them, gave rise to a deep split within the Croatian leadership that took the form of an intense factional struggle. That struggle raged through the summer and fall of 1971 and culminated in the victory of the antinationalist faction only when they appealed to and won the support of Tito. By demonstrating the openly anticommunist character of much of the nationalist argument and propaganda produced by Matica Hrvatska and by demonstrating the failure of the Croatian party leaders to take decisive action to oppose the nationalists or enforce agreements reached in the central party Presidium, the antinationalist faction in the Croatian leadership convinced Tito to move against the nationalists and the Croatian party leaders apparently in collusion with them by calling for their resignations and threatening them with armed intervention in Croatia.

Tito called the Croatian leadership to account in December 1971; in the following months hundreds of nationalist activists were arrested, and more than 1,000 party members were excluded or resigned from the party. At the same time Tito and his closest associates undertook a concerted effort to reestablish central authority in the party and party authority over society. They reconstructed the central party Presidium and its Executive Bureau in January 1972, and Tito took over direct personal leadership of the latter. With Secretary of the Bureau Dolanc as his chief executor, Tito began a process of purging all the regional organizations of leaders who opposed this dramatic recentralization of power and authority. In the fall of 1972 Tito intervened personally in a factional struggle that had broken out in the Serbian party during the summer to defeat the more liberal and independent-minded leadership and to help install a leadership more responsive to his own vision of the LCY. That leadership, in turn, proceeded to purge the Serbian party of more than 1,000 of its members over the course of the next year and one-half.

By the time the Tenth Party Congress convened in May 1974, the recentralization of authority in the party was complete. Eleven of the fifty-two members of the Presidium elected at the Ninth Party Congress in 1969 had been purged and replaced by obvious clients or supporters of Tito and his policies. Moreover a widespread turnover of party cadres at lower levels had also taken place, thus creating an effectively new party apparatus. That apparatus was now subjected to a widespread campaign to restore "the principles of democratic centralism," reversing the emphasis on "democratization" of relations in party life dominant since 1966.

Nevertheless, while personnel and organizational changes during this period were extensive and the authority of central party organs relative to that of the regional party leaderships undoubtedly was strengthened, the campaign to restore "the principles of democratic centralism" did not involve rejection of the principles of decision-making that had evolved in the party in the period since 1966. The report on the future tasks of the party delivered in January 1972 struck a careful balance between the need to strengthen the ability of central party organs to review and control the activity of both regional leaderships and local organizations on the one hand, and the need to preserve and protect the autonomy of the regional party organizations on the other. Even the Executive Bureau letter of September 1972 that marked the beginning of the campaign conceded that "it is necessary to oppose every attempt to transform democratic centralism into bureaucratic centralism, into the imposition of views without prior democratic discussions . . . into the rule of narrow groups. . . . " Tito, in his interview following distribution of the letter to all party organizations, emphatically rejected any "turning back" to Stalinism. In the report to the Tenth Party Congress he emphasized the need for strengthening unity and central authority in the party and affirmed "the equal participation and identical responsibility of republican and provincial organizations in the construction and execution of the unified policy of the LCY."

The recentralization of authority within the party in the period 1972–74 did not include the transfer to central organs of control over cadre assignments in the regions. The new party statutes adopted at the Tenth Party Congress retained the principle of composing central party organs of members elected by their respective organizations. The formula for the composition of central party organs remained "equal representation of the republics and corresponding representation of the provinces." A new element introduced in 1974, however, was the addition of a provision for "the corresponding representation" of the League of Communists of the Yugoslav People's Army. This reflected the increased political importance of the military during this period, arising out of its support of Tito and the antinationalist coalition during the "Croatian crisis" and its role as the only remaining "all-Yugoslav" integrative organization.

The strengthening of the central party leadership was carefully circumscribed by efforts to maintain the autonomous authority of the regional party organizations. The Tenth Party Congress, for example, replaced the Party Conference—established at the Ninth Party Congress in 1969 as the most authoritative decisionmaking body of the party between congresses—with a Central Committee. Whereas three-quarters of the 280 members of the Party Conference had been elected anew by local party organizations before each of its sessions, the membership of the reestablished Central Committee was to remain unchanged between congresses and included only 165 individuals. Both the smaller size and stable membership of the new Central Committee strengthened its autonomy. But that membership continued to be elected by the regional party organizations. Similarly the members of the smaller and more authoritative Presidium elected at the Tenth Party Congress were determined formally by the regional party organizations. And the presidents of each of the regional party organizations continued to be members of the Presidium by virtue of their positions.

Thus, while the Tito-led coalition established the right of central organs to determine independently their own internal organization and operation, to expel individuals from their ranks, and to remove regional leaders from office, the coalition did not establish the right of central organs to appoint independently either their own members or the leaders of regional organizations. That appointment power, as well as the power to control cadres appointments in lower level party organizations, remained in the hands of the regional leaderships. Even after the Tenth Party Congress the central party organs continued to be made up of individuals appointed by, and therefore responsible to, their respective regional or military party organizations.

Moreover the Tito-led coalition did not abandon the principle of consensual decisionmaking based on interregional consultation and "harmonization" of positions that had evolved in the period since 1966. The dramatic increase in the effectiveness of federal decisionmaking apparent in the months following the December 1971 purge of the Croatian leadership was achieved through the operation of institutions established by the 1971 amendments and operating on the basis of interregional consensus. During the period following the Tenth Party Congress, interregional negotiation and consensual decisionmaking practices became a central element in the effort to restore cohesiveness to the central party leadership as it moved ahead with the already-scheduled consideration of additional constitutional changes—the so-called second phase of the reforms first undertaken in late 1970. Changes in the organization and operation of state institutions adopted during this phase of constitutional reform completed the institutional and procedural requirements for the operation of a consensual system of political decisionmaking based on negotiation between representatives of the republics and provinces.

The Constitutional Order

The 1974 Constitution is an extraordinarily long document of some 250 pages in English translation, consisting of twenty-five pages of "basic principles" and 406 articles. It, like its predecessors, serves politically pragmatic as well as symbolic functions. In practical political terms, it preserves many of the provisions for federal decisionmaking contained in the 1971 amendments and reorganizes the central institutions of the federation to conform more closely to them, eliminating certain inconsistencies noted in practice in the period 1971–73. But it also reflects the changes that had taken place since the adoption of those amendments. It was written during the period of renewed emphasis on central power and authority, tempered by the continuing power and authority of the regions. This tension between center and regions is reflected in the institutional framework and statements of principle contained in the Constitution. It affirms the leading role of the LCY in society and the authoritative role of central institutions, but it preserves the role and authority of the republics and provinces in federal decisionmaking.

The new Constitution serves symbolic functions with respect to both the multinational condition and the socialist order. A large proportion of the text is devoted to an elaboration of the system of workers' self-management and the principles of social self-management. Embedded in these principles is a blueprint for the eventual assumption of most of the functions of government by workers and citizens formed into self-managing organizations and communities—thereby causing the withering away of the state. This represents "the hope for the future," a normative aspect of the Constitution that was only in small part realized in 1981. The Constitution also contains a broad range of concessions to the multinational character of the country, ranging from the comprehensive granting of linguistic and cultural rights to changes in the ritual expressions concerning the origins and character of the Yugoslav socialist state. Even the formal name of the federal parliament has been changed from "Federal Assembly" to "Assembly of the Socialist Federal Republic of Yugoslavia" in an attempt to convey the idea that there are no federal institutions per se, only the organized expressions of interregional cooperation, although in common usage it is still referred to as the Federal Assembly or Assembly.

The 1974 Constitution preserves the human and civil rights provisions and the system of constitutional courts established in 1963. The system of constitutional courts in Yugoslavia has become an important arena in which self-managing enterprises and organizations have protected their rights. But the courts have not served to protect from repression those individuals who engaged in activities perceived by the regime to threaten political stability or to challenge communist political power. Nationalists, Stalinists or neo-Stalinists, sympathizers of the Soviet Union engaged in such antiregime activity as the organization of an alternative, underground Communist Party, and dissident intellectuals and the civil libertarians who defend them remain without an effective defense against the regime.

One concession to multinationality that was not included in the new Constitution, however, was the elevation of Vojvodina and Kosovo from the status of autonomous provinces to the status of republics. Both regions remain formally subordinated to the Serbian republic. The relationship between Serbia and its provinces is formally regulated by the republican and provincial constitutions. But the provisions of these constitutions are decidedly vague on this point. In some areas, formal subordination is very real: the security police apparatus in the province of Kosovo, for example, where tensions between Albanians and Serbs are great and organized nationalist activity among Albanians has continued, remains under the direct administration of the republican apparatus. In other areas, however, the provinces enjoy extensive, and slowly expanding, autonomy. Moreover, even in policy areas formally subject to uniform solution throughout Serbia, the provincial leaders—primarily the Albanian-dominated leadership of Kosovo (for the leadership of Vojvodina remains heavily Serb)—exercise de facto veto power through their representatives in the republican parliament. The constitutional provisions for the organization and operation of the Serbian parliament have created a de facto federal structure for the republic.

The ambiguity of the concessions to Albanian nationalist sentiments in Kosovo reflected the constraints imposed on the regime by the national sensitivities of the Serbs. The province of Kosovo comprises territories and institutions that have enormous historical, symbolic, and emotional national significance for the Serb nation. Indeed Vojvodina also contains territory and institutions intimately associated with Serb national history. To separate either region from the Republic of Serbia, therefore, would be certain to trigger an intense Serbian nationalist response that would be very difficult for the regime to control. Consequently the leadership was retained as much of the symbolic subordination of these two regions as possible, while granting them effective political equality.

The court system of Yugoslavia is divided into a federal court, eight regional court systems, and constitutional courts for each of the republics and provinces and the federation. The Constitutional Court of Yugoslavia is composed of a president and thirteen members (two from each republic and one from each province) who are appointed by the federal parliament and serve for nonrenewable eight-year terms. The Constitutional Court is empowered to judge whether legislation is in "agreement" with the federal constitution and whether republican and provincial laws "conflict" with federal law. Republican and provincial laws need not, however, "agree" with federal laws. The court is also empowered to judge the constitutionality of federal regulations, to judge whether regulations and acts of other bodies "agree" or "conflict" with federal law, and to resolve disputes between the federation and the regions (or federal organs and regional organs) or among the regions (or regional organs) over their respective powers and authority. The court cannot, however, become involved in judgments concerning the regional constitutions; these are reserved to the individual constitutional courts of the republics and provinces. Hence the Constitutional Court of Yugoslavia does not serve as a court of appeal above the regional constitutional courts.

The functions of the regional constitutional courts parallel the functions of the federal court precisely. In order to maintain a certain degree of uniformity among the regional legal systems, the constitutional courts of the republics and provinces meet in regular consultative meetings to review their decisions and other issues. Through this device an informal but effective link has been established between courts that are otherwise entirely independent of each other. The case loads of these courts, judging from the experience of the Serbian court, is composed primarily of challenges to the constitutionality of regulations or other acts adopted by self-managing enterprises, communities, or other bodies rather than challenges to laws passed by governmental bodies. Cases in which one party claims that another has failed to fulfill a self-management agreement, but in which no challenge to the constitutionality of an act or regulation is made, are in the jurisdiction of the "self-management courts." The jurisdiction of these courts is limited only to self-management acts and does not include acts of governmental bodies or laws. Their decisions are not necessarily final; they may be taken to constitutional or regular courts for further action. A system of "economic courts" serves a parallel function for cases concerning economic or financial relations involving self-managing enterprises or other legal entities other than individuals.

The regular court system is divided into local, or communal, courts; courts that serve an area broader than one commune, corresponding to territorial divisions that have now been abolished; and supreme courts in each of the republics and provinces. There is also a Federal Supreme Court, whose jurisdiction is limited to federal legislation and other acts administered by federal agencies. Cases involving federal legislation and other acts administered by the republics and provinces fall within the jurisdictions of the regional court systems. The Federal Supreme Court does not serve as a court of appeal above the regional supreme courts, although it does resolve jurisdictional disputes between them. An entirely separate system of military courts exercises jurisdiction over all military personnel and certain categories of criminal activity with military significance (see Military Justice, ch. 5).

The electoral system established under the new Constitution has also increased party control over the political system. Direct elections to parliament at the local (commune), regional (republic and province), and federal levels have been eliminated in favor of a system of "delegations." Workers in the various sectors of society and citizens in local communities elect "delegations," or groups of representatives, who then elect "delegates" who enter either the Chamber of Associated Labor or Chamber of Local Communities, respectively, of the local or regional parliament. The third chamber of the local and regional parliaments is a "sociopolitical chamber" composed of "delegates" assigned ("delegated") to it by the major sociopolitical organizations of the commune or region: the party, the Socialist Alliance of Working People of Yugoslavia (SAWPY—see Glossary), the trade union federation, the veterans' organization, and the youth organization. The Socialist Alliance supervises the electoral process at each level, influencing the selection of members of each delegation in the country and determining the selection of every delegate to local, regional, and even the federal parliament. At the federal level, delegates to the Federal Chamber of the Assembly are elected by all three chambers of the commune assemblies, which constitute their delegations (see fig. 13). Delegates to the Chamber of Republics and Provinces—successor to the old Chamber of Nationalities—are elected by all chambers of the republican and provincial assemblies, which constitute their delegations. This system involves Yugoslavs in a massive participatory network. In 1974, the first year of the new system, there were over 70,000 delegations established and over 800,000 members. These delegation members, in turn, elected over 55,000 delegates to local and regional assemblies.

In theory every delegate in every assembly is bound to represent the views of his delegation on every issue, and his delegation is bound to collect and reflect the views of the constituency it represents. Since the establishment of this complex system in 1974, however, delegates have rarely consulted their delegations which, in turn, have rarely conveyed the views of their constituents, except at the federal level. There the new organization of the Assembly and the political practices introduced in it since 1974 ensure that "delegates" do consult and represent the views of their "delegations"—the republican and provincial leaderships.

The 1974 Constitution preserves the existence of the Assembly despite proposals by representatives of the regions engaged in early drafting of the text in the spring of 1972 to do away with it completely. The central party leadership intervened to ensure the establishment of a bicameral federal parliament composed of a Federal Chamber and a Chamber of Republics and Provinces (see fig. 14). The Federal Chamber is composed of an equal number of delegates elected by the commune assemblies in each republic and a smaller number from each province. It is intended to represent all citizens organized into self-managing organizations, institutions, and communities, and it is empowered to make decisions in all areas of autonomous federal authority on the basis of a simple majority

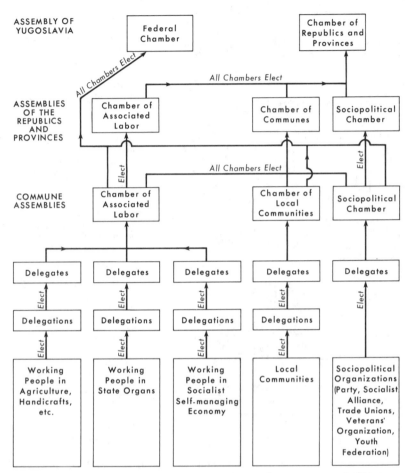

ASSEMBLY OF YUGOSLAVIA

ASSEMBLIES OF THE REPUBLICS AND PROVINCES

COMMUNE ASSEMBLIES

Source: Based on information from Jovan Djordjevic (ed.), *Drustveno-politicki sistem SFRJ*, Belgrade, 1975, p. 462.

Figure 13. The Delegate System of Elections

vote of its members. The Chamber of Republics and Provinces is composed of delegations elected by the republican and provincial assemblies. Although the republic delegations are composed of more members than the provincial delegations, this is of only technical significance. For on all questions requiring interregional consensus, voting in the chamber is by delegation, not by delegates, and requires unanimity. These questions comprise every problem affecting interregional relations, including all matters pertaining to the social plans, monetary and tax policies, investment and development policies, foreign trade and exchange policies, the organization and operation of the domestic market, and the size of the federal budget.

The Constitution continues the formal status of the Federal Executive Council as a subordinate executive body of the Assembly. In

195

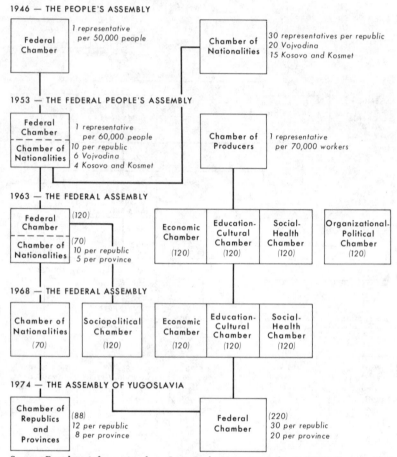

1946 — THE PEOPLE'S ASSEMBLY

| Federal Chamber | 1 representative per 50,000 people | | Chamber of Nationalities | 30 representatives per republic 20 Vojvodina 15 Kosovo and Kosmet |

1953 — THE FEDERAL PEOPLE'S ASSEMBLY

| Federal Chamber | 1 representative per 60,000 people | | Chamber of Producers | 1 representative per 70,000 workers |
| Chamber of Nationalities | 10 per republic 6 Vojvodina 4 Kosovo and Kosmet | | | |

1963 — THE FEDERAL ASSEMBLY

| Federal Chamber | (120) | Economic Chamber (120) | Education-Cultural Chamber (120) | Social-Health Chamber (120) | Organizational-Political Chamber (120) |
| Chamber of Nationalities | (70) 10 per republic 5 per province | | | | |

1968 — THE FEDERAL ASSEMBLY

| Chamber of Nationalities (70) | Sociopolitical Chamber (120) | Economic Chamber (120) | Education-Cultural Chamber (120) | Social-Health Chamber (120) |

1974 — THE ASSEMBLY OF YUGOSLAVIA

| Chamber of Republics and Provinces | (88) 12 per republic 8 per province | | Federal Chamber | (220) 30 per republic 20 per province |

Source: Based on information from Josip Sruk, *Ustavno uredjenje SFRJ*, Zagreb, 1976, pp. 329–32.

Figure 14.   The Evolution of the Federal Parliament as of 1981

theory, there is no separation of powers in the Yugoslav system. In fact, however, the council operates as the government of Yugoslavia and is a dominant presence in the Assembly and the federal decision-making process in general. It is composed of a president—in fact, he is the equivalent of a premier in a Western parliamentary cabinet—nominated by the collective Presidency. The premier, in turn, nominates the other members of the council and all are elected by the Assembly. It is composed of an equal number of members from each republic and province. The heads of the eight main federal bureaucracies—called secretariats—are members of the council ex officio; these include the secretaries for finance, foreign affairs, foreign trade, information, internal affairs (security police), justice and general administration, markets and general economic affairs, and national defense. In addition the ten presidents of various more specialized bureaucracies—called committees—are also members ex officio.

The council is organized into various internal commissions and committees for the purpose of preparing proposals for federal legislation and carrying out federal policy (see fig. 15). These commissions and committees provide institutional arenas for interregional negotiations over federal policy before it is submitted to the Assembly for consideration and provide important channels of access for other organized interests to participate in these early deliberations. The republican and provincial executive councils each send representatives to each of five interrepublican committees established by the 1971 amendments and continued in the Constitution as arenas in which interregional consensus might be established on policy in the historically most contentious areas: development policy, the monetary system, foreign trade and the foreign currency exchange system, the market, and finance. The deliberations in these committees play a decisive role in shaping the details of federal policy in these areas.

The regions are also represented in an internal consultative body of the council, called the Coordinating Commission of the Federal Executive Council. The Coordinating Commission is the central conflict-resolving body in the council and constitutes a higher arena for negotiations than any of the interrepublican committees. For key questions, the presidents of each of the regional executive councils participate directly in the commission's deliberations. The Permanent Commissions of the Federal Executive Council provide access points for organized interests other than the regional governments to participate in the formulation of federal policies. It is apparently in these commissions that the Federal Executive Council is able to determine an "all-Yugoslav" position on each issue, and it is from this perspective that its representatives in the interrepublican committees and the Coordinating Commission confront and negotiate with the regions.

The Federal Executive Council also can attempt to forge an "all-Yugoslav" position in another set of bodies called Federal Social Councils, also known by their earlier name as "federal councils." These councils were first established by federal statute in 1973 as joint bodies of the Federal Executive Council and the collective Presidency to provide arenas for the direct participation in the preparation of federal policies by organizations and interests that cut across regional boundaries. Although the Constitution does not provide explicitly for their existence, they were retained and expanded in number in 1974 because they had become one of the primary points for the exercise of direct political influence by the party leadership and the resolution of interregional political disputes over the broad outlines of federal policy. Because the councils include representatives of the major sociopolitical organizations (including the LCY) and the regional and federal governments, agreements reached in them are more easily enforced. Agreements

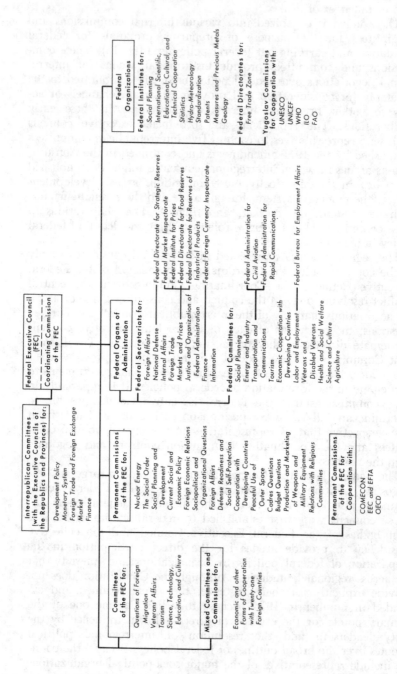

Figure 15. Organization of the Federal Executive Council and Federal Administrative Agencies, 1981

reached in these councils are very likely to ease the work of other bodies such as the interrepublican committees of the Federal Executive Council. Federal social councils have been established for international relations, for the protection of the constitutional order (state security), for questions of the social order, and for economic development and economic policy. The latter two councils in particular exercise enormous influence over the federal policymaking process.

One of the factors that make the federal social councils such authoritative bodies is that they are joint bodies of both the Federal Executive Council and the collective Presidency and include members of the Presidency in their membership. The collective Presidency has its origins in Tito's 1970 attempt to resolve the interregional deadlock in federal decisionmaking by creating an authoritative body composed of individuals from all the regions who would review and resolve interregional disputes from an all-Yugoslav perspective. First established in 1971 as a twenty-three-member body in order to permit each of the major nationality groups in each of the regions to be represented among its members, it included a mix of authoritative and not-so-authoritative individuals. The presidents of the regional assemblies, for example, were before 1974 members ex officio. In the interest of enhancing both its authority and effectiveness. the Presidency was reduced to nine members in the 1974 Const⁺.ution—one from each region, plus the president of the LCY. After the death of Tito, both the party statute and the Constitution were changed to mandate the membership only of an unspecified representative designated by the party.

The Presidency is the collective institutional inheritor of Tito's powers as president of the republic. An adviser to the Presidency has reported that it operates on a collegial basis and according to informal rules of consensual decisionmaking despite the fact that its formal internal rules of procedure specify that it is to make decisions on the basis of simple majorities or qualified majorities. Other key figures in the central political leadership of the country participate regularly in the routine meetings of the Presidency; included most often are the president of the Federal Executive Council and a representative of the party Presidium. Other federal officials responsible for particular areas participate in discussions of issues from their particular areas. Thus, as examples, the federal secretary (minister) for foreign affairs participates in discussions of foreign affairs, the federal secretary for internal affairs participates in discussions of internal security matters, and the leadership of the Assembly may be summoned to participate in discussions of Assembly matters. Not infrequently the Presidency may hold an expanded session to which a broad range of federal officials are invited. For "the most delicate questions of the internal and foreign policy of Yugoslavia," the Presidency meets in joint session with the LCY Presidium. Such joint sessions occur on an average of about once a month. On matters affecting the interests of the republics and provinces, the Presidency carries out "collaboration" and "cooperation" with the regional presidencies, including inviting their chairmen to participate in discussions of these matters in meetings of the Presidency.

The Presidency also has a number of internal working bodies. The most important of these are the Councils of the Presidency. There were in mid-1981 five such councils: foreign affairs, national defense, state security, economic questions, and the newly created Council for the Protection of the Constitutional Order, which unlike the Council for State Security is charged with overseeing the activities of the organs of state security—including the security services of the military—from the perspective of protecting human and civil rights of individuals and the self-managing rights of organizations and committees. These councils are vehicles for the organized cooperation and coordination of activity by the various federal agencies carrying out functions in these areas, and for the direct supervision of their activities by the highest political leadership. They are also forums for the discussion of policy questions in these areas and the preparation of policy recommendations to the Presidency itself. The commissions of the Presidency are more functionally specialized bodies with a decidedly less important role in the formulation of policy. Should the need arise, the Presidency also is empowered to create ad hoc working groups.

The collective Presidency constitutes one of the two most important institutions for the resolution of political conflicts. The other is, of course, the central party Presidium. Not only the Presidium but the LCY as whole continue to play a central role in the Yugoslav system. The Constitution for the first time defines the party as "the leading organized ideological and political force of the working class and of all working people in the creation of socialism" and stipulates that by "its guiding ideological and political action" the party "shall be the prime mover and exponent of political activity aimed at safeguarding and further developing the socialist revolution and socialist social relations of self-management . . . . " In order to facilitate the fulfillment of this task, the Constitution continues the practice established in 1963 of providing for the direct representation of "sociopolitical organizations"—that is, the LCY and the other major organizations that serve as its "front" or as vehicles for the carrying out of its policies and over which the party exercises decisive influences—in the sociopolitical chambers of representative institutions at local and regional levels. Moreover, in practice the delegates to the more powerful of the two chambers in the federal parliament—the Chamber of Republics and Provinces—are mostly elected from among these sociopolitical chambers and are themselves professional party cadres. The party also is represented in almost every other decisionmaking organ on the federal level. And where it is not formally represented as an organization, its influence is exercised through *aktivs*, small groups of dedicated Communists who are members of such organs, or through party cells established for Communists working in federal institutions. Thus the party is able to exercise substantial—indeed, when it is united, decisive—influence over the process of government.

The Process of Government

The process of government in the period since the adoption of the Constitution and the Tenth Party Congress in 1974 has reflected the continuing political tension between the center and the regions and ongoing conflict among the regions themselves. It has also reflected a growing tension between ideologically conservative and more liberal forces both in society and inside the party leadership. Federal decisionmaking during the late 1970s, and especially since the illness and death of Tito in 1980, suggests the existence of an emergent—but not yet completely established—political culture based on hard bargaining among conflicting interests. This bargaining is punctuated by frequent instances of public posturing, temporary deadlock, intransigent behavior, and other forms of pressure by representatives of one or another interest—be it a region, economic branch, or large self-managing enterprise. But there appears to be growing awareness among responsible actors in the political system of an imperative to agree in the end.

The Federal Executive Council is, unquestionably, the most important and most influential actor in the process of determining the details of general national policy directives established by the party. The bulk of interregional bargaining and other forms of conflict resolution takes place within its committees and commissions, in other consultative bodies on the federal level over which it presides, and in the committees and other bodies of the federal parliament in which it plays a dominant role. In all these arenas, the council acts as the representative of all-Yugoslav interests or as a mediator among conflicting interests. In the majority of instances, the council successfully defends its position against those taken by other parties to a particular policy conflict.

The power of the Federal Executive Council derives from a number of sources. First, the council enjoys an almost complete monopoly on the initiation of debate—the setting of the agenda—on federal policy. Although the LCY clearly sets priorities on the general issues to be dealt with, the council determines the program of work on specific legislative and policy proposals for implementing party directives and negotiates this program with representatives of the party leadership on a continuous basis. As a result the council has almost always been the only sponsor of legislation presented before the Assembly. The ability of the council to determine the federal decisionmaking agenda is based in large part on its control over the federal administrative bureaucracies and a virtual monopoly on policy-relevant, expert information. Representatives of the council need only argue that the government is not sufficiently prepared to deal with a particular issue in order to delay its appearance on the federal agenda.

The council's near monopoly on both information and expertise also gives it tremendous leverage against regional representatives or the representatives of other interests in debates over legislative or policy proposals once they are placed on the agenda. Thus, Yugoslav analyses of the decisionmaking process in the federal parliament, and especially in the committees of the Chamber of Republics and Provinces, generally report that the representatives of the council usually get their way in the end. The council's representatives are able to attack the substance of opposing positions with a wealth of data and analysis or play one regional representative off against another in order to reserve the council's own position. And when some change becomes necessary, the council can minimize its substance by developing less specific and more complicated formulations of the statement in contention. Alternatively, the council can attempt to link solutions to several issues together to form a package deal in which apparent concessions to various opposing positions in effect cancel one another out, leaving much of the council's own position intact.

The Federal Executive Council also appears to play a dominant role in the more confidential bargaining that constitutes the preliminary stages of preparation of federal policies. Regional representatives on interrepublican committees and functionaries of the council itself have reported in several lengthy interviews, for example, that the council is a powerful actor in the negotiations that take place in these committees. And the successful conclusion of an agreement in these committees provides almost irresistible leverage for the council in its dealings with the Assembly. Agreements in the interregional committees carry the endorsement of the regional executive councils who, in turn, exercise enormous influence over the regional delegations in the Assembly.

The Federal Executive Council is relatively less dominant in the federal social councils over which it presides. This is primarily because the social councils are dominated by representatives of the central and regional party leaderships. When the party leadership is divided within itself over an issue, the Federal Executive Council is unable to mediate between the opposing positions. Indeed, disagreement among regional party leaderships is sufficient to prevent the Federal Executive Council from proceeding with a proposal that it is prepared to present to the Assembly and in the support of which it is prepared to use all its resources. Although apparently intended when they were first established in 1973 to provide a formal governmental arena for the party to exercise directly its integrative influence over the general shape of policies, the federal social councils rapidly began to determine more than just the general shape of policies. The recommendations produced by the councils have become so extensive that the leadership of the Assembly has complained regularly since 1976 that the councils impinge significantly on the domain of the parliament, leaving delegates in the two chambers little to discuss. Although such statements constitute political hyperbole,

Parliament Building, Belgrade
Courtesy Embassy of Yugoslavia, Washington

they do suggest the enormously authoritative role played by these councils.

When a proposed piece of federal legislation or proposed federal policy statement has passed through the lengthy process of preliminary negotiations—a process that not infrequently takes as much as a year or more—it is sent to the Assembly for debate. It is important to point out that proposals both in areas that according to the Constitution remain in the autonomous jurisdiction of the federation and in areas that require interregional consensus are subjected to this preliminary process of negotiation. This is because during the late 1970s the principle of interregional negotiation and consensual decisionmaking was gradually extended to all areas of federal decisionmaking. The Federal Chamber of the Assembly, for example, was originally conceived as the place for representatives (delegates) of the working class and general citizenry to make decisions on issues in the autonomous jurisdiction of the federation independently of regional influence. Soon after the establishment of the Federal Chamber, however, individual delegates began to seek guidance for their activity from their respective regional governments. With time, the delegates from each region gradually organized themselves into de facto delegations subject to instructions from their regional leaderships, a relationship that has now been formalized in at least some of the republics.

Federal proposals in areas that formally require interregional consensus for passage are submitted by the Federal Executive Council to the Chamber of Republics and Provinces. The leadership of that chamber then sends the proposals on to the regional assemblies for their consideration and the formation of regional positions—a process hastened by the direct interregional negotiations already carried out in the committees of the Federal Executive Council. The formation of positions in the regional assemblies is more than a mere formality, however. The preliminary negotiations conducted at the federal level take place primarily among representatives of the regional executive councils, and although these executive councils exercise decisive influence over their respective assemblies, the assemblies themselves constitute the major institutionalized channel of access to the policymaking process for a whole host of economic, territorial, and political interests that were local and not represented at the federal level. Yugoslav politics has been characterized since the postwar period by strong local interests—sometimes organized into distinctive political "machines"—that sometimes impinge on national politics through their representatives in the regional parliament. A regional executive council, therefore, must sometimes argue in its assembly on behalf of federal proposals to which it has already assented through its representatives in the interrepublican committees, social councils, or other bodies at the federal level.

When each of the regional assemblies has considered a proposal, it instructs its delegation to the Chamber of Republics and Provinces on the position it shall take on the issue, and that delegation then returns to Belgrade to confront the delegations from the other regions in an attempt to reach final agreement. The positions of the regional delegations are sometimes still far apart even at this relatively late stage of decisionmaking process. This is especially true in cases when the Federal Executive Council has pushed a proposal through the preliminary negotiations without achieving complete interregional agreement. But it can also be true even when unanimous agreement on the general contours—or even the more detailed character—of a proposal has already been achieved. The discussions

Gathering of world dignitaries for Tito's
funeral, May 1980
Courtesy United Press International

in the chamber not only concern the very real details of committing resources to action, but also represent the last stage in the decision-making process—and, therefore, the last opportunity for a regional leadership to win a concession on the issue at hand.

It is usually the case that the regional representatives and representatives of the Federal Executive Council in the committees of the Chamber of Republics and Provinces are able to reach agreement. Such agreement tends to be most difficult to achieve on those proposals that commit large amounts of resources for long periods of time, such as social plans, and especially five-year social plans. A number of issues were especially contentious during the 1970s and in the year following Tito's death, namely, the quantity of resources allocated to investment in the underdeveloped regions in order to accelerate their development and the method by which they are secured and distributed, investment priorities and the federal tax and development policies designed to meet these priorities, access to foreign currency and its exchange, as well as issues affecting interregional economic relations. Conflicts over narrow proposals more limited in their potential effect on the distribution of capital resources generally prove to be easier to resolve.

Issues that cannot be resolved in the committees of the chamber are referred to meetings of the chamber's leadership—including the president of the Assembly, the president of the chamber, the chairmen of the regional delegations, the chairmen of the committees concerned, and representatives of the Federal Executive Council. It is often the case that the Chamber of Republics and Provinces will recess for a few days to permit the delegations to return to their respective regions to consult with their regional leaderships for further instructions on the issues at hand. If the conflict cannot be resolved in this way, discussion is transferred to the Federal Executive Council—probably its Coordinating Commission—for further direct negotiation. In some cases such a conflict might be referred to one of the federal social councils. In all but the most difficult cases, further negotiations under the auspices of the Federal Executive Council result in an interregional agreement.

When an issue cannot be resolved through repeated negotiation at all these levels, the collective Presidency may be consulted for advice. The Presidency cannot impose a solution to such conflicts. It must work through the powers of consultation and persuasion. In mid-1981 it continued to enjoy enormous moral and political authority as a result of its long identification with Tito and its constitutional role as his institutional successor. Even under these circumstances, however, the Presidency has proved reluctant to become too deeply embroiled in interregional conflicts over federal policies. It has generally responded to requests for advice with an injunction to continue negotiations until a solution is found. In an important sense its main function during its first year of operation was to place the imprimatur of legitimacy on agreements reached through hard-nosed, pragmatic bargaining in the parliament, government, and other federal bodies, and especially on agreements that depart from long-standing practices. This was its main role in the negotiations conducted during late 1980 over the formula for aid to the underdeveloped regions to be adopted in the social plan for 1981–85.

The amount of aid provided to the economically underdeveloped southern regions, the method by which resources for that purpose are secured, and the means by which and under what conditions those resources are made available to the underdeveloped regions have always been contentious issues within the Yugoslav leadership. As the regional leaderships gained increasing political power at the expense of the center during the late 1960s and early 1970s, the conflict between north and south became more intense. Indeed the linkage between regional economic issues and nationality issues was at the heart of the 1971 crisis. Since that time efforts by the leaderships of the developed regions to reduce the burden of aid to the underdeveloped have taken two directions: an effort to establish a definition of underdevelopment based on "objective criteria" or measures of the level of development, rather than on differences between the levels of development of a particular region and the Yugoslav average; and, an effort to change the basis of aid to those regions defined as underdeveloped from grants and low-cost loans of federal monies secured through taxation of the economy to direct investment of capital in various projects in the economies of the underdeveloped regions by self-managing enterprises from the developed regions.

The first of these efforts began during negotiations over preparation of the 1976–80 five-year plan. At that time, in return for continuing the status of the southern regions as underdeveloped for another five years, representatives of the developed regions won an agreement that "objective measures" of development would be established by 1978 and applied to the 1981–85 plan. The establishment of such measures, it was argued, held out the promise of eventually ending the underdeveloped status of at least some of the southern regions and thereby reducing the aid burden on the north. Because of intense conflict over the precise measures to be adopted, and especially over the question of abandoning "relative differences in the level of development in comparison to the Yugoslav average" as a measure of underdevelopment, a proposed set of measures could not be readied until July 1980. These were submitted to the Chamber of Republics and Provinces by the Federal Executive Council in an atmosphere of public contention between the leaderships of the developed and underdeveloped regions and were rejected by representatives of the underdeveloped regions. The leaderships then agreed to assign underdeveloped status once again to Bosnia, Macedonia, Montenegro, and Kosovo in the 1981–85 plan and to continue negotiations over the development of "objective measures." Such measures were scheduled to be developed by the end of 1982. In the interim, however, the issue remained an extremely sore point among representatives of the developed regions, especially Slovenia and Croatia.

The leaders of the developed regions have been somewhat more successful in their effort to change the basis of aid to the underdeveloped regions. Up to 1981 resources for aid had been secured through taxation of all the regional economies. These resources were then disbursed through a federal fund in the form of grants and low-cost or no-cost loans, according to proportions set by interregional consensus. According to a high-ranking member of a regional party leadership who discussed this issue in an interview in early 1981, representatives of the developed regions were then insisting that aid to the southern regions be carried out in the form of direct investment of capital by enterprises from the developed regions, and that taxation be abandoned completely. He reported that representatives of the underdeveloped regions, on the other hand, insisted on preserving the existing taxing mechanism. Press reports suggest that at least some of them were demanding an increased level of taxation while representatives of the developed regions were insisting that the time had come to reduce the level of aid. This regional party official reported that the issue was resolved only after long, hard bargaining that included, at the end and before final agreement, consultation with the collective Presidency.

That agreement calls for 1.83 percent of the annual social product (see Glossary) to be invested in the underdeveloped regions during 1981–85, a slight reduction from the 1.97 percent tax established for the 1976–80 period. One-half of that 1.83 percent is to be secured through taxation and disbursed by the federal fund, while the other half is to take the form of direct investments. This agreement represents an important, if only partial, victory for the developed regions and may constitute a form of compensation for their earlier defeat on the issue of establishing "objective measures" of development.

In the event that interregional agreement cannot be achieved on an issue that, in the judgment of the Presidency, requires resolution, the Presidency may authorize the Federal Executive Council to ask the Chamber of Republics and Provinces to pass a "temporary measure." Such a measure remains valid until a permanent agreement is achieved, but no longer than one year. It may be renewed one time. A temporary measure is not subject to regional veto in the chamber. It is adopted by a two-thirds majority of the delegates voting as individuals. No regional delegation—or even two regional delegations acting in unison—can block passage of such a measure.

The temporary measure is intended to provide an alternative to deadlock in the federal decisionmaking process. From the beginning of the 1974 constitutional period the leadership of the federal parliament argued that the government should not hesitate to employ it if necessary, but warned at the same time that too-frequent resort to such measures would be indicative of deeper problems in the system. The mere threat of using such a measure—implicit any time the Federal Executive Council turns to the Presidency for advice—has given the council important added leverage in bringing reluctant regional leaderships to agreement. It is, after all, better to conclude a negotiated agreement that represents only partial victory than to allow a potentially complete defeat to be imposed.

The council has been compelled to resort to such a measure only once, when in December 1979 it could not achieve interregional agreement on how a necessary reduction in the trade imbalances would be established in the social plan for 1980. The inability of the council to reach agreement on this issue did not bode well for decisionmaking in 1980. But the illness of Tito and his death in May placed enormous pressure on the leadership to avoid serious disagreement. And on a number of highly contentious issues the fear of having to resort once again to a temporary measure both so soon after its first use and at a time when the whole world was questioning whether Yugoslavia would survive for much longer impelled the leadership to come to agreement.

The experience of 1980 and early 1981 suggests, therefore, that the Federal Executive Council and collective Presidency can in fact resolve conflicts over the details of policy and its implementation even when these involve the direct economic interests of the regions. But state organs cannot do this without the support of the LCY leadership. They cannot define the broad outlines of policy. These must be defined in advance by the party leadership. Hence, the public process of federal decisionmaking that begins with the submission of a draft proposal to the Federal Assembly is unlikely ever to produce interregional agreement when none exists in the party itself. For under such circumstances the Federal Executive Council cannot be confident of the support of the coercive political power and authority of the LCY leadership that is sometimes necessary to reach agreement even over the details of policies about which there is general agreement. In mid-1981, however, the party remained deeply divided. To provide the support for the government that is necessary to the successful resolution of the conflicts inherent in the society and its political system, the LCY must first resolve corresponding conflicts and uncertainties in its own ranks.

The League of Communists

Although the Tito-led coalition in control of the LCY at the Tenth Party Congress in 1974 restored much of the basic organizational structure common to all ruling communist parties, the LCY did not reproduce the "shadow ministries" characteristic of other central party apparatuses, for it remained organizationally distinct from the state administration. It remained a highly federalized organization in which power and authority was divided between center and region. Changes adopted at the Eleventh Party Congress in 1978 reflected the continuing tension between center and region inside the party itself. These changes also suggested, however, the emergence of a renewed effort by at least some part of the leadership to further democratize inner-party life.

The Tenth Party Congress retained a large Presidium as the de facto leading organ of the party and created for it an Executive Committee of six secretaries drawn from the Presidium and six members drawn from the Central Committee. The Presidium was composed of four members from each republic, and two from each autonomous province and the party organization in the military. The presidents of each of the regional organizations were made members of the Presidium ex officio. The Central Committee, eliminated as the result of the changes of the late 1960s, was reestablished as the "highest organ of the LCY between two congresses."

Most of the delegates to the Tenth Party Congress were elected on a proportional basis according to party membership by commune party organizations. A certain number of delegates were appointed by the regional and military party organizations. This formula was retained in the rules adopted at that congress. Those rules also retained regional control over the selection of candidates for the Central Committee, Presidium, and Executive Committee. Moreover it is apparent that control over cadres' assignments in the party also remained in the hands of the regional leaderships.

The party structure adopted at the Tenth Party Congress in 1974 remained basically unchanged until the Eleventh Party Congress in 1978. The Presidium elected after the Eleventh Party Congress was significantly smaller than its predecessor. Prior to the congress it had consisted of forty-eight members; the post-congress Presidium, sitting in mid-1981, was composed of twenty-four: three from each republic, two from each province, one from the party organization in the military, and the president of the LCY. The new Presidium comprised the most authoritative individuals in political life, including the presidents of each of the eight regional party organizations. All had been members of the earlier Presidium. Their continuation in office required a change in the party statute exempting this organ, and all the regional presidiums as well, from the requirement that at least one-third of the membership of leading organs be "renewed" at each election. Dolanc was elected secretary of the Presidium, continuing the pattern of his increasing power that began in January 1972. Nine members of the Central Committee were selected to serve as "executive secretaries" of the Presidium but were not elected to Presidium membership (see fig. 16).

These changes partially confirmed earlier rumors about creation of a politburo-like central party organ, although the new Presidium was substantially larger than the rumored body. According to the statute adopted at the congress the new Presidium was to perform a primarily political/directive role. Each of its members is responsible for "specific issues and tasks." Each of the "executive secretaries" of the Presidium also has a "concrete responsibility for specific areas of work," but their role is limited to "operational work on the carrying-out of policy . . . ." This division of labor in the Presidium undoubtedly increased the operational efficiency of this smaller body and thereby strengthened it.

Other changes in the statute also reinforced the authority of the new Presidium. A lengthy and entirely new section on democratic centralism, for example, emphasized the authority of the central party organs "as the unified political leadership of the entire League of Communists of Yugoslavia." It also emphasized the "equal responsibility" of the republican, provincial, and military party organizations that elect the members of these organs "for the construction and execution of the unified policy of the League . . . ." The statute adopted at the Eleventh Party Congress also reversed the trend toward increasing emphasis on the influence of regional organizations over the central organs in the formation of policy that had been evident since 1964. It defined the role of the regional party

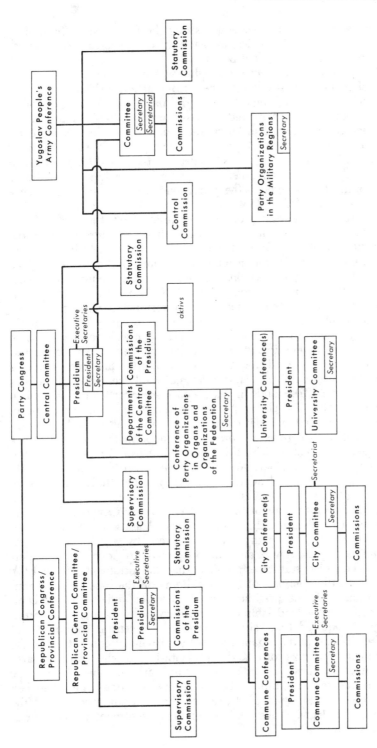

Figure 16. Formal Structure of the League of Communists of Yugoslavia, 1981

organizations in a manner emphasizing the influence of the unified party program and policies, as determined by central organs, over the formulation of regional policies.

The power of the central leadership was strengthened by the addition of two new subsections to the existing article on democratic centralism. The first of these permits the party leadership to "extend help to the membership and to basic organizations" of the party, and the second mandates "permanent and direct democratic communication" with sociopolitical, social, and self-managing organizations and delegations. Together, these additions increased the authority of the central party leadership to monitor developments throughout the party and society and to intervene wherever it decided to do so.

The new statute also prohibited exclusion from the party of any member of the Central Committee without the agreement of the committee itself. It required that when such an exclusion is under consideration, the Presidium must be informed and must be involved in the decision. This provision increased the relative autonomy of central party organs—including the Presidium—by insulating the members from punitive action by their regional party organization.

The manner in which these changes were carried out strengthened the importance of the formal rules of procedure. The decision to create a smaller Presidium with its own "executive secretaries" and to abolish the existing executive committee had been made as early as November 1977. That it was not implemented until the congress in June 1978 stands in sharp contrast to earlier periods, when even more sweeping changes in the organization of the central party had been carried out with little regard for existing rules of procedure. This adherence to formalities undoubtedly reflected a lack of urgency associated with this change. But it also ensured that this change would contribute to, rather than undermine, the authority of the central party leadership by emphasizing the importance of adhering to agreed-on rules of procedure.

As had been the case at the 1974 Tenth Party Congress, however, actions strengthening the central party leadership were accompanied at the Eleventh Party Congress by significant actions strengthening the power and authority of the regional party leaderships. The new statute established that the president of the LCY nominates the members of the Presidium "on the basis of prior consultations with the presidiums of the central and provincial committees" and the leadership of the military party organization. Similarly, it required that representatives of the central committees of the republican party organizations, the provincial committees of the provincial organizations, and representatives of the military party organizations must participate in determining membership changes in the central Presidium between regular elections, i.e., between congresses. These changes reaffirmed the continuing control of the regional leaderships over the power of appointment to the central organs of the party.

Changes in the statute increased the status of the Kosovo and Vojvodina party organizations in particular. Symbolically, they now were listed separately in the enumeration of "autonomous organizations in the unified League of Communists of Yugoslavia," although still designated in the next sentence as an "integral party" of the Serbian party organization. Substantively, they now were included with the republican organizations in the enumeration of organizations with which the president was mandated to maintain "permanent contact" and were allocated two positions on the Presidium in comparison to only one for the military party organization.

Other changes adopted at the Eleventh Party Congress suggest an attempt by regional leaders to weaken the power and authority of the central party organs directly. The statutory article defining the role of the Presidium requires it to "coordinate current ideo-political activity with the central and provincial committees" and the military party organization. Even more important, the provision concerning consecutive election to leading party organs and "executive-political functions" at all levels of the LCY was revised to prohibit entirely reelection to such positions, whereas the 1974 statute had only prohibited such election more than two times in succession. Consequently none of the secretaries elected to the Executive Committee of the Presidium at the Party Congress in 1974 was elected executive secretary of the Presidium at the Eleventh Party Congress. It is not surprising, therefore, that the new executive secretaries were selected from among younger and heretofore generally less powerful members of the Yugoslav elite, because the prohibition on reappointment to these positions precludes their using such positions to build up their own power. Such turnover among its secretaries is likely to undermine the power of the Presidium and its effectiveness as an executive organ.

An even more important weakening of the central party leadership and, indeed, of all leadership organs in the party, is contained in an important addition to the principles of democratic centralism contained in the new statute. An entirely new paragraph declared that democratic centralism is based on (among other things) "the obligation of members whose opinions and proposals remain in the minority in an organization or organ of the League of Communists to accept and carry out the decisions adopted by the majority, with freedom to retain [their] own opinion." This paragraph also stipulated that "any kind of activity which would make more difficult and interfere with the united action of communists . . . would represent a form of groupism and factional activity." Nonetheless the freedom of individual Communists to retain an opinion opposed to the positions adopted by party organs and organizations ultimately represents a serious formal limitation on the power of any central leadership to impose discipline on the broad party masses and thereby to forge the kind of unity necessary for the party to be able to fulfill the role of an integrative organization in society and politics.

This is especially true because in the year preceding the 1978 congress the leadership had come to some important conclusions about the nature of society itself and the party's role in it. After much discussion and controversy among the leadership, in June 1977 Kardelj presented a set of theses to the party Presidium for adoption as a basis for preparation for the upcoming party congress. After further discussion and apparent conflict and compromise in the leadership, these theses were published in the form of a book entitled *The Directions of Development of the Political System of Socialist Self-management.* In that book Kardelj suggested that in the future, politics in Yugoslavia will be characterized by continuing conflict among "a multitude of interests in society that arise out of class, economic, political, social, and other conditions of life, work, and the activity of people . . . . These differences and conflicts concern issues such as the further development of socialist society; the resolution of current economic, social, cultural, and other social problems; the direction and tempo of the further development of socioeconomic, political, and other relations; ideological and political differences that appear in connection with the treatment of concrete questions, etc." Kardelj characterized this state of affairs as "the pluralism of self-managing democratic harmonization of all the interests of these communities . . . . " "Since only that working man who is in a position not only to express his interests independently and democratically, but also to decide about them, can be a self-manager," Kardelj reasoned, "the very essence of self-management itself will impose the principle of interest pluralism as the basis for the system of self-managing democracy of a socialist society . . . . " "Every other political system," he asserted, "would be in fact a negation of self-management itself."

Unlike Western pluralists, however, Kardelj did not argue that the general social interest is defined by the accumulated interactions of particular or "partial" interests. Although he acknowledged that "it frequently is necessary to arrive at . . . the common social interest by means of the confrontation and selection of partial interests," he argued instead that

> when we talk about the fact that the system of self-managing democracy is based on the interest pluralism of self-managing subjects we are not then thinking only of partial interests (for example, the interests of organizations of associated labor or organized self-managing interest communities and other self-managing subjects or state organs), but also of the common social interests that must be the starting point for the determination of the strategy, directions, and method of the further economic, social, political, and cultural development of society as a whole. *Because a collection of partial interests does not in any way make up the common social interest.*

The common social interest, he insisted, is determined in a socialist self-managing society by the "subjective socialist forces," that is, by the League of Communists acting together with other sociopolitical organizations.

Despite the fact that mention of Kardelj's theory of "pluralism" was almost completely avoided at the Eleventh Party Congress, it is clear that his equation of the role of the party with the reconciliation of conflicting interests cut straight to the heart of the party's dilemma since 1966: How to define the obligations of individual Communists in nonparty organizations and institutions in a way that was consistent with both the principles of self-management and the maintenance of party unity?

At an earlier party conference devoted precisely to this question, one analyst had pointed out that individual Communists were required to participate in the decisionmaking processes of self-managing institutions and organizations from the perspective of the working class as a whole. He argued that "communists . . . cannot be 'advocates of partial interests,' but must articulate existing individual and group interests . . . so that each individual and group interest is brought to the level of the common [interest]; . . . so that these interests are integrated into the dominating interest of the working class as a whole . . . . "

Communists will be able to do this only when the principles of democratic centralism are observed, because democratic centralism ensures "the exclusion of potential possible role conflict in the activity of individual communists, organizations, and leaderships." Such role conflict, he pointed out, "arises precisely in situations when communists, organizations, or leaderships at a concrete level of decision-making find themselves faced with two forms of the manifestation of interest. One form . . . can be the interest of an individual branch, grouping, work organization, or some other interest structure such as a republic, commune, or province, and another [can be] the common interest—the interest of the entire movement . . . . "

Kardelj suggested that when the principle of democratic centralism is "applied faithfully," that is, when "not one communist, organization, or leadership can act in decisionmaking institutions . . . outside [the bounds of] decisions adopted in the League of Communists of Yugoslavia," such role conflict will be resolved in favor of the common interest. In other words, only the enforcement of strong party discipline will ensure that individual Communists perform an integrative role in society by advancing everywhere and in all institutions the common interest of the working class as defined by the party.

There are few substantive differences between this definition and Kardelj's later definition of the role of the individual Communist in the pluralism of self-managing interests. Kardelj argued quite simply that "the organized forces of socialist consciousness . . . must be the deciding factor of the consciousness of the delegate system." The decisionmaking process in self-managing organizations, he insisted, must be "open to the influence and cooperation of all those social forces that are able to bring into 'partial' self-managing decisionmaking elements of wider social perspectives, and in that way support the self-managing decisionmaking of the worker when he himself is not able to take such a perspective."

Kardelj's definition, however, shares with the earlier one a common underlying assumption about the internal character of the LCY. Both formulations posit the existence of a central party leadership that is both intent on and capable of overcoming the national and economic cleavages that divide it and of developing and enforcing a set of positions to provide guidance for individual Communists throughout the country. In short, both definitions call for the existence of a coherent leadership and a strongly disciplined party. And developments since the Eleventh Party Congress call into question the ability of that leadership to maintain such coherence and discipline for very long.

In November 1978, only a few months after the congress, a rotating chairmanship of the party Presidium was established. This was apparently in large part an attempt to prepare for Tito's succession by establishing a potential precedent for leadership arrangements after his death. By itself such an action need not undermine leadership coherence or its ability to maintain discipline. Shortly thereafter, however, Tito himself cited the establishment of this post and the long-standing practice of rotating the position of vice president of the collective Presidency, as precedents for undertaking a widespread campaign to apply the principles of rotation and shortened mandate periods to "other organs and organizations as well, starting from the commune up to the Federation." This suggestion quickly became known as the "Tito initiative."

By the spring of 1979, the initiative had been accepted by the leadership. In May the position of secretary of the Presidium was subjected to rotation on a two-year basis, and Dolanc voluntarily resigned from the position he had held for over eight years. In June the Presidium adopted a set of "conclusions" calling for "decumulation of functions" in party organs and the introduction of one-year mandates for the presidents of regional presidencies, assemblies at all levels, and other bodies, and two-year mandates for presidents of the executive organs of assemblies at all levels. The June 1979 conclusions also called for the application of rotation and one-year mandates to the regional party leaderships one year before the regional party congresses and conferences scheduled for 1982.

Implementation of these conclusions began almost immediately, with less powerful members of the state Presidency being dropped from simultaneous membership in the party Presidium. It continued over the course of the next year with the adoption of rotation and shortened mandate periods in local party organizations and nonparty sociopolitical organizations at all levels of the system. Application of the initiative to federal institutions, however, required amendment of the Constitution, and application of the initiative to the regional leaderships met with resistance from some of the regional leaderships. The Slovenian party secretary, for example, noted in November 1979 that the initiative was being implemented over some opposition within the Presidium itself. "Sometimes even we in the Central Committee," he suggested "catch ourselves talking

about the new method of work while working in the old way." From
the beginning, he observed, the representatives of Slovenia and the
Slovenian party organization in the Presidium and Central Committee accepted the idea of collective leadership, but "held to the
viewpoint that certain specific characteristics must be taken into account. The organs of the Federation are one thing, the organs of a
republic another, and the organs of a commune a third." While the
introduction of a one-year mandate on the level of the federation
was entirely appropriate and has been shown to be positive, the
Slovenian leadership, he reported, openly questioned whether this
formula was appropriate for the republics. Further evidence of differences among the regional leaderships could be found in the differences between the ways each approached the task of implementing
the June 1979 decisions.

The illness and death of Tito delayed debate and implementation
of the initiative until later in 1980. The process of constitutional
reform, which began with confidential discussions in January 1979
on the general outlines of the changes to be adopted, began in
earnest in late May. Although agreement was reached without great
difficulty on the principle of rotation and shortened mandates,
application of the initiative to the Federal Executive Council proved
to be a highly contentious issue. Representatives of the underdeveloped regions, convinced of the compulsory character of the conclusions adopted in June 1979 and committed to further "democratization" of the political system, pushed for the reduction of the
premier's term in office of two years and the elimination of his role
in selecting the other members of the government. Representatives
of the other regions, convinced of the need to ensure the continuing
decisionmaking effectiveness of the council, pressed to retain the
present arrangements.

Repeated negotiations and continuing interregional consultations
over the course of the summer and fall failed to produce agreement.
The conflicting views were reconciled only in October, when the
party Presidium intervened to decide the issue in favor of the status
quo. This suggests an awareness on the part of the party leadership
of the importance of strong central leadership to the Yugoslav
system. At the same time, however, the Presidium affirmed its commitment to apply the initiative to the regional party leaderships
before the Twelfth Party Congress, scheduled for spring 1982.

Changes carried out in the weeks immediately following the death
of Tito confirmed the already-established constitutional provisions
for succession in the state Presidency and demonstrated the continuing power of the regional leaderships in the LCY. Three hours after
Tito's death, a session of the state Presidency was convened, and
Lazar Kolisevski, who was at that time coming to the end of a one-
year term as vice president, was elected president of the Presidency
and Cvijetin Mijatovic was elected vice president. Ten days later, at
the conclusion of Kolisevski's original one-year term, Mijatovic was
elected president for a one-year term. Later that month, the order of

rotation among the regions was formally established for both positions. More important for the future stability of the country than the Presidency, however, is the central Presidium.

Since June 1979 the Presidency has taken a clearly secondary role to the party Presidium. The ability of the Presidium to intervene directly in federal policymaking even during the final stages of the process and thereby compel the reformation of policy demonstrates the superior authority of the LCY. In the month following Tito's death there was some uncertainty about whether a new president of the party would be elected to replace Tito. But that confusion was ended by a Presidium decision essentially to maintain the status quo, a decision that was ratified at the eleventh session of the Central Committee in June. The members of the Presidium decided to assign the power and authority granted in the party statutes to the president of the party to the Presidium as whole, and simply to change the title "Chairman of the Presidium" to "President of the Presidium." The new president of the Presidium would serve in the state Presidency in the name of the Central Committee. He would not, however, enjoy any of the authority of the old president of the party to nominate individuals for membership in the Presidium itself. For the exercise of this power, the Presidium established a special commission that would carry out its task on the basis of consultations with the regional party leaderships and the leadership of the party organization in the armed forces. In this way, the autonomous power of the regional leaderships was significantly enhanced in comparison to the state of affairs during Tito's tenure as president. Moreover that power was protected against encroachment by an ambitious "President of the Presidium," because the latter will serve for only one year, as had the chairman.

All the above changes are officially designated as "temporary" until confirmed or overturned at the Twelfth Party Congress, which was scheduled for early summer 1982. The leaders explicitly rejected the idea of convening an extraordinary congress of the party to alter the party statutes. They appeared to be both cautiously maintaining established principles and practices of decisionmaking and sustaining a relatively high level of unity. Whether the party leaders will be able to maintain in the future the unity displayed during the first year after Tito is, of course, the crucial question. Their plans to subject the regional party leaderships to rotation appeared incompatible with their ability to do so.

Other Sociopolitical Organizations

Yugoslavia is a highly organized society. In addition to the formal political structures of government, the party organization, and the organizations of the system of self-management in the economy that together involve hundreds of thousands of people to at least some degree in the political system, there are a number of important sociopolitical organizations that mobilize thousands more into organized activities that both support the established political order and provide important channels for the expression of particularistic interests. The roles of two of these organizations, the Socialist Alliance of Working People of Yugoslavia (SAWPY) and the trade unions, are formally defined in the Constitution.

The Socialist Alliance is the mass political front organization of the party. Established during World War II as an ostensible alliance of resistance forces fronting for the party's leadership, the Socialist Alliance functioned in the early period of communist power as a "transmission belt" for the exercise of party rule. As the party began to withdraw from direct involvement in the day-to-day management of society and formally abandoned its "ruling" function in favor of a "guiding" role in the development of society, the organizational structure of the Socialist Alliance increased in importance as an institutionalized channel for maintaining the party's direct contact with and influence over other nonparty organizations and social and political institutions. The statutes of SAWPY and the country's Constitution define the LCY as "the leading ideological and political force" in SAWPY and mandate SAWPY to "discuss social questions and take political initiative in all fields of social life." This includes submitting "proposals for the solution of social questions" and issuing "guidelines" for their solution to delegates in the local, regional, and federal assemblies; supervising the selection and election of candidates for membership in delegations and their delegates; overseeing the selection of candidates for all other public and social functions; overseeing cadres' policy; exercising a watchdog function over all self-managing, public, and social organs and institutions; facilitating political participation by the masses; and ensuring that "the working people and citizens" of Yugoslavia are kept informed. To enable SAWPY to perform these functions, the Constitution stipulates that it shall receive material and other support from the government.

The Socialist Alliance is organized on a federal principle. On the federal level, it is organized into a "conference" composed of regional delegations determined by the republican and provincial leaderships of SAWPY. The conference elects a Presidium, which includes a president, four vice presidents and a secretary, the presidents of the regional conferences and the conference for women ex officio, and representatives of the party leadership, the trade union leadership, the armed forces, the League of Socialist Youth of Yugoslavia, and other organizations and associations. The federal conference has also established a number of sections, or functional departments, for organizing discussions and formulating proposals for federal policy in a number of functional areas, such as socioeconomic relations in agriculture and the village; education, science, and culture; health and social policy; socioeconomic relations and development policy; sociopolitical relations, and other areas. During 1979 and 1980, as part of the campaign to implement the Tito initiative and in an effort both to distinguish the party more clearly from the government and to increase the party's ability to influence the governmental decisionmaking process, these sections have taken on increased importance as focal points in which the LCY has attempted to influence the development of social and economic policies. The Presidium of the federal conference has established a number of coordinating committees, other committees, commissions, and councils for both specific areas of governmental activity and more general social or ideopolitical issues. These include, for example, coordinating committees for cadres' policy in the federation and for people's defense and public self-protection; committees for the delegate system in the federation, for the concept of long-term development, for achieving housing policy, and for mass, ideological-educational, and sociopolitical work; councils for the mass media and for electing members of delegations; and numerous others. These bodies function as arenas for interregional consultation and coordination of policy and mass political action. Several are devoted to international ideological and political issues and to maintaining relations with the socialist or social-democratic parties and movements with which the LCY leadership prefers not to be associated officially.

This organization is reproduced in each of the republics and provinces in somewhat less elaborate form, modified by differences dictated by particular sociodemographic and economic conditions. It is also the general pattern at lower levels. Although in 1981 policy in both the Socialist Alliance and the LCY precluded individuals from holding positions in both organizations, the conferences of the Socialist Alliance at both the federal and regional levels are dominated by "professional political workers," that is, by party cadres, and in the presidiums that domination is almost total. This ensures that the Socialist Alliance remains a responsive, if not always effective, tool of party policies.

The trade unions are organized within the Confederation of Trade Unions of Yugoslavia, which is mandated by the Constitution to defend the political, social, and material interests and self-management rights of workers; advance the development of the economy; assist in the reconciliation of particularistic and common interests; oversee the selection and election of candidates for delegates to managing bodies in enterprises and delegations and delegates to assemblies; and assist in raising the class consciousness and sense of responsibility of workers. They are organized along the same general pattern as the LCY and Socialist Alliance, with the exception that—in keeping with the ideological principle that the working class is not divided by nation or region—the Council of the Confederation and its presidium do not appear to be divided into regional delegations. The presidium is, however, composed of both the heads of the federal committees of the confederation that constitute, in fact, the professional trade unions of Yugoslavia and the presidents of the regional trade-union councils.

Two other sociopolitical organizations deserve special mention because of their political importance. These are the Federation of

Reserve Officers and the Federation of Associations of Veterans of the National Liberation War (popularly known as SUBNOR). Both these organizations, but especially the latter, represent bastions of more conservative political views and have in the past been mobilized by the party leadership to support attempts to assert central authority in the party and party authority over society. The veteran's group is represented directly in the political system through the sociopolitical chambers of local and regional assemblies. As the wartime generation passes from the scene, however, the political clout of the veterans will certainly be reduced. The reserve officers' group, although clearly conservative in its orientation, has been decidedly more cautious politically than the veterans' group. Other organizations, such as the youth league, play a decidedly less significant role.

The Domestic Political Agenda

The post-Tito leadership is confronted with a number of economic problems that threaten the stability of the system. These include a serious balance-of-payments problem fueled in large part by the cost of imported energy but also by the limited ability of Yugoslav-manufactured goods to compete in Western markets; increasing foreign indebtedness and a concomitant mounting debt service burden; rampant inflation; excessive investment in industry at the expense of agricultural development; shortages of food, consumer goods, and raw materials; low productivity; and unemployment. The management of such problems would be difficult in any country. In Yugoslavia it is made even more difficult by the fact that actions intended to solve these problems must not only be effective, but must also be equitable in their impact on the various regions and nationalities if they are not to give rise to potentially explosive conflicts.

The energy problem appears to be susceptible to management through policies that are both economically rational and equitable, and therefore politically expedient. The major untapped sources of domestic energy are coal deposits in the underdeveloped areas, and their exploitation is being financed through direct investments from the electricity-deficient north. But the solutions to other problems appear to create at least as many problems as they solve (see Industry, ch. 3).

The current emphasis on increased investment in agriculture focuses on plans to aggregate small landholdings for more efficient cultivation. But geography, climate, and peasant resistance limit the amount that can be aggregated in the short or even medium term through outright purchase or creating cooperatives. Although some increases in production are likely to result, they may not outweigh the significant capital costs associated with these efforts. They are likely to be limited to a few regions containing the best land, and they certainly cannot come in time to alleviate present urgent problems of supplying cities, especially in the underdeveloped areas.

Attempts to increase the competitiveness and productivity of industry will hit an industrial work force already hard-hit by inflation and experiencing declining real incomes. The elimination of wasteful duplication will be particularly difficult to carry out equitably. The decision to improve trade balances by reducing imports of semifinished goods hits the highly profitable assembly industries of the north particularly hard. And finally, all these policies are very likely to increase unemployment—already a major problem.

The post-Tito party leadership is acutely aware of the potential for political crisis inherent in these conditions and has acknowledged it openly. Discussions at the first substantive Central Committee meeting following the death of Tito—convened in September 1980— included clear expressions of concern for the potential political consequences of dissatisfaction and frustration among workers caused by declining real incomes and worsening conditions. The leadership has also taken important steps toward bringing these problems under control with the more restrictive provisions of the five-year plan for 1981–85 and by securing a substantial amount of foreign credit from Western banks, oil-producing countries, and the International Monetary Fund. But Yugoslav five-year plans are not the products of Soviet-style central planners who can exercise determinative influence over the economy (see Role of Government, ch. 3). They are in large part political documents negotiated by representatives of the republic and provinces seeking official sanction for the protection of particularistic regional interests, and they require the continued support of regional leaders for implementation. Given the pressures of the economic problems of the 1980s, the representatives of the developed regions are likely to intensify their already determined, and as of 1981 partially successful, efforts to free their regions from the burden of forced transfers of capital resources from the north to the south. If they pursue this goal too vigorously they run the risk of intensifying interregional conflict. And if they are too successful, they will exacerbate the very real problems of the south.

The explosiveness of the economic problems, particularly in the underdeveloped regions, was underlined for the leadership by the outbreak of another series of violent, nationalist demonstrations by the Albanian population in Kosovo in the spring of 1981. These were forcefully suppressed by the central leadership. According to an interview with the federal secretary for internal affairs published in the aftermath of these demonstrations, a variety of Albanian nationalist activities and incidents had been taking place in Kosovo and those areas of Macedonia inhabited by Albanians throughout the 1970s. These incidents included the painting of nationalistic slogans on buildings, distribution of nationalistic pamphlets, and organization of secret societies—which resulted in the arrest, trial, and punishment of over 600 individuals.

With the illness and death of Tito in 1980, the secretary reported, the level and scope of such activities increased significantly. In mid-March 1981, frustration among the students of Pristina University over poor food and living conditions erupted in a series of violent demonstrations. These soon escalated into mass demonstrations, involving as many as 10,000 people at one time, in Pristina and at least six other nearby cities and towns. Demonstrations were characterized by slogans demanding, among other things, full republic status for Kosovo, the unification of all Albanian-inhabited territory in Yugoslavia, and even the separation of Kosovo from Yugoslavia and its annexation to Albania—demands that also had been raised in 1968. Other slogans protested the alleged economic exploitation of Kosovo by the Belgrade regime and decried the economic inequalities characteristic of society generally. The ferocity of these demonstrations was such that their suppression required the use of military, security police, and militia units drawn from other regions and backed up by tanks. Several deaths and many injuries occurred on both sides, as well as extensive property damage. They were followed by the arrest of dozens of alleged organizers of the demonstrations and summary judgments against hundreds of participants. One month later the Albanian president of the Kosovo party organization resigned his position.

These events shook the very foundation of the political order. Early attempts by the political leadership to restrict information about the events led to protests by Belgrade journalists asserting the rights of Yugoslav citizens to know what was going on in their own country and reminding the leadership of the importance of maintaining popular confidence in newspapers and other public institutions. They prompted some thoughtful reconsideration of certain disproportions in the patterns of social and economic development in the underdeveloped regions. Far too many students were being trained in intellectual disciplines in which there were simply not enough jobs for them, and too few were being trained in the skilled professions required by the economy. Moreover the technologically advanced and capital-intensive character of major development projects in the southern regions were not helping to alleviate the serious unemployment situation there. And, of course, these events reopened the sensitive issue of Serbian-Albanian relations in Kosovo and the status of Kosovo in the Republic of Serbia and the Yugoslav federation. These issues led, in turn, to serious questioning in Yugoslavia whether the country was returning to the situation of the late 1960s.

The events in Kosovo also affected Yugoslavia's relationship with Albania. The Albanian leadership, through its closely controlled press, expressed open support for the demands raised by the demonstrators in Kosovo, calling for the "liberation of Kosovo from the tutelage of Serbia," and raised thinly veiled irredentist demands of their own in Yugoslav territories. The Albanian press explained the demonstrations in terms of the "poverty and misery" and "lack of freedom" of the Albanian population in Kosovo and cited the backwardness of the province in comparison to the rest of Yugoslavia as evidence of discrimination. The Yugoslav leadership in Belgrade, in

Kosovo, and the other regions unanimously condemned the Albanian charges as "absurd and cynical" and contrasted the "Stalinist" character of the Albanian system to the more democratic nature of the Yugoslav political order. The polemical exchanges between the two countries were long and bitter and destroyed what little progress had been made in improving relations in previous years.

The Yugoslav leadership mounted an obvious campaign to reaffirm its commitment to accelerated development of Kosovo and to emphasize all that had, in fact, been achieved there. Nevertheless the eventual political repercussions of these events remained unclear in mid-1981. It was clear, however, that the central party leadership—indeed, the entire political leadership—must come to grips with the evident political failure of development policy and devise a response to the apparent implacability of Albanian nationalism.

Foreign Policy

The policy of nonalignment that has been the basis of Yugoslav foreign policy since the early 1950s was forced on the Yugoslav leadership by circumstance (see The Policy of Nonalignment, ch. 1). Following the break with Stalin, Tito was compelled to find some formula for guiding Yugoslavia's foreign policy that would differentiate it from the Soviet Union without surrendering its claim to leadership in the construction of a socialist order and that would generate international support without requiring it to draw too close to the capitalist camp. The emergence of assertive nationalist movements for independence and concomitant rapid decolonization of the Third World provided the opportunity to achieve these goals. Capitalizing on his prestige as the leader of a successful national liberation movement and an opponent of Stalin, Tito played an important role, along with India's Jawaharlal Nehru and Egypt's Gamal Abdul Nasser, in establishing a third force in international politics in 1961—the force of an organized political movement to the newly independent states or recently successful revolutionary regimes, ostensibly independent of either Soviet or Western domination. Although for many years it was argued that Yugoslavia's participation in founding and leading that movement constituted nothing more than proxy representation of Soviet interests, the policy of nonalignment and the creation of a movement behind it served Yugoslav national interests far more than Soviet interests.

Leadership of the nonalignment movement gave Yugoslavia—and Tito personally—enormous international prestige and influence, and it created a bloc of political supporters in the power politics of East-West relations that could be mobilized to support Yugoslav interests. At the same time, Yugoslav leadership of the movement provided a first-hand model for the leaders of the Third World of a socialist system independent of, and in some cases opposed to, the Soviet Union.

In practice, nonalignment was defined in terms of East and West, and not necessarily in terms of conflicts within the Third World itself. Consequently Yugoslav policy could be quite strongly aligned with one side or another in such a conflict, and such alignment could bring Yugoslavia into closer alignment with the Soviet Union than it might otherwise have chosen. No better example of such one-sidedness can be found than Yugoslav policy with respect to the Middle East. In large part as the result of Tito's personal friendship with Nasser, Yugoslav policy toward the Arab-Israeli conflict has always been decidedly pro-Arab. Moreover in later years, for reasons that are not entirely clear (but which may have much to do with Yugoslavia's decided enthusiasm for supporting so-called national liberation struggles, but certainly have nothing whatsoever to do with any anti-Semitic tendencies in Yugoslavia or among its leaders, for there are none of any significance at all), Yugoslavia's policy became strongly supportive of the Palestine Liberation Organization (PLO) and its policies. This pro-Arab tilt led Tito to permit the Soviet Union to cross Yugoslav airspace to resupply its Egyptian ally in time of war and later made Yugoslavia a strong supporter of the United Nations resolution condemning Zionism "as a form of racism." Indeed, this anomaly in Yugoslav policy eventually led to a situation in which the Yugoslavs were actually condemning the terrorist activities of Croatian and other émigré groups on the one hand while permitting PLO-associated terrorists to pass freely through Yugoslav territory to carry out their activities, on the other.

The death of Tito will surely reduce Yugoslav prestige and influence in the movement. Tito's presence was required in Havana in 1979 to counterbalance rising Cuban influence, and especially the powerful personal appeal of Fidel Castro, to an increasingly anti-Western, and particularly anti-American, movement. In Tito's absence, only the Soviet invasion of Afghanistan and the ongoing threat of invasion in Poland in mid-1981 seemed to prevent Yugoslavia's replacement by Cuba at the head of the nonalignment movement.

Like nonalignment, Yugoslav policy toward the Soviet Union has its roots in the break with Stalin and Nikita Khrushchev's eventual recognition of Yugoslavia's right to develop its own autonomous brand of socialism. Since 1956 the Yugoslavs had been careful to reaffirm at every opportunity the principles contained in both the Belgrade Declaration of 1955, reestablishing state-to-state relations, and the Moscow Declaration of 1956, reestablishing party-to-party relations on an equal basis. Yugoslav attitudes and policy toward the Soviet Union in the wake of the Soviet invasion of Czechoslovakia in 1968 are best captured in the reform of Yugoslav military and defense policies. The Yugoslavs adopted a strategy of preparing for aggression from all directions and established an "all-peoples territorial defense" force designed to impress on any would-be invader the certainty that such an invasion—unlike the invasion of Czechoslovakia—would be very costly (see Military Tactics, ch. 5).

Despite tentative steps toward a rapprochement during the early

1970s, highlighted by Leonid Brezhnev's acknowledgement of non-alignment and reaffirmation of the Moscow and Belgrade Declarations during his visit to Yugoslavia at the height of the Croatian crisis of 1971, Yugoslav-Soviet relations took another downturn in 1974 with the discovery by the Yugoslavs of a clandestine, anti-Titoist, pro-Soviet communist party operating inside Yugoslavia with the apparent support of the Soviet Union. Continuing differences between the Yugoslavs and the Soviets over the question of the international communist movement were emphasized again during preparations for the 1976 Berlin conference of European communist parties, when Yugoslavia sided with the Eurocommunists to insist on decisionmaking based on unanimity and to use those principles to eliminate all references to principles of "proletarian internationalism" calling for fealty to the Soviet Union.

Just as Yugoslav sensitivity to any Soviet attempt to reduce Yugoslavia's autonomy lies at the heart of Yugoslav-Soviet tensions, the improvement in United States-Yugoslav relations can be attributed to the finely crafted American statement of policy toward that country delivered by President Jimmy Carter in 1978. That statement has been read by the Yugoslav leadership as serving both countries' interests and, therefore, remains an important factor shaping Yugoslav perceptions of the United States.

* * *

The single finest study of the Yugoslav system up to 1966 is found in Paul Shoup's *Communism and the Yugoslav National Question,* which focuses primarily on the communist leadership's responses over time to the nationality conflicts that have divided the country. A more comprehensive survey of the development and character of the social and political order as it existed in 1960 is provided in George Hoffman and Fred Warner Neal, *Yugoslavia and the New Communism.* The impact of the break with Stalin on the political thinking and ideology of the Yugoslav leadership is examined in brilliant detail in A. Ross Johnson, *The Transformation of Communist Ideology.* For a good historical review and summary treatment of the system established in the postwar period and the 1950s, and for a detailed analysis of the political order established under the 1963 constitution, see Fritz W. Hondius, *The Yugoslav Community of Nations.* The momentous political events of the mid-sixties are described in a journalistic fashion in Paul Lendvai, *Eagles in Cobwebs.* An impressive political history of the contemporary period emphasized in this chapter is found in Dennison Rusinow, *The Yugoslav Experiment.* A sociological view of the system as it existed in the mid-seventies is found in Bogdan Denitch, *The Legitimation of a Revolution.* Readers interested in the background to the current gulf between the regime and its Marxist intellectual critics are directed to Gerson Sher, *Praxis: Marxist Criticism and Dissent in Socialist Yugoslavia.* (For further information see Bibliography.)

Chapter 5. National Security

Yugoslav People's Army

THE YUGOSLAV PEOPLE'S ARMY is a unique institution—the result of historical forces, strategic geographical realities, and economic constraints. It is a communist East European armed force not allied to the Soviet Union. Much of its military equipment—including submarines, jet fighters, and infantry weapons—has been locally produced, although many sophisticated components were acquired both from Western and Warsaw Pact sources. Its overall defense posture was to fight a guerrilla war in the event of a large-scale invasion, but it possessed sufficient fighting capability and heavy equipment to match any of its neighbors in a local military confrontation.

The National Defense Law of 1969 provided a new, important contribution to the nation's defense posture by instituting the Territorial Defense Force. By late 1980 this force, which was organized at the republic, provincial, and commune levels, had grown to about 1 million personnel and was expected to reach 3 million during the 1980s.

Two nationwide police forces—the State Security Service and the Public Security Service—possessed responsibility for the enforcement of law and order.

Development of Modern Forces

The present-day Yugoslav armed forces had their origin in the communist-led Partisan (see Glossary) guerrilla bands that began operations against German occupation forces in the summer of 1941. The Communist Party of Yugoslavia (CPY), outlawed since 1921, had operated underground during almost the entire interwar period. By the late 1930s it had organized small, armed bands composed largely of Communists, veterans of the International Brigade of the Spanish Republican Army, and left-wing intellectuals. Until the German invasion of the Soviet Union, these units engaged in training, acquired arms, and sabotaged the Yugoslav defense effort.

On receipt of the news that German forces had invaded the Soviet Union, communist Partisans took the field against Axis forces in Yugoslavia. Led by Josip Broz Tito, a Croatian Communist and veteran of the Russian Revolution and the Soviet Red Army, the Partisans were one of the better organized resistance forces that arose after the disintegration of the regular elements of the Yugoslav army. In late 1941 they reorganized into larger units called proletarian brigades; thereafter they did not limit activities to their region of origin but operated in various parts of the country.

The other major resistance movement was made up of anticommunist forces under the leadership of a former colonel of the Yugoslav army, Draza Mihailovic. This force—the Yugoslav Army of the Fatherland—including surviving units of the Yugoslav Royal Army, small landholders, students, and other resistance elements, was often loosely referred to as Cetniks, or guerrilla resistance forces. These forces initiated operations in the mountains of Bosnia shortly after the majority of the Yugoslav army was overwhelmed by the Axis forces in 1941. They later established themselves in the mountains of western Serbia, which remained their major stronghold (see fig. 1). In addition some independent Cetnik guerrilla units operated in other regions of the country.

During the first months of German occupation, Partisans and Cetniks fought side by side and gained some noteworthy successes in operations that resulted in the liberation of sizable areas. Because of differing political orientations and loyalties, however, conflicts developed into serious fighting by the end of 1941. Reconciliation proved impossible, and until the end of the war, open hostility between the groups resulted in periodic armed clashes.

Allied support was initially furnished only to the Cetniks, but by 1943 the Allies began to curtail that support and to furnish increasing quantities of supplies to the Partisans. In 1944 military aid was withdrawn from the Cetniks and thereafter was made available only to the Partisans (see The War: Occupation and Resistance, ch. 1).

By 1942 the Partisans had been established as the National Army of Liberation. At the end of 1943 the National Army of Liberation claimed a strength of over 300,000, most of whom served in some twenty-seven divisions of 4,000 to 7,000 men each, and Tito had been given the honorary title of Marshal of Yugoslavia by the National Liberation Committee. In late 1944 reverses suffered by German forces in other areas and strong pressures from Soviet forces and Yugoslav resistance units forced the withdrawal of Axis military units from the country. By October Belgrade had been occupied by Partisans, Soviet forces had withdrawn from the area, and Tito was able to entrench his control.

The National Army of Liberation was renamed the Yugoslav People's Army (YPA) on March 1, 1945, and Tito's supreme headquarters operated as the general staff for all forces—land, sea, and air. Negotiations were concluded with the Soviet Union for military assistance, including materiel and military advisers. Soviet military personnel infiltrated all echelons of the army in an attempt to transform the Yugoslav military establishment into a satellite communist force. Yugoslav objections to the Sovietization of the army, the power base for the Tito regime, became a major factor in the expulsion of Yugoslavia from the Communist Information Bureau (Cominform—see Glossary) in June 1948 (see The Break with Stalin, ch. 1). After the open break with the Soviet Union, all Soviet assistance ceased, and Tito was forced to turn to the West for assistance in order to continue the building up of the country's armed forces.

By the mid-1960s the costs of expanding, maintaining, and modernizing the YPA had become an issue of increasing concern to the country's economic and political decisionmakers. In 1966 and 1967 those leaders reviewed their assessments of the potential military threats and reexamined the country's resources and capabilities to repel an invasion. They concluded that the cost of equipping and maintaining sufficient conventional armed forces exceeded the state's ability. As they often did when confronted with serious problems, Tito and his closest colleagues turned for guidance to their wartime experience as Partisans. The invasion of Czechoslovakia in August 1968 served as reminder to all Yugoslavs of Soviet willingness to use force. The decision was made to augment the YPA with a massive paramilitary force manned by citizen soldiers. During the 1970s this new force—the Territorial Defense Force (TDF)—was expanded, and its relationship with the regular armed forces was established (see Missions and Organization, this ch.).

Attitudes Toward the Military

Although patriotism in the past was felt in the narrow, regional sense of loyalty primarily to the clan or national group, developments after the nation was formed in 1918—particularly the intense conflict during and after World War II—served to awaken a broader, more inclusive love of country. The patriotism and determination of Yugoslav troops when their country is endangered by foreign forces have been described as highly exemplary, and these traits are important factors in the adaptability of the average youth to military service.

Loyalty to the communist regime does not equal the soldier's loyalty to his country. Continued identification of the army with the communist-led Partisans who participated in the successful liberation of the country in World War II was still strong in 1981, however, and the sustained prestige of the military has influenced the conscripted soldier's attitude toward service under communist governmental leadership. The break with the Soviet Union in 1948 also raised the regard in which Tito and the military were held by the general population. The armed forces have remained loyal to central authority, and in general the military forces have been well regarded by the majority of the people.

As a result of the National Defense Law of 1969, every citizen is required to participate in national defense organizations. Political organs in the republics, provinces, and lower administrative entities are authorized to "organize national defense and to command the battle directly." The defense law gave a legal basis to territorial defense formations, establishing these citizen-militia units as legally and doctrinally coequal to the YPA. Observers believe that this new concept caused considerable discussion within the military leadership. Generally, two schools of thought developed. A so-called "romantic" Partisan school called for the recreation of the scattered organizations and small-unit operations of the World War II Partisan warfare; this view was also supported by some political figures in the republics, particularly in Croatia and Slovenia, who went as far as to advocate separate republican armies. The other school, conscious of the federalizing and unifying importance of the YPA, opposed any deemphasis or decentralization of the regular forces. Given Tito's overwhelming support for the latter, however, these differences were submerged without serious tension.

The modern Yugoslav state, composed of major culturally divergent nationality (see Glossary) groups, each having a separate military tradition, was developed through a long succession of wars dating back to the Greco-Roman conquests. After the Slav peoples entered the Balkan Peninsula in the sixth and seventh centuries, they fought against successive waves of Asian and other invaders; they fought Romans, Goths, Franks, Avars, Magyars, and Turks for over 100 years, sometimes winning victories and other times suffering terrible defeat (see Early Slav History, ch. 1). This almost constant warfare spawned proficient fighters with great traditions of heroism and valor. Notably individualistic and separated by religious, linguistic, and cultural differences, the South Slavs did not organize unified resistance to alien conquest. Warfare was conducted by clans, by guerrilla bands loosely associated on a regional basis, or more rarely by cohesive and unified resistance forces representing fairly large numbers of a single nationality group. A tradition of resistance that cut across nationality lines did not develop until after the middle of the nineteenth century. War became the principal occupation for many men for long periods of time, acquiring an esteemed status. Bravery, sacrifice, and death in battle were regarded as normal. Slav warriors have been memorialized in literature and folklore, and many villages have commemorated their heroes in songs and poems.

In 1389 Serbian, Albanian, Montenegrin, and Bosnian troops under the command of the Serbian Prince Lazar were defeated by the Turks at the Battle of Kosovo. This marked the beginning of Turkish dominance in the area, and with it came the greater part of the epic tradition. Ironically, though the Battle of Kosovo was a tragic defeat, legends of valor and heroic deeds by Serbian warriors have served to commemorate it as an important event in Serbian military history.

The long struggle against the Turks was vicious and bloody, and it was not uncommon for rebellious villages to be massacred. Heads were severed; inhabitants were impaled. Slow death was common. Christian boys were forcibly levied into the Turkish service, taken to Turkey to be made Muslims, and trained for service as shock troops known as Janissary units, which formed the elite, professional core of the Ottoman forces. This system of "child tribute" became more unbearable and cruel when, by the eighteenth century, Janissary troops were employed to suppress Slav revolts, thus contributing to continued subjugation by and the hatred of Ottoman rule.

Heroic resistance was not confined to any one national group. In 1593 a decisive defeat was administered to the Turks by the Croats. The Montenegrins, long embattled in their rugged homeland, were never completely conquered. Their relentless struggle against the

Turks established their reputation as redoubtable fighters with strong loyalties and remarkable courage, but the prolonged conflict exacted a heavy toll.

Austro-Hungarian armies began invading areas of the crumbling Ottoman Empire in the eighteenth century. Large numbers of Serbs, Croats, and Slovenes served in the Austro-Hungarian units and were considered among the best troops in the empire. Serbian units also fought well in the Serbo-Bulgarian war of 1885. Allied Serbian and Montenegrin troops were victorious in the Balkan wars of 1912–13, in which the Turks were forced out of most of European Turkey, and the military power of Serbia was greatly strengthened in southern Europe. In the initial stages of World War I the Serbs defended their territory victoriously against invasion by Austrian forces, but they were subsequently overcome by superior Austro-German forces. When the Kingdom of Serbs, Croats, and Slovenes (later changed to Yugoslavia) was established after World War I, the Serbian royal house ascended the throne, and its military organization was given a leading role in the new state. The Royal Yugoslav Army was structured along Serbian lines, with the Croats and Slovenes playing smaller roles in the policies affecting its development. This overwhelming Serbian influence tended to perpetuate and intensify traditional animosities between Serbs and Croats, both in the armed forces and among the people. This hatred was manipulated by the Germans when they invaded Yugoslavia in World War II. Pro-Nazi Croatian forces were used to assist Hitler in the occupation of the former Kingdom of Yugoslavia (see The War: Occupation and Resistance, ch. 1).

National Security Concerns

Yugoslavia acts as a geographic barrier between the Warsaw Pact nations of Hungary, Romania, and Bulgaria and the North Atlantic Treaty Organization (NATO) nations, Italy and Greece. Because the government has avoided military alliance with either East or West, it must be prepared to defend all its borders. The forbidding mountain ranges of southern Croatia, Bosnia and Hercegovina, and Montenegro act as natural barriers for the bulk of the Yugoslav western borders, severely limiting access to and from the Mediterranean and Adriatic seas (see fig. 17). The northern region of Yugoslavia facing Europe is most important economically, has a high population density, and its open terrain is without significant defensible natural borders.

The mountainous section south of the Danube-Sava line is broken up into numerous small areas—many of which are still economically underdeveloped and isolated from each other—making large-scale operations with heavy weapons at division—or even brigade—level difficult, if not impossible. These areas invite guerrilla warfare. Montenegrin mountain regions, the Black Mountains near Skopje, the North Albanian Alps, and the Dinaric Alps served as refuge for

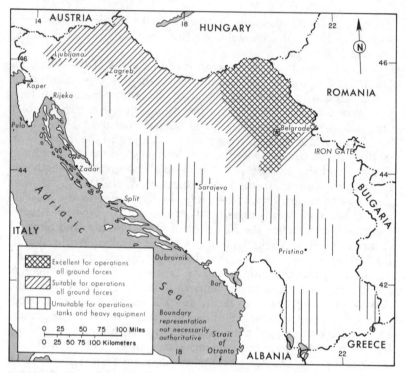

Figure 17. Terrain Considerations in Military Operations

the Partisans during World War II and would in any future internal Yugoslav military operations.

In addition to no serious natural barriers in the north, i.e., upper Italy, Yugoslavia is also extremely vulnerable in the east on the Pannonian Plains. This connecting route, known as the Julian/Laiback (Ljubljana) Gate, has historically acted as a trough for military forces pushing east or west, and probably would be exploited in any future conflict.

Yugoslavia shares a 1,700-kilometer frontier with the Warsaw Pact countries. The 623-kilometer Hungarian border is considered the most vulnerable area in the military-geographical sense, virtually a classical invasion route for tank formations. The only terrain features that would limit wide-scale armored maneuvers are the marshes east of Osijek at the mouth of the Drava River where it joins the Danube, the Slavonia Mountains, and the hilly region south of Novi Sad known as Frushka Gora. This strategic weakness on the Hungarian border, from the Yugoslav perspective, is magnified by the fact that the Soviet Union has forward-deployed and combat-ready tank and motorized rifle divisions that could cross into Yugoslavia with little warning. The 557-kilometer border with Romania must be classified as vulnerable in the northern sector; the absence of Soviet divisions in Romania and traditionally warm Yugoslav-Romanian relations probably tend to moderate Yugoslav military concerns, however, especially when compared to potential danger from Hungary. Despite this the Yugoslavs in their war plans must count on Soviet forces passing through Romania.

The 536-kilometer Bulgarian border may be considered secure in the military-geographical sense, but festering Yugoslav-Bulgarian enmity over Macedonian territorial and national issues compels Yugoslav strategic planners to commit and deploy forces defensively in this area. The Yugoslavs are also sensitive to the fact that at some future time Bulgaria, as a loyal Warsaw Pact member, could use Macedonia as a land bridge to link Albania with the Warsaw Pact, providing Soviet access to ports on the Adriatic for Soviet naval and maritime ships.

Except for short-term post-World War II guerrilla activity, the Yugoslavs have considered their borders with Greece relatively secure and have through the exchange of military visits by high-ranking Greek and Yugoslav military officers made a conscious effort to sustain good relations. For the Yugoslav leaders, the break with the Soviet Union made cordial relations with Greece and Italy an essential national security issue. Belgrade's relations with Athens and Rome, despite different social systems and ideologies, may be considered friendly, though Italian/Yugoslav competitive interest in Trieste and the Adriatic littoral remains a source of tension and probably continues as a factor in Yugoslav war planning.

Since the advent of nuclear weapons, the relatively narrow Adriatic Sea is no longer a tempting site for the development of large-scale military amphibian operations. The Dalmatian Coast has a number of first-class natural harbors with deep navigable channels, such as Kotor, Dubrovnik, Split, Sibenik, Bar, Rijeka, Pula, and Koper. The Dalmatian Islands could also be developed to a much larger degree as naval bases and air defense installations. The military use of these ports is limited from the Yugoslav standpoint by high mountain ranges—the Dinaric Alps—that separate the narrow coastal fringe from the hinterland. In terms of strategic mobility, this mountain wall not only acts as a restriction on sustaining forces in littoral areas of military operations but it also protects against landing operations from the sea. Strategically, however, it is believed that as the first line of defense of its Adriatic coast, the Yugoslavs would blockade the Strait of Otranto between Albania and Italy using sea mines, land-based aircraft, submarines, and torpedo boats and other light surface ships.

The integration of all peoples of Yugoslavia into a unified military establishment remained a continuing challenge to the central government in mid-1981. Historical enmity between Serbs and Croats, Roman Catholics and Eastern Orthodox, Muslims and Christians, Turks and Slavs still existed (see Peoples of Yugoslavia, ch. 2). Staffing of the military hierachy reflected this sensitivity to nationality problems. Key leadership positions generally reflected a proportionate balance of Serbian, Croatian, Macedonian, Bosnian, Slovenian, and Albanian representation. The language of the armed forces was Serbo-Croatian. Yugoslav patriotism and federal ideology were stressed. The military academies ensured that quotas for officer candidates were developed on a national (see Glossary) representational basis. Political training in the military organization pressed the theme that Yugoslav armed forces were to function as a unifying force for the state. Though there continued to be indications that national antagonism persisted at the lower tactical levels of the armed forces, there was much evidence in the early 1980s to support the successful development of officer leadership cadres that would represent a federal, centralized, Yugoslav ethos rather than narrower interests based on nationality and the republics.

During Tito's life a complete merger of all political and military authority existed: Tito was head of state, secretary general of the League of Communist of Yugoslavia (LCY), and supreme commander of the armed forces. He ensured that the armed forces served as the underpinnings for his federalization of Yugoslavia. His legacy to the armed forces consists of his mandate to the military to guarantee continued political unification and to act as a protector of the federalized state against internal as well as external enemies.

Missions and Organization

In late 1981 the Yugoslav national security organizational model continued to differ from most others because the Yugoslav forces consisted of two distinct elements—the YPA and the TDF—which were organizationally unified (see fig. 18). The TDF was essentially a regional command, each republic or province having considerable autonomy, but ultimately it was subordinated to the Federal Executive Council (see fig. 15). Consequently the TDF was not part of the Federal Secretariat for National Defense-YPA chain of command. Local TDF units fell under YPA tactical command only. When engaged in joint operations with YPA units on occupied territory, the TDF units would remain under regional defense commands. If an entire Yugoslav republic should be overrun by the enemy, that defense command would assume control of all military units in its territory—YPA as well as TDF units. Reverting in part to their World War II experience, the Yugoslavs have constructed a command and control mechanism to ensure that large-scale military resistance could continue even if the top of the military command structure were destroyed.

The army, as the predominant military force and largest element within the YPA, was specifically charged with the overall defense of the country and was assisted in this task by the Frontier Guard, the navy, and the air force. The Frontier Guard controlled all border areas, regulated the movement of all persons across the frontiers, and performed tasks relating to the maintenance of internal order and security.

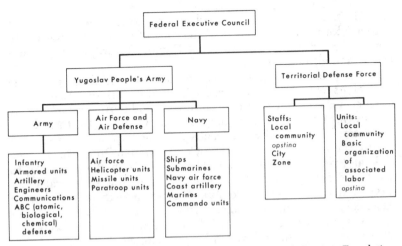

Source: Based on information from Joint Publications Research Service, *Translations on East Europe, Political, Sociological, and Military Affairs*, "Defense School: The Yugoslav Armed Forces—Bulwark of Our Defense," *Front*, Belgrade, Nov. 28, 1980, p. 44.

Figure 18. Organization of the Yugoslav Armed Forces

The naval forces were charged with guarding the coast and the seaward approaches to the country, as well as protecting and controlling the river lines of communication. In addition they provided sea lift and naval support to the ground force. The air force possessed the mission of nullifying or reducing the effectiveness of an enemy air attack and of providing close air support to ground forces. In carrying out this mission the Air Defense Force operated under administrative and operational control of the air force.

High Command

The officer corps can be best described as heterogeneous in composition and homogeneous in outlook. There has been occasional criticism that Serbs predominated in the officer corps, and it would appear in fact that over half of the officers are Serbs, though they comprise roughly 40 percent of the population. The proportion of generals and senior commanders of various nationalities is much closer to that in the general population—actually smaller in the case of Serbs and greater in the case of Croats. The compositions of high military staffs indicate a rough balance of nationalities.

Under the 1974 Constitution and the National Defense Law of April 1974, President Tito was the supreme commander of the armed forces. In this capacity the president exercised control over the military establishment through the federal secretary for national defense and his subordinate, the chief of the general staff, who acted as the immediate command element of the armed forces. This chain of command remained essentially in operation after Tito's death in

May 1980. The command channel passed directly from the federal secretary for national defense and the chief of the general staff to the commanders of military districts, the Frontier Guard, the navy, and the air and air defense forces.

In the event of a national emergency and the inability of the Federal Assembly to meet, the president (i.e., the president of the Presidency), is empowered to declare war, and during a state of war or an armed attack by a hostile force, he would, upon the recommendation of the Federal Executive Council, promulgate decrees having the force of law (see The Constitutional Order ch. 4). The Federal Executive Council was also vested with the authority to select personnel for key defense posts, including that of federal secretary for national defense. Because Tito nominated the president of the Federal Executive Council who in turn selected the other members, the decisions of the Federal Executive Council were, for all practical purposes, controlled by Tito himself.

The Federal Executive Council also appointed the National Defense Council (sometimes called the Military Council), a high-level peacetime advisory body to the president, responsible for mobilization of all national resources required for the national defense. The president of the republic was chairman of the council, and its membership included the federal secretary for national defense, the various assistant secretaries for national defense, the chief of the general staff, and many of the senior military commanders.

The Federal Secretariat for National Defense was the policymaking and directive body of the armed forces. To assist the federal secretary and his assistants in functions that apply to all the services, there were directorates charged with supervising activities in the fields of training, the rear services (logistics), communications, personnel, and the like. The chief of the general staff was the principal assistant to the federal secretary for national defense and took over his functions in his absence. The general staff, charged with formulation and coordination of plans and policies within the military establishment, was organized into general and special sections. The general section was concerned with intelligence, personnel, organization, and mobilization and operations; the special sections were assigned functions that related to the technical and administrative services.

Army Organization

Of the 190,000 personnel on active duty about 140,000 were conscripts. *The Military Balance 1981–82* reported that the army's field elements consisted of eight infantry divisions, eight independent tank brigades, sixteen independent infantry brigades, one mountain brigade, one airborne brigade, twelve field and twelve antiaircraft regiments, and six antitank regiments. For operational and administrative control of these combat forces, the country was divided into six military districts, each of which in turn was subdivided into two or more subdistricts. Each field headquarters operated in the

Soldiers engaged in field training exercises
Courtesy Embassy of Yugoslavia, Washington

general chain of command and had supervisory responsibility over the tactical units within its area for administration, training, or other military activities.

In September 1981 the Yugoslav press reported on proposed legislation to revise certain aspects of the 1974 National Defense Law. The proposed legislation assigns expanded emergency powers to the president of the Presidency and greatly increases the roles and powers of the federal secretary for national defense and the National Defense Council. If the legislation is adopted, the National Defense Council will possess "full control of the armed forces." Moreover, the council will consist of the federal secretary as chairman; the chief of staff of the YPA; the undersecretary and the deputy secretaries of the Federal Secretariat for National Defense; the chief inspector of the TDF; the president of the party committee in the YPA; and military commanders to be appointed by the federal secretary. There will, therefore, be no civilians on the council.

Because the types of equipment in infantry divisions differ, it is difficult to organize all divisions exactly the same way; nevertheless a typical Yugoslav rifle division could be expected to have three rifle regiments, an artillery regiment, and a tank regiment. Additionally there would be an engineer battalion and a signal battalion, as well as a military police company, a motor transport company, and a supply and maintenance company.

According to *The Military Balance 1981–82*, in late 1980 the ground forces possessed about 1,500 Soviet-made T–34/–54/–55 medium tanks and an unknown number of the Soviet PT–76 light tanks. Also in the ground forces inventory were about 650 American-made M–4 medium tanks. In addition to an unknown number of American- and Soviet-made scout cars and armored personnel carriers, the army inventory included newer Yugoslav-manufactured M–980 MICVs, with 700 more on order. The guns and howitzers inventory was of American, German, Soviet, and Yugoslav origin, but the self-propelled guns and howitzers reportedly were largely of Soviet origin (SU-76 and SU-100 mounting 105mm guns). The army also possessed unknown numbers of FROG-7 surface-to-surface missiles (SSM); the Snapper and Sagger antitank guided weapons (ATGW); SA–6/–7/–9 surface-to-air missiles (SAM); and ZSU–23–4 and ZSU–57–2 self-propelled antiaircraft (SP AA) guns, all of Soviet origin. By the 1970s the Yugoslavs were manufacturing their own antitank guns to replace older American and Soviet equipment.

Navy Organization

In 1981 the navy operated over 100 vessels. The 17,500 active duty personnel (of whom 6,000 were conscripts) included 2,500 marines. The larger vessels—including seven submarines, one frigate, three corvettes, and four coastal minesweepers—formed the major part of the Adriatic fleet. One submarine, one frigate, eight

fast attack craft [FAC (M)], and one landing ship, tank (LST) were
on order.

The other craft in the inventory either were in independent river
flotillas on the Danube, Sava, and Drava rivers or were attached to
the Adriatic fleet. These vessels included thirty-one FAC, sixteen of
which were equipped with surface-to-surface missiles; nineteen
large patrol craft; ten inland and thirteen river minesweepers; and
twenty-one minelayers. The navy operated one antisubmarine warfare (ASW) squadron, equipped with Soviet and Yugoslav helicopters, and one marine brigade. The navy also manned twenty-five
coast artillery batteries, which were equipped with surface-to-
surface missiles and 85mm, 130mm, and 152mm guns.

Since the early 1950s the country's shipyards and boatyards have
produced a significant segment of the vessels in service in 1981. The
submarines, corvettes, minesweepers, and most smaller craft were
locally manufactured. An example of recent manufacture is what
the Yugoslavs call the DJC 601, a polyester and fiberglass landing
craft, assault (LCA), capable of being carried on a new LST. The
first of these LCAs entered service in September 1976, and by June
1978 over 600 were in service.

Air Force Organization

The air force, a component of the YPA, in 1981 had about 341
combat aircraft in its inventory, consisting of a large number of jet
fighters, light bombers, reconnaissance and training aircraft, and
modern helicopters. Of the 45,000 active duty personnel in 1981,
only about 8,000 were conscripts. The aircraft were organized into
two air divisions (four air regions) having a total of about twenty-six
squadrons of conventional types. The air divisions and some of their
subordinate air regiments operated at the military district level.
Their locations were generally adjacent to major ground or naval installations, from which they received considerable support.

The airforce in 1981 operated nine interceptor squadrons that
used 126 MiG-21 F/DF/M. The twelve fighter, ground-attack
squadrons and two reconnaissance squadrons used some 165 domestically manufactured aircraft known as *Galeb/Jastreb*. Some eighteen MiG-21U and twenty *Jastreb* were used as trainers but possessed
combat capability. In 1981 the air force was awaiting delivery of
ninety-four domestically manufactured helicopters, known as the
Partisan, presumably to upgrade their three helicopter transport
regiments that had a total of seventy-nine helicopters, twenty of
them *Partisans*.

The air defense forces were under the control of the air force. In
their formative stages these were equipped with light- and medium-
caliber antiaircraft artillery weapons, but in the mid-1960s modern
surface-to-air missiles were acquired and construction was started
on missile launching sites to defend certain major cities and industrial areas.

Frontier Guard Organization

The Frontier Guard is an outgrowth of a pre-World War II frontier guard. Its new function under the Tito regime was to control the borders while the authority and power of the communist government were being consolidated. Its role also was to prevent the escape of defectors and the entry of undesirable refugees. In 1952 these orginal units were reorganized, renamed the Frontier Guard, and placed under direct control of the army.

In 1981 the 20,000 officers and men remained organized in brigades, each controlling a number of companies according to the assigned mission and extent of border responsibility. The units were primarily infantry, armed with light crew-served weapons. Diversified training, such as mountain climbing and skiing, was conducted within the organization in order to cope with the rugged terrain and weather conditions experienced in mountainous areas of the border. In times of war the Frontier Guard could readily be employed on general security duties in rear areas of the regular military forces.

The Territorial Defense Force

By mid-1981 the TDF had expanded to well over 1 million members; according to *The Military Balance 1981–82*, the force may have reached 3 million, about 15 percent of the total population. The TDF received the bulk of its financing through allocations from the respective regional budgets and other local funds. These subfederal channels were expected to provide one-half to 1 percent of national income for defense.

The TDF was developed by focusing on company-sized units at the local (commune) level. According to Yugoslav authorities, these TDF companies possessed operational missions within the boundaries of the commune. For example, many of these units received training for defense against airborne assault. In addition to these commune organizations, 'defense structures' have been developed in some 2,000 large factories and other economic enterprises. These establishments have been legally compelled to draw up local defense plans. Factory defense units were expected to perform civil defense functions, such as defending the plant in the event of attack by airborne or other enemy troops and then merging with the communal TDF if the factory were captured. The republics and provinces also formed battalion-sized mobile TDF units that could conduct operations throughout each republic.

In 1981 TDF units were organized at the communal and regional level under defense commands and were staffed by reserve YPA officers. The total of full-time headquarters personnel throughout the country in the mid-1970s was estimated at about 3,000. This functioned as the TDF's only permanent cadre. Communal commanders appeared to have two chains of command, being responsible to the communal political authorities as well as to the higher, republican territorial defense command.

Officer inspecting paratrooper equipment
Courtesy Embassy of Yugoslavia, Washington

In 1981, TDF units were armed mainly with Yugoslav-produced light antitank and antipersonnel weapons. Battalion-sized TDF units possessed heavier mobile antitank and antiaircraft weapons. There was considerable interest in more sophisticated weaponry for the TDF that should include infrared and laser-targeting devices and sensors. The utility of even obsolete weapons captured in World War II, however, was emphasized because most TDF forces were still not equipped with modern weapons. Weapons were stored in mobilization centers while personal military equipment was kept at home. Dispersal of light weapons on the Swiss pattern has been discussed but not carried out—probably because of the internal security problems it might cause. Yugoslavs claimed that half the existing TDF could be mobilized in three to six hours; the other half in a few days. Both claims were based on mobilization exercises and maneuvers.

Civil Defense

According to A. Ross Johnson, a highly respected military analyst, the focus on territorial defense has resulted in deemphasis on civil defense. Previous plans for massive evacuation of cities have been abandoned. According to the total defense doctrine, urban dwellers, like the population in the countryside, must defend their surroundings.

The TDF has assumed responsibility for intelligence and warning—formerly the responsibility of the civil defense organization. Civil defense forces retained an important role of incorporating, in some way, the entire able-bodied population not already included in the YPA or TDF. In the mid-1970s the civil defense organization numbered approximately 1.3 million. Each commune was legally required to form a civil defense organization, which was subordinate to the communal defense command. Primary missions of the civil defense organization were described as fire fighting, public health, shelter, and limited evacuation of the wounded children and the aged. The civil defense units were organized into engineering, sanitation, radiation-chemical-biological defense, fire fighting, veterinary, evacuation, and security elements.

Military Tactics

Yugoslav military analysts claimed that their rough terrain breaks up the fronts of large-scale attacks that employ tanks and motorized infantry. In 1980 they remained convinced that an invader could attack only along certain routes; these routes are narrow and are separated from one another by mountain ranges creating large intervals between them that cannot be traversed by heavy weapons. The Yugoslav government asserted that in these mountain areas they could defeat any enemy because it would be a "soldier-to-soldier" confrontation.

To stop enemy penetrations, the Yugoslavs pinned their hopes on a large antiarmor arsenal. They asserted they could shower all invasion routes with assorted bazookas with shaped-charge shells, recoilless guns, antitank guns, and self-propelled artillery. They would also expect to use air-to-surface napalm from aircraft to fight tanks. There were plans to use helicopters in this role as well. At close range the ground forces were expected to engage the enemy armor with guided missiles that would be organic to each infantry unit.

The artillery, both guns and howitzers, would engage the enemy armored units at ten to twenty kilometers. The Yugoslavs supposed that the artillery fire against the advancing tank forces would force the enemy machine gunners in tank turrets to withdraw within the protection of the armor. Once the machine-gun fire from the tanks had been suppressed, the Yugoslavs would employ helicopters with antitank weapons to destroy the enemy armor.

The Yugoslavs were ambiguous about use of their tank forces. Though categorical about refusing to commit tanks to a frontal engagement with enemy forces in the initial phases of an invasion, they were less specific about tactics for tank employment during the course of the battle. Assuming that the enemy would have a larger number of tanks during the initial phases, they therefore planned to withhold their tank forces during the early phases of battle until the enemy tank forces had been destroyed and weakened by artillery, bazookas, recoilless rifles, artillery, airplanes, and helicopters, and only then would the large Yugoslav tank formations go into battle. Yugoslav military analysts also carefully pointed out that in addition to large tank organizations, infantry units also have organic tanks for intervention in the most critical moments of battle. Military leaders were emphatic in their belief that tanks are the backbone of the battle wherever routes are passable for tanks, but that coordinated action of different areas and services was an absolute requirement for victory. According to Yugoslav tacticians, success in battle would belong to the side that was more skillful and faster in coordinated action.

Yugoslav strategy depended on the belief that an enemy would commence war operations with air attacks to damage transportation routes, to destroy communication centers and staffs, and to weaken the defensive strength of Yugoslav military units. In that case Yugoslav air defense forces would be striving to "pluck clean" those enemy air forces by using surface-to-air missiles and fighter interceptors. Yugoslav analysts claimed that they possessed sufficient reconnaissance radars to see far beyond their borders, had the capability to alert units in time to respond to attack, and that all air approaches were well covered by guided antiaircraft missiles. They also pointed out that all large ground force units have their own organic antiaircraft and air defense capability to deflect enemy air action.

Philosophically the YPA held to the tenet that the numerically weaker can conquer a numerically stronger adversary—if the former is more skillful, better trained, more flexible in command, and especially if able to utilize the advantages offered by terrain. From a practical standpoint, however, although the Yugoslavs were believed to have sufficient weapons and were expected to be courageous and resourceful fighters, their ability to sustain a mobile and successful defensive war was not promising when compared to the overwhelming number of determined Warsaw Pact forces.

Yugoslavia's security fundamentally depends on whether Soviet expansion toward the Adriatic Coast and the Balkans can remain confined. According to Yugoslav military writers, a blitzkrieg attack led by the Soviet Union appears to be the most likely invasion scenario. The Warsaw Pact forces would enjoy overwhelming military superiority on several lines of advance. They would have air superiority to cover a massive lightning mechanized invasion and to attempt to seize Belgrade, Zagreb, and other key cities quickly with airborne assault and helicopter-borne troops. The first mission of the YPA would be to blunt the attack to delay enemy penetration to buy time for the country to mobilize totally. YPA forces, falling back in order, would wage active defense in depth alongside the TDF. It was hoped that this would merge the front and rear and transform the entire country into a prepared defense zone. Converting the blitzkrieg invasion into a protracted conflict, YPA and TDF units would resist, using small unit and Partisan tactics. On territory seized by the enemy, TDF and paramilitary forces would fight strictly a Partisan-style war on the assumption that they could hold out until international forces came to their aid. Yugoslav military writers contend that an occupying force in excess of 8.5 soldiers per square kilometer, or roughly 2 million men, would be required to subjugate the country completely and that the Warsaw Pact would be unwilling and unable to commit such forces in southeastern Europe, given its strategic priorities in central Europe.

Logistics

The expulsion of Yugoslavia from the Cominform in 1948 gave impetus to the development of a domestic armament industry. Before that time the armed forces had equipped themselves with a heterogeneous mixture of military equipment and had drawn heavily on foreign sources, chiefly Soviet, for the continued supply of weapons and equipment. The embryonic armament industry, started in the early 1950s, had by the 1970s developed the capability of producing much of the light equipment needed by the ground forces, as well as light jet aircraft for the air force and a variety of small craft suitable for naval use. Its weapons industry developed to the extent that during the 1970–79 period it ranked eighteenth of the twenty-one major weapons exporters to Third World countries with the equivalent of roughly US$55 million worth of business. The military establishment remained dependent on outside sources, however, for modern, heavy weapons and the sophisticated, complex equipment needed by its components.

The logistics systems were highly centralized and self-contained in procurement, storage, repair, and issue of all supplies and equipment utilized by the armed forces. At the highest level they were controlled within the Federal Secretariat for National Defense by the Directorate of Rear Services, which was represented at each lower headquarters in the chain of command. The systems were directly responsible for procuring and storing all supplies and equipment needed for emergencies and mobilization, including fuels, lubricants, personal equipment, and rations. They also operated repair and maintenance shops at the major command level.

As the TDF has developed, it became necessary to equip it with up-to-date combat matériel, especially antitank weapons and air defense weapons. These weapons were procured from domestic production.

Manpower

Source and Quality

The principal source of manpower for the military services was the conscription system, which applied equally to all male citizens; no distinction was made between regions of the country or between national or religious groups. The armed services, consequently, formed a fairly representative cross section of the population, and they typified within their ranks the characteristics, attitudes, and qualities of the various sectors of the population. In the main the conscription system selected individuals who were physically fit, adaptable, and capable of performing general military duties.

Among the important military assets of the manpower inducted into the military service were youthfulness, physical toughness, and endurance. In 1981 probably about half of the recruits had rural backgrounds and were accustomed to the rigors of life in the open, taking care of themselves, and subsisting on simple foods. Most conscripts lacked technical training or extensive mechanical experience before induction into the service. In most instances, however, this shortcoming proved fairly easy to overcome because of the keen interest of the average soldier in learning and developing new skills that would help him to advance both in military service and later in civilian life.

Procurement

In 1980 there were approximately 5.9 million males between the ages of fifteen and forty-nine, of whom nearly 4.7 million were considered fit for military duty. Within this latter category about 189,000 males annually reached the military age of seventeen, about 60 percent of whom were eventually inducted into military service. Although all males between the ages of eighteen and fifty-five were subject to the draft, most conscripts were inducted between the ages of nineteen and thirty. Persons who were heads of families or who had completed two years of study at the university or advanced school level were required to serve only one year in the branch of service of their choice.

Youths registered at the age of seventeen, and most were inducted in the year of their nineteenth birthday. Induction and release usually took place biannually, in the spring and fall. Specialists, volunteers, and those previously deferred, however, were inducted at any time throughout the year. Deferments and exemptions were limited generally to those physically unfit or having severe hardship problems. Individuals who volunteered were enlisted for periods varying from three to nine years.

Noncommissioned officers within all three services were generally selected from two sources. At any time after completion of basic training, conscripts could be recommended by their unit commanders for training at a noncommissioned officers' school. The other source was those qualified individuals who requested school assignments and were selected to attend a noncommissioned officers' school directly from civilian life. In either case, upon successful completion of the course of instruction, candidates were graduated with the rank of sergeant, which became permanent after their first reenlistment.

Commissioned officers were obtained from two major sources— graduates of the military, naval, or air force academies; and from among those particularly well-qualified noncommissioned officers who successfully passed a regular officers' examination. Officers for the service branches, such as doctors, lawyers, pharmacists, and engineers, were commissioned directly from civilian life and were given further training in military branch schools.

Service Obligations

Compulsory military service was part of the military obligation of all citizens. It consisted of recruitment, doing military service (the compulsory term), and serving in the Reserve Force, and it covered all male citizens aged eighteen to fifty-five (for conscripts and reserve noncommissioned officers) and up to the age of sixty for reserve officers and warrant officers. Women were not subject to recruitment or compulsory military service.

Recruits were called up to do compulsory service in the course of the year in which they reached the age of nineteen, or eighteen in the event of war or an imminent danger of war. Military service could be deferred for pupils, students, sole breadwinners, and in certain specified cases. The obligation to do compulsory military service lasted until the end of the year in which a potential recruit reached the age of thirty. A recruit who had avoided conscription up to that age had to be inducted by the end of the year in which he was thirty-five. No one could be drafted after reaching the age of thirty-five. Exempt from military service were persons found to be permanently unfit for military service or who were unfit for military service in peacetime, and persons who had acquired Yugoslav citizenship (by naturalization or on the basis of international treaties) who had done military service in their country of origin or had reached the age of thirty years.

Compulsory military service in the army lasted fifteen months; in the navy eighteen months, but in 1981 this was scheduled to be reduced to fifteen months. A shorter term—one year—was served by persons who had completed intermediate school (two years postsecondary schooling), college, or university studies; by persons who had passed all examinations provided for the first two years of study at a college or university faculty, including examinations in the subject of defense and protection; and by persons who were sole breadwinners.

Soldiers could acquire the rank of private first class, corporal, or sergeant. Soldiers who distinguished themselves in work and by success in training were often given reward leave and an Exemplary Soldier badge, as well as other commendations and rewards. The proficiency of a soldier in military training and his behavior during compulsory military service were officially rated thirty days before its termination. All soldiers were entitled to free board and lodging, clothing and health care, and a specific amount of money for basic personal necessities. A disabled soldier was entitled to permanent disability allowance and a bulk sum in cash; in case of death these benefits accrued to his family. The family of a soldier who was their sole breadwinner was entitled to financial support while he was doing compulsory military service.

Soldiers are entitled to regular leave lasting from fifteen to twenty-one days, depending upon length of service. In addition they may be given a reward leave and a leave to take care of private affairs or to take part in sports competitions. Like other citizens, soldiers have the right to vote at elections for delegates to the assemblies of sociopolitical communities. Moreover a soldier who was employed prior to starting compulsory military service has the right to return to his job.

Training

From World War II until the break with the Soviet Union in 1948, the armed forces were trained in the Soviet pattern. Most of the concepts taught, as well as the doctrine, organization, and administrative procedures, were principally Soviet in nature, adapted to meet Yugoslav requirements. Considerable emphasis, for example, continued to be placed on the comprehensive experience gained in guerrilla warfare during the wartime period. Many officers and noncommissioned officers attended schools in the Soviet Union, and Soviet military advisers were present in considerable numbers in the country during the first few postwar years.

American military concepts and doctrines were introduced to a limited extent after the initiation of United States military assistance in 1951. Although the United States training program continued through 1958, the limitations placed on the manner in which it had to be carried out almost totally reduced its effectiveness. As a result much of the military thought and training in the armed forces has continued to reflect Yugoslav World War II experience and strong, early Soviet influence.

Since 1948 premilitary training has been obligatory for all physically fit males between the ages of seventeen and twenty. Its purpose was to prepare youths for later military service and to develop a pool of young men with some military knowledge who could be utilized in an emergency after a short term of professional training. Training drills embraced elementary military subjects and were conducted at rural training centers under the supervision of reserve officers and noncommissioned officers. Similar training was conducted in secondary schools and universities, but it was taught primarily as a school subject with little practical work.

Training in Military Schools

Military schools compared to civilian ones, i.e., secondary, intermediate, and higher military schools. Noncommissioned officers were trained in secondary military schools in two- to four-year courses. Courses for commissioned officers in higher military schools, i.e., military academies, lasted three to five years. These schools were classified by branch of service. Other schools of higher military education followed the studies in the military academies: command and staff academies, the High Military Political Schools, the National Defense School, and the Military Medical Academy.

For those wishing to enroll in military schools, the YPA offered general secondary vocational schools (formerly military gymnasiums). Additionally there were schools for reserve officers. Enrollment in military schools for active noncommissioned and commissioned officers was based on competitive admissions. Conditions for admission were in the main the same as those for admission to active military service. Cadets received free room and board, clothing and health care, and a monthly allowance for basic personal necessities.

Cadets who completed a school for active military personnel were directly admitted to active military service. A graduate from a military school for active military personnel was required to remain in the YPA twice as long as his schooling lasted, and not less than six years. Those trained to be pilots, however, had to remain not less than fifteen years.

Enlisted Training

In 1980 the basic training of conscripts was usually conducted in a training unit to which they were assigned shortly after induction. The new soldier generally underwent a twenty-week individual and small-unit training program, the first four to eight weeks of which were devoted to elementary subjects, including weapon familiarization and range firing. The remainder of the training cycle was devoted to instruction and testing in squad, section, and platoon tactics. This period of early training included a heavy proportion of communist political indoctrination classes covering such subjects as the country's role and activity in international relations, the socialist system in Yugoslavia, and the effectiveness of sociopolitical organizations in the international workers' movement.

Advance training usually took place in the units to which conscripts were permanently assigned after completion of basic training. Based on aptitudes and tests, certain conscripts were selected for specialist training before joining their permanent units, usually at nearby technical schools. Inductees selected for service in the navy and air force customarily followed similar training procedures and schedules at navy or air force installations. Training programs at all levels included periods allocated to political instruction.

Combat training and unit training usually took place at company, battalion, regimental, and brigade level. Exercises inolving larger units generally followed progressively and culminated in joint or combined maneuvers.

Officer Training

The training of officers in the armed forces included programs and formal school courses as well as a considerable amount of on-the-job and special course training for the development of individual skills. Political indoctrination courses were part of all military instruction programs. After receiving his initial commission, an

Member of TDF
Courtesy Embassy of Yugoslavia, Washington

officer in the army, navy, or air force was usually sent to a permanent unit for a period of familiarization in basic branch duties before selection for additional training. In certain cases, however, selected newly commissioned officers were sent directly to technical schools for specialized training in such fields as communications and engineering.

Advance training was provided within each of the services and consisted of schools that offered courses for both regular and reserve officers as well as enlisted personnel. In addition to the combat arms (infantry, artillery, and armor), each technical and administrative service operated a branch school that provided both basic and advanced courses. The student body at most of these schools was composed principally of lieutenants and junior captains.

The senior school in the military system, the Higher Military Academy, was composed of two schools: the Tactical School and the War Academy. The Tactical School offered a two-year staff course to senior captains, majors, and lieutenant colonels. The War Academy's one-year course of instruction was given to selected colonels who were subsequently assigned to high staff and command positions in any of the three armed forces.

Personnel Services and Support

Grades and Rank

Five general categories of military personnel were provided for in military regulations: general officers, senior officers, junior officers, noncommissioned officers, and soldiers. Corporals were usually classified as soldiers. Rank, insignia, and uniforms in the immediate postwar years were patterned closely after those in the Soviet forces, but in 1953 extensive changes were made to give them a more distinct, Yugoslav character.

Insignia for commissioned officers of all three services were worn on shoulder boards in the color corresponding to the individual service: grey-green for the army, blue for the air force, and black for the navy. In the case of senior and general officers of the army and air force, the shoulder boards also had distinctive piping (see fig. 19). Enlisted men wore standard chevrons to denote their ranks.

In the army and air force a junior lieutenant wore a single, five-pointed, gold star; a lieutenant, two stars; a captain, three stars; and a captain first class, four stars. In the senior officer category a major was denoted by a single gold star on a shoulder board piped with gold cord; a lieutenant colonel by two gold stars; and a colonel by three gold stars. Shoulder boards of general officers were piped with twisted gold cord and, in addition to gold stars, carried a symbol composed of a crossed cannon and a sword in a wreath. A major general was identified by one star; a lieutenant colonel general by two stars; a colonel general by three stars; a general of the army by four stars; and a general by five stars. The rank of marshal—which has been held only by Tito—was denoted by a red-bordered, grey-green

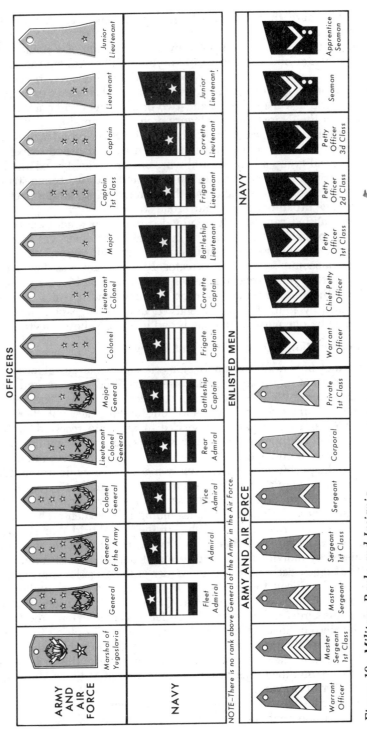

Figure 19. Military Ranks and Insignia

shoulder board that carried a large, red, five-pointed star and the country's national symbol.

In the navy, rank was denoted by a combination of a single gold, five-point star and gold stripes of varying widths. Among the junior officers a junior lieutenant wore one broad stripe; a corvette lieutenant one broad and one narrow stripe; a frigate lieutenant two broad stripes; and a warship lieutenant, two broad stripes and one narrow stripe. In the senior officer category a corvette captain was denoted by three broad stripes; a frigate captain by three broad stripes and one narrow stripe; and a warship captain by four broad stripes. In the admiral group a rear admiral wore one broad gold band and one broad stripe; a vice admiral, one broad band and two broad stripes; an admiral, one broad band and three broad stripes; and a fleet admiral, one broad band and four broad stripes.

The enlisted rank structure provided for seven grades above the rank of private. The insignia of a private first class was one red chevron worn on the upper arm; that of corporal, two red chevrons. In the noncommissioned officer category a sergeant was denoted by one inverted yellow chevron; a sergeant first class by two inverted yellow chevrons; a senior sergeant by three; and a senior sergeant first class by four. The senior enlisted rank of sergeant major was depicted by one narrow and one broad inverted yellow chevron.

Commendations, Decorations, and Ratings

Formal honors and symbols of merit and achievement occupied an important place in Yugoslav tradition, and officers and men received and wore awards with considerable pride. The regime granted numerous awards, and outstanding acts of heroism, courage, and particularly, of service to the state received prompt recognition by superiors. No awards or decorations for military personnel were peculiar to any of the three services. All recognition for outstanding achievement was usually made in the name of the state, and awards were granted by authority of the president.

Sixteen major decorations and six medals were awarded to both the military and civilians for outstanding achievement. The majority of these awards were established in the post-World War II period and were given for either war service or for notable assistance rendered by individuals in the creation of the communist state.

The highest decoration was the Order of the Yugoslav Star, usually conferred only on foreign heads of state for service in establishing friendly relations with Yugoslavia. Other awards, in order of status were: the Order of Freedom, the Order of People's Hero, the Order of the Hero of Socialist Labor, the Order of the People's Liberation, the Order of the Partisan Star, the Order of the Republic, the Order of Civil Merit, the Order of Brotherhood and Unity, the Order of the People's Army, the Order of Labor, the Order of Military Merit, and the Order of Bravery.

The six medals, in order of precedence, awarded to both military personnel and civilians, were the Medal for Bravery, the Medal for

Civil Merit, the Medal of Labor, the Medal for Military Merit, the Medal for Military Conduct, and the Medal for Merit. These medals were usually granted for lesser accomplishments not justifying one of the various orders.

Active military persons were evaluated to assess their service performance for promotion and assignment to duty and to encourage further professional development. Personnel were rated by a "routine" and "special" rating. Adjectival ratings were favorable, with degrees of "adequate," "good," "outstanding," and "especially outstanding," or unfavorable. Active military personnel were rated after one year spent in active military service, thereafter every three years up to the completion of ten years of active military service, and every four years after the completion of ten years of active military service. No rating was given after completion of thirty years of active military service.

Pay, Working Hours, and Leave

Pay in the military was determined by rank, length of service, marital status, and the number of dependents. Supplementary allowances were also granted for necessary travel, family separation, and other cost-of-living hardships imposed by emergency conditions. In addition special hazardous duty allowances were paid to pilots and airborne personnel, and incentive pay was granted to doctors, engineers, and other technicians having special skills and training.

Linked with an improving pay situation was a government program to accelerate the construction of military housing. Although pay and housing were major factors in the maintenance of military morale, other factors already in existence also influenced the general attitude toward military duty. Promotion in both the enlisted and officer ranks was generally equitable and fairly rapid; leave policies were generous; and retirement benefits were high, amounting in many cases to 55 percent of active duty pay.

The officer's pay with its special allowances and privileges has enabled the officer to live in equal or better circumstances than his civilian counterparts. The same situation did not prevail for enlisted men, whose pay was low by comparison.

Active military personnel, like other employed persons, had a regular working week of forty-two hours. Because of the nature and needs of service in the armed forces, however, they worked longer hours in actual practice.

Active duty military personnel were entitled to a twenty-four hours off duty period every seven days. They were entitled to paid annual holidays depending on length of service. Military men who had served more than thirty years or were over fifty years of age and women who had served more than twenty-five years or were over fifty years of age had their holidays increased by ten work days. A service member may also be granted other kinds of leave, such as reward leave, leave for passing examinations, compassionate leave (for those moved to another garrison), removal leave, or unpaid leave.

Military Justice

Military justice within the armed forces was carried out by special military courts that functioned as part of the overall judicial system, prosecuting military offenders under a uniform penal code. These courts were established by the Partisan forces during World War II and were reorganized in 1954, 1965, and 1969. The proceedings of military courts were generally open to the public, except in cases involving national security or the "interests of society." The jury system was not employed, and prosecution was carried out by members of the judge advocate general's office.

The military court system consisted of two categories or levels of courts, the Military Court of First Instance and the Military Supreme Court. The Military Supreme Court, which was also empowered to hear certain referred cases as a court of second instance, came under the Federal Supreme Court for appellate review, thus ensuring integration at the top of military courts and the regular court system.

Military court judges were appointed by the supreme commander of the armed forces. Appeal was provided for in the 1974 Constitution, and decisions of the Military Court of First Instance could be appealed to the Military Supreme Court and, ultimately, to the Federal Supreme Court.

As in the regular courts of the land, military judges comprised both professional and lay judges (citizens with no special legal training). Lay judges were usually service officers and functioned in a jury capacity at both court levels. The number of professional judges and lay judges in any court panel was determined by the seriousness of the charge and the severity of the sentence attached to it. Military offenders were guaranteed the right to their choice of military or civilian defense counsel.

Military courts exercised jurisdiction in all cases involving crimes and serious violations of disciplinary regulations on the part of military personnel and in most cases involving crimes against the state, whether committed by military or civilian personnel. Penalties, according to the law, were the same for all citizens, military or civilian. Military offenders convicted and sentenced to prison terms were generally confined in military prisons. Those sentenced to less than one year's confinement, however, were usually placed in special military institutions, where rehabilitation and early restoration to duty were stressed.

Practical questions of service relations concerning military and civilian personnel were generally regulated by administrative acts passed by competent commanding officers in conformity with laws and other rules. An appeal could be lodged against administrative acts or rulings. Legality was also ensured by the judicial supervision of administrative acts in litigious proceedings before the Military Supreme Court.

Active military persons were required to bear criminal and disciplinary responsibility and material liability for their acts and bore the same responsibility as other citizens for offenses committed outside the service. Military persons were tried before military courts for criminal offenses chargeable under the provisions of criminal laws (the Yugoslav Criminal Code and the republic and provincial criminal codes). As there was no separate military criminal code, proceedings before military courts were regulated by the Code of Criminal Procedure, as applied before other regular courts.

For minor breaches of discipline, active military persons were tried by military officers, and for disciplinary misdemeanors, by the disciplinary military court. In conjunction with material liability, active military persons were more or less treated in the same way as employed civilians. They were liable for damages to the federation for any loss caused in service intentionally or through neglect. For civil crimes, they were tried in the same way as for disciplinary misdemeanors.

Special Service-Related Rights and Duties

A variety of laws set forth rights and duties for service personnel. Most are of an inconsequential nature—i.e., the rights to wear a uniform and to bear arms—but others concern what might be called civil and political rights. For example an individual has the right to complain to a superior officer about working and living conditions. The officer to whom the complaint is made must respond to the complainant within thirty days. If the complainant is not satisfied with the response, he or she may appeal to a more senior officer, up to and including the commander in chief. The laws stipulate that regular meetings must be held within military units and installations to discuss living and working conditions. Military personnel select delegates to legislative assemblies at the commune, republic (and province), and federal levels. Moreover the military has self-management (see Glossary) communities of interest responsible for such matters as housing, health, pensions, and related subjects (see Problems of Workers' Self-Management, ch. 3).

With the consent of their superior officers, active duty personnel can work or engage in professional activities in the private sector. Permission is also required for travel abroad, acceptance of a foreign decoration, or membership in a foreign association or organization.

Service in the Yugoslav People's Army and in the Reserve by Civilians

Civilians could be employed both in the YPA and the TDF. Their status was regulated by special rules that were similar to those for workers in federal, republic, and provincial administrative agencies. Civilians who met general eligibility requirements prescribed by the Associated Labor Act and the special requirements prescribed for each individual job were employed by the YPA on the basis of public competition, advertisement of vacancies, and/or directly. A public competition was conducted by a commission, and the commanding officer concerned made a selection from among the candidates proposed by the commission.

Obligations to serve in the Reserve Force of the Armed Forces started for conscripts upon completing their compulsory term in the YPA and for noncommissioned and commissioned officers and warrant officers upon being transferred to the Reserve Force. Although not conscripted for active duty, women fit for military service were subject to service in the Reserve Force of the TDF, and women having qualifications for performing professional and technical services, e.g., nurses and communications technicians, in the Reserve Force of the YPA. Women subject to military service were called up only in the event of immediate danger to the country and during hostilities. Under exceptional circumstances they might be called up in peacetime to undergo training in the YPA by order of the federal secretary for national defense.

Recruits who were promoted to the rank of sergeant during active duty or in reservist training were placed in the Reserve Force in the rank of sergeant. Active noncommissioned officers were also placed in the Reserve Force as noncommissioned officers after completion of active duty. Reserve noncommissioned officers who completed school for reserve officers were transferred to the Reserve Force in the rank of second lieutenant, as were regular officers after completion of active military service. Persons who had graduated from a university could be promoted to the rank of second lieutenant, if by graduating they had satisfied their military obligation or completed their compulsory term and if they had spent the required time in a military unit and had successfully performed officer's duties.

The obligation to serve in the Reserve Force of the Armed Forces extended for conscripts and noncommissioned officers up to the end of the year in which they reached the age of fifty-five years (women—forty), and for reserve warrant officers to the end of the year in which they reached the age of sixty (women—fifty) years. The supreme commander of the armed forces was authorized to extend this obligation for male reserve officers and warrant officers in the event of immediate danger of hostilities and during wartime.

The quantity of persons given reserve noncommissioned and commissioned officers rank depended on the number of leadership personnel outlined in the war table of organization of the armed forces. Appointment to the rank of noncommissioned officer and warrant officer was within the jurisdiction of the federal secretary of national defense and other authorized army officers, and to the rank of reserve officers, of the supreme commander. As a rule, all persons in

Military Museum at Kalemegdan, Belgrade

the Reserve Force were covered by a war duty assignment and informed thereof.

Conscripts and reserve noncommissioned officers in the Reserve Force were called up for reservist training up to the age of fifty (women up to the age of forty) and reserve officers and warrant officers to the age of fifty-five (women up to age forty-five). Except for officers, reservist training could not total more than two months in the course of one year, and during the whole period of their obligation to serve in the Reserve Force, no more than six months. The total for reserve officers could be no more than twelve months. Every person in the Reserve Force was required to answer a summons to reservist training—failure to comply was a criminal offense. In certain cases specified by law, reservist training could be deferred.

During reservist training, individuals were entitled to an indemnity that equaled their average personal income during the preceding three months. Private craftsmen were entitled to an indemnity that equaled the base on which they paid contributions for pension and disability insurance. Peasant farmers were entitled to a monetary indemnity as prescribed by the Federal Executive Council. Reserve noncommissioned and commissioned officers and warrant officers, during reservist training, were entitled to all allowances corresponding to their rank. No monetary indemnity was paid if reservist training took place on nonwork days.

Promotion of noncommissioned and commissioned officers and warrant officers was largely determined by the fulfillment of the same requirements as applied to active military personnel. While on reservist training, persons belonging to the Reserve Force could be held responsible for breaches of military discipline. Individuals charged with a violation committed outside of military service that was detrimental to or involved gross negligence of the duties of reserve noncommissioned and commissioned officers or warrant officers were tried by courts of honor. Major violations included: commission of a criminal offense, antisocialist or nationalist (see Glossary) activity, violation of public morals, or flight from the country. There were first instance and higher courts of honor; their establishment, abolition, location, and territorial jurisdiction were regulated by republic or provincial laws. Disciplinary measures these courts of honor could impose were: reprimands, suspension of promotion from one to five years, and loss of rank or class. A person in the Reserve Force who wished to move abroad permanently had to obtain a permit from the commune organ in charge of national defense.

Public Order and Internal Security

The enforcement of law and order comprised the interlocking functions of two major, nationwide police organizations—the State Security Service (Sluzba Drzavne Bezbednosti—SDB) and a conventional people's militia known as the Public Security Service (Sluzba

Javne Bezbednosti—SJB). The people's militia was charged primarily with the customary duties of preserving law and order, but it also cooperated fully with the SDB in all matters that pertained to the discovery and suppression of political nonconformity or antiregime activity engaged in by those citizens considered to be "enemies of the state and of the Yugoslav people."

These two organizations represented modern-day versions of earlier security forces created as part of the Partisan forces by Tito and used by him to assist in the establishment and consolidation of communist authority throughout the country immediately after the cessation of hostilities. Although they ostensibly operated under a decentralized, self-management system at federal, republic, and local levels, the federal secretary for internal affairs in Belgrade exercised direct supervision over the operations of both police organizations and was empowered to issue binding instructions concerning all matters considered to be of major importance to the state.

The traditional independent attitudes of many of the nationalities within the country hampered the enforcement of law and order under Tito's system of federate republics from its earliest days. The security problem was further intensified in the early postwar years by resentment of the punitive methods by which the system maintained itself.

After expulsion from the Cominform in 1948, the Tito government sought to ease the security problem and to encourage acceptance of the communist regime by instituting a series of reforms that provided opportunities for wider popular participation in governmental affairs. Out of these reforms, which were based on a partial decentralization of authority, evolved the system of controls in 1981, which was intended to be sufficiently strong to assure perpetuation of the regime. Although the introduction of reforms has permitted the surfacing of dissension from time to time, the regime has continuously and strongly asserted the need to maintain communist one-party rule.

Public Order and Rights

Compared to any other communist country, the Yugoslavs in 1981 continued to enjoy broad freedom movement and access to most foreign noncommunist publications and to radio broadcasts. Given the extensive number of Yugoslavs working oustide the country, Yugoslavia evinced a solid record on freedom of emigration. The LCY, however, retained a monopoly on political power, and the government enforced specific restrictions on freedom of political expression. In particular it repressed public criticism of the late President Tito, the LCY, the theory of socialist self-management, Yugoslavia's nonaligned orientation, and statements advocating nationalism or separatism.

In mid-1981 Yugoslavia manifested an ongoing concern about the continued terrorism mainly employed by Croatian émigré political groups. The persistence of historic ethnic and national tensions within the country, economic difficulties exacerbated by regional economic disparities, and continued ideological and political differences with surrounding states were a continued source of internal problems. The LCY and the federal government had adopted a number of reforms that included the decentralization of political and economic institutions, and the encouragement of certain forms of cultural pluralism, e.g., encouragement of local languages in schools and media. Nevertheless the government continued to impose restrictions on many aspects of individual political behavior.

Article 176 of the Constitution provides for the "inviolability of the integrity of the human personality" and states that any extortion of a confession or statement is "forbidden and punishable." Other references in the Yugoslav Code of Criminal Procedure refer to this guarantee against torture.

Conditions within Yugoslav prisons reportedly were strict and sometimes harsh, but not inhumane. There were reports of harsh conditions in some prisons, i.e., that some prisoners had been held in solitary confinement for extended periods of time. The press manifested vigilence on this issue, reporting and editorializing against abuses of authority by the police and against excessive use of force. Medical care was available to prisoners, but there were many reports alleging denial of proper medical treatment to prisoners with special medical problems.

Amnesty International and the Western press have reported allegations involving the kidnapping of Yugoslav émigrés by the Yugoslav intelligence services for involuntary return to Yugoslavia for trial. There was no indication of a pattern of permanent or prolonged disappearance of persons, however.

Yugoslavs were in the main free from arbitrary arrest, although reportedly large numbers of suspects were detained for questioning after suspected acts of terrorism. According to the law a defendant must appear before a judge within twenty-four hours of arrest. This statute is designed to bring about "judicial awareness" of the reason for detention. As a rule arraignment quickly follows an arrest. The law stipulates that an indictment should be brought within three months, although an investigating judge may request an extension of three months or even longer from the court. Although the accused has the right to counsel from the time he or she is brought before a judge until an indictment is issued, consultations with an attorney occur in the presence of a court official. In most cases consular access was permitted to prisoners of foreign nationality, although in such cases notification of arrests was frequently delayed, and this and other problems usually occurred in cases where dual nationality was at issue.

Federal statutes contain detailed provisions for conducting searches, including the requirement for a court order except under certain limited circumstances. The 1974 Constitution stipulates that entry may be made without warrant only if this is indispensable for immediate arrest of a criminal, to protect life, or to guard property, or if it appears that evidence in criminal proceedings could not be secured otherwise. The Constitution states that illegal entry is "prohibited and punishable." In the early 1980s there was no evidence of widespread violations of these provisions, but dissidents believed that security police monitored their conversations and intercepted their mail.

According to Yugoslav law, dissidents may be charged with a variety of vaguely defined political crimes, e.g., hostile propaganda, counterrevolution, association against the state, and making statements prejudicial to brotherhood and unity. If convicted, an individual may be sentenced to prison terms of up to ten years. Yugoslavia also asserted its authority over its citizens outside the country, and on occasion arrested, charged, tried, and convicted persons for political offenses committed abroad, even if the acts in question were not crimes in the country in which they took place.

According to a 1981 report by the United States Department of State, the number of persons imprisoned in Yugoslavia in 1980 on political charges appeared to be within the range of 500–700 persons. Amnesties, although not routine, have been granted from time to time, usually on the occasion of Yugoslav National Day, November 29. The National Day Amnesty for 1979 involved fifty-one persons: nineteen were set free, and thirty-two had their sentences reduced. Of the latter number, two were identified as possibly being political prisoners. The 1980 National Day Amnesty involved eighty-two persons: forty-two were set free, and forty had their sentences reduced.

The Police System

The State Security Service

Under the 1966 Basic Law on Internal Affairs, the Federal Secretariat for Internal Affairs was responsible for coordinating and supervising the work of all elements of the SDB. The service was organized on a decentralized basis, units at each echelon operating under a chief of state security, who was responsible to the respective organs of internal security at the federal, republic or provincial, district, and commune level. The decentralized nature of the organization was intended to emphasize the government's principle of self-management, and the law stressed the fact that internal security was no longer an area under exclusive federal jurisdiction.

All units of the State Security Service had a common mission, which was described in Article 39 of the basic law as the gathering of data and other information for the purpose of discovering organized and secret activities aimed at undermining or subverting the constitutionally established order. Although the Federal Secretariat for Internal Affairs was authorized to establish general rules for the SDB, as well as the means and methods of operation, that office was expected to coordinate rather than to direct activities. Under Article 50 of the law, data concerning the internal organization and operation of the SDB were considered to fall in the category of official secrecy.

The Public Security Service

In 1981 the Federal Secretariat for Internal Affairs was also responsible for the supervision and coordination of all activities of the SJB. It also was organized on a similarly decentralized basis under the Basic Law on Internal Affairs, its units operating at the federal and all lower governmental levels. In addition to carrying out ordinary police functions, the SJB was also charged with enforcing traffic regulations, fire fighting, the conduct of criminal investigations, control of the movement of personnel across borders, and the furnishing of all penitentiary and prison guards. Special units were usually organized and trained as needed to perform these auxiliary functions.

The basic police unit was located at the local level—usually the commune—and, within its assigned area, operated the necessary number of police stations and substations. Usually police posts of various sizes were to be found in all cities, towns, and villages. At points of legal entry along the frontier, border posts were maintained to control sumggling and illegal infiltration of subversive elements and to assist in customs control.

The SJB was organized and uniformed as a military-type force. Although militiamen most frequently patrolled in groups of two to four men, units up to company size remained available for riot duty or for the control of large gatherings. Weapons were generally limited to sidearms, but in the case of serious disorders truncheons, rifles, submachine guns, tear gas equipment, and protective helmets were available for issue.

Candidates for enlistment in the SJB were required to be between the ages of eighteen and thirty and had to meet physical and mental standards generally similar to those of the YPA. After induction all recruits received a minimum of three months of basic training, which included instruction in military, criminal police, and political affairs. Additional training and indoctrination were provided periodically during the militiaman's term of service in the form of practical work and courses at special police schools. Militia officers were generally recruited from among army officers and reserve officers. Training, including political indoctrination and technical police subjects, was usually provided upon entry into service and, later, in schools conducted in the various republics and in Belgrade.

In early 1967 all insignia of rank were abolished within the SJB, and a general system of indicating function or service actually performed was substituted. Generally badges were worn and special insignia displayed on shoulder boards or on the upper left arm. Functions or status so represented included that of recruit, student trainee, militiaman, commander of a station, inspector, traffic militiaman, frontier militiaman, and penitentiary guard.

Criminal Procedures

Investigation of charges against an individual arrested as a criminal suspect was initiated by the public prosecutor, who was empowered to designate the investigative agency. In general, investigations of routine matters were delegated to the police, but in some major crimes the case was turned over to the appropriate court, which conducted an official judicial inquiry. Suspects could be held in custody for an extended period for investigation of serious charges, if such extended custody were approved by the judge having jurisdiction in the case. In cases involving minor infractions of the law, the accused was allowed bail until the results of the investigation were submitted to the public prosecutor.

After receiving the results of the investigation, the public prosecutor could either dismiss the case or bring an indictment against the accused and designate the court to hear the case. When designated a defendant by the public prosecutor, the accused could engage defense counsel or request the court to appoint one. The defense counsel was not permitted to be present during the early interrogation of the defendant or examination of witnesses, however, but was usually given the opportunity to examine the evidence if it had resulted in the filing of an indictment of the accused.

During trial proceedings the case was presented by the public prosecutor and the defense was permitted to examine witnesses. Both the prosecutor and the defense counsel presented concluding summaries before resting the case, and the accused was also permitted to present evidence on his or her own behalf at that time. No jury in the usual sense was provided, all cases being decided by a panel of regular and lay judges who voted on the verdict and sentence.

Criminal Courts

The criminal court system consisted of communal courts, district courts, the republic supreme courts, and the Federal Supreme Court (see The Constitutional Order, ch. 4). The jurisdictions of these courts corresponded closely to the country's administrative divisions and included all criminal cases not referred to the military courts and adjudicated by them. All four levels of courts were courts of first instance, the seriousness of the case determining at which level it would originally be heard.

The communal courts tried minor criminal cases for which a fine or a penalty of up to two years' imprisonment was provided as the principal punishment. Cases whose penalties exceeded two years' imprisonment, as well as all cases involving crimes carrying a mandatory death penalty, were heard orginally in district courts. In addition district courts functioned as appellate courts of review on judgments rendered by the communal courts. The six republic and two provincial supreme courts also usually functioned as courts of first instance in important criminal matters and also acted as courts of appeal in criminal cases introduced in lower courts.

The Federal Supreme Court, the highest court in the land, was the final appeals court for all four types of lower courts. Although holding unlimited general jurisdiction in all criminal affairs, it generally limited itself to the trial of certain important cases. Its major functions, besides appellate review, were to determine the constitutionality of decisions made in the lower courts, to supervise the uniform application of the laws, and to resolve jurisdictional conflicts between the various courts and the administrative departments of the government. It did not pass on the constitutionality of legislation nor did it interpret the Constitution, both of these tasks being reserved by law as functions of the special Constitutional Court.

Trials were generally open to the public except in cases involving military or national security questions when the judge had the authority to hold proceedings in camera. In cases of crimes relating to national defense and security and to matters concerning service in the military, civilians could be tried in military courts. The court could also, in cases involving classified materials, appoint a military officer as counsel for the defense rather than civilian counsel. The trial record does not necessarily provide a full transcript and all testimony was recorded in the words of the presiding judge. Government controls of the media also affected the degree and nature of publicity accorded the proceedings. The accused had the right to counsel, and lawyers often vigorously defended their clients. The government, however, had not always remained impartial in judicial proceedings, particularly in cases of political interest. There have been reports of the reluctance of some lawyers to take political cases for fear of reprisal. In ordinary criminal and civil proceedings, the courts acted according to the law and Constitution, and the defendants' civil rights were generally respected.

Verdicts could be appealed to the next higher court if the laws governing procedures were violated or if the evidence was considered in the next higher court. The public prosecutor, however, generally appealed the appellate decision to the Federal Supreme Court when the death penalty or life imprisonment had been imposed or confirmed by a republic supreme court or when the appellate decision was based on evidence that differed from that on which the original verdict was based.

The Penal System

Overall control and supervision of penal institutions were the responsibility of the Federal Secretariat for Internal Affairs, except for military prisons, which were administered by the Federal Secretariat for National Defense. By delegation of authority from the central government, the penal institutions of the various republics were administered by the respective republic secretariats for internal affairs. Penal institutions consisted of penitentiaries (for those sentenced to long terms for serious crimes), reformatories (for less dangerous criminals serving moderate terms), and jails (for petty offenders serving short sentences). Convicts sentenced to strict imprisonment were usually assigned to hard labor and subjected to a more strict regimen than those sentenced to simple imprisonment. Men and women were housed separately but in the same institutions.

Separate wards or sections were maintained for special categories of prisoners, such as alcoholics, pregnant women, juvenile offenders, and political prisoners.

All prisoners sentenced to strict imprisonment were required to work, if physically able, and the work schedule was prescribed as eight hours per day, six days a week. Although manual labor was usually ordered for prisoners undergoing strict imprisonment, those serving simple imprisonment were assigned work generally in keeping with their skills and aptitudes. Prisoners were allowed to work outside the prison on a supervised basis, but their wages were computed on a reduced scale. Prisoners were authorized to keep only part of their pay, one portion being withheld until discharge and the remainder going toward the support of dependents or relatives.

By law, prison inmates were entitled to free medical care, the right to correspond, and the privilege of receiving visitors and parcels. At various times the government pointed out that prison standards tend to vary among the republics and encourage prison officials to introduce more measures leading to the rehabilitation of inmates. Official reports have been released periodically concerning unsatisfactory conditions that were found in many prisons. Among those listed were overcrowding, inadequate sanitation, poor discipline, and the lack of training of supervisory personnel.

* * *

The Yugoslav government occasionally publishes remarkably detailed reports on various military and police rules, regulations, and activities that may be found in English in the *Joint Publications Research Service*. Radio Free Europe also publishes an occasional report on military affairs.

The many articles by A. Ross Johnson are valuable for themselves and for their bibliographies. Robin A. Remington's writings are always perceptive, and her article in the book edited by Catherine M. Kelleher is useful. The article and book by Adam Roberts provide excellent background material on the formation and operation of the Territorial Defense Force. For brief information on Yugoslavia's military equipment, manpower, and budget, the annual issue of *The Military Balance* should be consulted. The various *Jane's* publications may be examined for more detailed descriptions of the military equipment. (For further information see Bibliography).

Appendix

Table 1. Conversion Coefficients and Factors

When you know	Multiply by	To find
Millimeters	0.04	inches
Centimeters	0.39	inches
Meters	3.3	feet
Kilometers	0.62	miles
Hectares (10,000 m²)	2.47	acres
Square kilometers	0.39	square miles
Cubic meters	35.3	cubic feet
Liters	0.26	gallons
Kilograms	2.2	pounds
Metric tons	0.98	long tons
....	1.1	short tons
....	2,204	pounds
Degrees Celsius	9	degrees Fahrenheit
(Centigrade)	divide by 5 and add 32	

Table 2. Climate Data for Selected Cities

Cities	Elevation (in meters)	Average Temperature (°C)		Annual Precipitation (in centimeters)
		January	July	
Belgrade	132	−0.2	22.7	68.83
Osijek	94	−0.8	22.2	73.15
Jajce	341	0.1	19.7	128.0
Ljubljana	298	−1.4	19.7	161.80
Pristina	630	−0.9	21.1	60.71
Skopje	245	−1.7	23.3	48.77
Zagreb	163	0.0	21.7	88.92

Source: Based on information from Roy E.H. Mellor, *Eastern Europe: A Geography of the Comecon Countries*, New York, 1975, p. 28.

Table 3. Population 1961, 1971, and 1981,
and Population Density, 1981
(in thousands)

	Population						1981 Density	
	Actual (in thousands)			Percentage of Total			Per Square Kilometer	Percentage of Increase 1971–81
	1961	1971	1981	1961	1971	1981		
Republic								
Serbia	4,823	5,272	5,666	26.0	25.7	25.3	101	7.5
Croatia	4,160	4,422	4,576	22.4	21.5	20.5	81	3.5
Bosnia and								
Hercegovina ..	3,276	3,743	4,116	17.7	18.2	18.4	80	10.0
Slovenia	1,592	1,725	1,884	8.6	8.4	8.4	93	9.2
Macedonia	1,406	1,647	1,914	7.6	8.0	8.6	74	16.2
Montenegro	472	530	583	2.5	2.6	2.6	42	10.0
Autonomous Province								
Vojvodina	1,855	1,950	2,028	10.0	9.5	9.1	94	4.0
Kosovo	964	1,245	1,585	5.2	6.1	7.1	146	27.3
TOTALS ...	18,548	20,534	22,352	100.0	100.0	100.0	87	8.9

Table 4. Illiteracy, by Region, 1921
(five years old and older)

	Percent of Population		Percent of Population
COUNTRYWIDE	51.5	Macedonia	83.8
Bosnia and Hercegovina	80.5	Montenegro	67.0
Croatia	32.3	Serbia	65.4
Dalmatia	49.5	Slovenia	8.8

Source: Based on information from Joseph Rothschild, *East Central Europe Between the Two World Wars*, IX, Seattle, 1974, p. 276.

Table 5. Ethnic Composition of Officer Corps—Yugoslav People's Army, 1972
(in percentages)

Ethnic Group	Officers	Generals	Total Population
Serbs	60.5	46.0	39.7
Croats	14.0	19.0	22.0
Ethnic Muslims	3.5	4.0	8.4
Slovenes	5.0	6.0	8.3
Albanians	2.0	0.5	6.4
Macedonians	6.0	5.0	5.6
Montenegrins	8.0	19.0	2.5
Hungarians	0.5	0.5	2.5
Other	0.0	0.0	4.3
TOTAL*	99.5	100.0	99.7

*Totals may not add up to 100 because of rounding.

Source: Based on information from Bogdan Denitch, *The Legitimation of a Revolution: The Yugoslav Case*, New Haven, 1976, p. 114.

Table 6. Socioeconomic Indicators, 1975
(Index number: Yugoslavia = 100)

Region	Life Expectancy at Birth		Persons per Doctor	Persons per Hospital Bed	Average Area of Dwelling per Person	Proportion of Dwellings with Electricity	Proportion of Dwellings with Water and Sewerage	Literacy Rate			Proportion of Population over Ten Years Old Having Secondary or Higher Education
	Males	Females						Total	Males	Females	
Less Developed Regions											
Bosnia and Hercegovina ..	98	97	66	75	77	87	68	65	71	63	70
Kosovo	99	95	35	48	63	86	37	48	36	52	46
Macedonia	100	96	91	91	82	104	111	83	67	88	76
Montenegro	104	104	76	130	81	90	99	90	105	87	94
More Developed Regions											
Croatia	100	103	114	118	118	103	122	167	159	172	121
Serbia	103	102	120	108	100	102	97	85	103	81	103
Slovenia	100	104	133	127	127	109	133	1,250	667	1,667	144
Vojvodina	101	103	109	101	125	104	119	167	147	172	111

Source: Based on information from Martin Schrenk, Cyrus Ardalan, and Nawal A. El Tatawy, *Yugoslavia: Self-Management Socialism and the Challenges of Development*, Washington, 1979, pp. 288–89.

Table 7. *Federal Investment Fund Allocations, 1971-75*
(in percentages)

Region	1971	1972	1973	1974	1975
Bosnia and Hercegovina	31	33	32	32	32
Montenegro	13	11	12	12	12
Macedonia	26	22	23	23	23
Kosovo	30	34	33	33	33
TOTAL	100	100	100	100	100

Source: Based on information from Vajo Skendzic, "Accelerated Advancement of the Underdeveloped Regions of Yugoslavia," *Socialist Thought and Practice* [Belgrade], XVI, No. 2, 1976, p. 87.

Table 8. *Ethnic Composition by Percentage of Total Population,
Selected Years, 1953-81*

Ethnic Group	1953	1961	1971	1981
Serbs	41.7	42.1	39.7	36.3
Croats	23.5	23.2	22.0	19.8
Ethnic Muslims	--*	5.2	8.4	8.9
Slovenes	8.7	8.6	8.3	7.8
Albanians	4.4	4.9	6.4	7.7
Macedonians	5.3	5.6	5.8	6.0
Montenegrins	2.7	2.8	2.5	2.6
Yugoslavs	6.0	1.7	1.3	5.4
Other	7.7	5.9	5.6	3.6
TOTAL	100.0	100.0	100.0	100.0

*not recorded.

Source: Based on information from Paul Lendvai, "National Tensions in Yugoslavia," *Conflict Studies* [London], No. 25, August 1972, p. 2; and Gordon C. McDonald et al., *Yugoslavia: A Country Study*, Washington, 1970, p. 76; and Embassy of Yugoslavia.

Table 9. Private Farms, 1961 and 1971

Farm Size (in hectares)	Percentage of All Private Holdings	
	1961	1971
Less than 1.0	23	31
1.1 – 3.0	33	31
3.1 – 5.0	20	17
5.1 – 8.0	14	13
8.1 – 10.0	5	4
10.1 – 15.0	3	3
More than 15.0	2	1
TOTAL	100	100

Source: Based on information from Yugoslavia, Savezni Zavod za Statistiku, *Statisticki Godisnjak Jugoslavije, 1979*, Belgrade, 1979, p. 114.

Table 10. Workers' Council Membership by Occupation, Selected
Years, 1956–72
(in percentages)

	Blue-Collar			
	Unskilled, semiskilled	Skilled, highly skilled	White-Collar	Total
1956				
Work force	45	36	19	100
Workers' councils	23	52	25	100
1960				
Work force	38	32	30	100
Workers' councils	20	56	24	100
1964				
Work force	46	32	22	100
Workers' councils	20	54	26	100
1970				
Work force	37	32	31	100
Workers' councils	16	51	33	100
1972				
Work force	35	33	32	100
Workers' councils	15	50	35	100

Source: Based on information from Goldie Shabad, "Strikes in Yugoslavia: Implications for Industrial Democracy," *British Journal of Political Science* [Cambridge], 10, Part 2, April 1980, p. 299.

Table 11. Participation in Strikes, 1958-78

Strikers by Occupation	Percentage of All Strikers	Percentage of All Strikes
All Enterprise Employees	3	2
All Nonmanagerial Employees	2	4
All Nonprofessional Employees	15	7
Unskilled Workers	74	80

Source: Based on information from Goldie Shabad, "Strikes in Yugoslavia: Implications for Industrial Democracy," *British Journal of Political Science* [Cambridge], 19, Part 2, April 1980, p. 302.

Table 12. Wage Scales among Yugoslav Workers, Selected Years, 1951-61
(Index number: Unskilled workers' wages = 100)

	1951	1954	1957	1959	1961
White-Collar					
Professional	125	238	290	316	333
Semiskilled	125	155	170	186	190
Clerical	101	123	119	132	135
Blue-Collar					
Highly skilled	120	205	223	243	249
Skilled	120	146	149	159	160
Semiskilled	105	118	117	125	124
Unskilled	100	100	100	100	100

Source: Based on information from Frank Parkin, "Market Socialism and Class Structure: Some Aspects of Social Stratification in Yugoslavia," pp. 29–50 in Bernard Lewis Farber (ed.), *The Social Structure of Eastern Europe*, New York, 1976.

Table 13. Women in the Labor Force, by Region, 1979

	Percentage of Total		Percentage of Total
COUNTRYWIDE	35	Serbia	33
Bosnia and Hercegovina	31	Serbia proper	33
Croatia	39	Kosovo	20
Macedonia	30	Vojvodina	35
Montenegro	31	Slovenia	44

Source: Based on information from Vida Tomsic, *Women in the Development of Socialist Self-Managing Yugoslavia*, Belgrade, 1980, p. 194.

Table 14. Women in the Labor Force
by Economic Activity, Selected Years, 1954–78

	Percentage of Total Labor Force			
	1954	1964	1974	1978
Economic Activities	22	25	29	30
Manufacturing	24	30	33	34
Agriculture	23	19	21	22
Forestry	14	7	7	8
Construction	8	7	9	9
Transportation, Communication	11	12	14	14
Retail trade	32	42	47	49
Artisanal trades	21	21	25	21
Housing, Public utilities	59	39	31	31
Noneconomic Activities	42	52	57	58
Culture and social welfare	52	56	60	61
Public service and administration	27	42	48	50
COUNTRYWIDE	25	29	34	35

Source: Based on information from Vida Tomsic, *Women in the Development of Socialist Self-Managing Yugoslavia*, Belgrade, 1980, p. 194.

Table 15. Household Size, 1971

Persons per Household	Percentages of All Households			
	Total	Cities	Towns	Rural
1	13	18	13	9
2	16	18	16	14
3	19	23	19	15
4	21	23	23	18
5	13	9	14	15
6	8	4	7	11
7	4	1	3	7
8	2	1	2	4
9 or more	4	3	3	7
TOTAL	100	100	100	100

Source: Based on information from Centre for Educational Research and Innovation (CERI). *Child and Family: Demographic Development in the OECD Countries*, Organisation for Economic Co-operation and Development, Paris, 1979, p. 183.

Table 16. Housing, by Region, 1978

Republic	Average Dwelling Area per Person (in square meters)	Average Number of Persons per Dwelling	Number of Dwellings per 1,000 Population	Dwellings Built per 1,000 Population
Bosnia and Hercegovina 11.4	4.0	250.0	6.9	
Croatia 17.1	3.2	314.0	6.5	
Macedonia 11.7	4.8	209.0	5.6	
Montenegro 11.5	4.3	239.0	6.0	
Serbia 14.3	3.6	280.0	5.7	
Serbia proper 14.5	3.3	299.0	5.7	
Kosovo 8.7	6.6	151.0	4.8	
Vojvodina 17.9	3.1	326.0	6.3	
Slovenia 18.6	3.2	313.0	7.7	
COUNTRYWIDE 14.4	3.6	278.0	6.3	

Source: Based on information from Ivan Jeremic, "Housing, 1975–1979," *Yugoslav Survey* [Belgrade], XXI, No. 1, February 1980, p. 50.

Table 17. Physicians and Hospital Beds, 1971
(per 1,000 inhabitants)

Region	Physicians	Hospital Beds
Bosnia and Hercegovina	.68	4.3
Croatia	1.26	6.8
Macedonia	.92	5.4
Montenegro	1.13	6.5
Serbia proper	1.28	5.9
Kosovo	.40	2.6
Vojvodina	1.21	5.8
Slovenia	1.16	7.6
COUNTRYWIDE	1.06	5.7

Source: Based on information from Robert L. Berg, M. Roy Brooks, Jr., and Miomir
Savicevic, *Health Care in Yugoslavia and the United States*, Fogarty International
Center Proceedings, No. 34, National Institutes of Health, Bethesda,
Maryland, 1976, p. 86.

Table 18. Infant Mortality Rate, by Region, 1976

	Per 1,000 Live Births		Per 1,000 Live Births
COUNTRYWIDE	36.5	Serbia proper	29.9
Bosnia and Hercegovina	38.1	Kosovo	69.2
Croatia	23.7	Vojvodina	19.9
Macedonia	65.1	Slovenia	19.3
Montenegro	27.0		

Source: Based on information from Radmilo Feliks, "Public Health, Health Care, and
the Health Service," *Yugoslav Survey* [Belgrade], XIX, No. 3, August 1978,
p. 138.

Table 19. Workers' and Farmers' Use of Health Services, 1971

Service	Annual Use per Person	
	Workers	Farmers
Physician visits	3.82	0.99
Dental visits	1.20	0.19
Maternal care	0.24	0.05
Child health services	0.52	0.09
Youth and student health services	0.43	0.07
Tuberculosis services	0.18	0.08
TOTAL	6.39	1.47

Source: Based on information from Robert L. Berg, M. Roy Brooks, Jr., and Miomir
Savicevic, *Health Care in Yugoslavia and the United States*, Fogarty Interna-
tional Center Proceedings, No. 34, National Institutes of Health, Bethesda,
Maryland, 1976, p. 132.

Table 20. Federal Budget Summary, 1977–81
(in billions of dinars[1])

	1977	1978	1979[2]	1980[2]	1981[2]
Current Revenues					
Customs duties	39.7	23.4	24.1	20.4	24.1
Share of sales tax	0	26.3	38.2	47.9	73.3
Contributions from regions[3] ...	39.0	20.8	28.4	38.5	63.8
Other	1.3	2.1	3.1	3.0	3.1
Total Current Revenues	80.0	72.6	93.8	109.8	164.3
Expenditures					
National defense	38.1	42.6	55.0	76.3	101.9
Administration	10.9	13.1	15.1	8.8	11.1
Grants to regions[3]	6.1	7.0	10.5	14.3	16.3
Investments	0.6	0.6	0.7	0	0
Supplement to pension funds ...	10.4	12.4	14.8	24.7	31.9
Subsidies	22.3	1.4	0	0	0
Other	0.6	0.7	0.9	8.2	7.9
Total Expenditures	89.0	77.8	97.0	132.3	169.1
Allocations to Budget Reserves ...	0.3	0.3	0.2	n.a.	0
Debt Repayment and Other	4.2	4.0	5.0	n.a.	0
Budget Deficit	13.5	9.5	8.4	22.5	4.8
Financing of Deficit					
National Bank credit	9.5	9.5	8.4	9.2	4.8
Bond issues	4.0	0	0	13.3	0

n.a.—not available.
[1]For value of the dinar—see Glossary.
[2]Revised plan.
[3]Regions are the republics and autonomous provinces.

Source: Based on information from the Organisation for Economic Co-operation and
Development, *Economic Survey, Yugoslavia*, Paris, May 1981, p. 34.

Table 21. Consolidated Budget Summary of Public Sector[1], 1976–80
(in billions of dinars[2])

	1976	1977	1978	1979	1980[3]
Revenues					
Direct taxes[4]	134.6	175.5	232.5	279.6	351.4
Indirect taxes[5]	86.3	109.4	126.3	157.7	190.0
Other taxes and revenues	20.5	19.8	25.5	33.4	46.1
Total Revenues ....,....	241.4	304.7	384.3	470.7	587.5
Expenditures					
Defense and administration ...	57.5	71.5	83.9	103.8	n.a.
Education	38.1	43.7	57.4	67.5	n.a.
Social security and welfare	93.5	114.4	146.5	178.6	n.a.
Subsidies and enterprise losses ..	19.6	28.0	38.1	42.2	n.a.
Other expenditures[6]	44.6	54.3	63.4	77.7	n.a.
Total Expenditures	253.3	311.9	389.3	469.8	
Surplus (or − deficit)	− 11.9	− 7.2	− 5.0	0.9	n.a.
Foreign Financing (net)	− 1.5	− 0.1	− 0.1	0	n.a.
Domestic Financing (net)	13.4	7.3	5.1	0.9	n.a.

n.a.—not available.
[1]All units of government and communities of interest net of transfers between units.
[2]For value of the dinar—see Glossary.
[3]Preliminary estimate.
[4]Includes income taxes, social security contributions, enterprise payroll taxes, and property taxes.
[5]Includes taxes on goods and services including those in foreign trade.
[6]Includes those for housing and communal amenities and consumption subsidies.

Source: Based on information from the Organisation for Economic Co-operation and
Development, *Economic Survey, Yugoslavia*, Paris, May 1981, p. 33.

Table 22. Labor Force, Selected Years, 1968–80
(in thousands)

	1968	1975	1979	1980
Paid Domestic Employment				
Social Sector	3,487	4,667	5,506	5,681
Productive Activities	2,900	3,876	4,560	4,709
of which:				
Agriculture	(167)	(176)	(188)	(191)
Industry	(1,335)	(1,819)	(2,102)	(2,162)
Construction	(373)	(479)	(602)	(622)
Transportation and				
Communications	(275)	(346)	(387)	(399)
Trade	(317)	(476)	(558)	(582)
Nonproductive Activities	587	791	946	972
Private Sector[1]	100	91	109	117
Total Paid Domestic Employment	3,587	4,758	5,615	5,798
Registered Unemployed	311	540	762	785
Other Labor Force[2]	4,827	3,849	2,947	2,802
TOTAL[3]	8,725	9,147	9,324	9,385

[1]Excludes most or all private farmers.
[2]Includes private farmers and workers abroad.
[3]Midyear estimate of the economically active population.

Source: Based on information from the Organisation for Economic Co-operation and Development, *Economic Survey, Yugoslavia*, Paris, May 1981, p. 55.

Table 23. *Production of Major Minerals and Metals, Selected Years, 1948-78*

Commodity	Units	1948	1958	1968	1977	1978
Coal (all kinds)	million tons	10.6	19.0	26.7	39.1	39.7
Crude oil	-do-	neg.[1]	0.5	2.7	3.9	4.1
Iron ore	-do-	0.3	2.0	2.7	4.5	4.6
Pig iron	-do-	0.2	0.7	1.2	1.9	2.1
Crude steel	-do-	0.4	1.1	1.9	3.2	3.5
Copper ore	-do-	1.1	2.3	7.0	17.5	17.1
Zinc ore	-do-	0.9	1.8	2.7	4.2	4.1
Bauxite	-do-	0.1	0.7	2.1	2.0	2.6
Cement	-do-	1.2	2.0	3.8	8.0	8.7
Antimony ore	thousand tons	35	76	109	87	107
Chromium ore	-do-	63	114	45	2	2
Electrolytic copper	-do-	14	30	70	144	151
Refined lead	-do-	49	84	95	130	117
Zinc (refined and electrolytic)	-do-	3	31	79	99	95
Aluminum ingots	-do-	2	22	48	197	196
Antimony regulus	-do-	1.5	1.7	1.8	1.0	1.8
Rolled aluminum products	-do-	1	6	54	119	132
Rolled copper products	-do-	4	26	58	65	69
Asbestos ore	-do-	72	202	223	316	312
Asbestos fiber	-do-	0	5.4	10.4	9.0	10.3
Mercury	tons	377	423	510	108	n.a.[2]
Refined silver	-do-	47	117	94	146	159

[1]neg.—negligible.
[2]n.a.—not available.

Source: Based on information from Yugoslavia, Savezni Zavod za Statistiku, *Statisticki Godisnjak Jugoslavije, 1979*, Belgrade, July 1979, pp. 117–16.

Table 24. Imports by Major Commodity Groups, Selected Years, 1970–80
(in millons of United States dollars)

Commodity Groups*	1970	1978	1979	1980
Food, beverage, and tobacco	207	605	977	991
Raw materials	314	995	1,205	1,544
Mineral fuels	138	1,431	2,248	3,549
Chemicals	267	1,140	1,653	1,824
Base metals	427	835	1,151	1,313
Other semimanufactures	399	863	1,092	1,063
Machinery	629	2,833	3,993	3,450
Transport equipment	326	796	1,038	766
Other machinery	147	429	606	458
Miscellaneous	20	56	56	106
TOTAL IMPORTS	2,874	9,983	14,019	15,064

*Based on Standard International Trade Classification main commodity groups, cost, insurance, freight basis.

Source: Based on information from the Organisation for Economic Co-operation and Development, *Economic Survey, Yugoslavia*, Paris, May 1981, p. 58.

Table 25. Exports by Major Commodity Groups, Selected Years, 1970–80
(in millions of United States Dollars)

Commodity Groups*	1970	1978	1979	1980
Live animals and meat	159	313	300	352
Cereals and products	21	80	23	108
Other food, beverages, and tobacco	134	294	397	563
Wood	64	265	318	368
Other raw materials	93	186	301	297
Chemicals	97	469	636	1,011
Base metals	256	497	606	697
Other semimanufactures	236	762	1,000	1,297
Machinery	192	1,030	1,329	1,656
Ships	142	421	252	317
Other finished manufactures	261	1,147	1,358	2,023
Miscellaneous	24	204	274	289
TOTAL EXPORTS	1,679	5,668	6,794	8,978

*Based on Standard International Trade Classification main commodity groups, freight on board basis.

Source: Based on information from the Organisation for Economic Co-operation and Development, *Economic Survey, Yugoslavia*, Paris, May 1981, p. 58.

Table 26. Imports and Exports by Area, Selected Years, 1970–80
(in millions of United States dollars)

Area	1970 Imports	1970 Exports	1978 Imports	1978 Exports	1979 Imports	1979 Exports	1980 Imports	1980 Exports
Italy	378	255	827	531	1,146	716	1,117	833
West Germany[1].	567	198	1,801	472	2,887	739	2,500	778
Other EEC[2]	389	202	1,201	302	1,666	473	1,603	754
United States ...	160	90	615	371	1,059	373	1,015	393
Other OECD[3] countries	487	197	1,446	761	1,772	685	1,720	600
Soviet Union ...	193	242	1,375	1,394	1,793	1,401	2,698	2,489
Other communist countries	400	303	1,123	786	1,749	1,330	1,828	1,648
Africa	78	60	397	467	570	543	936	735
Middle East	70	35	536	234	993	454	1,093	635
Other developing countries	152	97	662	350	384	80	554	113
TOTAL .	2,874	1,679	9,983	5,668	14,019	6,794	15,064	8,978

Note: Imports c.i.f. (cost, insurance, and freight) and exports f.o.b. (freight on board).
[1]Federal Republic of Germany.
[2]European Economic Community countries.
[3]Organisation for Economic Co-operation and Development.

Source: Based on information from the Organisation for Economic Co-operation and Development, *Economic Survey, Yugoslavia*, Paris, May 1981, p. 59.

Table 27. Balance of Payments, 1976–80
(in billions of United States dollars)

	1976	1977	1978	1979	1980[1]
Imports (c.i.f.)[2]	− 7.37	− 9.63	− 9.99	− 14.02	− 15.06
Exports (f.o.b.)[3]	4.88	5.25	5.67	6.79	8.98
Balance of Trade[4]	− 2.49	− 4.38	− 4.32	− 7.22	− 6.09
Transportation (net)	0.43	0.57	0.58	0.73	0.83
Tourism (net)	0.72	0.75	0.93	1.03	1.37
Investment income (net)	− 0.28	− 0.26	− 0.30	− 0.63	− 1.08
Private and workers' remittances	1.42	1.43	1.74	1.71	1.54
Other services	0.36	0.31	0.10	0.73	1.14
Balance of Services[4]	2.65	2.80	3.06	3.56	3.80
Current Balance[4]	0.16	− 1.58	− 1.26	− 3.66	− 2.29
Long-term capital	1.09	1.40	1.35	1.08	1.92
Short-term capital	− 0.24	0.07	− 0.11	0.85	0.30
Exceptional financing	0.05	0.08	0.35	0.25	0.25
Capital Account[4]	0.90	1.55	1.59	2.18	2.47
Reserve movements (net)[4] ...	1.06	− 0.04	0.33	− 1.47	0.18
of which:					
Foreign exchange	(1.20)	(0.05)	(0.26)	(− 1.19)	(0.52)
IMF[5] credit	(0.19)	(− 0.11)	(− 0.07)	(0.29)	(0.34)

[1]Preliminary estimate.
[2]Cost, insurance, and freight.
[3]Freight on board.
[4]Totals may not add because of rounding.
[5]International Monetary Fund.

Source: Based on information from the Organisation for Economic Co-operation and Development, *Economic Survey, Yugoslavia*, Paris, May 1981, p. 11.

Bibliography

Chapter 1

Alexander, John. *Jugoslavia Before the Roman Conquest.* London: Thames and Hudson, 1972.

Alexander, Stella. *Church and State in Yugoslavia since 1945.* (Soviet and East European Studies series.) Cambridge: Cambridge University Press, 1979.

Arnakis, George G. "The Role of Religion in the Development of Balkan Nationalism." Pages 115–44 in Charles and Barbara Jelavich (eds.), *The Balkans in Tradition.* Berkeley: University of California Press, 1963.

Auty, Phyllis, *Yugoslavia.* New York: Walker, 1965.

Avakumovic, I. *A History of the Communist Party of Yugoslavia.* Aberdeen: Aberdeen University Press, 1964.

Barac, Antun. *A History of Yugoslav Literature.* Ann Arbor: Michigan Slavic Publications, 1976.

Bombelles, Joseph. *Economic Development of Communist Yugoslavia, 1947–1964.* Stanford: Hoover Institution Press, 1968.

Boppe, L.H. *La Croatie Militaire.* Paris: 1900.

Byrnes, Robert F. (ed.). *Yugoslavia.* New York: Praeger, 1957.

Castellan, Georges. *La Vie Quotidienne en Serbie au Seuil de l'independence, 1815–1839.* Paris: Hachette, 1967.

Chloros, A.G. *Yugoslav Civil Law: History, Family Property.* New York: Oxford University Press, 1970.

Clissold, Stephen. "Croat Separatism: Nationalism, Dissidence, and Terrorism," *Conflict Studies* [London], No. 103, January 1979, 1–21.

Clissold, Stephen (ed.). *A Short History of Yugoslavia: From Early Times to 1966.* Cambridge: Cambridge University Press, 1968.

_____. *Yugoslavia and the Soviet Union 1937–73: A Documentary Survey.* London: Oxford University Press, 1975.

Dedijer, Vladimir. *The Battle Stalin Lost: Memoirs of Yugoslavia, 1948–1953.* New York: Grosset and Dunlap, 1972.

_____. *Tito Speaks: His Self-Portrait and Struggle with Stalin.* London: Weidenfeld and Nicolson, 1953.

Dedijer, Vladimir, et al. *History of Yugoslavia.* New York: McGraw-Hill, 1974.

Denitch, Bogdan. *The Legitimation of a Revolution: The Yugoslav Case.* New Haven: Yale University Press, 1976.

Despalatovic, Elinor M. *Ljudevit Gaj and the Illyrian Movement.* Boulder: East European Quarterly, Columbia University Press, 1976.

Djilas, Milovan. *Conversations with Stalin.* New York: Harcourt, Brace and World, 1962.

_____. *The New Class.* New York: Praeger, 1957.

291

_____. *Njegos: Poet, Prince, Bishop.* (Trans., Michael B. Petrovich.) New York: Harcourt, Brace and World, 1966.

_____. *Tito: The Story from Inside.* (Trans., Vasilijekojic and Richard Hayes.) New York: Harcourt, Brace, Jovanovich, 1980.

_____. *The Unperfect Society: Beyond the New Class.* (Trans., Dorian Cooke.) New York: Harcourt, Brace, Jovanovich, 1970.

Djordjevic, Dimitrije (ed.). *The Creation of Yugoslavia: 1914–18.* Oxford, England: Clio Books, 1980.

_____. "The Serbs as an Integrating and Disintegrating Factor," *Austrian History Yearbook,* III, No. 2, 1967, 48–82.

Documents on German Foreign Policy, 1919–1945. Arlington, Virginia: Open-Door Press, 1976.

Doder, Dusko. *The Yugoslavs.* New York: Random House, 1978.

Dragnich, Alex N. *The Development of Parliamentary Government in Serbia.* Boulder: East European Quarterly, 1978.

_____. *Serbia, Nicola Pasic, and Yugoslavia.* New Brunswick: Rutgers University Press, 1974.

Dvornik, Francis. *The Slavs in European History and Civilization.* New Brunswick: Rutgers University Press, 1975.

Great Britain. Admiralty. Naval Intelligence Division. *Yugoslavia, II: History, Peoples, and Administration.* (Geographical Handbook series.) London: 1944.

Guldescu, Stanko. *The Croatian-Slavonian Kingdom, 1526–1792.* The Hague: Mouton, 1970.

Hamilton, F.E. Ian. *Yugoslavia: Patterns of Economic Activity.* New York: Praeger, 1968.

Haumant, Emile. *La formation de la Yugoslavie.* Paris: 1930.

Heppell, Muriel, and Frank B. Singleton. *Yugoslavia.* New York: Praeger, 1965.

Hoffman, George W., and Fred Warner Neal. *Yugoslavia and the New Communism.* New York: Twentieth Century Fund, 1962.

Hoptner, J.B. *Yugoslavia in Crisis, 1934–1941.* New York: Columbia University Press, 1962.

Hunter, Brian. *Soviet-Yugoslav Relations, 1948–1972: A Bibliography of Soviet, Western, and Yugoslav Commentary.* New York: Garland, 1975.

Jukic, Ilija. *The Fall of Yugoslavia.* (Trans., Dorian Cooke.) New York: Harcourt, Brace, Jovanovich, 1974.

Krekic, Barisa. *Dubrovnik in the 14th and 15th Centuries.* Norman: University of Oklahoma Press, 1972.

Lederer, Ivo. *Yugoslavia at the Peace Conference: A Study in Frontier Making.* New Haven: Yale University Press, 1963.

Lukic, Sveta. *Contemporary Yugoslav Literature: A Sociopolitical Approach.* Urbana: University of Illinois Press, 1972.

McDonald, Gordon C., et al. *Yugoslavia: A Country Study.* (DA Pam 550–99.) Washington: GPO for Foreign Area Studies, The American University, 1973.

Mackenzie, David. *The Serbs and Russian Pan-Slavism: 1875–1878.* Ithaca: Cornell University Press, 1967.

Maclean, Fitzroy. *The Heretic: The Life and Times of Josip Broz-Tito*. New York: Harper and Brothers, 1957.

McClellan, Woodford D. *Svetozar Markovic and the Origins of Balkan Nationalism*. Princeton: Princeton University Press, 1964.

Mellor, Roy E.H. *Eastern Europe: A Geography of the Comecon Countries*. New York: Columbia University Press, 1975.

Mousset, Jean. *La Serbie et son Eglise*. Paris: Droz, 1938.

Neal, Fred Warner. *Titoism in Action: The Reform in Yugoslavia after 1948*. Berkeley: University of California Press, 1958.

Paulowitch, Stevan. *Anglo-Russian Rivalry in Serbia, 1837–1839: The Mission of Colonel Hodges*. Paris: Mouton, 1961.

Petrovich, Michael. *A History of Modern Serbia, 1804–1918*. New York: Harcourt, Brace, Jovanovich, 1976.

Remac, Joachim. *The Origins of World War I*. New York: Holt, Rinehart and Winston, 1967.

Ristic, Dragisa N. *Yugoslavia's Revolution of 1941*. University Park: Pennsylvania State University Press, 1966.

Roberts, Walter R. *Tito, Mihailovic, and the Allies: 1941–1945*. New Brunswick: Rutgers University Press, 1973.

Rothenberg, Gunther. *Military Border in Croatia, 1740–1881: A Study of an Imperial Institution*. Chicago: University of Chicago Press, 1966.

Rusinow, Dennison. *The Yugoslav Experiment, 1948–1974*. Berkeley: University of California Press, 1977.

Schrenk, Martin, Cyrus Ardalan, and Nawal A. El Tatawy. *Yugoslavia: Self-Management Socialism and the Challenges of Development*. Washington: International Bank for Reconstruction and Development, 1979.

Seton-Watson, Hugh. *Eastern Europe Between the Wars, 1918–1941*. Hamden: Anchor, 1962.

Shoup, Paul. *Communism and the Yugoslav National Question*. New York: Columbia University Press, 1968.

Singleton, Frederick B. *Twentieth-Century Yugoslavia*. New York: Columbia University Press, 1976.

Stokes, Gale. *Legitimacy Through Liberalism: Vladimir Jovanovic and the Transformation of Serbian Politics*. Seattle: University of Washington Press, 1975.

Sugar, Peter. *The Industrialization of Bosnia-Hercegovina*. Seattle: University of Washington Press, 1963.

———. *Southeastern Europe under Ottoman Rule: 1354–1804*. Seattle: University of Washington Press, 1977.

Temperley, Harold H.V. *History of Serbia*. New York: Howard Fertig, 1969.

Tomasevich, Jozo. *Peasants, Politics, and Economic Change in Yugoslavia*. Stanford: Stanford University Press, 1955 and 1976.

———. *War and Revolution in Yugoslavia: 1941–45: The Cetniks*. Stanford: Stanford University Press, 1975.

Ulam, Adam B. *Titoism and the Cominform*. New York: Greenwood, 1971.

Vucinich, Wayne S. *Serbia Between East and West: The Events of 1903–1908.* Stanford: Stanford University Press, 1954.

Vucinich, Wayne S. (ed.). *Contemporary Yugoslavia: Twenty Years of Socialist Experiment.* Berkeley: University of California Press, 1969.

Wilson, Duncan. *Tito's Yugoslavia.* Cambridge: Cambridge University Press, 1980.

Wolff, Robert L. *The Balkans in Our Time.* Cambridge: Harvard University Press, 1974.

Chapter 2

Adler, Philip. "Nation and Nationalism Among the Serbs of Hungary 1790–1870," *East European Quarterly,* XIII, No. 3, Fall 1979, 271–338.

Alexander, Stella. *Church and State in Yugoslavia since 1945.* (Soviet and East European Studies series.) Cambridge: Cambridge University Press, 1979.

_____. "Church-State Relations in Yugoslavia: Recent Developments," *Religion in Communist Lands* [Keston, Kent, England], 5, Winter 1977, 238–40.

_____. "Yugoslavia: New Legislation on the Legal Status of Religious Communities," *Religion in Communist Lands* [Keston, Kent, England], 18, No. 2, Summer 1980, 119–24.

Andrassy, Juraj. "Working Paper No. 15." Pages 172–82 in Boris Visinski (ed.), *The Ohrid Seminar on Minorities: United Nations Seminar on the Promotion of Human Rights of National, Ethnic, and Other Minorities, Ohrid, Yugoslavia, 1974.* Skopje: Macedonian Review Editions, 1977.

Avakumovic, Ivan. "The Serb Peasant Party, 1919–1945." Pages 57–78 in Ivan Volgyes (ed.), *The Peasantry of Eastern Europe Vol. I: Roots of Rural Transformation.* New York: Pergamon Press, 1979.

Bakali, Mahmut. "Thirty Years of the Socialist Development of Kosovo," *Socialist Thought and Practice* [Belgrade], XVL, No. 1, 1976.

Baric, Lorraine. "Levels of Change in Yugoslav Kinship." Pages 1–24 in Maurice Freeman (ed.), *Social Organization.* Chicago: Aldine, 1967.

_____. "Traditional Groups and New Economic Opportunities in Rural Yugoslavia." Pages 253–78 in Raymond Firth (ed.), *Themes in Economic Anthropology.* London: Tavistock Publications, 1967.

Barton, Allen H., Bogdan Denitch, and Charles Kadushin (eds.). *Opinion-Making Elites in Yugoslavia.* (Praeger Special Series in International Politics and Government.) New York: Praeger, 1973.

Baucic, Ivo. *The Effects of Emigration from Yugoslavia and the Problems of Returning Emigrant Workers,* II. (European

Demographic Monographs series.) The Hague: Martinus Nijhoff, 1972.

_____. "Regional Differences in Yugoslav External Migration." Pages 217–43 in Huey Louis Kostanick (ed.), *Population and Migration Trends in Eastern Europe*. Boulder: Westview Press, 1977.

Beeson, Trevor. *Discretion and Valour: Religious Conditions in Russia and Eastern Europe*. Glasgow: Fontana Books, The British Council of Churches, 1974.

Benz, E. *The Eastern Orthodox Church: Its Thought and Life*. New York: Doubleday, 1963.

Berent, Jerzy. "Causes of Fertility Decline in Eastern Europe and the Soviet Union," *Population Studies: A Journal of Demography* [London], XXIV, 1970, 35–58.

Berg, Robert L., M. Roy Brooks, Jr., and Miomir Savicevic. *Health Care in Yugoslavia and the United States*. (Fogarty International Center Proceedings series. No. 34.) Bethesda, Maryland: National Institutes of Health, 1976.

Bergman, Theodor. *Farm Policies in Socialist Countries*. (Trans., Lux Furtmüller.) Lexington, Massachusetts: Lexington Books, D.C. Heath and Co., 1975.

Bertsch, Gary K. "Ethnicity and Politics in Socialist Yugoslavia." Pages 88–99 in the *Annals of the American Academy of Political and Social Sciences*. (Vol. 433.) Philadelphia: 1977.

_____. "Participation, Change, and Stability: Yugoslavia in Comparative Perspective." Pages 119–46 in Teresa Rakowska-Harmstone (ed.), *Perspectives for Change in Communist Societies*. Boulder: Westview Press, 1979.

_____. *Values and Community in Multinational Yugoslavia*, XVII. (East European Monographs series.) Boulder: East European Quarterly, 1976.

Bertsch, Gary K., and Karen L. Persons. "Workers' Education in Socialist Yugoslavia," *Comparative Education Review*, 24, No. 1, February 1980, 87–97.

Besemeres, John F. *Socialist Population Politics: The Political Implications of Demographic Trends in the USSR and Eastern Europe*. White Plains: M.E. Sharpe, 1980.

Bezdanov, Atevan, Dragutin Frankovic, and Berislav Sefer. "The Policy and System of Education," *Yugoslav Survey* [Belgrade], XXI, No. 3, August 1980, 115–46.

Bjelajac, Slobodan. "A Critical Appraisal of a Housing Project in the City of Split, Yugoslavia," *Ekistics* [Athens], 45, No. 270, June 1978, 225–29.

Brailsford, H.N. *Macedonia: Its Races and Their Future*. London: Methuen, 1906.

Brocic, Manojlo. "The Position and Activities of the Religious Communities in Yugoslavia with Special Attention to the Serbian Orthodox Church." Pages 351–67 in Bohdan R. Bociurkiw and

John R. Strong (eds.), *Religion and Atheism in the USSR and Eastern Europe*. London: Macmillan, 1975.

Broekmeyer, M.J. (ed.). *Yugoslav Workers' Selfmanagement: Proceedings of a Symposium Held in Amsterdam, 7-9 January, 1970*. Dordrecht, The Netherlands: D. Reidel Publishing, 1970.

Bukowski, James B. "The Catholic Church and Croatian National Identity: From the Counter-Reformation to the Early Nineteenth Century," *East European Quarterly*, XIII, No. 3, Fall 1979, 327–38.

Bulatovic, Ranko N. "New Trends in Educational Reform in Yugoslavia," *Prospects-Quarterly Review of Education* [Paris], United Nations Educational, Scientific and Cultural Organization, VI, No. 4, 1976, 644–49.

Burg, Steven L. "Decision-Making in Yugoslavia," *Problems of Communism*, 29, No. 2, March–April 1980, 1–20.

_____. "Ethnic Conflict and the Federalization of Socialist Yugoslavia: The Serbo-Croat Conflict," *Publius*, 7, No. 4, Fall 1977, 119–43.

Buric, Olivera. "The Zadruga and the Contemporary Family in Yugoslavia." Pages 117–38 in Robert F. Byrnes (ed.), *Communal Families in the Balkans: The Zadruga*. Notre Dame, Indiana: University of Notre Dame Press, 1976.

Byrnes, Robert F. (ed.). *Communal Families in the Balkans: The Zadruga*. Notre Dame, Indiana: University of Notre Dame Press, 1976.

_____. *Yugoslavia*. New York: Praeger, 1957.

Centre for Educational Research and Innovation (CERI). *Child and Family: Demographic Developments in the OECD Countries*. Paris: Organisation for Economic Co-operation and Development, 1979.

_____. *Educational Financing and Policy Goals for Primary Schools: Country Reports*, II. Paris: Organisation for Economic Co-operation and Development, 1979.

Clark, Cal. "Commune Policies and Socio-Economic Parameters in Yugoslavia." Pages 148–75 in Daniel N. Nelson (ed.), *Local Politics in Communist Countries*. Lexington: University of Kentucky Press, 1980.

Clark, Cal, and Karl F. Johnson. "Development's Influence on Yugoslav Political Values," *Sage Publications* (Sage Professional Papers in Comparative Politics, No. 01-058.) Beverly Hills: Sage Publications, 1976.

Clissold, Stephen. "Croat Separatism: Nationalism, Dissidence, and Terrorism," *Conflict Studies* [London], No. 103, January 1979, 1–21.

Cohen, Leonard. "The Social Background and Recruitment of Yugoslav Political Elites, 1918–48." Pages 25–68 in Allen H. Barton, Bogdan Denitch, and Charles Kadushin (eds.), *Opinion-Making Elites in Yugoslavia*. New York: Praeger, 1973.

_____. "Partisans, Professionals, and Proletarians: Elite Change in

Yugoslavia, 1952–78," *Canadian Slavonic Papers* [Ottawa], XXI, No. 4, December 1979, 446–78.

Comisso, Ellen Turkish. *Workers' Control under Plan and Market: Implications of Yugoslav Self-Management.* New Haven: Yale University Press, 1979.

Connor, Walter D. *Socialism, Politics, and Equality: Hierarchy and Change in Eastern Europe and the USSR.* New York: Columbia University Press, 1979.

Costa, Nicholas J. "An Ethnomusicalogical Study of the Land of the Eagle," *East European Quarterly,* XV, No. 2, 1981, 251–59.

Cviic, K.F. "Yugoslavia's Moslem Problem," *World Today,* 36, No. 3, March 1980, 108–14.

Dahlquist, Paul William. "The Politics of Balance in Tito's Yugoslavia." (M.A. thesis.) Monterrey, California: Naval Postgraduate School, March 1979.

Davis, James C. "A Slovene Laborer and His Experience of Industrialization, 1888–1976," *East European Quarterly,* X, No. 1, Spring 1976, 2–20.

Denich, Bette S. "Sex and Power in the Balkans." Pages 243–62 in Michelle Zimbalist Rosaldo and Louise Lamphere (eds.), *Women, Culture, and Society.* Stanford: Stanford University Press, 1974.

_____. "Social Mobility and Industrialization in a Yugoslav Town." (Unpublished Ph.D. dissertation.) Berkeley: Department of Anthropology, University of California, 1969.

_____. "Urbanization and Women's Roles in Yugoslavia," *Anthropological Quarterly,* 49, No. 1, January 1976, 11–19.

Denitch, Bogdan. "Mobility and Recruitment of Yugoslav Leadership: The Role of the League of Communists." Pages 95–119 in Allen H. Barton, Bogdan Denitch, and Charles Kadushin (eds.), *Opinion-Making Elites in Yugoslavia.* New York: Praeger, 1973.

_____. "Religion and Social Change in Yugoslavia." Pages 366–87 in Bohdan R. Bociurkiw and John R. Strong (eds.), *Religion and Atheism in the U.S.S.R. and Eastern Europe.* London: Macmillan, 1975.

_____. "The Evolution of Yugoslav Federalism," *Publius,* 7, No. 4, Fall 1977, 107–17.

_____. *The Legitimation of a Revolution: The Yugoslav Case.* New Haven: Yale University Press, 1976.

_____. "The Relevance of Yugoslav Self-Management." Pages 268–79 in Gary K. Bertsch and Thomas W. Ganschow (eds.), *Comparative Communism: The Soviet, Chinese, and Yugoslav Models.* San Francisco: W.H. Freeman, 1976.

Djilas, Milovan. *Tito: The Story from Inside.* (Trans., Vasilije Kojic and Richard Hayes.) New York: Harcourt, Brace, Jovanovich, 1980.

Djuranovic, Veselin. "Socio-Economic Development of Montenegro" (Trans., D. Rouge.), *Socialist Thought and Practice* [Belgrade], XVL, No. 11, 1976, 81–108.

Dobos, Manuela. "The Nagodba and the Peasantry in Croatia-Slavonia." Pages 79–107 in Ivan Volgyes (ed.), *The Peasantry of Eastern Europe Vol. I: Roots of Rural Transformation.* New York: Pergamon Press, 1979.

Dyker, David A. "Yugoslavia: Unity Out of Diversity?" Pages 66–100 in Archie Brown and Jack Gray (eds.), *Political Culture and Political Change in Communist States* (2d ed.) New York: Holmes and Meier, 1977.

Eterovich, Francis H., and Christopher Spalatin (eds.). *Croatia: Land, People, Culture,* I and II. Toronto: University of Toronto Press, 1970.

Feliks, Radmilo. "Public Health, Health Care, and the Health Service," *Yugoslav Survey* [Belgrade], XIX, No. 3, August 1978, 137–56.

Fine, John V.A., Jr. *The Bosnian Church: A New Interpretation,* X. (East European Monographs series.) Boulder: East European Quarterly, 1975.

Fodor, Eugene (ed.). *Fodor's Yugoslavia, 1980.* New York: David McKay, 1980.

Franolic, Branko. "Language Policy and Language Planning in Yugoslavia with Special Reference to Croatian and Macedonian," *Lingua* [Amsterdam], 51, No. 1, 1980, 55–72.

Frey, Cynthia W. "Yugoslav Nationalisms and the Doctrine of Limited Sovereignty," *East European Quarterly,* X, No. 4, Winter 1976, 427–57.

———. "Yugoslav Nationalisms and the Doctrine of Limited Sovereignty," *East European Quarterly,* XI, No. 1, Spring 1977, 79–108.

Gaffney, Christopher C. "Kisker: The Economic Success of a Peasant Village in Yugoslavia," *Ethnology,* 18, No. 2, April 1979, 135–51.

Gasinski, Thaddeus Z. "The National Minority Policy of Today's Yugoslavia," *Nationalities Papers,* VIII, No. 1, Spring 1980, 29–51.

Georgeoff, John. "Current Educational Reforms in Yugoslavia," *Slavic and European Education Review,* No. 1, 1980, 1–10.

Gitelman, Zvi. "Federalism and Multiculturalism in Socialist Systems." Pages 157–70 in Daniel J. Elazar (ed.), *Federalism and Political Integration.* Ramat Gan, Israel: Turtledove Publishing, 1979.

Great Britain. Admiralty. Naval Intelligence Division. *Yugoslavia, I. Physical Geography.* (Geographical Handbook series.) London: 1944.

Gross, Mirjana. "On the Integration of the Croatian Nation: A Case Study in Nation Building," *East European Quarterly,* XV, No. 2, 1981, 209–25.

Gruenwald, Oskar. "The Praxis School: Marxism as a Critique of Socialism?" *East European Quarterly,* XV, No. 2, 1981, 227–50.

Halpern, Joel M. "Demographic and Social Change in the Village of

Orasac: A Perspective over Two Centuries." Pages 37–124 in Barbara Kerewsky Halpern and Joel M. Halpern (eds.), *Selected Papers on a Serbian Village: Social Structure as Reflected by History, Demography, and Oral Tradition.* Amherst: Department of Anthropology, University of Massachusetts, 1977.

———. "Farming as a Way of Life: Yugoslav Peasant Attitudes." Pages 356–84 in J. Karez (ed.), *Soviet and East European Agriculture.* Berkeley: University of California Press, 1967.

———. *A Serbian Village.* New York: Harper and Row, 1967.

———. "Some Perspectives on Balkan Migration Patterns (with Particular Reference to Yugoslavia)." Pages 77–116 in Brian M. Du Toit and Helen I. Safa (eds.), *Migration and Urbanization: Models and Adaptive Strategies.* The Hague: Mouton, 1975.

———. "Town and Countryside in Serbia in the Nineteenth Century, Social and Household Structure as Reflected in the Census of 1863." Pages 401–27 in Peter Laslett (ed.), *Household and Family in Past Time.* London: Cambridge University Press, 1972.

———. "Yugoslavia: Modernization in an Ethnically Diverse State." Pages 316–50 in Wayne S. Vucinich (ed.), *Contemporary Yugoslavia: Twenty Years of Socialist Experiment.* Berkeley: University of California Press, 1969.

Halpern, Joel M., and David Anderson. "The Zadruga, A Century of Change," *Anthropologica* [Ottawa], XII, 1970, 83–97.

Halpern, Joel M., and John Brode. "Peasant Society: Economic Changes and Revolutionary Transformation," *Biennial Review of Anthropology,* 1967, 46–139.

Halpern, Joel M., and E.A. Hammel. "Serbian Society in Karadjordje's Serbia: An Anthropoligical View." Pages 1–36 in Barbara Kerewsky Halpern and Joel M. Halpern (eds.), *Selected Papers on a Serbian Village: Social Structure as Reflected by History, Demography, and Oral Tradition.* Amherst: Department of Anthropology, University of Massachusetts, 1977.

Hammel, E.A. "The Balkan Peasant: A View from Serbia." Pages 75–98 in Philip K. Bock (ed.), *Peasants in the Modern World.* Albuquerque: University of New Mexico Press, 1969.

———. "Economic Change, Social Mobility, and Kinship in Serbia," *Southwestern Journal of Anthropology,* 25, No. 2, Summer 1969, 188–97.

———. "The Pink Yo-Yo: Occupational Mobility in Belgrade, ca. 1915–1965." (Research paper for Institute of International Studies, University of California, Research Series, No. 13.) Berkeley: University of California, 1969.

———. "The Zadruga as Process." Pages 335–74 in Peter Laslett (ed.), *Household and Family in Past Time.* London: Cambridge University Press, 1972.

Hammel, E.A., and Charles Yarbrough. "Preference and Recall in Serbian Cousinship: Power and Kinship Ideology," *Journal of Anthropological Research,* 30, Summer 1974, 95–115.

———. "Social Mobility and the Durability of Family Ties," *Journal* of *Anthropological Research*, 29, No. 3, Autumn 1973, 145–63.

Heppell, Muriel, and Frank B. Singleton. *Yugoslavia*. New York: Praeger, 1965.

Hodges, Donald C. *The Bureaucratization of Socialism*. Amherst: University of Massachusetts Press, 1981.

Hodza, Hajredin. "Working Paper No. 22." Pages 234–49 in Boris Visinski (ed.), *The Ohrid Seminar on Minorities: United Nations Seminar on the Promotion of Human Rights of National, Ethnic, and Other Minorities. Ohrid, Yugoslavia, 1974*. Skopje: Macedonian Review Editions, 1977.

Hoffman, George W., and Ronald L. Hatchett. "Policy and Population in Yugoslavia and Bulgaria." Pages 99–124 in Huey Louis Kostanick (ed.), *Population and Migration Trends in Eastern Europe*. Boulder: Westview Press, 1974.

Hoffman, George W., and Fred Warner Neal. *Yugoslavia and the New Communism*. New York: Twentieth Century Fund, 1962.

Horvat, Branko. *The Yugoslav Economic System: The First Labor Managed Economy in the Making*. White Plains, New York: International Arts and Sciences Press, 1976.

Jackson, George D., Jr. *Comintern and Peasant in East Europe 1919–1930*. (East Central European Studies of Columbia University series.) New York: Columbia University Press, 1966.

Jambrek, Peter. *Development and Social Change in Yugoslavia*. Lexington, Massachusetts: Lexington Books, D.C. Heath, 1975.

Jancar, Barbara. "Yugoslavia: The Case for a Loyal Opposition under Communism." Pages 205–20 in Gary K. Bertsch and Thomas W. Ganschow (eds.), *Comparative Communism: The Soviet, Chinese, and Yugoslav Models*. San Francisco: W.H. Freeman, 1976.

Jelavich, Barbara. "The British Traveller in the Balkans: The Abuses of Ottoman Administration in the Slavonic Provinces," *The Slavonic and East European Review* [London], XXXIII, No. 81, June 1955, 396–413.

Jelavich, Charles, and Barbara Jelavich (eds.). *The Balkans in Transition: Essays on the Development of Balkan Life and Politics since the Eighteenth Century*. (Russian and East European Studies series.) Berkeley: University of California Press, 1963.

Jeremic, Ivan. "Housing, 1975–1979," *Yugoslav Survey* [Belgrade], XXI, No. 1, February 1980, 37–52.

Johnson, A. Ross. "The Role of the Military in Communist Yugoslavia: An Historical Sketch." (Rand Research Paper series, No. P–6070.) Santa Monica: Rand Corporation, 1978.

———. "Yugoslavia: The Non-Leninist Succession." (Rand Research Paper series, No. P–6442.) Santa Monica: Rand Corporation, January 1980.

Joncic, Koca. "Working Paper No. 14." Pages 156–72 in Boris Visinski (ed.), *The Ohrid Seminar on Minorities: United Nations Seminar on the Promotion and Protection of Human Rights of*

National, Ethnic, and Other Minorities. Ohrid, Yugoslavia, 1974. Skopje: Macedonian Review Editions, 1977.

Jovanov, Neca. "Strikes and Self-Management." Pages 339–73 in Josip Obradovic and William N. Dunn (eds.), *Workers' Self-Management and Organizational Power in Yugoslavia.* Pittsburgh: University Center for International Studies, University of Pittsburgh, 1978.

Kadic, Ante. " 'The Democratic Spirit' of the Poljica Commune." Pages 201–14 in Robert F. Byrnes (ed.), *Communal Families in the Balkans: The Zadruga.* Notre Dame, Indiana: University of Notre Dame Press, 1976.

Kinzer, Frederick D. "Educational Reforms in Yugoslavia," *Educational Record,* 59, No. 1, 87–104.

Klein, George, and Patricia V. Klein. "Land Reform in Yugoslavia: Two Models." Pages 39–60 in Ivan Volgyes (ed.), *The Peasantry of Eastern Europe Vol. II: 20th Century Developments.* New York: Pergamon Press, 1979.

Klones, N.J. "Tito and the Yugoslav Movement." Pages 121–26 in Gary K. Bertsch and Thomas W. Ganschow (eds.), *Comparative Communism: The Soviet, Chinese, and Yugoslav Models.* San Francisco: W.H. Freeman, 1976.

Klosterman, Peter, et al. "The Effect of Differences in Local Entitlement on Utilization." Pages 113–22 in Robert L. Berg (ed.), *Health Care in Yugoslavia and the United States.* Bethesda, Maryland: National Institutes of Health, 1976.

Kohn, Robert, and Kerr L. White. *Health Care: An International Study.* London: Oxford University Press, 1976.

Kosinski, Leszek A. "Urbanization in East Central Europe after World War II," *East European Quarterly,* VIII, No. 2, June 1974, 129–53.

Kraus-Delpin, Herma. "The Yugoslav Woman and Her Status in Society," *Review of International Affairs* [Belgrade], 27, No. 622, May 3, 1976, 6–7.

Kunitz, Stephen J. "Health Care and Workers' Self-Management in Yugoslavia," *International Journal of Health Services,* 9, No. 3, 1979, 521–37.

_____. "The Recruitment, Training, and Distribution of Physicians in Yugoslavia," *International Journal of Health Services,* 10, No. 4, 1980, 587–609.

Laslett, Peter, and Marilyn Clarke. "Houseful and Household in an Eighteenth-Century Balkan City." Pages 375–400 in Peter Laslett (ed.), *Household and Family in Past Time.* London: Cambridge University Press, 1972.

Lendvai, Paul. "National Tensions in Yugoslavia," *Conflict Studies* [London], No. 25, August 1972, 1–17.

Lockwood, William G. "Albanian." Pages 19–23 in Richard V. Weekes (ed.), *Muslim Peoples: A World Ethnographic Survey.* Westport, Connecticut: Greenwood Press, 1978.

_____. "Bride Theft and Social Maneuverability in Western Bosnia," *Anthropological Quarterly*, 47, July 1974, 253–69.

_____. "Converts and Consanguinity: The Social Organization of Moslem Slavs in Western Bosnia," *Ethnology*, XI, 1972, 55–79.

_____. "The Peasant-Worker in Yugoslavia." Pages 281–300 in Bernard Lewis Farber (ed.), *The Social Structure of Eastern Europe: Transition and Process in Czechoslovakia, Hungary, Poland, Romania, and Yugoslavia.* New York: Praeger, 1976.

_____. "Social Status and Cultural Change in a Bosnian Moslem Village," *East European Quarterly*, IX, No. 2, Summer 1975, 123–34.

Lottman, Nerbert R. "Yugoslavia: Worth A New Look," *Publishers' Weekly*, September 5, 1980, 28–38.

Lukic, Radomir. "Yugoslav Social Structure and the Formation of Public Opinion." Pages 69–94 in Allen H. Barton, Bogdan Denitch, and Charles Kadushin (eds.), *Opinion-Making Elites in Yugoslavia.* New York: Praeger, 1973.

McDonald, Gordon C., et al. *Yugoslavia: A Country Study.* (DA Pam 550–99.) Washington: GPO for Foreign Area Studies, The American University, 1970.

Mackenzie, David. "The Background: Yugoslavia since 1964." Pages 446–56 in George W. Simmonds (ed.), *Nationalism in the USSR and Eastern Europe in the Era of Brezhnev and Kosygin.* Detroit: University of Detroit Press, 1977.

Mackenzie, G. Muir, and A.P. Irby. *The Slavonic Provinces of Turkey-in-Europe.* London: Alexander Strahan, 1866.

Majstorovic, Stevan. *Cultural Policy in Yugoslavia.* (Cultural Policy series.) Paris: United Nations Educational, Scientific and Cultural Organization, 1972.

Manojlovic, Petar, and Vojislav Petrovic. "Social Welfare," *Yugoslav Survey* [Belgrade], XVIII, No. 2, May 1977, 89–102.

Markovich, Stephen C. "Whither the League of Communists?" *Canadian Slavonic Papers* [Ottawa], XII, No. 1, March 1980, 92–98.

Matley, Ian M. "Transhumance in Bosnia and Herzegovina," *Geographical Review*, 58, No. 2, April 1968, 231–61.

Mellor, Roy E. H. *Eastern Europe: A Geography of the Comecon Countries.* New York: Columbia University Press, 1975.

Mihajlov, Mihajlo. "The Dissident Movement in Yugoslavia," *Washington Quarterly*, 2, No. 4, Fall 1979, 64–73.

Miko, Francis T. "Yugoslavia after Tito." Library of Congress, Congressional Research Service, 77–2–F. Washington: January 25, 1977.

Milenkovitch, Deborah D. "The Case of Yugoslavia," *American Economic Review*, 67 No. 1, February 1977, 55–60.

Miljkovic, Dusan. (Trans., S. Petnicki.) "The Socio-Economic Development of Yugoslavia 1947–1978," *Socialist Thought and Practice* [Belgrade], XIX, No. 11, 1979, 47–71.

Milojenic, B.C. *Yugoslavia, Geographical Survey.* Belgrade: Committee for Cultural Relations with Foreign Countries, 1958.

Moore, John H. *Growth with Self-Management: Yugoslav Industrialization 1952–1975.* (Hoover Institution Publication 220.) Stanford: Hoover Institution Press, 1980.

_____. "La politique yougoslave de développement régional, 1952–1971," *Revue D'Etudes Comparatives Est-Ouest* [Paris], XI, No. 2, June 1980, 5–46.

Moore, Patrick. "Macedonia: Perennial Balkan Apple of Discord," *The World Today* [London], 35, No. 10, October 1979, 420–28.

Moore, Roy. "Self Management in Yugoslavia," *Fabian Research Series* [London], No. 281, January 1970, 1–33.

Mosely, Philip E. "The Peasant Family: The Zadruga, or Communal Joint-Family in the Balkans, and Its Recent Evolution." Page 95–108 in Caroline F. Ware (ed.), *The Cultural Approach to History.* New York: Columbia University Press, 1940.

Obradovic, Josip, and William N. Dunn. *Workers' Self-Management and Organizational Power in Yugoslavia.* Pittsburgh: University Center for International Studies, University of Pittsburgh, 1978.

Oleszczuk, Thomas. "The Commanding Heights and Liberalization: The Case of Yugoslavia," *Comparative Politics*, 13, No. 2, January 1981, 171–85.

_____. "Convergence and Counteraction: Yugoslavia's 'Antitechnocratic' Campaign and Electoral Results: 1957–1974," *Comparative Political Studies*, 13, No. 2, July 1980, 205–35.

_____. "Group Challenges and Ideological De-Radicalization in Yugoslavia," *Soviet Studies* [Glasgow], XXXII, No. 4, October 1980, 561–79.

_____. "Managerial Elitism under Workers' Self-Management: An Analysis of the Causes of Power Inequality in the Yugoslav Enterprise." (Ph.D. Dissertation.) Madison: University of Wisconsin, 1977.

Organisation for Economic Co-operation and Development. *The Agricultural Policy of Yugoslavia.* (Agricultural Policy Reports series.) Paris: 1981.

_____. *Economic Survey, Yugoslavia.* Paris: 1980.

Parkin, Frank. "Market Socialism and Class Structure: Some Aspects of Social Stratification in Yugoslavia." Pages 29–50 in Bernard Lewis Farber (ed.), *The Social Structure of Eastern Europe: Transition and Process in Czechoslovakia, Hungary, Poland, Romania, and Yugoslavia.* New York: Praeger, 1976.

Pecujlic, Miroslav. "The University of the Future," (Trans., S. Petnicki.) *Socialist Thought and Practice* [Belgrade], XX, No. 9, 26–53.

Pejovich, Svetozar. *Social Security in Yugoslavia.* (Studies in Social Security and Retirement Policy.) Washington: American Enterprise Institute, 1979.

Pervan, Ralph. *Tito and the Students: The University and the*

University Student in Self-Managing Yugoslavia. Nedlands, Australia: University of Western Australia Press, 1978.

Petrin, Tea, and Jane Humphries. "Women in the Self-Managed Economy" (Zene u samoupravnoj privredi), *Ekonomska Analiza* [Belgrade], XIV, No. 1, 1980, 69–91.

Popovic, Vesna. "Social Mobility and Political Activity of Public Opinion-Makers." Pages 120–54 in Allen H. Barton, Bogdan Denitch, and Charles Kadushin (eds.), *Opinion-Making Elites in Yugoslavia.* New York: Praeger, 1973.

Popovski, Dusan. "Respect for the Rights of Ethnic Minorities" (Trans., V. Bambic.) *Socialist Thought and Practice* [Belgrade], XVL, No. 12, 1976, 58–71.

Pounds, Norman J.G. *Eastern Europe.* Chicago: Aldine, 1969.

———. *Geographical Essays on Eastern Europe.* Bloomington: Indiana University Press, 1961.

Prasnikar, Janez. "The Yugoslav Self-Managed Firm and Its Behaviour" (Jugoslovansko samoupravno podjetje in njegovo obnasanje). *Ekonomska Analiza* [Belgrade], XIV, No. 1, 1980, 1–32.

Ra'anan, Gavriel D. *Yugoslavia after Tito: Scenarios and Implications.* (Westview Special Studies on the Soviet Union and Eastern Europe.) Boulder: Westview Press, 1977.

Raditsa, Bogdan. "Nationalism in Croatia since 1964." Pages 458–72 in George W. Simmonds (ed.), *Nationalism in the USSR and Eastern Europe in the Era of Brezhnev and Kosygin.* Detroit: University of Detroit Press, 1977.

Radivojevic, Biljana. "Marriage and Divorce," *Yugoslav Survey* [Belgrade], 21, No. 2, February 1980, 61–70.

Rakicenic, Tomislav L. *Yugoslavia: Land and People.* Belgrade: Yugoslav Illustrated Magazine Review Press, 1968.

Reed, Mary E. "The Anti-Fascist Front of Women and the Communist Party in Croatia: Conflicts within the Resistance." Pages 128–39 in Tova Yedlin (ed.), *Women in Eastern Europe and the Soviet Union.* New York: Praeger, 1978.

Remington, Robin Alison. "Civil-Military Relations in Yugoslavia: The Partisan Vanguard," *Studies in Comparative Communism,* XI, No. 3, Autumn 1978, 250–64.

Rheubottom, David B. "Time and Form: Contemporary Macedonian Households and the Zadruga Controversy." Pages 215–31 in Robert F. Byrnes (ed.), *Communal Families in the Balkans: The Zadruga.* Notre Dame, Indiana: University of Notre Dame Press, 1976.

Roberts, Adam. "Yugoslavia: The Constitution and the Succession," *World Today* [London], 34, No. 4, April 1978, 136–46.

Robinson, Gertrude Joch. "Mass Media and Ethnic Strife in Multi-National Yugoslavia," *Journalism Quarterly,* 51, Autumn 1974, 490–97.

———. *Tito's Maverick Media: The Politics of Mass Communications in Yugoslavia.* Urbana: University of Illinois Press, 1977.

Rogel, Carole. *The Slovenes and Yugoslavia, 1890–1914*, XXIV. (East European Monographs series.) New York: East European Quarterly, 1977.

Rosefielde, Steven. *World Communism at the Crossroads: Military Ascendancy, Political Economy, and Human Welfare*. Boston: Martinus Nijhoff, 1980.

Rosenblum-Cale, Karen. "After the Revolution: Women in Yugoslavia." Pages 161–82 in Ivan Volgyes (ed.), *The Peasantry of Eastern Europe Vol. II: 20th Century Developments*. New York: Pergamon Press, 1979.

Rothschild, Joseph. *East Central Europe Between the Two World Wars*, IX. (History of East Central Europe series.) Seattle: University of Washington Press, 1974.

Rus, Veljko. "Self-Management Egalitarianism and Social Differentiation," *Praxis* [Zagreb], 6, No. 1–2, 1970, 251–67.

Rusinow, Dennison I. *The Yugoslav Experiment 1948–1974*. Berkeley: University of California Press, 1977.

_____. *Educational Reforms in Austria and Yugoslavia*. (American Universities Field Staff. Fieldstaff Reports. Southeast Europe Series. XXII, No. 3.) Hanover, New Hampshire: AUFS, 1977.

_____. *Nationalism Today: Carinthia's Slovenes, Part I: The Legacy of History*. (American Universities Field Staff. Fieldstaff Reports. Southeast Europe Series. XXII, No. 4.) Hanover, New Hampshire: AUFS, 1977.

_____. *Notes from a Yugoslav Party Congress*. (American Universities Field Staff. Fieldstaff Reports. Europe Series. No. 41.) Hanover, New Hampshire: AUFS, 1978.

_____. *Yugoslav Domestic Developments*. (American Universities Field Staff. Fieldstaff Reports. Europe Series. No. 25.) Hanover, New Hampshire: AUFS, 1978.

_____. *Yugoslavia and the World, 1978*. (American Universities Field Staff. Fieldstaff Reports. Europe Series. No. 43.) Hanover, New Hampshire: AUFS, 1978.

Schrenk, Martin, Cyrus Ardalan, and Nawal A. El Tatawy. *Yugoslavia: Self-Management Socialism and the Challenges of Development*. Washington: International Bank for Reconstruction and Development, 1979.

Shabad, Goldie. "Strikes in Yugoslavia: Implications for Industrial Democracy," *British Journal of Political Science* [Cambridge], Vol. 10, Part 2, April 1980, 293–315.

Sharp, Samuel L. "Ethnicity and Migration in Yugoslavia," *Studies in Comparative International Development*, X, No. 3, Fall 1975, 63–70.

Sher, Gerson S. *Praxis: Marxist Criticism and Dissent in Socialist Yugoslavia*. Bloomington: Indiana University Press, 1977.

Shoup, Paul. *Communism and the Yugoslav National Question*. New York: Columbia University Press, 1968.

Simic, Andrei. "Acculturation to Urban Life in Serbia." Pages 331–54 in Bernard Lewis Farber (ed.), *The Social Structure of*

Eastern Europe: Transition and Process in Czechoslovakia, Hungary, Poland, Romania, and Yugoslavia. New York: Praeger, 1976.

_____. "Country 'n' Western Yugoslav Style: Contemporary Folk Music as a Mirror of Social Sentiment," *Journal of Popular Culture* X, No. 1, Summer 1976, 156–66.

_____. *The Peasant Urbanities: A Study of Rural-Urban Mobility in Serbia,* I. (Studies in Anthropology.) New York: Seminar Press, 1973.

Simon, Gerhard. "The Catholic Church and the Communist State in the Soviet Union and Eastern Europe." Pages 190–221 in Bohdan R. Bociurkiw and John W. Strong (eds.), *Religion and Atheism in the USSR and Eastern Europe.* London: Macmillan, 1975.

Singleton, Fredeick B. "Yugoslavia Without Tito," *The World Today* [London], 36, No. 6, June 1980, 204–08.

_____. *Twentieth-Century Yugoslavia.* New York: Columbia University Press, 1976.

Sirc, Ljubo. *The Yugoslav Economy under Self-Management.* New York: St. Martin's Press, 1979.

Skendzic, Vajo. "Accelerated Advancement of the Underdeveloped Regions of Yugoslavia," (Trans., Kordia Kveder.) *Socialist Thought and Practice* [Belgrade], XVI, No. 2, 1976, 77–91.

Soljan, Niksa Nikola. "The Concept of Self-Management and the Socio-Economic Background of Decision-Making in Education: The Yugoslav Model," *Comparative Education,* 14, No. 1, March 1978, 65–69.

_____. "The Reform of the System of Pre-Service and In-Service Teacher Training in Yugoslavia: Towards the Educating Community," *International Review of Education* [Hamburg], XXIV, 1978, 75–80.

Spangler, Michael A. "Time and Social Change in a Yugoslav City." (Ph.D. Dissertation.) Madison: University of Wisconsin, 1979.

Stamp, L. Dudley. *A Regional Geography, V: Europe and the Mediterranean.* New York: Wiley, 1960.

Stankovic, Slobodan. "Yugoslavia." Pages 93–106 in Richard F. Staar (ed.), *Yearbook on International Communist Affairs, 1980.* Stanford: Hoover Institution, 1980.

Stipetic, Valdimir, and Vidosav Trickovic. "Agriculture, Nutrition, and Development in Yugoslavia," *Food Policy* [Sussex, England], 5, No. 3, August 1980, 168–87.

Thiel, Mira. "Eine neue Schulreform in Jugoslawien," *Ost-europa* [Stuttgart], 27, No. 12, December 1977, 1023–37.

Tomasevich, Jozo. *Peasants, Politics, and Economic Change in Yugoslavia.* Stanford: Stanford University Press, 1955.

_____. "The Tomasevic Extended Family on the Peninsula of Peljesac." Pages 187–200 in Robert F. Byrnes (ed.), *Communal Families in the Balkans: The Zadruga.* Notre Dame, Indiana: University of Notre Dame Press, 1976.

_____. "Yugoslavia During the Second World War." Pages 59–118 in Wayne S. Vucinich (ed.), *Contemporary Yugoslavia: Twenty Years of Socialist Experiment*. Berkeley: University of California Press, 1969.

Tomsic, Vida. *Women in the Development of Socialist Self-Managing Yugoslavia*. Belgrade: Jugoslovenska Stvarnost, 1980.

Trgo, Fabijan. "Military Strategy and the National Factor in the Liberation War," (Trans., Nada Kronja-Stanic.) *Socialist Thought and Practice* [Belgrade], XVL, No. 3, 1976, 89–102.

Triska, Jan F., and Ana Barbic. "Evaluating Citizen Performance at the Community Level: The Role of Party Affiliation in Yugoslavia." Pages 54–89 in Daniel N. Nelson (ed.), *Local Politics in Communist Countries*. Lexington: University of Kentucky Press, 1980.

Trouton, Ruth. *Peasant Renaissance in Yugoslavia, 1900–1950*. London: Routledge and Kegan Paul, 1952.

Tulasiewicz, Witold, "Political Education in Yugoslavia: Practice in Self-Management," *Cambridge Review of Education* [Cambridge, England], 9, No. 1, 1979, 36–42.

Ulrih-Atena, Ela. "National Linguistic Minorities: Bilingual Basic Education in Slovenia," *Prospects-Quarterly Review of Education* [Paris], United Nations Educational, Scientific and Cultural Organization, VI, No. 3, 1976, 430–38.

Vanek, Jaroslav. *The Labor-Managed Economy: Essays by Jaroslav Vanek*. Ithaca: Cornell University Press, 1977.

_____. "The Theory and Practice of Self-Management: An American Perspective." Pages 260–72 in Steven Rosefielde (ed.), *World Communism at the Crossroads: Military Ascendancy, Political Economy, and Human Welfare*. Boston: Martinus Nijhoff, 1980.

Van Valkenburg, Samuel, and Colbert C. Held. *Europe*. New York: Wiley, 1952.

Verba, Sidney, and Goldie Shabad. "Workers' Councils and Political Stratification: The Yugoslav Experience," *American Political Science Review*, 72, No. 1, March 1978, 80–95.

Visinski, Boris (ed.). *The Ohrid Seminar on Minorities: United Nations Seminar on the Promotion of Human Rights of National, Ethnic, and Other Minorities. Ohrid, Yugoslavia, 1974*. Skopje: Macedonian Review Editions, 1977.

Vrcan, Srdan. "Some Comments on Social Inequality," *Praxis* (International Ed.) [Zagreb], 9, No. 2–3, 1973, 217–42.

Vucinich, Wayne S. "A Zadruga in Bileca Rudine." Pages 162–86 in Robert F. Byrnes (ed.), *Communal Families in the Balkans: The Zadruga*. Notre Dame, Indiana: University of Notre Dame Press, 1976.

Vucinich, Wayne S. (ed.). *Contemporary Yugoslavia: Twenty Years of Socialist Experiment*. Berkeley: University of California Press, 1969.

Vuskovic, Boris. "Social Inequality in Yugoslavia," *New Left Review*, No. 95, January–February 1976, 26–44.

Wesson, Robert. *The Aging of Communism.* (Praeger Special Studies.) New York: Praeger, 1980.

Wilson, Duncan. *Tito's Yugoslavia.* Cambridge: Cambridge University Press, 1979.

Wolff, Robert L. *The Balkans in Our Time.* Cambridge: Harvard University Press, 1956.

Woodsworth, David E. *Social Security and National Policy: Sweden, Yugoslavia, Japan.* Montreal: McGill-Queen's University Press, 1977.

Woodward, Susan Lampland. "Socialization for Self-Management in Yugoslav Schools." Pages 307–19 in Gary K. Bertsch and Thomas W. Ganschow (eds.), *Comparative Communism: The Soviet, Chinese, and Yugoslav Models.* San Francisco: W.H. Freeman, 1976.

World Health Organization. *World Health Statistics.* Geneva: 1980.

"Yugoslavia." Pages 335–44 in *Worldmark Encyclopedia of the Nations*, V. New York: Harper and Row, 1967.

Yugoslavia. Jugoslovenska Stvarnost. *Facts About Yugoslavia.* Belgrade: Federal Secretariat for Information, 1979.

Yugoslavia. Savezni Zavod za Statistiku. *Statisticki Godisnjak Jugoslavije, 1979.* (Godina XXVI series.) Belgrade: 1979.

Zaninovich, M. George. "Leadership and Change in Yugoslavia," *Current History*, 80, No. 465, April 1981, 173–77, 186.

Zukin, Sharon. *Beyond Marx and Tito: Theory and Practice in Yugoslav Socialism.* London: Cambridge University Press, 1975.

Zwerdling, Daniel. *Workplace Democracy: A Guide to Workplace Ownership, Participation, and Self-Management Experiments in the United States and Europe.* New York: Harper and Row, 1980.

Chapter 3

Artisien, P.F.R., and S. Holt. "Yugoslavia and the EEC in the 1970s," *Journal of Common Market Studies*, 18, No. 4, June 1980, 355–69.

Blagojevic, Steve. "The System and Level of Investment, 1974–1978," *Yugoslav Survey* [Belgrade], XXI, No. 4, November 1980, 47–62.

Burg, Steven L. "Decision-Making in Yugoslavia," *Problems of Communism*, 29, No. 2, March–April 1980, 1–20.

Comisso, Ellen Turkish. *Workers' Control under Plan and Market: Implications of Yugoslav Self-Management.* New Haven: Yale University Press, 1979.

Dovring, Folke. "Land Reform in Yugoslavia," *Land Reform* (U.S. Department of State, Agency for International Development), X, Spring 1970, 1–63.

Dubey, Vinod. *Yugoslavia: Development with Decentralization.*

Baltimore: Johns Hopkins University Press for the World Bank, 1975.

Farkas, Richard P. *Yugoslav Economic Development and Political Change: The Relationship Between Economic Managers and Policy-Making Elites.* New York: Praeger, 1975.

Horvat, Branko. *The Yugoslav Economic System: The First Labor Managed Economy in the Making.* White Plains, New York: International Arts and Sciences Press, 1976.

International Bank for Reconstruction and Development. "World Development Indicators." Pages 5–63 in *World Development Report.* Washington: August 1981.

International Monetary Fund. "Yugoslavia." Pages 454–58 in *Annual Report on Exchange Arrangements and Exchange Restrictions, 1981.* Washington: 1981.

Jankovic, Nevenka. "Social Policy and Its Implementation," *Yugoslav Survey* [Belgrade], XXI, No. 4, November 1980, 3–28.

Joint Publications Research Service—JPRS (Washington). The following publications are from the JPRS series:

Translations on East Europe Economic and Industrial Affairs.

"Agricultural Combine Director Interviewed on Prospects," *Duga*, Belgrade, October 25, 1980. (JPRS: 77157, No. 2081, January 12, 1981, 96–100.)

"Agricultural Plan Unfulfilled," *Ekonomska Politika*, Belgrade, January 12, 1981. (JPRS: 77435, No. 2097, February 23, 1981, 57–58.)

"Agricultural Production Capacities to 1979," *Prerade I Plasmana*, Belgrade, October 1980. (JPRS: 77078, No. 2076, December 30, 1980, 62–77.)

"Agriculture-Food Production, Needs Forecast to 1985," *Glasnik Poljoprivredne Proizvodnje, Prerade I Plasmana*, Belgrade, April 1980. (JPRS: 75963, No. 2020, June 30, 1980, 133–57)

"Average Private Farm Income, Expenditures in 1979," *Ekonomska Politika*, Belgrade, September 1, 1980. (JPRS: 76655, No. 2055, October 20, 1980, 56.)

"Bleak Prospects for Agriculture Detailed," *Duga*, Belgrade, January 31, 1981. (JPRS: 77747, No. 2112, April 3, 1981, 49–53.)

"Capital Accumulation of Organizations of Associated Labor," *Jugoslovenski Pregled*, Belgrade, May 1979. (JPRS: 75963, No. 2020, June 30, 1980, 158–75.)

"Causes of Meat Supply Shortages Analyzed," *Duga*, Belgrade, November 8, 1980. (JPRS: 77425, No. 2096, February 20, 1981, 114–18.)

"Changes in Banking System Still Incomplete," *Vesnik Investbanka*, Belgrade, February 1980. (JPRS: 76104, No. 2026, July 24, 1980, 112–15.)

"Data on Expansion of Socialized Agricultural Sector," *Glasnik Poljoprivredne Proizvodnje, Prerade I Plasmana*, Belgrade,

November 1980. (JPRS: 77105, No. 2078, January 5, 1981, 35–43.)

"Data on Farm Associations, Pensions, Production, 1979," *Glasnik Poljoprivredne, Prerade I Plasmana*, Belgrade, June 1980. (JPRS: 76264, No. 2034, August 20, 1980, 93–102.)

"Data on Numbers of Workers, Families Abroad," *Ekonomska Politika*, Belgrade, June 8, 1981. (JPRS: 78620, No. 2154, July 28, 1981, 60.)

"Data Showing Role of Consumer Credits, 1976–80," *Ekonomska Politika*, Belgrade, April 20, 1981. (JPRS: 78261, No. 2135, June 9, 1981, 98–103.)

"Development of 380-KV Transmission Network 1980–2000," *Elektroprivreda*, Belgrade, May–June 1980. (JPRS: 76786, No. 2064, November 7, 1980, 99–119.)

"Electric Power Capacity, Needs, Plans," *Ekonomska Politika*, Belgrade, April 14, 1980. (JPRS: 75995, No. 2021, July 7, 1981, 153–57.)

"Electric Power Production, Consumption," *Ekonomska Politika*, Belgrade, March 23, 1981. (JPRS: 78041, No. 2124, May 11, 1981, 82–83.)

"Electric Power Status, Plans," *Privredni Pregled*, Belgrade, January 7, 1981. (JPRS: 77415, No. 2095, February 19, 1981, 61–62.)

"Energy Outlook," *Privredni Pregled*, Belgrade, September 13–15, 1980. (JPRS: 76626, No. 2053, October 15, 1980, 128.)

"Energy Plan for 1981," *Privredni Pregled*, Belgrade, January 28, 1981. (JPRS: 77473, No. 2100, February 27, 1981, 59.)

"Export of Food—Problems, Possibilities," *Prerade I Plasmana*, Belgrade, October 1980. (JPRS: 77078, No. 2076, December 30, 1980, 78–86.)

"Exports of Livestock, Meat for 1979, 1980 Given," *Glasnik Poljoprivredne Proizvodnje, Prerade I Plasmana*, Belgrade, April 1981. (JPRS: 78307, No. 2137, June 16, 1981, 70–72.)

"Failures of Fragmented Electricity System Faulted," *Duga*, Belgrade, January 3, 1981. (JPRS: 77635, No. 2108, March 20, 1981, 67–69.)

"Ferrous Metallurgy in 1979 Foreign Trade," *Celik*, Belgrade, May–June 1980. (JPRS: 76061, No. 2025, July 17, 1980, 91–100.)

"Financing of Smederevo Ironworks Remains Controversial," *Nedeljne Informativne Novine*, Belgrade, May 18, 1980. (JPRS: 76155, No. 2029, August 1, 1980, 123–26.)

"Fish Production, Consumption to 1985," *Agronomski Glasnik*, Zagreb, March 1980. (JPRS: 76335, No. 2038, August 29, 1980, 98–104.)

"Foreign Exchange Needs Discussed," *Vjesnik*, Zagreb, April 25, 1981. (JPRS: 78307, No. 2137, June 16, 1981, 66–69.)

"Fuel, Power Situation, Outlook Discussed," *Privredni Pregled*,

Belgrade, July 26–28, 1980. (JPRS: 76626, No. 2053, October 15, 1980, 121–23.)

"Gas Consumption, Imports," *Privredni Pregled*, Belgrade, August 16–18, 1980. (JPRS: 76404, No. 2041, September 10, 1980, 114.)

"Granfil Discusses Bank for International Cooperation," *Privredni Pregled*, Belgrade, March 26, 1980. (JPRS: 75765, No. 2010, May 23, 1980, 201–205.)

"Investments in Fixed Assets in First Quarter," *Privredni Pregled*, Belgrade, May 27, 1980. (JPRS: 75963, No. 2020, June 30, 1980, 130–32.)

"Iron, Steel Production in 1980, 1981," *Celik*, Belgrade, December 1980. (JPRS: 78001, No. 2122, May 6, 1981, 19–23.)

"Kraigher Interviewed on Economic System," *Ekonomska Politika*, Belgrade, May 11, 1981. (JPRS: 78426, No. 2144, July 1, 1981, 30–54.)

"Lack of Foreign Exchange Hits Metals Industry," *Privredni Pregled*, Belgrade, April 10, 1981. (JPRS: 78418, No. 2143, June 30, 1981, 53.)

"Law on Permanent Funds to Finance Underdeveloped Regions, 1981–85," *Sluzbeni List SFRJ*, Belgrade, December 31, 1980. (JPRS: 77805, No. 2115, April 10, 1981, 59–64.)

"Law on Supplemental Funds for Republics, Provinces, 1981–85," *Sluzbeni List SFRJ*, Belgrade, December 31, 1980. (JPRS: 77805, No. 2115, April 10, 1981, 65–67.)

"Low Price Reduces Sugar Beet Acreage, Production," *Privredni Pregled*, Belgrade, August 30–September 1, 1980. (JPRS: 76483, No. 2044, September 24, 1980, 121–22.)

"Natural Gas Production, Outlook, Imports from USSR," *Vjesnik*, Zagreb, April 19, 1981. (JPRS: 78261, No. 2135, June 9, 1981, 104–107.)

"Need to Unify Ferrous Metallurgical Development Seen," *Celik*, Belgrade, October 1980. (JPRS: 77614, No. 2107, March 18, 1981, 45–49.)

"Non-Economic Investments," *Sedam Dana*, (supplement to *Vjesnik*), Zagreb, October 4, 1980. (JPRS: 76719, No. 2058, October 29, 1980, 105.)

"Oil Refining, Refinery Operating Conditions, 1979–1980," *NAFTA*, Zagreb, June 1980. (JPRS: 76264, No. 2034, August 20, 1980, 79–85.)

"Oil Supply in 1981," *Privredni Pregled*, Belgrade, January 8, 1981. (JPRS: 77312, No. 2089, February 4, 1981, 149.)

"Organization of Private Farmers Lagging," *Vjesnik*, Zagreb, August 27, 1980. (JPRS: 76655, No. 2055, October 20, 1980, 53–55.)

"Other Republics Said to Earn Hard Currency from Croatian Goods," *Vjesnik*, Zagreb, September 13, 1980. (JPRS: 76655, No. 2055, October 20, 1980, 60–67.)

"Problems of Steel Industry Analyzed in Interview," *Nedeljne Informativne Novine*, Belgrade, February 15, 1981. (JPRS: 77747, No. 2112, April 3, 1981, 45–48.)

"Production Figures Listed for Products of Mining, Metallurgy," *Tehnika*, Belgrade, No. 3, 1981. (JPRS: 78261, No. 2135, June 9, 1981, 110–11.)

"Professor Horvat Queried on Origins of Current Economic Situation," *Student*, Belgrade, March 25, 1981. (JPRS: 78426, No. 2144, July 1, 1981, 55–64.)

"Project for Oil Refinery in Serbia Raises Controversy," *Nedeljne Informativne Novine*, Belgrade, February 8, 1981. (JPRS: 77747, No. 2112, April 3, 1981, 41–44.)

"Prospect for Completion of Smederevo Ironworks Reviewed," *Duga*, Belgrade, January 3, 1981. (JPRS: 77635, No. 2108, March 20, 1981, 70–75.)

"Reduced Heat in Belgrade," *Borba*, Belgrade, October 7, 1980. (JPRS: 76719, No. 2058, October 29, 1980, 104.)

"Reduced Steel Production," *Privredni Pregled*, Belgrade, October 8, 1980. (JPRS: 76719, No. 2058, October 29, 1980, 104.)

"Results of Private Farm Survey on Farm Size, Future," *Agronomski Glasnik*, Zagreb, November–December 1980. (JPRS: 78060, No. 2125, May 13, 1981, 68–82.)

"Socialized Agriculture," *Ekonomska Politika*, Belgrade, June 30, 1980. (JPRS: 76264, No. 2034, August 20, 1980, 104.)

"Status, Aid in Underdeveloped Areas Discussed," *RAD*, Belgrade, July 18, 1980. (JPRS: 76264, No. 2034, August 20, 1980, 61–68.)

"Status, Outlook for Natural Gas Production," *Privredni Pregled*, Belgrade, July 5–8, 1980. (JPRS: 76404, No. 2041, September 10, 1980, 102–08.)

"Steel Needs, Production, Imports, Prices," *Privredni Pregled*, Belgrade, February 13, 1981. (JPRS: 77597, No. 2106, March 16, 1981, 61–63.)

"Thermoelectric Power Complex in Obilic," *Jedinstvo*, Pristina, March 11, 1980. (JPRS: 75765, No. 2010, May 23, 1980, 206–209.)

"Unemployment Rates," *Komuna*, Belgrade, November 1980. (JPRS: 77110, No. 2079, January 6, 1981, 87.)

"Varied Business of Federal Economic Council Outlined," *Privredni Pregled*, Belgrade, September 27–29, 1980. (JPRS: 76728, No. 2059, October 30, 1980, 60–62.)

Markovic, Zarko. *An Informative Presentation of Yugoslav Laws.* Belgrade: Institute of the Yugoslav Chamber of Economy for Economic Publicity, 1979.

Moore, John H. *Growth with Self-Management: Yugoslav Industrialization, 1952–1975.* (Hoover Institution Publication 220.) Stanford: Hoover Institution Press, 1980.

Obradovic, Josip, and William N. Dunn (eds.). *Workers' Self-Management and Organizational Power in Yugoslavia.* Pittsburgh:

University Center for International Studies, University of Pittsburgh, 1978.

Organisation for Economic Co-operation and Development. *The Agricultural Policy of Yugoslavia.* (Agricultural Policy Reports series.) Paris: 1981.

_____. *Economic Survey, Yugoslavia.* Paris: May 1981.

_____. *Economic Survey, Yugoslavia.* Paris: May 1980.

_____. *Economic Survey, Yugoslavia.* Paris: May 1979.

_____. *Economic Survey, Yugoslavia.* Paris: May 1978.

_____. *Economic Survey, Yugoslavia.* Paris: May 1977.

Petrovic, Jovan. "Monetary Effects of Bank's Foreign Currency Transactions," *National Bank of Yugoslavia Quarterly Bulletin* [Belgrade], December 1980, 15–25.

Prasnikar, Janez. "The Yugoslav Self-Managed Firm and Its Behavior," *Economic Analysis and Workers' Management* [Belgrade], 14, No. 1, 1980, 1–32.

Privredno Finansijski Vodic. *Banks and Other Financial Institutions.* Belgrade: 1979.

Ribnikar, Ivan. "The Yugoslav Monetary System," *Association for Comparative Economic Studies Bulletin* (ACES), XXIII, No. 1, Spring 1981, 67–78.

Sapir, Andre. "Economic Growth and Factor Substitution: What Happened to the Yugoslav Miracle?" *The Economic Journal* [London], 90, June 1980, 294–313.

Schrenk, Martin, Cyrus Ardalan, and Nawal A. El Tatawy. *Yugoslavia: Self-Management Socialism and the Challenges of Development.* Washington: International Bank for Reconstruction and Development, 1979.

Selucky, Radoslav. *Economic Reforms in Eastern Europe: Political Background and Economic Significance.* New York: Praeger, 1972.

Shabad, Goldie. "Strikes in Yugoslavia: Implications for Industrial Democracy," *British Journal of Political Science* [Cambridge], Vol. 10, Part 3, July 1980, 293–316.

Sirc, Ljubo. *The Yugoslav Economy under Self-Management.* New York: St. Martin's Press, 1979.

Sondermayer, Roman V. "The Mineral Industry of Yugoslavia." Pages 1045–60 in Albert E. Schreck (ed.), *Minerals Yearbook, Volume III, 1978–79.* Washington: U.S. Department of the Interior, Bureau of Mines, 1981.

_____. "The Mineral Industry of Yugoslavia." Pages 1189–1206 in Albert E. Schreck (ed.), *Minerals Yearbook, Volume III, 1976.* Washington: U.S. Department of the Interior, Bureau of Mines, 1980.

Stiblar, Franjo. "Personal Savings in Yugoslavia—Test of Existent Hypotheses and the Role of Data Source," *Economic Analysis and Workers' Management* [Belgrade], 14, No. 2, 1980, 219–50.

Trifunovic, Vladimir. "Maize Production and Consumption,

1966–1979," *Yugoslav Survey* [Belgrade], XXI, No. 4, November 1980, 63–72.

Tyson, Laura D'Andrea. *The Yugoslav Economic System and Its Performance in the 1970s.* (Research Series No. 4.) Berkeley: Institute of International Studies, University of California, 1980.

U.S. Congress. 95th, 1st Session. Joint Economic Committee. Laura D'Andrea Tyson. "The Yugoslav Economy in the 1970s: A Survey of Recent Developments and Future Prospects." Pages 941–96 in *East European Economies, Post-Helsinki.* Washington: GPO, 1977.

U.S. Congress. 97th, 1st Session. Joint Economic Committee. John H. Moore. "Self-Management in Yugoslavia." Pages 215–29 in *East European Economic Assessment Part 1—Country Studies, 1980.* Washington: GPO, 1981.

U.S. Congress. 97th, 1st Session. Joint Economic Committee. Laura D'Andrea Tyson and Gabriel Eichler. "Continuity and Change in the Yugoslav Economy in the 1970s and 1980s." Pages 139–214 in *East European Economic Assessment Part 1—Country Studies, 1980.* Washington: GPO, 1981.

Vanek, Jaroslav. *The Labor-Managed Economy: Essays by Jaroslav Vanek.* Ithaca: Cornell University Press, 1977.

Wilson, Duncan. "Self-Management in Yugoslavia." *International Affairs* [London], 54, No. 2, April 1978, 253–63.

The Yugoslav Bank for International Cooperation. *The Law on the Yield and on Joint Financial Organization.* Belgrade: 1978.

Yugoslavia. Federal Secretariat for Information. *Facts About Yugoslavia.* Belgrade: 1979.

Yugoslavia. Federal Statistical Office. *Statistical Pocket-Book of Yugoslavia, 1980.* Belgrade: May 1980.

———. *Statistical Yearbook of the Socialist Federal Republic of Yugoslavia, 1978.* (Translation key. 25 Issue series). Belgrade: 1978.

Yugoslavia. Savezni Zavod za Statistiku. *Statisticki Godisnjak Jugoslavije, 1979.* (Godina XXVI series.) Belgrade: 1979.

(Various issues of the following periodicals were also used in the preparation of this chapter: *Energy in Countries with Planned Economies* [Berne]; *Financial Times* [London]; Foreign Broadcast Information Service (FBIS) *Daily Report Eastern Europe; National Bank of Yugoslavia Quarterly Bulletin* [Belgrade]; *New York Times*; *Radio Free Europe Research*; and *Yugoslav Survey* [Belgrade].)

Chapter 4

Atlagic, David (ed.). *13 Sednica CKSKJ: Aktuelna pitanja idejno-politicka pitanja.* Belgrade: Komunist, 1980.

———. *15 Sednica CKSKJ: Idejno-politicka pitanja drustveno-ckonomskog iazvoja.* Belgrade: Komunist, 1980.

Baletic, Milovan, and Zdravko Zikovec (eds.). *Deseta Sednica*

Centralnog Komiteta Saveza Komunista Hrvatska. Zagreb: Vjesnik, 1970.

Bilandzic, Dusan. *Ideje i praksa drustvenog razvoja Jugoslavije 1945–1973*. Belgrade: Komunist, 1973.

Blagojevic, Borislav (ed.). *Mesto i uloga odbora i komisija predstavnickih tela*. Belgrade: Institute za Upredno Pravo, 1969.

Burg, Steven L. *Conflict Regulation, Decisionmaking, and Institutional Change in a Multinational State: The Case of Yugoslavia Since 1966*. (Ph.D. Dissertation.) Chicago: Department of Political Science, University of Chicago, 1980.

_____. "Ethnic Conflict and the Federalization of Socialist Yugoslavia: The Serbo-Croat Conflict," *Publius*, 7, No. 4, Fall 1977, 119–43.

_____. "Yugoslavia since Tito: Decision Making in the Party and the State in a Transitional Period." (Paper presented at 12th Convention of AAASS, Philadelphia, 1980.)

_____. "Yugoslavia Without Tito: Prospects for Stability." (Paper presented at 22d Annual ISA Meeting, Philadelphia, 1981.)

Cohen, Leonard J. "Conflict Management and Political Institutionalization in Socialist Yugoslavia." Pages 122–65 in Albert F. Eldridge (ed.). *Legislatures in Plural Societies*. Durham: Duke University, 1977.

Denitch, Bogdan. *The Legitimation of a Revolution: The Yugoslav Case*. New Haven: Yale University Press, 1976.

Djordjevic, Jovan (ed.). *Drustveno-politicki sistem SFRJ*. Belgrade: Radnicka Stampa, 1975.

Djurovic, Dragoljub (ed.). Zapazanja iz vada Veca republika; pokrajina skupstine SFRJ," *Biblioteka Skupstine SFRJ* [Belgrade], 14, No. 6, 1977.

Djurovic, Dragoljub, et al. (eds.). *The Constitution of the Socialist Federal Republic of Yugoslavia*. Belgrade: Secretariat of the Federal Assembly Information Service, 1974.

Draskovic, Dragomir. "Integrativna funkcije demokratskog centralizma i avangardno delovanje SK." Pages 53–64 in Atif Purivatra (ed.), *Demokratski centralizam u teoriji i praksi SKJ*. Sarajevo: Studijski Centar Gradske Konferencije SKBiH, 1975.

Fisk, Winston. "The Constitutionalism Movement in Yugoslavia: A Preliminary Survey," *Slavic Review*, 30, No. 2, June 1971.

Hoffman, George W., and Fred Warner Neal. *Yugoslavia and the New Communism*. New York: Twentieth Century Fund, 1962.

Hondius, Fritz W. *The Yugoslav Community of Nations*. The Hague: Mouton, 1968.

Johnson, A. Ross. *Yugoslavia: In the Twilight of Tito*, II, (The Washington Papers series.) Beverly Hills: Sage Publications, 1974.

_____. *The Transformation of Communist Ideology: The Yugoslav Case, 1945–1953*. Cambridge: MIT Press, 1972.

Kardelj, Edvard. *Pravci razvoja politickog sistema socijalistickog samoupravljanja*. Belgrade: Komunist, 1977.

Lendvai, Paul. *Eagles in Cobwebs.* Garden City, New York: Anchor Books, 1969.

Martinovic, Savo. *Deveti Kongres Saveza komunista Jugoslavije: Stenografske beleske,* I–VI. Belgrade: Komunist, 1970.

Martinovic, Savo (ed.). *Ustavne promene: sestnavsta sednica Predesednistva SKJ (Dokumenti).* Belgrade: Komunist, 1971.

Milenkovitch, Deborah D. *Plan and Market in Yugoslav Economic Thought.* New Haven: Yale University Press, 1971.

Nikolic, Pavle. *Savzne Skupstina u Ustavnom; Politickom Sistem u Jugoslavije.* Belgrade: Savezudruzenja Pravnika Jugoslavije, 1969.

_____. "Skupstinski sistem." Pages 270–82 in Jovan Djordjevic (ed.), *Drustveno-politicki sistem SFRJ.* Belgrade: Radnicka Stampa, 1975.

Poslovnik Saveznog Izvrsnogveca. Belgrade: Sluzbeni List, 1979.

Prifti, Peter. *Kosovo in Ferment.* Cambridge: MIT Center for International Studies, 1969.

Rojc, Emil, et al. (eds.). *Deseti Kongres SKJ: Dokumenti.* Belgrade: Komunist, 1974.

Rusinow, Dennison I. *Anatomy of a Student Revolt.* (American Universities Field Staff, Fieldstaff Reports. Southeast Europe Series, XV, Nos. 4 and 5.) Hanover, New Hampshire: AUFS, 1968.

_____. *The Yugoslav Experiment, 1948–1974.* Berkeley: University of California Press, 1977.

Savez komunista Hrvatske. Centralni Komitet (CK). *Izvestaj o stanju u Savezu komunista Hrvatske u odnosu na prodor nacionalizma u ujegove redove.* Zagreb: Informativna Sluzba Centralnog Komiteta SKH, 1972.

Savez komunista Jugoslavije. *Aktuelmi problemi daljeg razvoja naseg politickog sistema.* Belgrade: Komunist, 1970.

_____. *Referat i zavrsna rijec Predsjednika Tita, Rezolucije, Statut SKJ: XI Kongresa SKJ.* Belgrade: Komunist, 1978.

_____. Predsednistvo. *Osma Sednica Predsednistva SKJ.* Belgrade: Komunist, 1970.

_____. Centralni Komitet. *Ceturti plenum Centralnog Komiteta saveza komunista Jugoslavije.* Belgrade: Komunist, 1966.

_____. Centralni Komitet. *Deveta Sednica Centralnog Komiteta.* Belgrade: Komunist, 1968.

_____. Centralni Komitet. *Nacrti dokumenata za Deveti Kongres SKJ.* Belgrade: Komunist, 1969.

_____. Centralni Komitet. *Osma Sednica Centralnog Komiteta SKJ.* Belgrade: Komunist, 1967.

_____. Centralni Komitet. *Pripreme 9. Kongresa.* Belgrade: Komunist, 1967.

Savez komunista Srbije. Centralni Komitet. *Aktivnost SKS poste ceturte sednice CK SK Jugoslavije.* Belgrade: Sedma Sila, 1966.

_____. Centralni Komitet. *Reorganizaeija i izbor organa Centralnog komiteta Saveza komunista Srbije (sedma sednica CK SK Srbije).* Belgrade: Sedma Sila, 1966.

_____. *Sesti Kongres Saveza komunista Srbije*. Belgrade: Komunist, 1968.

Sher, Gerson S. *Praxis: Marxist Criticism and Dissent in Socialist Yugoslavia*. Bloomington: Indiana University Press, 1977.

Shoup, Paul. *Communism and the Yugoslav National Question*. New York: Columbia University Press, 1968.

Skupstina SFRJ. *Ostvarivanje delegatskog skupstinskog sistema, sa poschnim osurtom na Federaciju*. (Biblioteka Skupstine SFRJ.) Belgrade: 1980.

Socijalisticki Savez Radnog Naroda Kosova. Pokrajinska Konferencije. *Dokumenti*. Prizren: SSRN Kosova, n.d.

Socijalisticki Savez Radnog Naroda Bosne i Hercegovine. *Prva Sjednica SSRNBiH*. Sarajevo: Republicki Komitet SSRNBiH, 1975.

Sruk, Josip. *Ustavno uredjenje SFRJ*. Zagreb: Informator, 1976.

Staar, Richard F. (ed.). *Yearbook on International Communist Affairs 1978*. Stanford: Hoover Institution Press, 1978.

Stjepanovic, Nikola. *Upravno Pravo SFRJ*. Belgrade: Privredni Pregled, 1973.

Sukovic, Mijat. "Delegatski Sistem." Pages 242–69 in Jovan Djordjevic (ed.), *Drustveno-politicki sistem SFRJ*. Belgrade: Radnika Stampa, 1975.

U.S. Central Intelligence Agency. National Foreign Assessment Center. *Directory of Yugoslav Officials*. Washington: 1981.

Vukovic, Ilija. *Socijalisticki Savez Radnog Naroda u politickom sistem u SFRJ*. Belgrade: Savremena Administracija, 1975.

Yugoslavia. Savezni Zavod za Statistiku. *Statisticki Kalendar Jugoslavije 1976*. Belgrade: 1976.

Zecevic, Middrag (ed.). *Ustav SFRJ: Strucno objasnjenje*. Belgrade: Institut za politicke studije FPN and Privredni Pregled, 1975.

(Various issues of the following [Belgrade] periodicals were also used in the preparation of this chapter: *Informativni Bilten Savezne Skupstine; Komunist; Nedeljne Informativne Novine; Politika*; and *Sluzbeni List SFRJ*.)

Chapter 5

Alexander, Stella. *Church and State in Yugoslavia since 1945*. (Soviet and East European Studies series.) Cambridge: Cambridge University Press, 1979.

Barton, Allen H., Bogdan Denitch, and Charles Kadushin (eds.). *Opinion-Making Elites in Yugoslavia*. (Praeger Special Series in International Politics and Government.) New York: Praeger, 1973.

Bebler, Anton. "Development of Sociology of Militaria in Yugoslavia," *Armed Forces and Society*, 3, No. 1, Fall 1977.

Bird, Christopher. "From a Reporter's Notebook," *Problems of Communism*, XVIII, Nos. 4 and 5, July–October 1969, 77–88.

Code of Criminal Procedure. Belgrade: Union of Jurists Associations of Yugoslavia, 1954.

Cotic, Duran. "Juvenile Delinquency," *Yugoslav Survey* [Belgrade], IX, No. 1, February 1968, 83–94.

Dean, Robert W. "Civil-Military Relations in Yugoslavia, 1971–1975," *Armed Forces and Society*, 3, No. 1, Fall 1976.

Denitch, Bogdan. *The Legitimation of a Revolution: The Yugoslav Case*. New Haven: Yale University Press, 1976.

"Development of the Yugoslav People's Army," *Yugoslav Survey* [Belgrade], II, No. 7, October–December 1961, 919–27.

Gjupanovich, Fran, and A. Adamovitch. *Legal Sources and Bibliography of Yugoslavia*. New York: Praeger, 1964.

Gsovski, V., and K. Grzybowski. *Government, Law, and Courts in the Soviet Union and Eastern Europe*. New York: Praeger, 1969.

Heppel, Muriel, and Frank B. Singleton. *Yugoslavia*. New York: Praeger, 1966.

Jane's All the World's Aircraft, 1980–81. (Ed., John W.R. Taylor.) New York: Jane's, 1980.

Jane's Fighting Ships, 1980–81. (Ed., John Moore.) New York: Jane's, 1980.

Jane's Weapon Systems, 1979–80. (Ed., Ronald T. Pretty.) New York: Jane's, 1980.

Johnson, A. Ross. "The Role of the Military in Communist Yugoslavia: An Historical Sketch." (Rand Research Paper series, P–6070.) Santa Monica: Rand Corporation, January 1978.

––––––. *The Transformation of Communist Ideology: The Yugoslav Case, 1945–1953*. Cambridge: MIT Press, 1972.

––––––. *The Yugoslav Doctrine of Total National Defense*. Santa Monica: Rand Corporation, 1971.

––––––. "Yugoslav Total National Defense," *Survival*. [London], XV, No. 2, March–April 1973, 54–58.

––––––. *Yugoslavia: In the Twilight of Tito*. (The Washington Papers series.) Beverly Hills: Sage Publications, 1974.

Joint Publications Research Service—JPRS (Washington). The following publications are from the JPRS series:

Translations on East Europe, Political, Sociological, and Military Affairs.

"Armed Forces Role in Defense System Analyzed," *Jugoslovenski Pregled*, Belgrade, May 1969. (JPRS: 49121, No. 148, 1969.)

Army Fiscal Plan for Current Year Review," *Vojnoekonomski Pregled*, Belgrade, January 1970. (JPRS: 50552, No. 216, 1970.)

"Defense Scenario Against Aggressor Sketched," *Nedeljne Informativne Novine*, Belgrade, August 3, 1980. (JPRS: 76675, No. 1820, October 22, 1980, 76–80.)

"Defense School: The Yugoslav Armed Forces—Bulwark of Our Defense," *Front*, Belgrade, November 28, 1980. (JPRS: 77319, No. 1847, February 4, 1981, 89–93.)

"Defense Training in Croatian, Slovenian Secondary Schools Reviewed," *Obrana i Zastita*, Belgrade, January–February 1970. (JPRS: 50302, No. 204, 1970.)

"Information Offered on Military Schools," *Front*, Belgrade, April 24, 1970. (JPRS: 50627, No. 220, 1970.)

"Law on Decorations," *Sluzbeni List SFRJ*, Belgrade, November 7, 1969. (JPRS: 49666, No. 176, 1970.)

"Need to Intensify War on Crime," *Ekonomska Politika*, Belgrade, February 1970. (JPRS: 50232, No. 200, 1970.)

"Reduction of Prisons in Croatia," *Vjesnik*, Zagreb, May 1968. (JPRS: 45745, No. 3, 1968.)

"Republics' Agreement on Army Development, Defense Goals, 1981–85." *Sluzbeni List SFRJ*, Belgrade, December 31, 1980. (JPRS: 77612, No. 1859, March 18, 1981, 33–46.)

"Republics' Agreement on Military Weapons, Equipment, Production, 1981–85." *Sluzbeni List SFRJ*, Belgrade, December 31, 1980. (JPRS: 77612, No. 1859, March 18, 1981, 47–53.)

"Revised Law on Military Courts Enacted," *Sluzbeni List SFRJ*, Belgrade, November 27, 1969. (JPRS: 49666, No. 87, 1969.)

"Role of Seapower in Nationwide Defense Discussed," *Pormorstvo*, Rijeka, October–December 1969. (JPRS: 49929, No. 187, 1970.)

"Statistics on Recent Juvenile Delinquency," *Borba*, Belgrade, February 1970. (JPRS: 49994, No. 190, 1970.)

Sociological Translations on East Europe.

"The Basic Law on General Courts," *Sluzbeni List SFRJ*, Belgrade, February 1965. (JPRS: 30829, No. 299, 1965.)

"Disciplinary Centers for Minors," *Socijalna i Zdravstvena Politika*, Belgrade, November–December 1964. (JPRS: 29715, No. 286, 1965.)

"Juvenile Delinquency," *Naroda Milicija*, Belgrade, November 1963. (JPRS: 23367, No. 200, 1964.)

"Yugoslav Basic Law on Internal Affairs," *Sluzbeni List SFRJ*, Belgrade, December 1966. (JPRS: 40277, No. 421, 1967.)

Military Information on East Europe.

"Basic Law on the Internal Affairs Service," *Sluzbeni List SFRJ*, Belgrade, November 1964. (JPRS: 28170, No. 98, 1965.)

"The Law on National Defense," *Sluzbeni List SFRJ*, Belgrade, July 1965. (JPRS; 31866, No. 118, 1965.)

"Law on the Yugoslav People's Army," *Sluzbeni List SFRJ*, Belgrade, December 31, 1964. (JPRS: 29403, No. 105, 1965.)

"The New Law on the Yugoslav People's Army," *Radna i Drustvena Zajednica*, Belgrade, January 1965. (JPRS: 30888, No. 112, 1965.)

"Ukase on Military Courts," *Sluzbeni List SFRJ*, Belgrade, February 17, 1965. (JPRS: 29386, No. 104, 1965.)

Kelleher, Catherine McArdle (ed.). *Political-Military Systems Comparative Perspectives*. Beverly Hills: Sage Publications, 1974.

Kraus, Bozidar. "Changes in Criminal Procedure and the Enforcement of Criminal Law Sanctions," *Yugoslav Survey* [Belgrade], IX, No. 4, November 1968, 61–68.

Lellenberg, Jon L. "Yugoslav Concept of General People's Defense." (Stanford Research Institute research paper, SRI 8974.) Menlo Park, California: November 1972.

Lendvai, Paul. "National Tensions in Yugoslavia," *Conflict Studies* [London], No. 25, August 1972, 1–17.

The Military Balance 1980–81. London: International Institute for Strategic Studies, 1980.

Pantelic, M. "The Role of the Armed Forces in the System of National Defense," *Yugoslav Survey* [Belgrade], 1967.

————. "The President of the Republic," *Yugoslav Survey* [Belgrade], V, No. 19, October–December 1964, 2717–20.

Rainer, Mennel. "Defence and Military-Geographical Analysis of Yugoslavia," (Trans., Director General, Intelligence and Security, National Defense Headquarters, Ottawa, January 14, 1975.) *Wehrkunde*, [West Germany], No. 6, June 1974, 291–94.

Remington, Robin Alison. "Civil-Military Relations in Yugoslavia: The Partisan Vanguard," *Studies in Comparative Communism*, XI, No. 3, Autumn 1978, 250–64.

Roberts, Adam. Nations in Arms: *The Theory and Practice of Territorial Defense.* New York: Praeger, 1976.

————. "The Yugoslav Experiment in All-People's Defence." Pages 109–27 in *R.U.S.I. and Brassey's Defence Yearbook.* London: Brassey's Publishers, 1978.

Rothschild, Joseph. *East Central Europe Between the Two World Wars*, IX. (History of East Central Europe series.) Seattle: University of Washington Press, 1974.

Roucek, Joseph S., and Kenneth V. Lottick. *Behind the Iron Curtain.* Caldwell, Idaho: Caxton Printers, 1964.

Shoup, Paul. "The Evolution of a System," *Problems of Communism*, XVIII, Nos. 4,5, July–October 1969, 67–77.

Stockholm International Peace Research Institute. *World Armaments and Disarmaments: SIPRI Yearbook 1980.* London: Taylor and Francis, 1980.

"The Treatment of Persons Serving a Prison Sentence," *Yugoslav Survey* [Belgrade], III, No. 8, January–March 1962, 1098–1103.

U.S. Central Intelligence Agency. National Foreign Assessment Center. *Factbook 1981.* Washington: January 1981.

U.S. Congress, 89th, 1st Session. Senate. Committee on the Judiciary. *Yugoslav Communism: A Critical Study.* Washington: GPO, 1961.

U.S. Department of State. "Yugoslavia." Pages 920–28 in *Country Reports on Human Rights Practices.* (Report submitted to the Committee on Foreign Relations, U.S. Senate and Committee on Foreign Affairs, U.S. House of Representatives, February 2, 1981.) Washington: GPO, 1981.

Yugoslavia. *National Defense Law of the Socialist Federal Republic of Yugoslavia.* Belgrade: Joint Translation Service, 1969.

Yugoslavia. Savezni Zavod za Statistiku. *Statisticki Godisnjak Jugoslavije 1969.* (Godina XXVI series.) Belgrade: 1979.

Zaninovich, M. George. *The Development of Socialist Yugoslavia.* Baltimore: Johns Hopkins Press, 1968.

Zdenko, Antic. "The Chief of Staff of the Yugoslav Army," *Radio Free Europe Research*, August 1, 1967.

_____. "National Structure of the Yugoslav Army Leadership," *Radio Free Europe Research*, April 12, 1972.

_____. "Yugoslav Federal Budget: Striving for Stabilization," *Radio Free Europe Research* (RAD Background Report–292/80), 5, No. 61, December 4–8, 1980.

Glossary

Cetniks—Resistance group led by Draza Mihailovic, who did not wish to surrender to the German invaders but who successfully avoided war against them. Frequently engaged in attacks against the Partisans (*q.v.*).

Cominform—Communist Information Bureau, a joint organization formed in 1947 of the communist parties of the Soviet Union, its East European allies, France, and Italy. Yugoslavia was expelled in 1948.

Comintern—Third Communist International. Established in 1919 to coordinate and direct communist parties throughout the world. Abolished in 1943 in response to complaints from the Soviet Union's wartime allies, Britain and the United States.

dinar—National currency unit consisting of 100 paras. The dinar has been devalued frequently over the years. The average yearly value for conversion purposes expressed in dinars per one United States dollar was:

1970. . .12.50	1974. . .15.91	1978. . .18.64
1971. . .15.17	1975. . .17.39	1979. . .19.00
1972. . .17.00	1976. . .18.19	1980. . .24.91
1973. . .16.19	1977. . .18.30	

fiscal year—same as calendar year.

gross material product (GMP)—Also called social product. Consists of the value added by the productive sectors before deduction of depreciation. GMP excludes such nonproductive activities as defense, public administration, finance, education, health, and housing.

LCY—League of Communists of Yugoslavia, the sole political party of Yugoslavia. Each republic and province has a league of communists, such as the League of Communists of Slovenia; there is also a League of Communists of the Yugoslav People's Army. All these leagues are part of the LCY.

nation, national, and nationality—Nation refers to those ethnic groups most of whose traditional territorial homeland lies within Yugoslavia's modern boundaries, i.e., Serbs, Croats, Slovenes, Montenegrins, Macedonians, and ethnic (or Bosnian) Muslims. Nationality or national minority designates those groups whose homelands lie outside Yugoslavia; the principal national minorities are Albanians and Hungarians. Although relevant legislation gives full equality to minorities in culture, public life, and language, the juridical distinction between nation and nationality plays a significant role in Yugoslavia's political life.

nationalism, nationalistic—In contemporary Yugoslavia both refer to the efforts of the various nations and nationalities (*q.v.*) in support of their own cultures and interests and opposed to those of the country as a whole. The regime views nationalism as a fragmentary force threatening the country's internal stability; nationalistic tendencies are, therefore, roundly condemned.

Partisan—Popular name for resistance forces led by Josip Broz Tito during World War II. In 1942 adopted formal name of National Liberation Army, but members better known as Partisans.

Republic of Ragusa—An area along the Adriatic Coast; existed from February 18, 1358, to January 31, 1808; officially known as Republica Ragusina throughout the Middle Ages (in Serbo-Croatian, Dubrovacka Republika). The republic varied in size from one period to another with Ragusa (Dubrovnik) as its capital and principal center.

SAWPY—Socialist Alliance of the Working People of Yugoslavia, also known as Socialist Alliance. Front organization for the LCY (*q.v.*).

self-management—Concept that the employees of firms (or participants in organizations) possess extensive decisionmaking rights within the framework of broad guidelines. *See* socially owned.

social product—*See* gross material product.

Socialist Alliance—*See* SAWPY.

socially owned—A legal concept introduced by the Yugoslavs along with workers' self-management (*q.v.*). When most of the economy was nationalized in the late 1940s, the state became owner of the assets exercising ownership rights for the people. In the 1950s the legal distinction was made that the nationalized means of production were owned by all of the people and not by the state or other organizations or institutions. Nevertheless workers' self-management organizations were granted certain legal rights, such as registered rights to use farmland, without actual ownership. Workers were also legally responsible for maintaining the socially owned assets in their care. It was not clear how claims were handled for socially owned assets when a bankrupt workers' self-management unit was liquidated.

sociopolitical communities—Yugoslav term used to refer collectively to the republics, provinces, and communes as territorial-political units.

ustase (sing. *ustasa*)—From the word *ustanak*, a rising or rebellion. Members of an extremist Croatian movement that adopted fascist guidelines and collaborated with German and Italian occupation forces during World War II. Engaged in genocidal practices against Serbs resident in Croatia and Bosnia and Hercegovina.

World Bank—Group of three institutions consisting of the International Bank for Reconstruction and Development (IBRD), the International Finance Corporation (IFC), and the International Development Association (IDA); established in 1945, the World Bank in 1981 was owned by the governments of approximately 141 countries, which subscribe the institutions' capital. The IFC works with the private sector in developing countries. The IDA operates in the same sectors and with the same policies as the IBRD but provides credits only to the poorer developing countries and on easier terms than those of conventional IBRD loans.

Published Country Studies
(Area Handbook Series)

550–65	Afghanistan		550–21	India
550–98	Albania		550–154	Indian Ocean Territories
550–44	Algeria		550–39	Indonesia
550–59	Angola			
550–73	Argentina		550–68	Iran
			550–31	Iraq
550–169	Australia		550–25	Israel
550–176	Austria		550–182	Italy
550–175	Bangladesh		550–69	Ivory Coast
550–170	Belgium			
550–66	Bolivia		550–177	Jamaica
			550–30	Japan
550–20	Brazil		550–34	Jordan
550–168	Bulgaria		550–56	Kenya
550–61	Burma		550–81	Korea, North
550–83	Burundi			
550–50	Cambodia		550–41	Korea, South
			550–58	Laos
550–166	Cameroon		550–24	Lebanon
550–159	Chad		550–38	Liberia
550–77	Chile		550–85	Libya
550–60	China			
550–63	China, Republic of		550–163	Malagasy Republic
			550–172	Malawi
550–26	Colombia		550–45	Malaysia
550–91	Congo		550–161	Mauritania
550–90	Costa Rica		550–79	Mexico
550–152	Cuba			
550–22	Cyprus		550–76	Mongolia
			550–49	Morocco
550–158	Czechoslovakia		550–64	Mozambique
550–54	Dominican Republic		550–35	Nepal, Bhutan & Sikkim
550–52	Ecuador		550–88	Nicaragua
550–43	Egypt			
550–150	El Salvador		550–157	Nigeria
			550–94	Oceania
550–28	Ethiopia		550–48	Pakistan
550–167	Finland		550–46	Panama
550–155	Germany, East		550–156	Paraguay
550–173	Germany, Fed. Rep. of			
550–153	Ghana		550–185	Persian Gulf States
			550–42	Peru
550–87	Greece		550–72	Philippines
550–78	Guatemala		550–162	Poland
550–174	Guinea		550–181	Portugal
550–82	Guyana			
550–164	Haiti		550–160	Romania
			550–84	Rwanda
550–151	Honduras		550–51	Saudi Arabia
550–165	Hungary		550–70	Senegal

550–180	Sierra Leone
550–184	Singapore
550–86	Somalia
550–93	South Africa
550–171	Southern Rhodesia
550–95	Soviet Union
550–179	Spain
550–96	Sri Lanka (Ceylon)
550–27	Sudan
550–47	Syria
550–62	Tanzania
550–53	Thailand

550–178	Trinidad and Tobago
550–89	Tunisia
550–80	Turkey
550–74	Uganda
550–97	Uruguay
550–71	Venezuela
550–57	Vietnam, North
550–55	Vietnam, South
550–183	Yemens, The
550–99	Yugoslavia
550–67	Zaire
550–75	Zambia

☆ U.S. GOVERNMENT PRINTING OFFICE   1982-0-361-658   (512)